D1261610

SPIES AND SABOTEURS

Spies and Saboteurs

Anglo-American Collaboration and Rivalry in Human Intelligence Collection and Special Operations, 1940–45

Jay Jakub, D.Phil
Professional Staff
House Permanent Select Committee on Intelligence
United States Congress

Foreword by Sir Douglas Dodds-Parker

First published in Great Britain 1999 by
MACMILLAN PRESS LTD
Houndmills, Basingstoke, Hampshire RG21 6XS and London
Companies and representatives throughout the world

A catalogue record for this book is available from the British Library.

ISBN 0–333–72150–0

First published in the United States of America 1999 by
ST. MARTIN'S PRESS, INC.,
Scholarly and Reference Division,
175 Fifth Avenue, New York, N.Y. 10010

ISBN 0–312–21327–1

Library of Congress Cataloging-in-Publication Data
Jakub, Jay, 1963–
Spies and saboteurs : Anglo-American collaboration and rivalry in
human intelligence collection and special operations, 1940–45 /Jay
Jakub ; foreword by Sir Douglas Dodds-Parker.
p.   cm.
Includes bibliographical references (p.   ) and index.
ISBN 0–312–21327–1 (cloth)
1. World War, 1939–1945—Secret service. 2. World War, 1939–1945–
–Military intelligence.   I. Title.
D810.S7J27   1998
940.54'86—DC21   97–51695
                                                                            CIP

This book is printed on paper suitable for recycling and made from fully managed and
sustained forest sources.

10   9   8   7   6   5   4   3   2
08   07   06   05   04   03   02   01   00   99

Printed and bound in Great Britain by
Antony Rowe Ltd, Chippenham, Wiltshire

To my loving wife Eleni, without whose steadfast support this book would not have been possible.

Also to my friends and colleagues at Oxford, the British Special Forces Club, the Central Intelligence Agency, and to those veterans of OSS, SOE, and the Secret Intelligence Service whose sacrifices and larger-than-life exploits inspired this work.

Contents

Foreword by Sir Douglas Dodds-Parker, Chief of British
Special Operations in the Western and Central
Mediterranean (1943–45)   xi

Preface   xvii

Acknowledgments   xxi

Key Terms and Acronyms   xxiii

**1   Planting the Seeds: 'Wild Bill' Donovan's Two
European Missions, 1940–41   1**
Introduction   1
Roosevelt's 'Unofficial Representative,' July–August 1940   2
    Background   2
    The Visit   5
    The Aftermath   7
The Navy Department's 'Observer,' December 1940–March 1941   10
    Background   10
    Bermuda and London   13
    The Middle East   14
    The Balkans   16
    Back in London   18
    The Aftermath   18
Conclusions   20

**2   An Unequal Partnership: The Coordinator of Information and
British Mentoring, 1941–42   22**
Introduction   22
From Concept to Reality: The Birth of COI and
the British Role   23
    British Intervention   24
    A Bureaucratic Breakthrough   27
From Birth to War   28
    Together Through the Washington Minefield   28
    Establishing COI's First Overseas Station   32
Bumps in the Road   33
    Problems in London   33
    Robert Solborg and COI's Special Operations Capability   38
    Wallace Phillips, and COI's Secret Intelligence Capability   40
    Looking to the Far East   42
Conclusions   45

3   **Trial by Fire: London and the Proving Grounds of North Africa**
    and Burma, 1942–43   **48**
    Introduction   48
    The Anglo-American Intelligence Protocols of June 1942   49
    London, 1942   53
       Background   53
       SO London   55
       SI London   60
    North Africa, 1942–43   66
       Background   66
       Operation 'TORCH'   69
       The French Dynamic   72
       The MASSINGHAM Controversy   74
    The SO-SOE Operational Revisions of January 1943   79
    Burma and India: Success and Mistrust   83
    Conclusions   90

4   **Coming of Age: London, Norway, and the Jedburgh-Sussex**
    Negotiations, 1943   **93**
    Introduction   93
    OSS-SOE, Norwegian Operations, and the Jedburgh Plan   94
    OSS-SIS, Joint Chiefs Directives, and Operation SUSSEX   100
    Conclusions   109

5   **The Yugoslav Morass: A Case Study in Anglo-OSS**
    Divergence, 1942–44   **110**
    Introduction   110
    Background   111
    Early Maneuvering   113
    Down the Slippery Slope in 1943   121
    The Huot Affair and OSS Bari   133
    SOE's Formal Break with Mihailovic   135
    Deepening Divisions in 1944   139
    Conclusions   143

6   **The Liberation of France: A Case Study in**
    Anglo-OSS Convergence, 1943–44   **146**
    Introduction   146
    Background, 1940–43   147
    The Maquis and the Special Inter-Allied Missions   157
    Semi-Integrated Organizational Collaboration   161

The Jedburgh Plan 170
Operation SUSSEX 174
OSS Operational Groups and British Special Forces 180
Conclusions 182

7 Key Findings **185**
Introduction: A Relationship of Four Themes 185
Indirect Mutual Dependence 185
Direct Mutual Dependence 188
Restricted Independence 191
Unrestricted Independence 194
Final Observations 196

Notes 198

War Chronology of Key Events 245

Bibliography 254

Index 262

Foreword

by Sir Douglas Dodds-Parker

Dr Jay Jakub's book on the origins of the Anglo-American 'special relationship' in human intelligence and special operations during the Second World War is of substantial present value. His friendly and sustained industry has been rewarded as he picked his way through the minefields of the records and memories of nationalist, ideological, Service, political and personal events and prejudices, genuine if sometimes conflicting. His explicit conclusions are the more valuable with their freedom from bias. Future researchers will find this a reliable, unique source from which to judge these seminal years and efforts of Anglo-American association in secret services.

Useful mention can also be made of the situations which preceded and influenced the critical years of 1940 to 1945 covered in this survey, and of the differing positions and aims of the main protagonists: Britain with its Empire, and the United States of America. Broadly speaking, Britain believed in an Empire to create free-standing units as Empire became Commonwealth, as has occurred, the final stages being hastened by the events of the Second World War. Conversely, the United States advocated independence to be given without waiting for the administrative and economic structures which sustain true independence. This put the two sides at odds and complicated the relationship between the British and American secret services.

I accepted with some diffidence Dr Jakub's flattering invitation to write this foreword. As a junior officer, I had first been concerned – by the chance of my employment since 1935 – in the need for Imperial organizations for action to withstand the hostile activities of dictatorships worldwide. My Sudan service in the late 1930s on the Ethiopian frontier and in the Public Security Department in Khartoum led me later to witness the first victory over fascism, with the restoration in 1941 of the Ethiopian Emperor Haile Selassie. In Ethiopia the British secret services were involved throughout, from secret intelligence (SI), through clandestine action (SO), to paramilitary and regular forces, and military government.

On my return to the United Kingdom, I was charged with the supervision for the Special Operations Executive (SOE) in London of air and sea transport into and out of the Continent of Europe. Our map room showed by May 1941 only two parachute drops into France, both 'blind.' By May 1944, this number had increased to one thousand dropping points ready for action. It would have been difficult, and certainly undesired, to show to whom the credit for this achievement was due; such was the close cooperation of all three main allies – British,

American, and French. Reading this book will give some idea of the success of their association, and the difficulties which had to be overcome in building the groups under the conditions of occupation.

For the secret services herein recorded, the British Secret Intelligence Service (SIS) was long-term, professional, with a great record of past success. SOE was created from the 'D-Section' of SIS and the military research section of the War Office Intelligence section (MIR). This took place in July 1940, for the short term, as it turned out. It was designated 'Executive' not 'Service,' implying, as in the Civil Service, subordination to Higher Authority. Its members were recruited from employments in which they had shown aptitude and gained experience, to meet many challenges ahead. All were anxious to return to their normal employment once the survival of Britain and the Commonwealth was assured, and after helping – with our allies – in the liberation of the occupied countries from the Axis powers. Never was heard any suggestion that SOE should continue thereafter, or that they sought employment therein. SIS regarded SOE at the outset with some apprehension as being 'amateurish'. A similar view was held, together with SOE, of the newborn American organizations, Coordinator of Intelligence (COI) and the Office of Strategic Services (OSS), in 1941 and 1942 respectively.

SIS thus had duties which stretched beyond the war's end, whereas SOE knew that their tasks would be short-lived. On the other hand, the American Services were being created and led by General Bill Donovan, with his vast and varied experience, who foresaw the place of the United States in the future world order. He therefore urged the need for a permanent organization, combining intelligence and action, befitting its economic strength and political stature.

In the years between the wars the world had been split into many authoritarian groups of Left and Right. The Left, Communists and various Socialists; the Right, Fascists, broadly representing the status quo, and capitalists. The Right had been strengthened on the Continent by the knowledge of the bloodstained Russian revolution, and episodes like Bela Kun in Hungary. The result was more anti-Communists than anti-Fascists in Europe before and after 1939. Another factor was the weakness of the Democracies in the later 1930s. They had estimated that there could not be another European war without ten years warning. Then Germany had rearmed with unexpected swiftness, under an obvious aggressor. All others wished to avoid a repeat of the slaughter of 1914/1918. They admired President Teddy Roosevelt's dictum 'Speak softly, but carry a big stick.' They spoke softly – appeasement – but pursued disarmament, not a big stick.

Yet again there had been a seismic change in conflict. Until 1918, wars had been fought between armies, leaving out the civilian populations. The 'Troubles' in Ireland and Russia after 1917, and later conflicts in China, Ethiopia, and Spain, had shown that there could well be resistance against outside occupation, in which the new facilities – air transport and wireless radio – could play a vital role. Against this background, it was difficult for us to understand the account of the American opposition to Donovan's first plans to help Britain. These resulted in protection for the United States itself. His aim, for which he fought untiringly, was to create an organization to gather intelligence and to take clandestine action. Dr Jakub has described many details of the domestic difficulties, even obstruction, that Donovan had to overcome in Washington, from suspicion to bureaucracy. From the embryo of the COI was born the OSS – forerunner to the Central Intelligence Agency – its birth marked by its immediate launch into combat. So when the United States became a full ally in December 1941, SIS and SOE had already made headway, with hidden help from the Americans.

Donovan had made two visits to Britain and the Mediterranean area in 1940 and 1941, before the United States had entered the war. He convinced Washington that Britain would fight on, but must be given substantial help. Lend-Lease was one result. Donovan found, also, that many were aware that unless the submarine war against Allied shipping in the North Atlantic could be won, Britain might still be defeated. This fear was only finally resolved in 1943. Until war's end there remained the apprehension that there might, again, be a Nazi/Communist Pact, as in 1939.

The contribution which Donovan made for freedom for all Allies, before and after Pearl Harbor, can never be overestimated. None will ever forget the day when the United States entered the war, to know them as colleagues, not just as helpful friends, like David Bruce whom I used to brief on our activities at SOE. From then on until the end of the war, all on the working level were involved together, day and night. Action under the occupation never ceased. The working level never knew when a signal might report success or disaster. Perhaps we thus lived closer to the occupied. As the numbers of the OSS and some other Allies increased, I cannot recall any American on joining who did not work, and was not accepted, as 'one of us'. They understood, even if they could not fully share, the underlying feeling of the British who, from contacts with those from the occupied countries, realized what horrors Britain had not had to endure. Dr Jakub records clearly the growing independence of the American Services from the British. For the working level it was the opposite, until the short-term military victories were won. For this, great credit must be given to General Eisenhower himself. He always radiated cooperation. Woe betide any who complained about another colleague with a different passport! 1943 in Algiers was his greatest year for welding all together. The original Allied Forces Headquarters (AFHQ) was the best headquarters to work in and for during these years, 1940 to 1945, of joint warfare.

Next, in late 1942, an SOE mission went to Algiers to work under General Eisenhower. Its target was southern France and Italy. In January 1943, I was appointed 'deputy,' under Colonel Eddy of OSS. Thus I was involved in the expansion of SOE/OSS and the full cooperation, indeed its integration, with a cooperative French element, which only ceased with the liberation of France late in 1944.

From our joint base in Algiers, following the freeing of Corsica and the Italian Armistice in late 1943, further bases were created in Corsica, Naples and Bari in

Italy. From the last was given air support to Poland and Central Europe, and to much of the Balkans, both of which groups were at first out of the AFHQ area. All this gave wide experience of SOE/OSS cooperation.

Two episodes in this phase mentioned by Dr Jakub show Allied misunderstandings, or differing judgements, but not antagonism. First, OSS's Louis Huot, whose controversial Balkan operation from Italy is discussed in Chapter 5. Following the Italian Armistice, an Allied base for special operations was set up in Brindisi. The local situation was fluid. Seventy thousand Allied prisoners of war were freed in Italy. The Adriatic was wide open, until weeks later the Germans closed the eastern side. War stores were being brought by sea from the Polish base in Tunisia. Little prevision was allowed, to safeguard the security of the Allied landing at Salerno. We were faced with the problem of forwarding military stores to the all too willing recipients in Yugoslavia; local ships were available. From 'On High' arrived Louis Huot, with the magic of real American dollars. Gerry Holdsworth, an SOE sailor in charge of the Brindisi base, set Louis to work, to carry the first load, which he did bravely, adding President Franklin Roosevelt's compliments, and was sent for from Cairo to report to OSS. He did not return. Four decades later I heard when in the United States that Huot was still trying to justify his action, which I offered to help, having encouraged him in a splendid operation to supply Tito's Partisans. It seems that such crossing of the Area lines (supplying Yugoslavia from Italy) had not been agreed with Roosevelt, Churchill, and Stalin. Had this been known, Huot could have been described as an officer from the joint SOE/OSS headquarters in Algiers, and omitted the President's compliments.

The second episode had longer term effects – the support for Draza Mihailovic and the Chetniks in Yugoslavia. In 1940, SOE had agreed with the nationalist Yugoslav leader in Belgrade, General Dusan Simovic, to 'leave behind' the then Colonel Mihailovic in the event of occupation by the Germans. This occurred in 1941. The usual instructions were to keep the powder dry, to carry out sabotage, etc., without attracting reprisals, until support was needed for the approach of liberating armies. This Mihailovic did, with varying success in controlling disparate elements in a divided country, until the appearance of Tito after the Soviet Union was attacked. Thereafter began differences of opinion by the admittedly ill informed decision-takers in Cairo, about whether – while agreeing on the policy of supporting Tito – support should be withdrawn from Mihailovic on the grounds that he was not active enough. The decision was finally taken to withdraw support and the British officers assigned to help the Chetniks, despite Mihailovic's representatives in Italy saying that, now that the Allies were winning the war, the enemy of his country was Communism, against which he needed any support he could get (a view shared by the West within four years).

In 1940 the only groups left with clandestine organizations had been the Poles and the Communists. So, as spontaneous resistance to Nazi occupation everywhere increased, most groups had a Communist element in control, with clear postwar aims. Policy had been to support groups regardless of this; under Allied military authorities who were bound to regard the Communists as part of their Soviet ally. It was possible in most countries, as the war progressed, to balance pro-Communist groups with anti-Communists. Thus in Greece a handful of British officers were able to hold a bridgehead for Democracy. Under General Donovan's guidance, such an attempt was made in Yugoslavia after the withdrawal of British aid to Mihailovic. It will be for future historians, drawing on the evidence put up by Dr Jakub's book, to decide the merits of these differing judgements.

Near the end of military operations in the Mediterranean in October 1944, Colonel Hewitt from our Bari headquarters estimated that at the peak of special operations, clandestine and paramilitary groups – working from bases at Algiers, Corsica, Naples, and Bari – totalled 2700 individuals of all ranks. Among these numbered a large Air Force contingent commanded by a Major General, an Air Marshal, and numerous Brigadiers, with men and women from a score of nationalities, supplying a dozen countries, from France to Poland to Greece. These 2700 were responsible for directing up to a million men and women, ready to march before or when liberating armies approached. It was quite an organization. Few could have been able, or wished, to tell who had contributed most to this international coalition for the Free Society. But all would have paid tribute to General Donovan and our General Gubbins for their original vision and unremitting application to turn visions into reality. Similar tributes would have been paid by all who served in General Koenig's EMFFI headquarters, supporting the Normandy landings, and in the Special Operations Center for the southern assault on France. Also by the integrated groups such as the Jedburghs, the Path-finders and the Sussex intelligence successes, and by the British SAS and the OSS Operational Groups who often linked regular with irregular action.

In East Asia, cooperation was not so marked; starting from different bases, often independent, with different 'imperial' aims, political and economic, for victory and after. Comparatively little was accomplished before the atomic bomb brought an end to the anti-Axis series of hostilities. But some actions added to the later contests in 'Indo-China'. For Ho Chi Minh, after being put into North Vietnam by OSS for anti-Japanese action, was directed later against the French. When the French were also expelled, Ho turned against the American crusade against Communism. This conflict was only to cease three decades after VJ-Day.

The independence of India was probably little affected by differences of Allied opinions. But other failures to agree may have had some adverse effect in Burma and Thailand. Less than a decade later, I was to find General Donovan in Thailand, and happy to try to work with him in the nascent rise of the drug menace from the region.

Before leaving London in November 1942, the Minister of State at the Foreign Office, Dick Law, the Canadian-born son of the Prime Minister Bonar Law, told me in friendly advice: 'Try to involve the Americans in all our responsibilities, but try to retain control.' I took this to be in line with Churchill's speaking at the end of the Second World War of the 'changing of the guard', to defend the Free Society which Britain by its own lights had sought to do for past centuries.

With the anticipated changes from Empire to Commonwealth, and the subsequent reduction in the power of the United Kingdom, these two realized that such defence must pass to the only power – unwilling though at times it might seem – able and with the same outlook to take on the task. In his generation, Donovan did as much as any other, long-term, to hasten the transfer of these responsibilities. Much of the explanation for this claim lies in the pages of this excellent exposition of Donovan's many achievements by Dr Jay Jakub.

Preface

The genesis of my interest in exploring in depth the secret transatlantic linkages that not only facilitated the war effort, but also resulted in the establishment of a truly independent US intelligence entity, can be found in the belief that the historical record remains incomplete. This record emphasizes quantity over quality, and is so large and varied as to be somewhat intimidating, not just to the interested reader or scholar, but even to the intelligence historian. This poses problems in that it is becoming increasingly difficult to sort out the real from the imaginary, the informative from the purposely misleading, the facts from the sensationalism.

Much of what has been written on Second World War clandestine matters is based either upon personal recollection or incomplete primary sources, or are compilations of largely secondary source material. There are numerous personal accounts of adventure and heroism, for example, especially in the realm of special operations, and this has been substantially augmented in recent years as a result of nostalgia brought on by the 50-year commemorations of the war in 1989–95. Many first-hand accounts, particularly those of Bickham Sweet-Escott, Michael Lees, Sir William Deakin, Sir Douglas Dodds-Parker, Stewart Alsop, Thomas Braden, Sir Peter Wilkinson, Joan Bright Astley, and H. Montgomery Hyde, are indispensable to the serious researcher. However, many others are superficial, inconsistent, or embellished from fading memories. The best of the broader scholarly accounts of the wartime British and American secret services, moreover, were written more than a decade or two ago, before the mass declassification of primary source material in the 1980s and 90s added so much to public repositories that academe's ability to exploit it fully has yet to be realized in the smallest sense. Limited access to privileged information is a chronic problem in intelligence research, and is certainly to blame for many of the problems encountered by researchers prior to this 'bonanza' of new material.

The mass declassification of OSS documents in recent years, in fact, has enabled historians for the first time to utilize the nearly complete raw record of a modern intelligence organization to make objective judgments such as those made in this book. As intelligence historian Bradley Smith has observed:

> Until now, all of us have had to play by different rules than those individuals studying other organizations . . . Scholars pursuing serious intelligence history have been compelled to content themselves with memoirs, memories, [and] documentary traces . . . All of our work has been lamed by second handedness and the impossibility of ever judging particular features or facts against an overall pattern of the activities of the organization we were trying to study . . . The appearance of [the OSS records] launches a new phase of serious historical study of intelligence activities and organizations.[1]

My observation that there has been an emphasis on quantity over quality in most intelligence writing produced between the war and the appearance of the OSS records, however, should not in any way be construed as an indictment of the historical record, nor does it detract from those works that have filled important gaps in our knowledge. There are indeed very useful secondary resources and personal accounts available, and these works stand out precisely because of the mass of their considerably less useful counterparts. Michael Foot's *SOE in France*, for example, is now thirty years old, yet remains essential for assessing British special operations across the English Channel. Sir Harry Hinsley's officially-sanctioned account of British intelligence during the war – published in five volumes beginning almost two decades ago – is also both useful and contextual although, like Foot, Hinsley's team did not address OSS in any detail. Former CIA officer Thomas Troy's recent reprint of his formerly classified paper on the early ties between Donovan and William Stephenson is also helpful, but covers a narrow period and much of the research was completed some 25 or more years ago. Troy's 1981 book, *Donovan and the CIA*, remains perhaps the most important resource on what was happening to Donovan's organization in Washington during the war – particularly regarding bureaucratic infighting – but was never intended to be a book about Anglo-OSS affairs, although some aspects of the relationship are discussed. Bradley Smith's 1983 book, *The Shadow Warriors*, and R. Harris Smith's 1972 book, *OSS*, both examine the evolution of OSS in a broad and useful way, but were written before most of the OSS operational records were publicly available and focus more on how Donovan's wartime organization evolved into CIA than on how it worked with its British counterparts. David Stafford, Mark Wheeler, Robin Winks, Arthur Funk, Richard Aldrich, Max Corvo, Fabrizio Calvi, and some others have also provided well documented accounts of specific aspects of the wartime secret services, but these are limited either to a specialized subject, a short time period, or to a single country or region. Christopher Andrew's history of the British Secret Services is also helpful background, but covers a very broad period of time and therefore only briefly discusses the Anglo-OSS relationship. The official OSS war report, published in two declassified volumes, remains useful, but is very much a 'sanitized' publication, omitting names, dates, and other important details.

In examining the Anglo-OSS relationship in a selective, case-study approach, I establish the fact that this association was often as much a rivalry as a partnership and examine its evolution largely through the use of documentary evidence, much of it released in 1990–92. That which is primarily related to OSS was found at the US National Archives in Washington, DC, the Central Intelligence Agency's Historical Intelligence Collection, the US Army Military Historical Institute in Pennsylvania, the Franklin Roosevelt Memorial Library in New York, and the Hoover Institute Archives in California. British documentary sources came principally from the Public Record Office at Kew, the Imperial War Museum archives, the archives of Churchill College, Cambridge, and Balliol College,

Oxford. The nearly comprehensive secondary resources on wartime intelligence held by the Special Forces Club in London, where the author was made an honorary, then full member by invitation in 1994, were also used for background and to check the accuracy of other sources. Original Serbian military documents held at the Archive of the Military Historical Institute in Belgrade were used, along with resources held at the Bodleian and British Libraries, and at the US Library of Congress. While much of the primary source material cited herein is not sourced elsewhere, some of it will certainly be familiar to the expert reader. The story it tells, however, is I believe both unique and important in adding to the field of scholarly work in this area. It is a story, moreover, that has ramifications for the way in which future scholars will examine the intelligence aspects of the Anglo-American association during the Cold War and post-Cold War periods.

Specifically, I make extensive use of previously inaccessible or under-utilized archival material, which includes the first ever public use of the personal papers of SOE's Bickham Sweet-Escott. My research strategy was developed only after extensive consultations with US National Archive archivists John Taylor, Larry MacDonald, and Amy Schmitt, archivists at Hoover, the PRO, and the FDR Library, the President of the Veterans of OSS, Geoffrey Jones, the first President of the British Special Forces Club, Sir Douglas Dodds-Parker, a Serbian historian familiar with the Military Historical Archive in Belgrade, and Imperial War Museum archivist Mark Seaman. The material in US National Archives Record Group 226, especially in the vast collection under Entry 190 containing the papers retained by Donovan's office whilst he was the director of OSS, as well as in other record groups and microfilm collections relevant to OSS, form the core of my primary sources. As Donovan was a notorious micromanager of OSS activities, documents found under this entry were particularly relevant and likely to be representative of the bulk of material found in the overwhelmingly large holdings of the 226 record group; they also include many documents specifically representing British views. Donovan's extensive personal papers retained after he left government service were also consulted, as were the papers of OSS's M. Preston Goodfellow, Leland Rounds, Paul van der Stricht, Norwood Allman, J. Russell Forgan, David Wooster King, Oliver J. Cadwell, Franklin A. Lindsay, Kostas Kouvaras, and Gero von Schultze Gaevernitz. The papers of intelligence historians Joseph Persico and R. Harris Smith were reviewed, as were Donovan's correspondence with Franklin Roosevelt, and the personal collection of Ward Warren held at CIA, which includes an important report by OSS's Hans Tofte. British Security Coordination's H. Montgomery Hyde's papers and Admiral John Godfrey's diaries were consulted, as were the papers of a senior veteran of OSS who wishes to remain anonymous. Virtually all of the material used from RG 226 and the PRO, as well as much of that taken from the Carlisle, Hoover, and FDR Library holdings and from Mr Warren, are declassified documents, although they are not specifically sourced as such in the book when the classification does not appear on the actual items. Where classification is visible on original material, however, it has been specifically sourced as such in the foot-notes.

Interviews with secret service veterans also played a role in my research. When used, these were rigorously cross checked for accuracy, as were diary entries, memoirs, letters, and secondary sources. Those interviewed include Sir Douglas Dodds-Parker, former head of SOE in the Western Mediterranean, Geoffrey Jones, an OSS veteran of French and Far Eastern operations, the late CIA director and OSS veteran William Colby, and Colonel Carl Eifler, former head of OSS Detachment 101 in Burma and India. Fisher Howe, OSS London's first executive officer, was also interviewed, as were Henry Hyde, who played a leading role in OSS espionage while in Algiers and London, Dr William Morgan, OSS psychiatrist and Jedburgh, Peter Lee of SOE and SIS counterintelligence, Sir Patrick Reilly, administrative assistant to SIS chief Sir Stewart Menzies, the late Dr Stephen Mann of Bletchley Park, and Professor Michael Foot, who served in the British special forces. Gwen Lees, who served in SOE Cairo and SOE Bari, was consulted, as were Vera Adkins from SOE London, Sir Peter Wilkinson, a deputy to SOE's chief Colin Gubbins, and Crown Prince Alexander of Yugoslavia. Cetnik veterans were interviewed in Belgrade, including Dusan Marinkovic, Mihailo Protic, and Dusko Topalovic, and Zvonomir Vuckovic of the Chetnik Ravna Gora Division was consulted by post. Transcripts and taped interviews with other OSS and SOE veterans were used selectively.

This book is not intended to be a history of the strategic decisions governing military operations in the various theaters in which the US and British secret services operated, nor is it a history of the war, only of a relatively narrow aspect of it. When specific military operations are discussed, such as Operation TORCH in North Africa, the Burma campaign in 1942–3, Allied support for the Cetnik and Partisan movements in Yugoslavia, or Operation's OVERLORD and ANVIL / DRAGOON in France, these should be seen as background for the various Anglo-OSS interrelationships analyzed therein. They are not an attempt to document historically the operations in either a political-military or a strictly military sense. This book also does not attempt to cover the Anglo-OSS relationship comprehensively, leaving signals intelligence to others,[2] and focuses only upon the critical areas where the relationship prospered or foundered.

Acknowledgments

There are many who deserve my thanks for all they have done to support my work on this book. First and foremost is my wife, Eleni, who steadfastly endured along with me the ordeal of my research every step of the way, and supported my decision to leave the US Government for Oxford University. My friend and mentor, Professor Robert J. O'Neill, the Chichele Professor of the History of War at All Souls College, Oxford, is also worthy of special praise. His incisive comments and suggestions during the drafting and refining process turned this book into much more than it might have been without him.

There are so many more. Sir Douglas Dodds-Parker, for example, not only nominated me for membership in the Special Forces Club that he helped to found after the Second World War, but agreed to be interviewed by me on several occasions and has kindly written the foreword to this book. He provided useful material, important introductions and valuable suggestions. Without his support, I would have been very hard pressed, indeed, to proceed as I did. Terry Message, Chris Moorhouse, Sue Rodgers, and Perry Morton of the Special Forces Club were also extraordinarily helpful in making the written and human resources of the Club available to me. Geoffrey Jones, the President of the Veterans of the OSS, first introduced me to Sir Douglas and the Club, seconding my nomination for membership. Without his assistance in arranging introductions and interviews with OSS veterans, in addition to providing other guidance, I would truly have been at a great disadvantage. Ward Warren, the curator of the Historical Intelligence Collection at CIA, a 30-year veteran of the clandestine service, is yet another who deserves special mention as it was he who introduced me to Mr Jones, provided access to CIA's archive at Langley and to his personal papers, and answered a myriad of questions from me along the way. American archivists John Taylor, Larry MacDonald, and Amy Schmitt helped me to find my way around the enormous new public holdings on OSS in the National Archives and to formulate an efficient and effective research strategy, and Mark Seaman of the Imperial War Museum in London directed me to the under-utilized audio record of his interviews with SOE and SIS veterans. Gervase Cowell, while the SOE Adviser to the British Government, also helped with my research strategy and expedited the opening of the Bickham Sweet-Escott papers for my use. His able successor as SOE Adviser, Duncan Stuart, provided me with previously unavailable material for my use with the support of his enormously helpful and good-humored P.A., Valerie. HRH Crown Prince Alexander of Yugoslavia and his staff led me to veterans of the Mihailovic movement who agreed to be interviewed and who provided useful archival material. These included Duka Marinkovic, who also arranged to translate primary source material from the Yugoslav Military Archive in Belgrade, Bata Protic, Dusan Topalovic, and Zvonomir Vuckovic.

This book is dedicated to the men and women of the Office of Strategic Services, the Special Operations Executive, and the Secret Intelligence Service, who either gave their lives during the war or served their country in its time of most urgent need, without regard to the personal risks involved. They have forgone public recognition and have sometimes endured controversy, but have always remained true and loyal to their cause. It is also dedicated to their successors, who carried the spirit, dedication and lofty goals of the wartime secret services through the Cold War and post-Cold War periods. The late Freddie Woodruff, an admired friend, was one of those 'great gamesmen' who recently sacrificed his life for his country and its ideals.

Key Terms and Acronyms

Archive codes

AMHI	United States Army Military Historical Archive, Carlisle, Pennsylvania.
AMHIB	Archive of the Military Historical Institute, Belgrade, Yugoslavia.
BOA	Balliol College Archive, Oxford University.
CCA	Churchill College Archive, Cambridge University.
FDRL	Franklin D. Roosevelt Memorial Library, Hyde Park, New York.
HIA	Hoover Institute Archives, Stanford University, Palo Alto, California.
HIC	Historical Intelligence Collection, Central Intelligence Agency, Langley, Virginia.
IWM	Imperial War Museum Archive, London.
NARA	United States National Archives and Records Administration, Washington, DC.
SFC	Special Forces Club Library, London.
UKPRO	United Kingdom Public Record Office, London.

ACRU	*Air Crew Rescue Unit.* Established in 1944 to rescue downed Allied airmen in Yugoslavia, the ACRU was staffed by OSS personnel.
AFHQ	*Allied Forces Headquarters (Mediterranean).*
Agent provocateur	Individual used to penetrate an opposing organization by posing as a member of that group or as a suitable recruit.
ANVIL	First code name for Allied invasion of southern France in 1944. See DRAGOON.
AS	*Armée Secrète* (French). A compilation of various resistance groups that focused upon sabotage activities and included the *Maquis*, the *Sédentaires*, and the *Francs Tireurs et Partisans* (FTP). AS was the 'interior' resistance arm of the Gaullists, although the FTP retained its independence.
Baker Street	Often used to refer to SOE or its London headquarters in Baker Street.

BCRA   *Bureau Central de Renseignements et d'Action.* Gaullist intelligence service.

Big Bill   Nickname for William Donovan within the British and American intelligence establishments.

Black propaganda   Information which is non-attributable to the government which is disseminating it. Usually disinformation.

Blind Drop   Clandestine insertion by parachute without a reception committee.

BRAL   *Bureau de Renseignements et d'Action Londres.* London office of BCRA.

Brissex   Nickname for British SUSSEX teams. See Ossex.

Broadway   Often used to refer to SIS, which was headquartered in London's Broadway.

BSC   *British Security Coordination.* Based in New York and led by William Stephenson from 1940–45, BSC supervised the combined activities of Britain's intelligence, security, and propaganda elements in the Western Hemisphere.

C   Code name for the chief of the British SIS.

CCS   *Combined Chiefs of Staff.* Anglo-American military body for joint strategic planning and operations during the war.

CD   Code name for the chief of the British SOE.

CE   *Counterespionage.* Secret operations to penetrate foreign intelligence services or to identify and thwart their activities.

Cetniks   Used herein to denote Yugoslav resistance fighters loyal to Draza Mihailovic.

CFLN   *Comité Français de la Liberation Nationale* (France). Based in Algiers, the CFLN was initially co-chaired by de Gaulle and Giraud. It coordinated French 'exterior' resistance activities and in theory oversaw the CNR. De Gaulle ousted Giraud from the CFLN in November 1943 and exercised complete dominance over the Committee from March 1944 onward.

CI   *Counterintelligence.* Activities designed to thwart or identify foreign intelligence service counterespionage activities.

CIA   *Central Intelligence Agency.* Established in 1947 by President Truman. CIA, in many ways, took over for OSS, but emphasized SI and R & A activities over predominantly wartime SO work.

CNR   *Conseil Nationale de la Résistance* (French). CNR was formally established in May 1943 at de Gaulle's behest under Jean Moulin to coordinate all resistance elements inside France.

COSSAC   *Combined Operations Staff Supreme Allied Command.* In 1943, COSSAC was designated the operational headquarters in charge of planning OVERLORD. Also denotes the Chief of Staff to the Supreme Allied Commander.

COI   *Coordinator of Intelligence.* Created in July 1941, COI was the first centralized, coordinated US intelligence organization. It was led by William Donovan and was replaced by OSS in June 1942.

COS   *Chiefs of Staff* (British).

D   SIS department responsible for SO activities prior to the creation of SOE in 1940.

D-Day   The Allied invasion of France in Normandy on 6 June 1944.

Detachment 101   Code name for the first COI/OSS paramilitary unit. Operated mostly in Burma.

Deuxième Bureau   G-2 (intelligence) section of the French General Staff. As part of EMFFI from June 1944, this bureau was responsible for CI and false documents.

DF   SOE branch responsible principally for the exfiltration of field agents.

DNI   *Director of Naval Intelligence* (British and US).

DRAGOON   Revised code name for the Allied invasion of southern France in 1944. See ANVIL.

801 Bomb Group   Cover designation for OSS aircraft squadrons operating from the UK.

ENIGMA   Machine encryption device used by the Germans in World War II. ENIGMA worked somewhat like a typewriter, with internal rotating drums that would change position when a key was struck, creating an infinite number of mathematical variations. British codebreakers, with help from their Polish counterparts, broke many different ENIGMA codes during the war. ENIGMA intelligence was called ULTRA.

EMFFI   *Etat Major Forces Françaises de l'Intérieur* (French). Created by SHAEF in May–June 1944 to direct French resistance activities for OVERLORD and DRAGOON. Gaullist organization comprised of six bureaus, which covered personnel and administration (*Premier Bureau*), tactical intelligence, CI and false documents (*Deuxième Bureau*), operations and air transport (*Troisième*

	Bureau), planning, arms, and supplies (*Quatrième Bureau*), W/T (*Cinquième Bureau*), and training, Jedburghs, OGs, and special Allied missions (*Sixième Bureau*). Dissolved 23 September 1944.
ETO	*European Theater of Operations.*
ETOUSA	*European Theater of Operations United States of America.*
F Section	SOE branch responsible for independent French resistance groups.
FBI	*Federal Bureau of Investigation.* US internal security service led by J. Edgar Hoover during the war.
FFI	*Forces Françaises de l'Intérieur.* Gaullist-controlled groups inside France as designated for military operations in spring 1944.
FIS	*Foreign Information Service.* Branch of COI led by Robert Sherwood that conducted 'white' propaganda operations. FIS became part of OWI after COI was dissolved in June 1942.
FNB	*Foreign Nationalities Branch.* COI and OSS unit established to debrief returning travelers and refugees from Axis or Axis-occupied areas.
FTP	*Francs Tireurs et Partisans* (French). Militant section of the French Communist Party. FTP was part of the Armée Secrète.
G-2	*US Army Intelligence.* Also used elsewhere to denote military intelligence.
HUMINT	*Human Intelligence.* Term used to denote intelligence derived from clandestine collection by humans rather than via technology or other means.
JCS	*Joint Chiefs of Staff.*
Jedburghs	Joint Allied special operations (paramilitary) teams created for OVERLORD, but also used elsewhere in 1944–5.
JIC	*Joint Intelligence Committee.* Part of the US JCS; Britain also had its own JIC.
Little Bill	Nickname for William Stephenson within the American and British intelligence establishments.
MAGIC	Allied code name for intelligence derived from broken Japanese ciphers.
Maquis	The Maquis groups operated mostly in southern France, but later established themselves throughout the country. Members lived as outlaws in the wild to escape Vichy mobilization orders or German labor deportation efforts.

	They resisted through various acts of aggression, including sabotage, ambush, etc.
MI-5	Responsible for CI and internal security on the territory of the United Kingdom.
MI-6	Cover designation for the British SIS.
Milice	*French Militia.* Set up by pro-Nazi Joseph Darnand on 30 January 1943 to help the Germans to capture French resistance elements and to round up Jews.
MEW	*Ministry of Economic Warfare* (British). SOE fell under the auspices of MEW.
MO	*Morale Operations Branch.* OSS element responsible for the conduct of subversion, including black propaganda.
MOI	*Ministry of Information* (British). Equivalent of the American OWI. PWE fell under the auspices of MOI.
N.A.T.O.	*North African Theater of Operations.* American designation used in 1942–44 for military operations in North Africa.
NCO	*Non-Commissioned Officer.*
OG	*Operational Group.* OSS commando unit trained in all types of SO. OGs were composed of four officers and thirty NCOs divided into two sections. They were dispatched on missions of sabotage or guerrilla fighting.
OLIVA	Code name for a COI plan devised in 1942 to establish an SO base in China.
ONI	*Office of Naval Intelligence* (British and US).
ORA	*Organisation Résistance de l'Armée* (French). Composed of pro-Giraud groups, ORA members usually came from the original French Army of the Armistice and worked independently of other resistance elements until ORA was integrated into the consolidated forces of French resistance.
OSS	*Office of Strategic Services.* Established in June 1942 to replace COI, OSS was led by William Donovan until it was disbanded in 1945 by President Truman.
Ossex	Nickname for American Sussex teams. See Brissex.
OVERLORD	Code name for the Allied invasion of northern France in June 1944.
OWI	*Office of War Information* (American). Equivalent of the British MOI.
Partisans	Used herein to denote Yugoslav resistance fighters loyal to Josip Broz Tito.
Passy	Code name for Andre Dewavrin, head of the BCRA throughout the war.

Pathfinders　Name given to OSS/SI and SIS personnel sent into occupied France in advance of OVERLORD and of the dispatch of Sussex agents. They made advance preparations for the arrival of Sussex personnel by establishing local informer networks, recruiting reception committees, locating safe houses, etc.

PCO　*Passport Control Officer.* Cover title for British SIS officers serving abroad in official British diplomatic missions.

PURPLE　Japanese diplomatic cipher broken by the US Army in 1940. Intelligence derived from PURPLE was called MAGIC, although MAGIC would later encompass intelligence from other broken Japanese codes.

PW　*Psychological Warfare.* Subversion and propaganda activities.

PWE　*Political Warfare Executive.* Principle British wartime organization for the dissemination of propaganda.

Q　British code name for William Donovan.

R & A　*Research and Analysis.* Branch of COI and OSS.

RF Section　SOE branch that worked with Gaullist resistance groups.

SA/B　*Special Activities/Bruce.* SI branch of COI and OSS named for its wartime chief David Bruce. Later changed to SI Branch.

SA/G　*Special Activities/Goodfellow.* SO branch of COI and OSS named for its wartime chief M. Preston Goodfellow. Later changed to SO Branch.

SAS　*Special Air Service.* British commando organization.

SCAEF　*Supreme Commander Allied Expeditionary Force.*

SEAC　*Southeast Asia Command.*

Sédentaires　Resisters who lived at home and pursued their normal civilian occupations, but were armed, organized, and ready to fight in conjunction with the Allied invasion.

SHAEF　*Supreme Headquarters Allied Expeditionary Forces.*

SI　*Secret* or *Special Intelligence.* Used herein to denote HUMINT activities. Also used to describe the part of OSS that was responsible for HUMINT.

SI London　Term used to describe the OSS Secret Intelligence element based in London.

SI Washington　Term used to describe the OSS Secret Intelligence headquarters element.

SIGINT　*Signals Intelligence.* Intelligence derived from intercepted communications.

SIS	*Secret Intelligence Service.* British organization for intelligence. Also known as Broadway and MI-6.
SO	*Special Operations.* Used herein to denote sabotage, subversion, and guerrilla warfare. Used also to denote OSS element responsible for SO work.
SO London	Term used to describe the OSS Special Operations element based in London.
SO Washington	Term used to describe the OSS Special Operations headquarters element.
SOE	*Special Operations Executive* (British). Created in 1940 to conduct SO activities against targets in Axis or Axis-occupied/controlled territory. Dissolved in 1946.
Special Forces Unit No. 4	First designation for the Jedburghs in 1943.
SPOC	*Special Projects Operations Center.* Formed in Algiers by AFHQ on 23/25 May 1944 as an Anglo-American HQ staffed by SOE and SO to implement AFHQ's directives regarding the use of resistance to support ANVIL/DRAGOON.
SUSSEX	Joint Allied intelligence collection operation directed at occupied France to help lay the groundwork for and to support OVERLORD.
TORCH	Code name for the Allied invasion of French North Africa in November 1942.
ULTRA	Intelligence derived from ENIGMA decryptions.
White propaganda	Information attributable to the government that is disseminating it.
Wild Bill	Nickname for William Donovan earned during combat in the First World War.
W/T	*Wireless Transmitter.* Used to denote both the transmitting sets and the operators.
X-2	OSS counterintelligence/counterespionage branch. Obtained intelligence on enemy espionage organizations and agents.
Z	British code name for Claude Dansey, deputy to C at SIS during the war.

1 Planting the Seeds: 'Wild Bill' Donovan's Two European Missions, 1940–41, and their Impact on Anglo-American Intelligence Cooperation

> In 1940 [Bill Donovan] was sent on a fact-finding mission to England and in 1941 to the Balkans and the Middle East . . . [Afterwards he] recommended to the President . . . the need of a service to wage unorthodox warfare and to gather information through every means available . . . The seeds which Bill planted bore fruit.　　　　　　　　　　(Allen Dulles, CIA Director, 1959)[1]

INTRODUCTION

In likening the impact of William 'Wild Bill' Donovan's two European missions (1940–41) on the development of Anglo-American intelligence cooperation to the 'planting of seeds which later bore fruit,' Allen Dulles, former OSS operative and CIA director, captured the essence of what was to become a truly 'special relationship.' This transatlantic bond was perhaps unique in modern history,[2] with one sovereign Great Power at war agreeing to tutor another sovereign Great Power at peace in the ways of the spy and saboteur, which had hitherto remained private and subject to the most closely observed rules of national secrecy. This relationship developed over the course of the war into a true partnership, breaking down many of the barriers of secrecy between Britain and America and in so doing facilitating the Allied victory over the Axis powers and serving a useful purpose to the present day.

While traveling in 1940–41 at the behest of the President – but as a private citizen – Donovan performed the multiple functions of intelligence collector, liaison officer, covert diplomat, analyst, and disseminator of information. He accomplished this feat at a time when what little existed of the US intelligence 'community' was disorganized, decentralized, generally ineffective, and largely ignored by the key decision-makers in Washington. Donovan provided the President with an independent, penetrating, and informed view of events in Britain, the Mediterranean, and the Balkans during the critical period before America's entry into the war. His 1940 mission coincided with the onset of the 'Battle of Britain,' the

1

outcome of which helped him to convince American decision-makers and the US public that aiding the British was a good gamble; that Britain would not be overrun by the Nazi's, as had been Poland, Norway, the Low Countries, and France. His Mediterranean-Balkan journey in 1941 was used, *inter alia*, to help to convince some of Britain's wavering 'allies' and the leaders of neutral states that America 'was determined that Great Britain should win the war and . . . only [those] countries genuinely supporting her . . . could expect sympathy at the Peace Conference'[3] that would follow.

Donovan's reputation with the British as a war hero, anti-Nazi, Anglophile, and confidant of Roosevelt opened doors to him in the secret world of British intelligence and special operations that were closed to others. His experiences on the two missions covered in this chapter gave him unparalleled insights into the functions of intelligence and unorthodox warfare. They clarified his views and strengthened his conviction that there was an urgent need for a centralized American intelligence entity with a special operations component. They also helped to pave the way for this entity's creation, and Donovan's appointment by President Roosevelt as the 'Coordinator of Information' (COI) in July 1941.[4] As the official OSS war report explains:

> Through COI [and its successor, the Office of Strategic Services 'OSS'], the US was beginning its first organized venture into the fields of espionage, propaganda, subversion and related activities . . . The significance of COI/OSS was in the concept of the relationship between these varied activities and their combined effect as one of the most potent weapons in modern warfare . . . This concept evolved from two missions performed for President Roosevelt in 1940 and 1941 by William Joseph Donovan.[5]

Donovan's two missions also forged a personal relationship with key members of the British government and secret services. The introduction of this element of trust proved crucial in helping to make the coordination of clandestine work by OSS and the British Secret Intelligence Service (SIS) and Special Operations Executive (SOE)[6] both possible and productive.

ROOSEVELT'S 'UNOFFICIAL REPRESENTATIVE,' JULY–AUGUST 1940

You are like unto rivers of water in a dry place
(Radiogram from Lord Beaverbrook to Donovan evaluating the latter's July–August mission to England, September 1940)[7]

Background

After France's dramatic collapse in the spring of 1940, Britain stood alone against Hitler's military machine. Churchill was charismatically defiant, but pessimism in Washington about Britain's chances for survival – stoked by reports from

Joseph P. Kennedy, the defeatist US Ambassador to the Court of St James – left America deeply divided. At issue was whether or not to give Britain war materiel which was needed at home by the underequipped US military. Kennedy strongly advised Roosevelt not to risk 'holding the bag in a war in which the Allies expect to be beaten,'[8] and 'his pessimistic outlook and lack of appreciation of the strength of British public morale and determination to fight . . . [called for] an independent and objective assessment by a prominent American.'[9] As the influential director of British Naval Intelligence, Admiral John Godfrey, later observed, 'The object of Bill Donovan's mission was to discover if we were in earnest about the war, and if we were worth supporting.'[10] The general mood of isolation was very strong in America and Britain was desperate.

At the same time, concern was also growing in America about Nazi 'Fifth Column' subversive activities in the Western Hemisphere. These fears were both shared and cultivated by the British, who had dispatched the Canadian businessman William Stephenson on behalf of SIS to America earlier in the year to assess the situation. Stephenson reported that the Germans were attempting to sabotage the British resupply effort and advocated creating a British intelligence entity in the US – later named 'British Security Coordination (BSC)'[11] – which he returned to lead. BSC, Stephenson argued:

> should cover a considerably wider field than the collection of secret intelligence by the old and well-tried methods . . . It should comprise everything that . . . could not be done by overt means to assure sufficient aid for Britain, to counter the enemy's subversive plans throughout the Western Hemisphere and eventually to bring the US into the war. This included counterespionage, political warfare, and 'special operations.'[12]

Stephenson identified Donovan, who was very close to Navy Secretary Frank Knox and War Secretary Henry Stimson, as a friend of Britain who could further his objectives, foremost with regard to materiel assistance, but also in US intelligence coordination. With a future transatlantic military partnership on the horizon, the intelligence issue increasingly preoccupied the forward-thinking Stephenson. Donovan had traveled widely before the war,[13] was well versed in international affairs, a war hero, and a public figure. Perhaps most importantly for the longer-term, he 'shared Stephenson's concern regarding US weakness in the field of wartime intelligence and the absence of any US organization responsible for coordinating information derived from a variety of sources.'[14] Both men were convinced of the need for a non-military central authority for the collection, evaluation, and distribution of intelligence. Summarizing the role played by Stephenson in these early days, a BSC staffer wrote in 1944 that:

> Stephenson's discussions with . . . Donovan before and after the latter's historic visit to London and the Continent in July 1940, and early in 1941, were largely instrumental in bringing about a clearer conception of the need for a

properly coordinated American intelligence service . . . Donovan's proposals for the establishment of a service for strategic information . . . were to a considerable extent based on his conversations with Mr. Stephenson and his colleagues.[15]

Stephenson later told his biographer H. Montgomery Hyde that his cultivation of Donovan to further British goals proved to be absolutely correct.[16]

The choice of Donovan to visit Britain as Roosevelt's unofficial representative was a natural one for the reasons previously outlined. American and British historians, however, differ somewhat on precisely who was the real driving force behind the choice of Donovan and the mission itself. The OSS war report notes that in July 1940, Navy Secretary Knox 'proposed to the President . . . that [Donovan] be sent to England to study the situation, with particular reference to the work of the German Fifth Column.'[17]

Donovan had helped to prepare Knox – in the former's Georgetown home – for his Senate confirmation hearings earlier in July, and the two agreed on the threat posed to US interests by Nazi aggression, both in Europe and North America. Donovan was summoned to the White House in July, where he met with Knox, Stimson, and Secretary of State Cordell Hull, and was asked to travel to Britain with a mandate 'to learn about Britain's handling of the Fifth Column problem.'[18] Donovan's biographer Corey Ford explained the motives behind his visit as an effort by the Donovan-Knox-Stimson triumvirate to gather the evidence necessary to convince Roosevelt to 'bypass Congress' and sanction the transfer of 50 First World War-era destroyers to the Royal Navy to bolster Britain's resupply effort in its time of most dire need.[19]

Stephenson, meanwhile, claimed to have first suggested to Donovan that he 'pay a visit to Britain with the object of investigating conditions at first hand and assessing for himself the British war effort, its most urgent requirements, and its potential chances for success.'[20] Stephenson had the motive to do so, provided he had recognized Donovan's potential at this point. When asked in 1944 to comment on a written British account of his relationship with Stephenson, however, Donovan contradicted the assertion that Roosevelt sent him to London 'as a result of' discussions between him and Stephenson by scribbling in the margin, 'Did not know S[tephenson] then. I met him only after return.'[21] This challenges the claims of Hyde and Stephenson's BSC deputy, Dick Ellis, which imply that Donovan and Stephenson exchanged views prior to the 1940 mission. Perhaps, as CIA historian Thomas Troy argues, '[Stephenson's] subsequent close connections with Donovan have understandably caused him to push the line of collaboration further back than the facts justify, to convert . . . advance knowledge into inspiration of the trip.'[22] One might also argue that Donovan, a busy man in 1944, simply got it wrong.

In any event, it is not disputed that Stephenson played a key role in ensuring that Donovan was well received in Britain. When Donovan read an OSS statement in

1944 that Lord Lothian, Britain's Ambassador to the US, first arranged for him to see Churchill, he replaced Lothian's name with Stephenson's.[23] As BSC's Ellis explained in his unpublished memoir: 'Stephenson strongly urged that Donovan be accorded every facility and the most frank and complete confidence as one who was not only influential in the highest circles but who possessed the ear and good will of the President.'[24] And as Stephenson himself told Hyde, 'I endeavored to marshal my friends in high places to bare their breasts [to Donovan],'[25] whom the BSC chief evidently saw as an important interlocutor.

The Visit

On 14 July 1940, Donovan left the US for England – via Lisbon – on a Flying Clipper, armed with letters of introduction from Knox, Hull, and others with important British contacts.[26] He arrived at the onset of the Battle of Britain, and coincidentally was in England on 22 July when SOE[27] was established with the objective, in Churchill's words, to 'set Europe ablaze.'[28] His visit was arranged without informing Ambassador Kennedy, who later protested vehemently to Undersecretary of State Sumner Welles. 'Wild Bill,' as he was known to the world from his First World War exploits, was determined to make an independent assessment without interference from Kennedy. He left Britain in August with a full appreciation of the war on its central front and of the various secret efforts to fight it.

Donovan arrived in England on 17 July and wasted little time. He met the King, was briefed by 'C' (Stewart Menzies, chief of SIS) on the overseas organization of SIS, met Colin Gubbins – who took control of SOE's subversion activities, then of SOE itself in September 1943 – and Sir Frank Nelson, an old SIS-hand tipped to be SOE's first chief. He met Paddy Beaumont-Nesbitt, Director of Military Intelligence, Desmond Morton, Churchill's secretary for liaison with the British intelligence community, and then he saw the Prime Minister himself.[29]

Donovan's appointment diary for 22 July–1 August 1940 is filled with entries for other senior British officials. He saw the First, Second, and Third Sea Lords, the Assistant Chief of the Naval Staff, the Director of Naval Intelligence, the Minister of Information, the Secretary of State for Air, various Air Commodores, Parliamentary Secretaries, and lesser functionaries.[30] He made sure to fully debrief the US military attaché, Raymond Lee, and his staff, who were generally in agreement that the British would weather the storm in the near term (Lee himself put the odds in favor of British survival at 2:1).[31] Donovan also met with the War Cabinet and many other persons of authority,[32] some of whom, like Lord Beaverbrook, asked him to use his influence to obtain for Britain specific technical assistance.[33] As Ellis later observed:

He quickly won the confidence of his hosts by his forceful personality, tact and understanding, and had not only been given every facility to visit military training centers, dockyards, and war factories . . . but also to study the workings of

intelligence and security organizations and the various war-time 'special services' [for] propaganda, counterpropaganda, and clandestine operations.[34]

Ford supports this assertion:

> Because he was Bill Donovan, the British showed him things no American had
> seen before: their top-secret invention of radar, their newest interceptor planes,
> their coastal defenses. He was made privy to some of Britain's ingenious propa-
> ganda devices . . . They unlocked their safes, and initiated him into the myster-
> ies of [SIS] and the techniques of unorthodox warfare.[35]

Indeed, Donovan's contacts with intelligence functionaries during the London
trip were far from insignificant. It has even been suggested that Menzies personally helped to arrange his schedule.[36] And in a note to Donovan dated 25 July 1940,
an unidentified contact wrote:

> I understand you have already taken notes in Colonel Menzies' department and
> I am told by one of his people that you do not wish to take back with you any
> bulky information . . . If however you do want anything further . . . you may be
> sure Lord Swinton will do all he can to help and indeed myself of course too.[37]

That Broadway – as SIS was also known – gave a foreigner access to some of its
most closely guarded secrets is remarkable, even with the blessing of so many in
British government, given its traditional suspicious attitude and security concerns. Such was the trust the British placed in Donovan; a trust that later characterized much of the Anglo-US clandestine relationship. London's desperation at this
time also broke down barriers which would have been considerably stronger had
Hitler not been on Britain's doorstep.

Donovan's intelligence role was further enhanced by Navy Secretary Knox's
request that he approach Admiral Godfrey to propose intelligence cooperation between the US and British Navies. Donovan first met with Godfrey on 15 July and
offered to 'recommend direct liaison' between the two naval offices, and to arrange for the British to receive consular reports from American diplomatic missions abroad, particularly from those operating in French ports. The former's
proposal must have struck a chord, for the two men met again on 22 July, and on 25
July for dinner.[38] Godfrey subsequently showed Donovan 'the part of [his] department which is accommodated in the sub-ground,'[39] and invited him to spend the
evening of 3 August – Donovan's last night in Britain – at his estate, where the two
men 'sat up to 2 a.m. . . . talking.'[40] Donovan's commitments to Godfrey were
passed on to Knox, and on 5 September, 'a presidential order was issued authoriz-
ing the British attaches in Washington to receive copies of all State Department
and consular reports that contained information of value to them.'[41] This cooperation was soon extended, and Donovan was able to assure Stephenson that he

'would be given every assistance in obtaining information on any topics he might raise.'[42]

Donovan's friendship with Godfrey later proved of considerable use to the former's fledgling COI apparatus. Godfrey's note to Donovan on 20 July 1941 illustrates the feelings of mutual trust and spirit of collaboration prevailing at that time between the two men:

> As always you can count on my help in every way, and if at any time you feel that our experience on any particular subject would be valuable, I shall be only too glad to send across the expert by the quickest possible means.[43]

Godfrey later wrote that:

> It was obvious that we had a good friend in Donovan, and one who had the ear of the President and knew how to work with the British . . . Before [the visit] he was told that he would find us 'difficult,' secretive and patronizing. His actual experience, so he said, was exactly the opposite.[44]

The fruits to be harvested from the seeds planted by Donovan in London were many and varied.

In assessing Britain's capacity to fight a conventional and covert war, Donovan was by mid-1940 already acting as his country's *de facto* 'Coordinator of Intelligence.' This role was recognized and encouraged by the British. Donovan's behavior in Britain, moreover, clearly illustrates how advanced his thinking already was on intelligence coordination. According to CIA's Troy:

> To nearly everybody he spoke to he had addressed a request for documents, a report, a study, or answers to questions put forth in his own name or at the behest of some official in Washington. Thus, he had asked for copies of training syllabi . . . militia regulations, even for stories about RAF experiences. He had asked for reports on the European food situation, on economic controls in Britain, and for reports on [the Ministries of] Supply, Information, and Economic Warfare.[45]

The Aftermath

Donovan returned to the US on 4 August 1940, 'confident of [Britain's] ability to survive, . . . convinced that American aid could have a decisive impact on the war's outcome'[46] and that 'Fifth Column activity had become a factor of major importance in modern warfare.'[47] He saw Knox, met with senior members of the military and Administration, including the Chief of Naval Operations and the Secretary of War, and briefed Roosevelt on 9 August. He met with members of both houses of Congress, co-wrote a series of articles on Nazi Fifth Column activities for the *Chicago Daily News*, and gave a celebrated nationwide radio interview.[48] The theme of his reports, according to Ellis, was as follows: 'The will [of the British] to resist Nazi aggression was accompanied by a capacity to do so provided the equipment could be made available to supplement what was being produced by their own efforts.'[49] Donovan recommended transfers of war materiel at once, starting with the fifty old destroyers.

Donovan's personal papers from this period are filled with letters of appreciation from those who benefited from his supply of information obtained in Britain. One of the first letters Donovan received after returning to the US was from Edward Stettinius, Jr., then a member of the Defense Advisory Commission:'I handed the President a digest of the British material, . . . describing how it had all come about and that it was available [due to] your fine efforts . . . He was most pleased and promised to review the material immediately.'[50]

The Assistant Chief of Staff for Army Intelligence (G-2), Brigadier General Sherman Miles – who later tried to undermine efforts to establish a centralized intelligence organization – wrote to Donovan several times in the autumn of 1940, expressing gratitude for information on the British Army, Ministry of Information, and the European food situation.[51] On 1 October, Donovan advised Roosevelt of a report on British economic controls, and on 5 October, received a note of thanks from the US Director of Naval Intelligence for information from Britain's Ministry of Economic Warfare.[52] Such activities later left little doubt in the minds of Donovan's supporters on both sides of the Atlantic about his usefulness and suitability for coordinating intelligence.

The British credited Donovan with facilitating the process of US materiel assistance and turning the tide of opinion in Washington decisively toward Britain. As Godfrey later observed: 'Not only did Mr. Roosevelt accept Donovan's appreciation of our war effort, but he approved in principle the supply of material on a large scale, which developed into 'lend lease' and later full alliance.'[53]

Donovan told Stephenson on 22 August that the plan for transferring the destroyers had been approved. After Roosevelt's closest advisor, Harry Hopkins, visited Britain shortly thereafter: 'a million rifles, [some] 75mm guns, and ammunition were delivered to England and shipments of aircraft and spare parts were expedited.'[54]

BSC's Ellis concluded that these shipments 'bridged the gap between the heavy losses sustained at Dunkirk and the expansion of British aircraft and armament production.'[55]

While acknowledging the important role Donovan played in increasing the flow of supply to the UK, it is important to note that his was not the only American assessment mission to Britain at this time, nor was his the only voice arguing for closer Anglo-US ties. Shortly after the fall of France, 'a procession of official American emissaries . . . began to descend on London.'[56] Among the most important of these were visits by US Army Air Corps Lt. Colonel Carl Spaatz[57] to discuss bombing techniques in June 1940, and a visit a month later by the US 'Special Observers Group,' comprised of the Assistant Chief of Naval Operations, the Chief of the Army Air Corps Plans Division, and the Army Assistant Chief of Staff for Plans, to investigate Britain's ability to replace the materiel losses sustained at Dunkirk.[58]

All of these activities facilitated closer Anglo-US collaboration. The reports of the Special Observers Group, for example, prompted Roosevelt to authorize secret military staff talks in Washington in late 1940.[59] An exchange of scientific missions in the late summer and autumn of 1940 led to broad 'collaboration in technical matters.'[60] Nonetheless, Donovan's reports certainly 'strengthened Roosevelt's resolve' to assist the British and helped to override the reluctance of senior US Army officials to do so.[61]

The goodwill that Donovan earned from the British on this first mission can be clearly gleaned from the record, as can the constructive working relationship that was rapidly established. Lord Halifax, as Foreign Secretary, wrote to Anthony Eden at the War Office and Archibald Sinclair at the Air Ministry in December to explain that, in his view, Donovan was:

> thoroughly reliable to the extent that it was decided that certain secret information might be disclosed to him . . . Since his return to Washington he has been most helpful to our cause in every way, and for this we have [to thank] the nature of the welcome which was accorded to him in London.[62]

Some of the 'secret information' noted by Halifax included material from Hugh Dalton on his new SOE, which Donovan duly passed on to James Forrestal at the White House.[63] In letters exchanged between Donovan and Sir Ronald Tree of the British Ministry of Information (MOI) in August and September, the progress the former had made on matters discussed in London was addressed as was Tree's responsiveness to requests by Donovan for more information.[64] On 27 August, Donovan advised Churchill's Secretary, Brendan Bracken, that:

> I think my estimate [of Britain's ability to hold out] has had a healthy effect on the attitude of mind of our people in authority here . . . They are going to do their best to comply with [your] request as to these items [weapons, ammunition, spare parts, destroyers] for which there is such pressing need.[65]

Cabling Bracken again a month later, Donovan reported: 'Papers received and am very grateful for superb job you have done.'[66]

Robert Vansittart's 28 October letter to Donovan is yet another example of the degree of friendship Donovan often managed to achieve with influential British interlocutors at this time: 'My friendship for you is a really affectionate one, and you are one of the people of whom I have always felt it was a pity that fate laid our ways so far apart.'[67] This was presumably in response to Donovan's letter of 26 September, which reported: 'The things I promised [to] urge upon the President I did, and all of them have now been done . . . Opinion here is rapidly moving in support of Britain.'[68]

In addition to his work on general assistance to Britain, Donovan returned to Washington determined to convince Roosevelt to create an intelligence 'clearinghouse' to deal with the vast amount of secret information useful in US war preparations. Roosevelt encouraged Donovan to work closely with Stephenson and to 'sound out senior U.S. officials of government departments and the armed services'[69] on the centralization of intelligence; the two soon established an informal means passing key items from BSC to the President. This included information on Nazi subversive activities in the Western Hemisphere, which was often also passed to J. Edgar Hoover of the Federal Bureau of Investigation (FBI), with whom Stephenson had already established a working relationship.[70] Donovan and Stephenson – 'Big Bill' and 'Little Bill' as they would be remembered in intelligence folklore – forged a pupil–tutor relationship which laid the groundwork for future collaboration. This cooperation born of mutual trust contributed to Britain's willingness in December to share even more of its secrets with Donovan when the latter embarked on a second special mission, this time to London, the Mediterranean, and the Balkans.

THE NAVY DEPARTMENT'S 'OBSERVER,' DECEMBER 1940–MARCH 1941

'Many congratulations upon all you are doing.' (Churchill to Donovan, January 1941)[71]
'All I have tried to do is to make it clear that the President meant what he said.'
(Donovan's reply)[72]

Background

The winter of 1940–41 was a very difficult one for Britain, despite its victories against the Luftwaffe in the summer, the Italian navy at Taranto and army at Sidi Barrani in the autumn, and over Ambassador Kennedy, who resigned on 1 December. German U-boats were tightening their stranglehold on the British resupply effort, the German 'Afrika Korps' was deploying in Libya to rescue the Italians and press the attack, Hitler was turning his attentions to the Balkans, and Britain was still virtually alone in the war. Churchill argued convincingly for increased involvement by the US, especially the provision of US naval escorts for his badly depleted merchant fleet and for more war materiel, which he could divert to the hard pressed Middle East and Balkan fronts. But America remained wary about provoking Germany into a precipitate declaration of war and was generally undecided about its next move.

Against this backdrop, Stephenson pressed Donovan to use his influence in Washington once again to help ameliorate the situation. He convinced the American with little effort that Berlin would be unlikely to declare war on Washington short of direct US aggression as long as Britain remained undefeated, and that 'for the American Navy to participate in convoy duty should be regarded as an essential step in the US policy of playing for time . . . until American preparedness was sufficiently advanced to meet the German challenge.'[73]

Knox, Stimson, and Hull, however, were not satisfied that the potential gains from increased aid to Britain outweighed the risks of more direct US involvement. They required more information and responded positively to Donovan's overture that he go again to Britain, then to the Mediterranean, to gather supporting evidence.[74] As early as August, Donovan corresponded with the US Naval Attaché in London about the Mediterranean region, probably in an effort to gather information to justify a trip, and was advised as follows: 'The Mediterranean shows signs of becoming a vital area, especially Egypt . . . Some think that this may actually be the most vital area within a few weeks.'[75] In his role as an 'unofficial US government representative,' Donovan was to call on: 'leading civil and service people so that as an experienced soldier and politician he can form a judgment of the situation, and find out what special assistance the United States might be able to give.'[76] To enhance his standing, Donovan was also appointed as an official US Navy representative.

Some on the British side who were familiar with Donovan's prior mission, particularly Stephenson, Ambassador Lord Lothian, and Foreign Secretary Lord Halifax, took steps to ensure that Donovan would be received warmly by British officials throughout his travels. Stephenson 'drafted the appropriate cables . . . so that Donovan would be granted every possible facility for this journey, [noting that] it was impossible to overemphasize the importance of Donovan's visit.' He characterized Donovan's contribution to Britain's interests as 'vital,' and warned that the actions of the American would be inconsistent with and outside the normal channels of orthodox diplomacy.[77] Lothian, meanwhile, cabled the Foreign Office as follows: 'Donovan . . . has done splendid work for us since he [last] visited England [and should be] looked after'[78] . . . '[He] is a valuable champion of our cause and is on the inside of all pro-British activities.'[79]

Halifax, meanwhile, characterized Donovan in a letter to Duff Cooper as: 'one of our best and most influential friends in America [who] carries a great deal of weight both with the Service Departments and the Administration.'[80]

Donovan saw Godfrey, who – at the behest of Stephenson – had advised the Commander-in-Chief of the Mediterranean Fleet, Admiral Cunningham, of the impending mission. According to BSC's Hyde, the Godfrey-Stephenson signal 'made it abundantly clear to the Admiral and his staff that Donovan was the most important emissary that they were ever likely to meet in this world or the next.' This communication, in fact, explained clearly why the British were so willing to work closely with Donovan, who was still without a government portfolio:

Donovan exercises controlling influence over Knox, strong influence over Stimson, friendly advisory influence over the President and Hull . . . Being a Republican and a Catholic of Irish descent he has a following of the strongest opposition to [Roosevelt] . . . [He] was responsible for getting us the destroyers, the [Sperry] bomb-sight and other urgent requirements . . . There is no doubt that we can achieve infinitely more through [him] than through any other

individual . . . He is receptive and should be made fully aware of our requirements and deficiencies and can be trusted to represent our needs in the right
quarters, and in the right way in the U.S.A.[81]

After the trip, Donovan told Stephenson that 'he had never been treated in such
royal and exalted fashion and that the red carpet had been thicker and wider than
he thought it was possible to lay.'[82] Indeed, Churchill left no doubt as to his wishes
that Donovan be accorded every confidence when he had his Chiefs of Staff advise
the various relevant authorities as follows:

> Donovan is visiting the Mediterranean as an observer for President Roosevelt
> with whom he has great influence . . . [He] is one of our best friends in the
> U.S.A. His object is to study and report [on] our strategic situation in the Medi-
> terranean, but his terms of reference are very wide . . . Prime Minister directs
> that every facility should be afforded to [Donovan], who has been taken fully
> into our confidence.[83]

Interestingly, the record also indicates that in early December 1940 – despite
what was shared with Donovan in July – not all were convinced in London, including Churchill, that British secrets should be made so readily available to the
Americans. In a letter from Archibald Sinclair, Secretary of State for Air, to Lord
Halifax on 7 December, for example, Sinclair advised:

> [Donovan's] visit must, if it is to be equally successful [as his last visit], be con-
> ducted in a similar atmosphere . . . If it is not, the effect will be deplorable . . .
> The Prime Minister and Lord Beaverbrook, [however,] have recently expressed
> strong views against giving the Americans secret information. I think, there-
> fore, that you should perhaps mention [this] to the Prime Minister and obtain
> from him directions on how far we should take Colonel Donovan into our con-
> fidence.[84]

Other British documents of 7 December further illustrate the uncertainty surrounding this issue. A memorandum from a Foreign Office functionary to his
superior, for example, noted:

> [Sinclair's] private secretary has mentioned that if Colonel Donovan is to dis-
> cuss the military situation in the Near East during his visit to this country it will
> be of the greatest importance that a decision should be taken as to what exactly
> he may be told, since our military strategy in this part of the world is being kept
> very secret.[85]

This particular matter was evidently settled via a note scribbled at the bottom
which said, 'As far as we are concerned I think he [Donovan] can be told anything.'[86]

A diary entry in late December 1940 by Vivian Dykes, assigned by Churchill to
be Donovan's minder and traveling companion for much of the Mediterranean

trip, is also illuminating as regards the mixed feelings on Donovan and the 'secrets question.' Dykes expressed his fear that Donovan might in the end prove to be less a friend to Britain than the mutual self-interest in wartime collaboration might otherwise indicate. He may have been taking a longer view of British imperial interests in competition with American interests abroad, as perhaps were Churchill and Beaverbrook, when he wrote:

> Donovan put over the American point of view very interestingly. He urged for both sides looking at the [war] from the standpoint of mutual self-interest only. The violently pro-English American [is] liable to be one of this country's worst friends in America.[87]

Dykes may simply have been suggesting that because Donovan was so widely perceived to be an Anglophile, he did not have credibility with Americans who were more skeptical of the British. If he was predicting that Donovan would put America's interests above all else, however, he was to be proven correct. This was especially evident in 1943–5, when Donovan steered his service on an independent course when US and British interests clashed in the Balkans and Far East.

Despite the debate, Donovan and his British supporters – Stephenson and Godfrey in particular – won the day. Donovan was recognized at the highest levels in Britain as a key player in London's efforts to move Washington from the role of passive partner to wartime co-belligerent. As such, he could count on increasing assistance and frankness in the most sensitive areas of intelligence and special operations. His mission to the Mediterranean and Balkan areas increasingly took on an intelligence character, was recognized and promoted as such by the British, and was welcomed by Donovan. British Passport Control Officers (PCOs) – SIS undercover operatives posted abroad – were even charged for the expenses incurred by Donovan along the way, by instruction from London.[88] Donovan almost certainly consulted with these officers about intelligence matters, including possibly operations, during his journey. Dykes' diary refers to contacts with PCOs in Madrid, Athens, Sofia, and in Belgrade, where Dykes also had discussions about the 'D Organization,'[89] in reference to SOE and its SIS predecessor, Section D. The British were educating Donovan as part of their investment in the future.

Bermuda and London

As a sign of the importance the British placed on Donovan's trip, Stephenson chose to accompany him as far as London. The pair left for Bermuda – the first leg of their journey – on 6 December 1940. Bermuda, a British colony, had become the center of Stephenson's hemispheric censorship campaign, since all airborne mail from North America was routed through the island's airport. It was also a convenient transit point to Europe via Lisbon. When bad weather delayed by two weeks their onward flight to Portugal, Donovan almost certainly was briefed on BSC mail censorship and other Bermuda-based operations.

When the two men reached London, they immediately launched into a whirl-wind series of meetings, which rivaled those of Donovan's July visit. They met Churchill, who requested that Donovan also visit the Balkan front as a guest of the British, had meetings with the chiefs of the armed services and a panoply of other officials, including the heads of the Ministry of Economic Warfare (MEW), SOE, and the Political Warfare Executive (PWE).[90] Donovan went on to visit various British military installations, including a naval signals school, a dockyard where some of the transferred US destroyers were receiving refits, a training depot, com-bined and air operations headquarters, a flying-boat station, radio direction find-ing facility, and beach and anti-aircraft defenses. He learned about the origins of the Special Service Battalions – which developed into the Commandos – and even experienced an air raid on Plymouth.[91]

The intelligence-related contacts that Donovan made in July 1940 proved particularly useful to him in December. In his substantive discussions with SOE, British special operations in Latin America were addressed and 'policy decisions taken,' including the coordination of Caribbean-based operations under the aus-pices of Stephenson's BSC. What authority Donovan had to make 'policy de-cisions' on clandestine operational matters concerning the Western Hemisphere remains unclear, as Hoover's FBI had jurisdiction from the American side. This Anglo-US coordination, nonetheless, 'provided the necessary framework for in-telligence and communications as well as a channel for collaboration with the US services where this was possible.'[92] Donovan and the British most likely viewed the former's informal mandate from the President liberally, and both sides made the most of this opportunity for face-to-face discussions. On his return to London in late February 1941, Donovan's relationship with SOE – and introduction to the covert war effort – was further enhanced by a full briefing on the functions of the Executive and visits to SOE training facilities.[93] The extent of Donovan's contacts with SIS in December are less clear, but it is known that he met with and 'talked freely' with Menzies,[94] who in turn attended Donovan's London debrief in Feb-ruary.[95] Knox's 'special observer' was rapidly acquiring a framework of know-ledge upon which he could base subsequent proposals for the establishment of an American special operations and intelligence collection capability.

The Middle East

After tours of British facilities in Gibraltar and Malta, including discussions with the garrison and fleet commanders, Donovan spent a week in Cairo and the West-ern Desert. There he met with General Archibald Wavell, who had defeated the Italians at Sidi Barrani.[96] He saw Air Chief Marshal Longmore and Generals Rich-ard O'Connor and Henry Maitland Wilson, debriefed various other senior of-ficers, toured Army intelligence establishments, and learned of commando operations.[97] On his return to the region via Cyprus and Palestine (5–23 February), Donovan met the Chief of the Imperial General Staff, Field Marshal Sir John Dill, visiting Australian Prime Minister Robert Menzies, and Admiral Andrew Cunningham.

Throughout his journey, Donovan made the most of his time and acquired useful material from the British – much of which was secret. In Cairo, for example, he drafted a report on anti-aircraft defense of the Suez Canal gleaned from a discussion with a British Brigadier.[98] Whilst in the Western Desert, he acquired a memorandum on long-range penetration activities.[99] He later distributed this intelligence to consumers in Washington who were short of reliable information about the areas he visited, and in so doing, further enhanced his credibility with all concerned. Donovan also passed information gleaned from his various meetings back to the British, with his own often forceful and compelling analysis of events. Briefing Dill after returning to Cairo from the Balkans leg of his journey, Donovan 'put a good deal of stiffening into [him about the importance of keeping a foothold in the Balkans].'[100] And he insisted on fully coordinating the field reports he drafted and sent back to Washington with Wavell and Longmore, lest they disapprove or be embarrassed by anything contained therein.[101] Thus, Donovan earned the working trust of these key players on the British side both with his frankness and his discretion. These relationships paid dividends later when Donovan needed the cooperation of senior British field commanders for his intelligence and special operations work.

In addition to his various intelligence collection efforts, Donovan played the role of secret diplomat, cajoling and sometimes intimidating his non-Allied interlocutors in discussions about American intentions. His meetings throughout the Middle East included many substantive ones with British and American diplomats, some of whom briefed him on British interests in Iraq, Palestine, and Syria, where in some cases officials were flirting with the Axis Legations. He met with such personages as the Grand Mufti of Jerusalem, the Iraqi Regent, Prime and Foreign Ministers, and King Farouk of Egypt, warning them all in no uncertain terms that:

(1) America was determined at all costs to ensure the defeat of Germany, which menaced her own security; (2) No [US] war materiel would go to countries not definitely in the Allied camp; [and] (3) Any such countries would get no mercy from America at the peace conference [to follow the defeat of the Axis].[102]

The implication of this message was clear: America would help Britain to the utmost, Britain's friends were America's friends, and America would retaliate against Axis collaborators.[103] He carried the warning to all of his non-Allied interlocutors, with some degree of effect, particularly in the Balkans. At the end of the mission, Foreign Secretary Eden advised Churchill as follows:

Donovan has devoted himself to making it clear where the United States stand and that the President means what he says. His courageous and downright speaking and his wise handling of men has been of very great value to us at a critical moment in the Balkans and the Middle East.[104]

The Balkans

Donovan left Cairo for the Balkans on 15 January 1941, stopping first in Athens for meetings with the Greek leadership (16–17 January). He then proceeded to Sofia for talks with the Bulgarian regime (20–22 January) and to Belgrade for meetings with Yugoslav leaders (23–24 January), before going back to northern Greece to view the Albanian front (25–28 January) and thence to Ankara (31 January–4 February) for discussions with the Turks. He had extended his mission to the Balkans at Churchill's request; the Prime Minister 'was anxious to find some means of upsetting Hitler's timetable for the subjugation of the Balkan countries.'[105]

In Athens, Donovan saw Greece's King George, General Ioannis Metaxas, who was Greece's virtual dictator, and the Commander-in-Chief of the Greek Army, General Alexander Papagos, as well as senior British officials. He encouraged the Greeks to keep fighting, gave assurances that 'the U.S. would see the Allies through,' and asked for a list of Greek materiel requirements for consideration under the US Lend-Lease Bill provisions.[106] Once again, Donovan's intervention paid political dividends for Britain. After meeting Donovan one evening: '[Papagos] changed his attitude during the night and was now more disposed to favor acceptance of [Britain's] offer of troops . . . [Previously, he would only agree to accept supplies for fear of provoking the Germans into intervening]'.[107] Donovan's later detour back to northern Greece and the Albanian border area proved to be less eventful, but gave him a thorough appreciation of the tactical situation. His first-hand account of the Albanian Front and other experiences added to his credibility in Washington, as evidenced in a diary entry for 20 March 1941 by Roosevelt's Treasury Secretary Henry Morgenthau:

> Donovan is the first man I have talked to that I would be willing to really back . . . He has been for a week actually in the trenches up in Albania . . . He was down in Libya when they took that last town . . . He was with Wavell for over a week [and] was with Eden in Cairo.[108]

In Sofia, Donovan encountered a regime all but cowed into submission by German threats. Nonetheless, he carried his 'straight-talking' message about US intentions to King Boris and his ministers, with little effect. The menacing presence of seventeen German divisions just across Bulgaria's border with Romania left Boris with little choice but to acquiesce in Hitler's demands. While he was unable to drive a wedge between Sofia and Berlin, Donovan's 'arguments caused [Boris] to hesitate before allowing German troops to [transit Bulgaria] in order to attack the British forces who were seeking to gain a foothold in Greece . . . Churchill had indicated he would be happy with a delay of twenty-four hours; Donovan secured a delay of eight days.'[109] From an intelligence collection perspective, the trip proved valuable in that Donovan could make a personal appraisal of German influence in Bulgaria and of the key political figures there. His findings assisted

Washington in assessing the state of play in the Balkans and was particularly useful to the British, whose interests were most directly threatened.

Donovan's visit to neighboring Yugoslavia proved, perhaps, to be more worthwhile to Anglo-American interests than anything he had accomplished on the mission to date. Arriving in Belgrade, he found the regime to be nearly as intimidated by Hitler as King Boris had been, with Prince Paul poised to collaborate with Berlin on the transit of troops. One of Donovan's interlocutors, however, was the nationalist Yugloslav Air Force chief, General Dusan Simovic, who led a secret group of opponents to the collaborationist regime. Donovan responded to the General's queries about British capabilities and American intentions by reassuring him of America's support as best he could and conveying a clear message: America would enter the war, and with the help of her Allies, would defeat the Axis and treat collaborators mercilessly.

Accounts of this crucial moment in Yugoslavia's turbulent history vary, with some arguing that Donovan influenced Simovic's decision to launch his coup d'état, others attributing it to British scheming, and still more claiming that the coup would have happened in any event. Those who ascribe to the 'Donovan theory' include Stephenson's biographer Hyde, BSC's Ellis, and Donovan's biographer Ford. All three have written unequivocally that Simovic's decision to move against Prince Paul was a direct result of Donovan's personal assurances that America would enter the war.[110]

The arguments put forth by Professor Harry Hinsley about the coup are somewhat more convincing, although there is no mention of Donovan's meeting with Simovic in his 3000-page official account of Britain's wartime intelligence activities. Hinsley attributes Simovic's actions to a combination of factors, including the persuasiveness of the British Minister in Belgrade, the encouragement of British attachés and special operations officers, and Yugoslav internal politics. 'While British participation in the [coup] plans no doubt contributed to their success,' Hinsley has argued, 'it is clear that even without direct British encouragement there would still have been a coup.'[111] SOE's Bickham Sweet-Escott agrees:

> SOE was entitled to take some credit for the pro-Allied coup d'état . . . by the Serb Peasant Party, because our Minister had encouraged our people to keep in touch with the leaders of the Party, which we had been financing, but most of us thought the coup would have happened if SOE hadn't existed at all.[112]

A recently declassified SOE document titled, 'Report to SO – On Certain SO2 Activities in Yugoslavia,' appears to support the Hinsley/Sweet-Escott line. It discusses British activities leading up to the Simovic coup and confirms that special operations officers were indeed working to overthrow Prince Paul's government: 'The work of SO2 [the precursor to SOE] during these days . . . was essentially that of urging the necessity of action for a coup d'etat upon all our friends and everyone with whom we had contact [in Yugoslavia].'[113] These documents conclude, however, that: 'There is no doubt at all that the coup d'etat was carried out and the Prince overthrown as a definite rejection of his policy of the [Tripartite] Pact.'[114] This verdict implies that the coup plotters were motivated by far more than British overtures. It is interesting also that Donovan scribbled the word 'No' in the margin of an internal OSS document next to the following statement: 'There is no doubt that it was entirely due to the line [Donovan] took . . . that General Simovic was persuaded to eject the then pro-German Government.'[115]

The fact that Donovan met with Simovic at the decisive moment is nonetheless significant, as is the fact that the British secret services were simultaneously attempting to influence events to similar ends. With British and US interests coinciding in this way, it is very probable that the events surrounding the Simovic coup afford a very early example of proactive collaboration between Donovan and British intelligence. Whatever his precise role, Donovan's actions almost certainly added to his credibility with both the British and Roosevelt by demonstrating that he could be useful both in unorthodox diplomacy and intelligence collection.

Back in London

After brief stops in Turkey, Spain, and Portugal, Donovan routed through London on his way home to pass on the fruits of his labors to his British hosts and to continue the business of information acquisition that he had so skillfully begun in July. The British were more than grateful for Donovan's substantial efforts, and numerous telegrams emanating from their diplomatic and military facilities in Cairo, Baghdad, Athens, and elsewhere[116] praised his work and paved the way for a warm welcome in London. His interlocutors in the battered British capital again included the top echelon of government. His opinion was requested on the decision to aid Greece and he continued his dialogue with the various intelligence services, especially SOE. He met with the Director of Censorship, the Chief of Home Security, and again with Godfrey, SOE chief Nelson, and with Menzies of SIS. He solidified his British contacts, again gathered together all of the information he could on anything that would be of interest to his Washington sponsors – especially in the area of intelligence – and headed for home.[117]

The Aftermath

Donovan finally arrived back in America on 18 March 1941. He was greeted by a policy community hungry for his first-hand accounts of the war in the Mediterranean and the Balkans, the state of Britain's ability to hold out and carry the fight to the Axis, and for all manner of other data on such matters as British food stocks, Balkan politics, etc. He first met with Knox, then with Hopkins and Roosevelt. He saw Henry Stimson on the 19th, and briefed Stimson's staff the next day.[118] On the 26th, he addressed the nation on the radio – as he had after his first mission – pressing Britain's need for supplies and above all for shipping. He was in great demand.

Donovan almost certainly met with Stephenson shortly after his return, and the BSC chief played a critical role in guiding him through the web of intelligence-related activities in which the former found himself (willingly) ensnared in the spring of 1941. Stephenson's primary mission of staving off British collapse via the acquisition of adequate US supplies had largely been achieved with the passage of the Lend-Lease Act on 11 March, and he could now look to the next step – overt US involvement in the war – where Donovan could be and had already been of great assistance.[119] The best means to achieve this end was thought to be via the provision of intelligence about enemy activities and intent to the President and his key advisors. Stephenson had been attempting to do this, with some success, since his initial arrival in America a year earlier. Using Donovan as a focal point for such intelligence dissemination (and later collection) efforts must have been rather attractive to Stephenson and his colleagues; after all, 'Wild Bill' was in the unique position of being trusted by all concerned.

Stephenson, in fact, made sure to boost Donovan's 'intelligence credentials' in the aftermath of his second mission, in the hope that he would one day be appointed by Roosevelt to undertake the creation of an effective counterpart to the British secret services. He provided the information which allowed Donovan to draft a letter to Knox on 26 April – the earliest written record of Donovan's formal ideas for a centralized, coordinated American intelligence entity – explaining the broad workings of the British intelligence establishment. Donovan used the letter also as a vehicle to express his view that an American intelligence organization should eschew work related to the duties of the FBI or armed services, but should have 'sole charge of intelligence work abroad . . . [coordinating] the activities of the military and naval attaches and others in the collection of information . . . [and should] classify and interpret all information' for the President and other relevant Government entities.[120]

Donovan was experiencing at first-hand the problems associated with information overload. He sought – with Stephenson's help – a means by which some order could be imposed on the bureaucratic chaos that loosely formed the US intelligence community. He observed the phenomenon of a government acquiring information on multiple subjects, and in great quantities, without the benefit of more than fragmentary compilation, analysis, and dissemination. As the OSS war report observed:

> The greatest victim of the situation in Washington was the President. In the summer of 1941 he appointed a committee of Cabinet members . . . to consider the intelligence problem generally and recommend a plan of action. The committee consulted with Donovan and he expounded to it his concept of an overall intelligence agency with propaganda and subversive attributes. The committee's report to the Present recommended the establishment of such an organization.[121]

Donovan's letter to Knox provided the framework for the formal proposal Donovan submitted to Roosevelt on 11 June – one month before he was appointed Coordinator of Information.

CONCLUSIONS

Perhaps the most important results of the two missions by Donovan under examination – for the development of the transatlantic secret service relationship to
come – were the role Donovan assumed for himself, the impression he made on his
British interlocutors, and equally, the impressions the British and their special operations made on him. Acting unofficially and very much in an *ad hoc* fashion,
Donovan performed with extraordinary diversity and competence the multiple
roles of field collector of intelligence, liaison officer, covert diplomat, analyst, and
disseminator. He used his missions not only to learn and to report, but also to identify influential collaborators among his interlocutors for future endeavors, assessing them – and they him – much like the modern day intelligence 'case officer.'

The coincidence of interest between Donovan's perception of America's needs
and Britain's view of its own goes a long way in explaining Donovan's effectiveness. In 1940–41, Britain needed all the materiel help it could get. Donovan facilitated materiel support and earned a great deal of good will in the process. He was
seen by the British to be a suitable conduit for channeling additional resources into
the British-led subversive effort, and by the President as a conduit for channeling
British intelligence to US consumers. As Britain pursued a peripheral grand strategy, which eschewed decisive confrontation between armies and focused instead
upon weakening the enemy through a variety of less costly means – including subversion – the work of SOE and SIS took on increasing importance for London's
decision-makers, as did Donovan's potential role. While 'setting Europe ablaze'
from within began at British initiative, its goals would have to be shared by the
Americans, whose naivety at this time about 'ungentlemanly warfare' made
Donovan and that handful of prescient men like Knox in Washington the exception rather than the rule. It was War Secretary Stimson, after all, who as Secretary
of State in 1929 had dismantled the 'Black Chamber' – America's most important
cryptographic capability – because he (naively) believed that 'gentlemen should
not read each other's mail.'[122]

Donovan's missions were just a step, albeit a large one, in the process of development for the Anglo-US intelligence alliance. His goal of creating the organizational infrastructure necessary to (1) put America's 'intelligence house' in order;
(2) combat unorthodox as well as orthodox warfare with unorthodox means; and
(3) stand shoulder to shoulder with Britain as an equal partner in the covert war
effort, was not achieved immediately. The seeds Donovan and the British planted
in the summer of 1940 and the winter of 1940–41 took some time to mature. The
US did not even enter the war until December 1941, but when it did, it had the
means by which important aspects of the war effort could be coordinated with
Britain. Donovan's missions, moreover, created momentum for the unprecedented intelligence cooperation that followed. Intelligence exchanges became
more substantive and regularized and joint planning moved ahead apace.
Stephenson and his staff were at Donovan's side with advice, information, and

practical assistance, and continued this role for much of the war. Just four months after returning from the Mediterranean, Donovan was appointed to lead America's first centralized intelligence entity. The formal apparatus was now in place to address America's multifaceted intelligence requirements, which were rapidly becoming more complex and important as the US became a full participant in the war.

2 An Unequal Partnership: The Coordinator of Information and British Mentoring, 1941–42

> From my point of view COI was essentially a long-term investment and for some time it required more help than it could give in return.[1]   (William Stephenson, Chief of BSC)

INTRODUCTION

The momentum generated by Bill Donovan's two missions previously addressed toward creating a centralized American intelligence entity – linked firmly to the British – culminated on 11 July 1941 in the formal establishment of the office of Coordinator of Strategic Information (COI) with Donovan as its first and only chief. This was accompanied by increasingly close collaboration between Donovan's neophytes – who were directed immediately to expand COI's activities to include propaganda, research, analysis, human intelligence collection, and special operations, *inter alia* – and the various British intelligence services.[2] These new ties played an important role in both the establishment and early survival of Britain's intelligence protégé in Washington. Anglo-COI collaboration took place in New York and Washington with British Security Coordination, and in London with SIS, SOE, the Political Warfare Executive (PWE) and various other relevant British Government entities. It also took place at British-run intelligence and special operations training facilities throughout the United Kingdom and in Canada, and as far afield as Vichy North Africa and the neutral states of Europe.

Donovan's fledgling secret service was in need of mentoring, and its prime contribution during its eleven-month lifespan was in the fields of propaganda and research, rather than in intelligence collection or special operations. This was mainly because of the considerable preparatory work necessary to recruit and train officers, and to build agent networks. The British, who had the experience COI lacked and were desperately in need of US resources, were more than willing to play the role of tutor. This enabled Donovan to build the foundation of an organization capable of conducting complementary – then independent – operations in much less time than would otherwise have been possible.

Yet, the road to a true wartime partnership between the two countries in intelligence proved to be not altogether a smooth one. Significant bureaucratic obstacles to cooperation needed to be overcome on both sides of the Atlantic. In Washington, COI came under assault immediately by government entities which resented its sudden intrusion into what had hitherto been their territory. They included the Federal Bureau of Investigation (FBI), State Department, Offices of Inter-American and Civilian Affairs, and the military services, who put aside many of their traditional differences to form a loose anti-COI alliance. Such circumstances forced the British to walk a fine line between COI – upon which they had already expended great energy – and the rest of the US Government with which they had to collaborate closely to achieve their wider war aims.

The skill of Britain's spymasters, saboteurs, soldiers, politicians, and diplomats proved equal to this task. London found a way in 1941–2 to further ties to COI without jeopardizing other interests. America was not able to contribute much of informational substance to the transatlantic partnership, but compensated by aiding the British via the Lend-Lease program and by using COI to funnel financial resources to BSC, SOE, and SIS. Over time, Donovan found creative ways to protect his organization during its most vulnerable period, making its work and worth clearly apparent to the President and COI's intelligence-hungry consumers, surviving the transition from peace to war. Working as apprentices to the British master-craftsmen of intelligence, Donovan and his recruits constructed a base upon which they could build to make a substantial and independent contribution to the war effort. When the new wartime Anglo-American part of the Grand Alliance reorganized its war-fighting establishments in the spring and summer of 1942 to facilitate joint strategy and military operations, COI was reorganized as well. It became the more focused Office of Strategic Services (OSS), which undertook to fight a secret global war, dividing the world with its British counterparts for this purpose.

FROM CONCEPT TO REALITY: THE BIRTH OF COI AND THE BRITISH ROLE

> The handsomest gift of all from Britain via [Bill] Stephenson was the concept of a central, co-ordinated intelligence system. This idea, once articulated, could not be destroyed. It survived the war and eventually formed the core concept of a peacetime intelligence system under a Central Intelligence Agency.[3]   (Ray S. Cline, OSS veteran and former Deputy Director of CIA)

The period between the end of Donovan's Mediterranean mission in March 1941 and the formal establishment of COI in July saw some hope for a future Anglo-American alliance, as well as for greater British involvement in US intelligence matters. The passage of the Lend-Lease bill on 11 March, for example, constituted an important step forward in the overall relationship, as did Roosevelt's public pledge four days later to support Britain, Greece, China, and all of the democratic governments-in-exile. The conclusion of secret Anglo-US staff talks on 27 March, moreover, reached 'broad agreement on plans for strategic cooperation in the event of US entry into the war'[4] with Germany as first priority. Yet, these moves did little in the near-term to blunt the Axis consolidation and expansion of its victories in Europe and Asia, its advance through the Balkans, and the crippling attacks against British shipping in the North Atlantic. When British advances in North Africa were reversed in the summer of 1941 and the USSR reeled under a crushing Nazi invasion, the desperation that had driven the British to make unprecedented overtures to Donovan in 1940 had returned.

It was against this backdrop of increased US participation on the one hand, and a desperate military situation on the other, that men like Stephenson and John Godfrey accelerated their efforts to help Donovan to build a useful secret service. It was Britain's view that only through the secret information and integrated analysis of a well organized and vigorously led US secret service could Roosevelt and his advisors hope to appreciate fully the grave danger Germany posed to US interests and act decisively to prepare the country for war. For the British leadership especially, the US was their hope for near-term survival and ultimate Allied victory.

British Intervention

By spring 1941, the British believed that they had found in Donovan the perfect person with whom to share privileged information; someone who could establish a counterpart organization to SIS and SOE with which they could collaborate on propaganda, spying, and sabotage, *inter alia*. They believed Donovan to be well suited to influence Roosevelt on Britain's behalf, to help to expedite America's entry into the war, or at least to better prepare it for the eventuality of war. British exertions – in conjunction with the energetic and well-connected Donovan – laid the groundwork for the construction of an imperfect but dynamic intelligence capability hitherto unavailable to the President, the country, and the Allied cause.

In those critical months in the run-up to the formal establishment of COI, the British, especially Stephenson and Godfrey, intervened decisively on behalf of and with Donovan. In early May, Stephenson advised London that he had been 'attempting to maneuver Donovan into accepting the job of coordinating all US intelligence.'[5] Godfrey, meanwhile, added an additional dimension to Stephenson's efforts when he visited New York and Washington in June to make a personal assessment of America's intelligence capabilities. In his official postmission report he confirmed that the British were, indeed, using what influence they had in Washington to 'marry' Donovan and the nascent concept of a coordinated American intelligence entity:

> In cooperation with Mr. Stephenson . . . Donovan was persuaded to increase his personal interest in Intelligence, and details as to how US Intelligence could be improved in the common cause were worked out in collaboration with him and certain other senior officers of the government. The question was also discussed with the President direct and Colonel Donovan's qualifications as coordinator of Intelligence were advocated to Mr. Roosevelt.[6]

That Donovan needed some persuading, as Godfrey suggests, is plausible. He was a regular soldier who had been considered by two Presidents for the War Secretary's post and probably wanted to be in on the actual fighting when the US went to war. The British, however, had other plans which were not to prove incompatible with Donovan's desire to be 'in the thick of things.'

Godfrey's mission in late-spring and early-summer 1941 is crucial to any assessment of Britain's role in establishing COI in that it indicates the extent to which London was willing to go to get Washington moving toward a more effective clandestine capability and to place its man in the top job. Godfrey's initial contacts with the military intelligence chiefs and the FBI director left him disillusioned with the state of affairs within the US intelligence community:

> After a fortnight, it became clear that I was up against a brick wall . . . we already knew that relations between the US Army and Navy were bad, but we did not realize how bad until we tried to get them to see eye to eye and collaborate with each other and with the State Department about this supremely important matter of intelligence and its allied activities.[7]

Godfrey consulted Stephenson, who in turn asked for advice from Sir William Wiseman, a British businessman living in New York from where he had supervised all of Britain's intelligence activities in the US during World War I. Wiseman was well connected and well informed; he strongly suggested that Godfrey see the President, who was in his opinion 'the only person who could and would handle this question [of intelligence centralization] with any hope of success.'[8]

With Wiseman's help, Godfrey was invited in early June to the White House, where he made his pitch for a centralized intelligence service. 'At last I got a word in edgeways,' Godfrey recalled. 'I said it a second time, and a third time – one intelligence security boss, not three or four.'[9] Godfrey, ever the shrewd counsel, chose not to discuss directly with Roosevelt his preference that Donovan lead any new organization. Instead, he put his friend John Winant – who had succeeded Joseph Kennedy as US ambassador in London and was himself an admirer of Donovan – forward for the task. Winant's views were greatly respected by Roosevelt, and he was 'the sort of man,' said Godfrey, ' one could talk to about anything with great frankness.' Winant – who was also a confidant of Stephenson – conveniently visited Washington for 'consultations' whilst Godfrey was still in America, and 'the thing,' as Godfrey put it in reference to Donovan's appointment a month later as COI, 'could not have been arranged without [Winant's] cooperation. Someone had to suggest Donovan and obviously it would have been unwise for me [Godfrey] to do so.'[10] At about the same time, David Eccles of Britain's Ministry of Economic Warfare (MEW) 'briefed Donovan on the British blockade of continental Europe and its effects on the delicate balance of power in the western Mediterranean,'[11] presumably as another step in preparing him for his coming job. Thus, with Stephenson and Godfrey working on Donovan, Eccles briefing him, and Godfrey – at Wiseman's suggestion – attempting to influence Roosevelt indirectly through Winant, it is clear that the British sought rather successfully and with premeditated intent to orchestrate the birth and leadership of COI.

Nonetheless, Donovan's appointment appeared far from certain. He had been offered the job of Administrator for the State of New York for the Defense Savings Program by an insistent Treasury Secretary Morgenthau. There were also bureaucratic enemies, who saw Donovan's White House connection and behind the scenes activities as a threat to their parochial interests. One notable example was General Sherman Miles,[12] who wrote to his Chief of Staff, General George Marshall, less than a month after Donovan's return from the Mediterranean, to warn him that 'there is a movement on foot, fostered by Colonel Donovan, to establish a super agency controlling all intelligence [that would be] disadvantageous, if not calamitous' for the War Department.[13] Marshall knew very little about Donovan's thoughts on centralizing intelligence, but '[he] had been conditioned as a professional soldier to rely [solely] on military intelligence together with the intelligence of the other services and the FBI.'[14] Miles hoped that his powerful chief might be persuaded to nip such a 'movement' in the bud, but Marshall was too busy at that time to give the warning much consideration. The full story of the intra-governmental maneuverings of Donovan's many Washington enemies and the intriguing against him in the weeks before July 1941 is a fascinating tale of bureaucratic warfare at its worst, told splendidly by Thomas Troy[15] and others, and will therefore not be repeated here.

Some historians have suggested that the President had actually decided not to appoint Donovan to head COI because he was considered to be too close to the British, but changed his mind at the last moment.[16] In fact, there is ample evidence to suggest quite the opposite: that Donovan was the perfect man for the job in Roosevelt's eyes because he knew the British, the British trusted him, and America badly needed guidance in a murky world of propaganda, espionage, subversion, and sabotage to which it was as unaccustomed as the British were dedicated. In the memorial book at his funeral in 1959, Donovan was lauded for these very reasons as 'the only American who combined the necessary knowledge and know-how, the confidence of foreign friends, the qualities of leadership to forge this new instrument of war, and the ability to drive ahead despite the jealousies and animosities of other government agencies.'[17] According to Otto Doering, COI's first General Counsel, '[Roosevelt] respected Donovan; he respected his ability and his integrity and independence.'[18] Probably, the answer to the question of why Donovan was not immediately appointed to lead COI once Roosevelt decided to move forward was simply that the President was being pulled in many directions by the frantic efforts then underway to begin preparing America for war. Centralizing intelligence was important, but certainly was not at the top of the President's pressing agenda, which included coping with his political opponents and the isolationist movement, making Lend-Lease a reality, and retooling the US economy for war. There really was no other serious candidate for the top COI position.

A Bureaucratic Breakthrough

COI was borne of necessity from the tireless efforts not only of men like Donovan, Stephenson, and Godfrey, but also of a committee of three Americans – War Secretary Stimson, Navy Secretary Knox, and Attorney General Robert Jackson – who were appointed early in 1941 by Roosevelt to 'look at the intelligence problem generally and recommend a plan of action.'[19] Donovan consulted with them, and his friendship with Knox ensured that his views were given a full airing. While it was the committee that formally proposed the creation of what later became COI, the concept belonged to Donovan and his British 'advisors.' Donovan's watershed paper, 'Memorandum of Establishment of Service of Strategic Information,' was drafted at the behest of Roosevelt and was delivered to him a month before the order establishing COI was issued. It concerned the necessity of creating what he called 'a central enemy intelligence organization [to] collect pertinent information,' analyze and interpret it using 'specialized trained research officials in the relative scientific fields,' and undertake to conduct 'psychological attacks' on the enemy's 'spiritual defenses.'[20] The paper almost certainly was co-ordinated if not co-authored with Stephenson, Godfrey, and Godfrey's assistant Ian Fleming. Godfrey, in fact, was a guest in Donovan's New York apartment at the time the paper was purportedly drafted.

The ideas outlined in Donovan's memo formed the broad basis of the President's Executive Order of 11 July, which authorized COI to:

> collect and analyze all information and data which may bear upon national security; to correlate such information and data and to make such information and data available to the President and to such departments and officials of the Government as the President may determine; and to carry out, when requested by the President, *such supplementary activities as may facilitate the securing of information important for national security not now available to the Government.*[21]

It was the last part (my italics) which gave Donovan the broad and ambiguous mandate to conduct 'supplementary activities,' which in turn led him into areas as diverse as propaganda and other forms of subversion, secret intelligence gathering, special operations, and research and analysis, and which contributed to COI's many external and internal struggles. This ambiguous mandate was to pit the influential Robert Sherwood – who became Donovan's deputy and propaganda chief – against his new boss, ultimately resulting in the undoing of COI after less than a year.[22]

The British, as might be expected, were rather pleased with themselves when the COI deal was finalized. While the formal announcement of the COI order came in July, Donovan negotiated his terms of reference with Roosevelt on 18 June – insisting that he be answerable only to the President. He reported this arrangement to Stephenson, who in turn cabled London the same day, adding at the end of his message that 'Donovan had accused him of having intrigued and driven him into the job' and that 'you can imagine how relieved I am after three months of battle and jockeying for position in Washington . . . that our man is in a position of such importance to our efforts.'[23] In London, Churchill's personal secretary for liaison with his security services, Desmond Morton, could not conceal his delight in a note to a colleague:

> Another most secret fact of which [Churchill] is aware but not the other persons concerned, is that to all intents and purposes US security is being run for them at the President's request by the British. A British officer sits in Washington with [the FBI and with Donovan] for this purpose and reports regularly to the President. It is of course essential that this fact should not become known in view of the furious uproar it would cause if known to the Isolationists.[24]

SIS's Menzies, meanwhile, kept a discreet distance from Donovan so as not to bring the wrath of COI's Washington enemies down upon his activities. 'C' (Menzies) advised 'Colonel Z' (his deputy Claude Dansey) to congratulate the new COI chief on his behalf: 'I read [the news] with great pleasure,' Dansey wrote, 'for I think we shall have every reason to be thankful to your President's selection, which cannot fail to bring fruitful cooperation. Good luck to you.'[25]

FROM BIRTH TO WAR

> I believe that Donovan placed more emphasis on cooperation with his British . . . counterparts than with his bureaucratic rivals in Washington.[26]
> (William Henoeffer, Curator of CIA's Historical Intelligence Collection in 1988)
> I should think from his past utterances that David [Bruce] will make it clear in his introduction [to my biography] that I did more to further the cementing of good working Anglo-American relations in the war years than any other individual involved.[27]   (Bill Stephenson)

Together Through the Washington Minefield

With Donovan safely installed by Roosevelt in July 1941, the British turned their attention to the question of how to help COI to survive and flourish in the bureaucratic minefield in Washington which lay ahead. Godfrey, who returned to Britain earlier in the month, was optimistic about COI's chances of making good over the long term. Two passages in his mission report reveal both the depth of confidence the British – or at least Godfrey – had in COI's future, and the extraordinary level of Britain's commitment to help Donovan when it mattered most to his bureaucratic survival. Godfrey concluded first that:

> If Donovan assumes his duties as Coordinator of Intelligence with vigor and speed, and if he accepts a full measure of advice and cooperation from British Intelligence, there is no reason why U.S. Intelligence should not perhaps by the end of 1942, have developed into an extremely valuable offensive weapon.[28]

He explained further that:

> Donovan has been supplied with memoranda on a great variety of aspects on intelligence and he has been offered any degree of collaboration he may require with British Intelligence organizations . . . Stephenson will continue to work in the closest cooperation with him, and the Intelligence Staff of the Joint Staff Mission will act as his liaison with the [Joint Intelligence Committee] and with Service Intelligence Departments in London.[29]

Such a willingness to render this level of support to a still-neutral America – with little hope of a near-term *quid pro quo* in kind – is perhaps a reflection of London's desperate plight in the months before Pearl Harbor more than any sense of altruism on the part of Britain's secret services. The immediate *quid pro quo* for London in fact had nothing at all to do with intelligence, but came instead in the form of substantial American Lend-Lease aid; British support for COI might be considered both an investment and a partial repayment.

Godfrey left behind Ian Fleming to further assist the new Coordinator and to monitor COI's progress. Fleming immediately began the process of disseminating additional privileged British material to Donovan – ensuring the latter's unique access to the President, to whom Donovan passed a tantalizing selection. Fleming also advised Donovan on how first to proceed in his new job, drafting at least two memoranda for him. The first was on 'how a new US intelligence service might cooperate with the British,' which recommended that Donovan post intelligence officers to 'U.S. embassies in sensitive foreign capitals, where they should come under the command of the local SIS representative until they [are] fully trained.' In this document, he also suggested that COI 'should be under the protection of a strong government department and it should be insured by every means possible against political interference or control.' Moreover, Fleming described his view of the perfect intelligence officer, who should have 'trained powers of observation, analysis and evaluation; absolute discretion, sobriety, devotion to duty; language and wide experience, and be aged about 40 to 50.'[30]

After the war, Fleming claimed to have written a second paper in 1941. This was 'on how to create an American Secret Service,' in which he allegedly advised Donovan on 27 June:

> to make an early attack on the inertia and opposition which will meet you at every step . . . move against the opposition to your appointment . . . get good men, who will not be going begging for much longer . . . and get certain sections of the organization started immediately if they are to put up any kind of show, should America come into the war in a month's time.[31]

This document has yet to be found, but it would have been logical for the British to make such suggestions. Interestingly, Donovan gave Fleming a .38 revolver at this time, with the inscription 'For Special Services,' which led Fleming – according to his biographer Andrew Lycett – 'to claim [that] he had written the blueprint for the Central Intelligence Agency.'[32] As far as all were concerned in the summer of 1941, however, the main goal was to keep up the momentum generated by COI's creation. In this the British found that Donovan needed little encouragement.

Donovan moved rapidly to establish COI in many areas in an effort to explore what was within the realm of the possible and the as yet undefined limits of his authority. In addition to recruiting a staff to organize capabilities in the diverse fields of propaganda, research, analysis, presentation, debriefing, etc., Donovan and his team began to contemplate creating a capability to gather secret intelligence, conduct special operations, and undertake commando activities. There seemed to be no limit to Donovan's energy and no end in sight to his ambitious plans. 'He had to keep shoving and probing, exploiting his access to the White House, to extend the range of activities until he reached at least the outer boundaries of informational coordination. He was a new kind of official in a new kind of war, and it was inevitable that he [made] others nervous.'[33]

Donovan did, indeed, make others nervous, with a skill borne of a man used to getting his way and getting things done. As Fleming, Stephenson, and Godfrey had feared, COI faced an assault from 'a host of predatory government agencies [which] forgot their internecine animosities and joined in an attempt to strangle this unwanted newcomer.'[34] Foremost among these were the State Department, which feared COI encroachment on its overseas diplomatic functions, the FBI, which had overseas ambitions, and the War Department, which had its own intelligence agenda. Intra-governmental battles raged behind the scenes in Washington over the broad mandate claimed by COI in the realm of propaganda, espionage, counterespionage, special operations, and research, *inter alia.* Donovan's nickname 'Wild Bill' soon became synonymous in government circles not with the bravery for which it was earned in combat, but with the threatening and unfocused way in which his opponents believed he 'ran amuck' in Washington.[35]

In the face of these formidable bureaucratic enemies, the support Stephenson's BSC provided to Donovan in the months preceding Pearl Harbor was the principal reason that COI survived its first Christmas. BSC helped Donovan to build COI from scratch, enhance its reputation among its Washington-based consumers – Roosevelt first and foremost – and to navigate the bureaucratic minefield which lay ahead. Donovan and Stephenson consulted very closely during this period, as is evident from the appearance of the latter's name thirty-six times in the former's calendar of appointments and telephone calls between 9 August and 29 September 1941.[36] Moreover, the most experienced of BSC's staff was put at COI's disposal. Barty Pleydell-Bouverie, who handled BSC's liaison with the FBI out of a small office in Washington, became the first day-to-day link between BSC in New York and COI Headquarters, using his telex line to Stephenson to facilitate and enhance dialogue.[37]

By August 1941, Stephenson had assigned his own deputy, Ellis, to Washington to act for the rest of the war as a focal point for passing intelligence directly to

Donovan's staff. In his unpublished memoir and biography of Stephenson, Ellis cogently characterized the nature of the growing partnership between COI and the British during this time:

> The close and easy relationships between British and American personnel that marked the work of [the secret] services [in 1940–41], and the beneficial impact on the other [from the] qualities of each partner were largely due to the early contacts that were established long before Pearl Harbor in liaison duties and associations in training establishments in Canada, Britain, and the [US].[38]

One of Donovan's most important deputies, David Bruce, later praised Ellis' contribution, claiming that without his help, '[we] could not have gotten off the ground.'[39] This accolade, coming from Donovan's top spymaster and a future respected diplomat, could not be more telling.

COI opened an office in New York – alongside BSC – to further facilitate contact after Pearl Harbor and to enlarge the activities of Edward Buxton's Oral History Unit, which debriefed anyone with personal knowledge of Axis-controlled areas. Donovan recruited a fellow attorney, Allen Dulles, to run this very active section, which helped the American and British organizations to stay in regular contact at the working level. Dulles devised 'a system for collecting foreign intelligence from the cosmopolitan business, financial, and scholarly communities of New York and [for recruiting] agents.' From refugees his staff procured 'road maps, worn clothing, ration and identity cards . . . mundane items of rare value for future American agents infiltrating behind enemy lines.' Once COI became OSS, the New York office began interviewing 'arriving sailors about what they had seen in European ports . . . Through such means American naval strategists assembled accurate and detailed information about [many Axis] ports.'[40]

Dulles went on to play an even more significant role in American intelligence, both as chief of OSS Switzerland and later as director of the Central Intelligence Agency. But in 1941, his diplomatic training,[41] legal skills, and social contacts served him well in COI New York, where his staff and BSC could compare notes and share information, leads, and techniques. Moreover, as the funds for Dulles' activities were unvouchered – like those of COI as a whole – his New York office almost certainly was used to secretly transfer funds to BSC, SOE, and SIS.

The existence of a multi-function COI also prompted Stephenson to enlarge BSC. Before the end of July 1941, he had returned to London for consultations and found a receptive ear for his expansion proposals. SOE, which wanted to enhance its role in Latin America, was the British organization most eager to establish close ties to COI,[42] and BSC now had to step up its operational and informational support to Donovan on a day-to-day basis; these activities required more manpower and resources. Stephenson got his mandate and soon 'returned to New York with instructions to enlarge his SOE activities, to give Donovan the fullest assistance possible in turning COI into a full-fledged intelligence organization, and to create a strong framework for the Anglo-American alliance in secret warfare.'[43]

The material passed to Donovan by BSC, supplemented by information on a variety of topics provided by Donovan's growing list of personal contacts, casual informants, and staff, was scrutinized and a selection passed to the President. This included not just secrets, but analysis and personal observations that gave Roosevelt a feeling for world events that he could not get elsewhere. Between August and December 1941, Roosevelt received COI reports on British strategic planning,[44] Polish–Soviet relations,[45] German morale[46] and perceptions of Soviet-US relations,[47] the Soviet transport system,[48] the sinking of the German battleship *Bismarck*,[49] and the origin of the British commandos.[50] In the aftermath of the Pearl Harbor attack, COI saw an opportunity to raise its profile still further, and increased its output accordingly.[51]

Establishing COI's First Overseas Station

One of Donovan's early priorities as COI was to establish a presence in London, where his nascent organization could reap the full benefits of British tutelage and privileged information, and where it could stage for a future active role in the war. In addition to being at the center of the Allied war effort in 1941, London had geographical proximity to SOE and SIS training facilities, to future COI target areas in Europe, and to British armed forces and government entities. Moreover, it gave convenient access to the Allied governments-in-exile, which were expected to provide support, intelligence, and recruits in future. Donovan was also aware of the need to prove COI's worth to Roosevelt: London provided an early opportunity.

Donovan began by recruiting an old Justice Department colleague, William Whitney, and sent him to London with Bob Sherwood in September 1941 on a fact-finding mission. Whitney and Sherwood 'inspected all British installations of the type of SOE, SIS, PWE [Political Warfare Executive], MOI [Ministry of Information], and MEW [Ministry of Economic Warfare].' According to Whitney:

> [We] were acting in the capacity of general observers and had no particular liaison purpose in mind. [Our] intent was to gain some idea of how the British were fighting the irregular war of black propaganda, secret intelligence and special operations.[52]

In late October, Donovan and Whitney met with Roosevelt and presented a strong case for sending Whitney back to London to open COI's first permanent overseas office. The President sent a letter to Churchill, which explained: 'In order to facilitate the carrying out of the work of [COI] with respect to Europe and the occupied countries, I have authorized Colonel Donovan to send a small staff to London.'[53] The reasons behind Whitney's selection for this job – so critically important to COI's future role – are indicative of the premium put on British goodwill by Donovan at this time. Whitney was an American, but had a British wife and was an alumnus of Oxford. He had joined the British Army in 1939 and was made a

Major, serving for a short time in the British Expeditionary Force in France and even working in a minor capacity for British military intelligence.[54] It was not unreasonable for the British to think that Whitney saw the UK almost as an adopted country and could be relied upon to look out for their interests. Menzies, in fact, thought Whitney to be 'an ardent Anglophile' if not a British agent.[55] Donovan, in turn, almost certainly expected that the British would be more forthcoming with Whitney for the same reasons.

The first COI offices were officially located on the top floor of the US Embassy, but were in fact maintained in the British War Cabinet building, where Whitney and his small staff could communicate with Washington through secure British channels. In these early days, access to COI's liaison contacts were tightly restricted by Donovan to Whitney and COI London's executive officer, Fisher Howe.[56] All COI communications from London went through SOE operators and equipment, and thence via BSC's Washington office led by Ellis – a remarkable level of trust and dependence. According to Howe, 'We [in COI] were so primitive at that time . . . totally subordinate to their communications.'[57] Howe was even assigned an SOE secretary, who worked at the heart of COI London for nearly a year, probably keeping an eye on her new American employers in addition to her clerical duties. Whitney and Howe almost certainly were concerned more with the job at hand – getting their station established – than with any proprietary considerations at this early stage.

The Howe story bears additional telling, as his work sheds light on the *ad hoc* nature of COI, as well as on the early financial relations between COI and the British. When Howe was recruited in September 1941, he was dispatched with Whitney, having had 'no training whatsoever,' save for a brief meeting with Stephenson and Ellis.[58] One of his first official acts was to pass $100 000 in small denominations to SOE 'for them to use.'[59] The disbursement – along with other almost certainly unvouchered cash transfers to BSC in 1941 – is a first indication of a tangible COI return on Britain's intelligence investment, since the early privileged material forwarded by US sources to the UK 'added little to what Whitehall already knew.'[60]

BUMPS IN THE ROAD

> COI was larger and greater in scope than OSS [yet] smaller in staff [and] somewhat uncertain in theory and power . . . COI was naturally unable to accomplish much.[61]   (Bill Whitney)

Problems in London

While the British generally looked at their assistance to COI as an investment in the future, the subject of the *quid pro quo* was indeed an issue from the outset and affected Whitney's ability to operate. One of his earliest frustrations was in trying to make the Anglo-American intelligence relationship more equitable. In a report prepared for Donovan a week before Pearl Harbor, Whitney complained:

> [I] am impressed by the embarrassing fact that all favors requested by us appear to have been met promptly but that we have not accomplished any of their requests . . . I am convinced that defaults have now accumulated to such an extent that the time has come when we ought either (a) really to tell our friends that we can carry out these requests or alternatively (b) to tell them why we cannot do so. Am sure they will be understanding but at present they are simply puzzled and hurt . . . Situation has been rendered worse by the fact that they have advised their Overseas representatives at Gibraltar, Cairo, Singapore, etc., that we were about to do great things.[62]

Such 'favors' included using the US diplomatic pouch to transmit secret material to and from various places where the British faced operational restrictions. London also wanted French francs for operational purposes, diplomatic assistance concerning an agent arrested in Vichy, and for help with the Polish government-in-exile's recruiting work in the US;[63] low-level matters, certainly.

Whitney was aware that he was vulnerable in London to charges that COI was holding out, or even worse, that his organization was irrelevant.[64] He pressed Donovan to assign someone 'of real ability . . . to devote himself exclusively to carrying out London's requests [by getting] about among other American departments and our own staff.' He also stressed that 'the lives and effectiveness of many individual men working in the field' were dependent upon his ability to 'produce the goods' when asked. British requests, he noted, 'appear here to serve as a test as to whether our organization is likely to be practical, useful, and effective.'[65]

Whitney's correspondence with Donovan in December 1941 gives another insight into his pre-Pearl Harbor activities and Britain's goodwill, even in the face of continued 'imbalances.' Whitney's requests for detailed information from the British on 'broadcasting stations in the east,' on 'propaganda material to be dropped by [the] RAF,' on a 'plane from Newfoundland,' and for British 'aid in bringing cipher machines from Stockholm,' for example, were promptly met.[66] The British certainly had cause for concern, and with the notable exception of Stephenson and BSC, many in senior British government circles must have questioned the utility of dealing directly with COI London, which complicated Whitney's work considerably.

All told, COI London had mixed results after its first two months in existence. Whitney's initial objective, in his own words, was:

> to contact in London all the British agencies engaged in the more irregular aspects of war – white propaganda, secret intelligence, special operations, in a word, the whole field of psychological warfare for which the United States had made no other preparations.[67]

He did so, using his 'connections' to advantage. He contacted Churchill, then worked his way down the governmental and military hierarchy, while Howe worked feverishly to establish an administrative infrastructure and helped wherever possible. Whitney's activities 'were arranged and maintained on a highly personal basis.'[68] He established contact with the British Joint Intelligence Committee, which became a principal source of information, and worked with SIS, SOE, and the Ministry of Economic Warfare. His contact with the British Chiefs of Staff was via General Hastings Ismay,[69] who was concerned enough about Whitney's access to suggest to Churchill in November that he and Desmond Morton act as 'watch-dog[s]' on the American's interests. Churchill agreed and directed that the COI man be watched 'vigilantly.'[70] Whitney pressed on with his work, establishing, *inter alia*, the practice of compiling a daily intelligence summary largely derived from information passed to him by liaison interlocutors for use by Donovan. 'Quite often . . . Donovan would show this report to President Roosevelt.'[71]

His special access notwithstanding, Whitney ran into trouble from the start. He confused the British authorities over the exact nature and scope of his activities, as COI seemed to try to cover everything from liaison, secret intelligence, and research and analysis to special operations and propaganda. The US State Department – continuing its efforts to undermine COI – was wary about the organization's claim to responsibility for US-initiated propaganda broadcasts from London and may have prompted its British counterpart to complain, which the Foreign Office did before the end of the year by questioning COI's jurisdiction in propaganda matters. Ismay, meanwhile, gave orders that Whitney should be shown 'nothing which relates to future [military] operations or which is derived from "Most Secret" sources such as ULTRA.'[72] A frustrated Whitney returned to COI headquarters shortly after Pearl Harbor to consult with Donovan about COI's new wartime role. He recommended that the organization focus its activities, cede some of its myriad functions to other agencies, and he warned prophetically that 'COI could not last under the Roosevelt Administration with presidential favor but without cabinet representation.'[73]

The balance of Whitney's tenure in London was spent principally in support of Sherwood's propaganda effort, rather than on the secret intelligence and special operations work which dominated the activities of his successors. Continued British unease about COI's place within the US establishment, confusion about its mission, and concern for relations with COI's US opponents were largely to blame. Some also feared that Donovan's prying eyes in London might uncover too much about British operations. Whitney reported in February 1942: 'We are fully occupied, but that means that we spend 95 percent of our time on [propaganda] . . . For all practical purposes there is no representation in London of [SI and SO] departments . . . We make no contribution to this work [at] present.'[74] Whitney described the months in London leading up to the dissolution of COI in June 1942 as 'extremely uncertain [with] little of value . . . accomplished.'[75]

Whitney returned to the US twice during his London stint, and both times found that the British obstructed his staff's work in his absence. When he met with

Donovan in Washington during December 1941, for example, COI London's 'intelligence surveys became less frequent and contained less material [than before],'[76] despite the fact that its staff had been augmented by five officers and four clerks on 8 December. Before Whitney could rectify the situation, he fell ill and returned briefly to the US for treatment. Percy Winner[77] took over temporarily and found his work severely curtailed by General Ismay, who commented that he 'wanted nobody as bright as Winner with access to the inner offices of British power' and suggested to Desmond Morton that he should 'ride him off.'[78] Ismay evidently felt that Whitney posed less of a threat than Winner, either because he was less capable or more easily managed.

When Whitney returned to London, he encountered more difficulties. Most pressing was his rapidly diminishing access to British agencies. He wrote to Bruce on 28 February that: 'The representatives of [our] War and Navy Departments, (as indeed of the other US Government Departments) are very jealous of their functions here, and we are unable to go directly to the British [with whom] they are in contact.'[79] US entities had established bilateral links and procedures for exchanging information with their British opposites, who in turn saw no advantage in duplicating these channels by dealing bilaterally with Whitney. They probably assumed that COI London was kept informed by COI Washington, which received pertinent information via BSC, and were loath to antagonize their other liaison partners by appearing to favor Donovan's London-based interlopers.

COI London's work was complicated further by two other developments. First, Whitney discovered in February 1942 that COI Washington was not providing him with information that it was getting from BSC which was crucial to his work. He asked Bruce to assign an officer to improve the flow of information on intelligence and special operations matters.[80] The second issue concerned Whitney's efforts to establish independent links to the governments-in-exile in London. Menzies' deputy at Broadway, Claude Dansey, was particularly anxious:

> [Dansey] was horrified to discover that [Whitney] . . . had been in direct contact with the other Allied intelligence services in London without telling him. He was alarmed at the opportunities for confusion created by such independent action, and pointed out the dangers to Donovan, who agreed that, although American Intelligence could not be controlled by the authorities of another state, he would take care to maintain the closest collaboration with the SIS.[81]

Thus began the precarious nature of the relationship between Donovan's representatives and the enigmatic Dansey, which put SIS's relations with OSS into some difficulty once the latter felt ready to demonstrate its independence. For the time being, however, SIS was to be kept informed and differences were glossed over. In March, Bruce advised Whitney that: 'In regard to our direct contacts with foreign secret services . . . we have kept our British friends here advised of what we propose to do in that respect and our suggested plan has met with their complete approval.'[82]

There were other instances where COI Washington failed to adequately support Whitney. These were due more to the unfocused and disorganized way in which COI was evolving, however, than to the fault of any individual involved. Whitney described one problem as follows:

> [Your] response to our inquiry whether the US Government had developed some oil figures to reciprocate the figures which we had been sending in detail and which we obtained from [the British]. The response . . . said 'corresponding facts and figures go from us to British in Washington, hence should be available in London.' The word 'British' really does not help us at all. The whole question is as to what *department* of the British Government . . . [You] did not stop to think about our problems and needs.[83]

Thus, COI London found itself – during the first part of 1942 – to be out of the information mainstream. Since Whitney had little purpose other than to ferret out information from the British, he was generally considered to be a nuisance by most non-COI concerned entities.

COI Washington was not indifferent to COI London's problems, and found a sympathetic ear in Stephenson. In March, Bruce responded to Whitney's pleas for support by approaching BSC and promising COI London that it would soon get more information and advice on intelligence and special operations matters. BSC agreed to 'advise their headquarters to supply [Whitney] with a greater volume of information than they have been doing,' and a better system of coordination was worked out between BSC New York and COI Washington with regard to information sharing. Bruce was soon able to advise Whitney that: 'COI in general is stronger beyond all comparison than it was when you last left here, and I think future developments will demonstrate that in the field of intelligence at least, it is the outstanding agency of the government.'[84]

Whitney left COI London permanently on 30 April 1942, putting the station in the hands of Fisher Howe until June. Whitney Shepardson soon took over the intelligence and liaison functions in London and was the temporary station chief until William Phillips – a former US Ambassador to Italy – arrived shortly thereafter to take overall charge, with Dick Heppner leading special operations. By this time, COI London had ceased to rely on the British for secure communications, and Allen Dulles' New York station was producing many excellent operational leads. Dulles added to his responsibilities all COI 'contacts with foreign agencies,' and worked somewhat under COI London's supervision.[85] Donovan's organization was beginning to look like more than a weak appendage of the British secret services.

Shepardson picked up where Whitney had left off, but with more success. This was partially due to the evolution of COI towards what was soon known as OSS, and also to the new working agreements concluded with SOE in June 1942, which established global operational areas and lines of authority. In his first month in

London – and COI's last in existence – Shepardson acquired useful material from his interlocutors, which included a French report on the Allied secret services in North Africa. In addition, he arrived at an 'understanding with [British] military attaches on [intelligence] going direct to British military sources,'[86] thereby breaking down a considerable barrier to COI's work during Whitney's tenure. Shepardson, moreover, reestablished a link with Churchill's office, which had been forged by Whitney but had lain dormant since the latter's departure in April. He fostered very useful ties to the head of the British Joint Intelligence Committee, William Cavendish-Bentinck, who soon '[made] intelligence available to [Shepardson] on most generous terms [and furnished] notes and comments on various special memoranda submitted to his office.'[87]

Robert Solborg and COI's Special Operations Capability

As COI struggled in the second half of 1941 to expand its ability to process, analyze, and disseminate information, and to establish effective linkages of all kinds, Donovan turned his attention to special operations. This was to develop into one of OSS's most important capabilities. SOE, which wanted to collaborate with COI – partly because of its own ambitious expansion plans – had encouraged Donovan to establish a counterpart capability. COI had only a vague mandate 'to carry out . . . such supplementary activities as may facilitate the securing of information important for national security,'[88] which only under the broadest of interpretations might include fomenting resistance, spreading black propaganda, and conducting sabotage.

The fact that Donovan was held in high esteem by SOE – one officer at Baker Street called him 'an almost legendary figure to us'[89] – created high expectations for COI in special operations. These expectations, however, were initially left unfulfilled:

> Our hopes that America's entry into the war would at once [allow] us to obtain the facilities we so urgently needed were disappointed . . . Many more months had still to go before Donovan's position and functions were clarified. Until this took place we could expect little material help from his organization because as yet it did not exist . . . Every month – every week almost – seemed to bring him a new presidential directive. In the meantime he could make no progress in creating an organization until it was settled what exactly he was to do.[90]

Donovan had to find the right man to build a special operations capability, and saw that it would take more time than anticipated to make a significant contribution to the unequal partnership.

The 'right man' was found by the British in the person of Robert Solborg. At the suggestion of BSC's Ellis and with the support of Preston Goodfellow – then the US Army G-2's liaison officer with COI – Solborg was chosen by Donovan on 9 October 1941 to manage 'Special Activities – K and L Funds,' which was created to conduct 'espionage, subversive activities (including sabotage) and guerrilla units.'[91] Solborg was asked to build upon Donovan's three-phase concept of conducting intelligence infiltration operations, undertaking sabotage and subversion, and fomenting resistance through guerrilla and commando activities.[92]

Both Ellis and Goodfellow claimed friendship with Solborg, whose First World War combat experience in the Russian Tsar's Army and espionage work for the British in 1939–40 – and to a lesser extent for the US Army in 1940–41 – made him a logical, if unusual, choice for the job. Solborg was wounded on the Eastern Front in World War I,[93] worked as an aide to the Tsarist head of the North American military purchasing commission in New York, and became a US citizen after the 1917 Bolshevik Revolution. He was hired by the American Rolling Mill Company (Armco) – which later provided a cover for his British espionage work – joined the US Army, served briefly as the US military attaché in Paris in 1919, and rejoined Armco in Europe, where he rose to be Managing Director of the company's British operations by 1939.

It was upon the outbreak of war in 1939, according to his own account, that Solborg first came into contact with SIS – and probably with Ellis – after volunteering his services to the British. His credentials as an American businessman gave him access to German industry, and he was directed to acquire secret information on the German midget submarine program, which he did with some success.[94] His work for the British appears to have ended – at least temporarily – when he was called up by the US Army, whose Military Intelligence Division (MID) sent him back to Europe and North Africa in 1940–41 to survey the situation clandestinely. It was his report on North Africa for MID which brought him again into contact with Ellis, who asked Donovan for a copy; Ellis recommended Solborg for COI's 'SOE' job on 14 September 1941.[95]

From the British perspective, Solborg was the perfect choice. He was one of their former secret agents and presumably could be relied upon to keep their interests at the forefront and to ensure that they were fully informed of COI plans and activities. Probably with the help of Ellis, Solborg prepared a paper for his interview with Donovan on 6 October in which he outlined his initial views on how COI's intelligence and special operations arms should be organized. After his appointment by Donovan, he met with BSC's SOE experts, where he 'quickly produced some preliminary ideas,'[96] and was dispatched to London shortly thereafter. It was Stephenson who arranged for Solborg to undergo 'extensive training in British [special operations] schools,'[97] and he was under instructions from Donovan to 'survey the British subversive warfare setup'[98] with the purpose of assembling America's own such capability. Solborg toured the SOE schools and developed his own thoughts on how to get his unit up and running; Japan's attack on Pearl Harbor further encouraged him to make the most of this opportunity. Thus, by the end of COI's first six months, Solborg was well prepared to move forward, but no actual operational activities had been conducted by his element and few had been recruited to help him.

When Solborg finally returned to Washington in early January 1942, he advised that: '[COI operations] should include . . . black propaganda, the sabotage of enemy transport, communications, and military installations . . . fomenting, organizing, equipping, training, and leading of disaffected elements under enemy rule.'[99] BSC and SOE London augmented Solborg's work by undertaking their own exploratory studies on how and where to recruit and train Solborg's personnel. It was soon agreed that COI should begin training a cadre of special operations officers at BSC's 'Camp X' clandestine training facility in Canada, and at SOE schools in the UK.[100]

In February 1942, Donovan dispatched Solborg to Portugal to establish a COI foothold, survey the operational environment, and explore means of operational coordination with field-deployed SOE units. Anxious to return to North Africa with plans to subvert elements of the Vichy regime, however, Solborg took it upon himself to visit Casablanca against Donovan's wishes,[101] and lost his job shortly thereafter. Posing as an advisor to Roosevelt,[102] Solborg had met with Vichy French officers loyal to General Henri Giraud – who later competed with Charles de Gaulle for the leadership of the French resistance – and promised them US backing, and that French North Africa would remain under their control after the arrival of the Allied armies. Solborg had the authority neither to meet with the Giraud group nor to make any such promises.

Solborg's letters from Portugal and Morocco to Goodfellow discuss his relationship with SOE and indicate that he was indeed exceeding his authority. In March 1942, Solborg wrote about 'a series of conferences with the British who came to meet [him in Lisbon] from London, Madrid and Tangier,' presumably to help him to get started in Iberia and North Africa:

> The first few days [were] tough, but we have now reached an amicable basis and get along quite well together . . . [SOE] put quite a little work on my shoulders, [but] I can take it. There is lots to be done in this part of the world to improve our position, and I can see that I shall be kept very busy.[103]

Solborg detailed his efforts to work with the Giraud group in another letter to Goodfellow, and said that he was too busy to comply with Donovan's request that he meet him and Stephenson in London. The British, meanwhile, backed de Gaulle and feared that Solborg's work with the Giraudists was known to the Germans; this charge provoked an angry denial from Solborg.[104] When Solborg returned to the US shortly thereafter, he was fired and replaced by Goodfellow.

Wallace Phillips and COI's Secret Intelligence Capability

At almost the same time that Dick Ellis brought Solborg to Donovan's attention in early-autumn 1941, the Coordinator was negotiating with the hitherto hostile US Army and Navy intelligence arms about centralizing America's human intelligence collection effort under COI's auspices and had discovered an opening which he aggressively exploited. Following Godfrey's blistering report on the unpreparedness of America's military establishment for intelligence activities – which included the evaluation that 'too many amateurs were running around playing spy . . . [and] intelligence being collected was hopelessly wrong'[105] – the US Office of Naval Intelligence and its US Army counterpart had come under increasing pressure from the White House and Whitehall to get their houses in order. By September 1941 – with prodding from Donovan's supporters Stimson and Knox, and with the belief that COI's ties to SIS would give it some advantage – the 'establishment' had begun to warm to the idea of giving responsibility for unconventional activities, such as intelligence collection, to Donovan.

On 5 September, Stimson sent a memorandum titled 'Undercover Intelligence Service' to Donovan's long-time antagonist General Miles (G-2) explaining the War Department's 'new thinking,' which turned the tide inexorably in COI's favor on this matter:

> The military and naval intelligence services have gone into the field of undercover intelligence to a limited extent. In view of the appointment of [Donovan], it is believed that the undercover intelligence of the two services should be consolidated under [COI] . . . An undercover intelligence service is much more effective if under one head rather than three, and a civilian agency, such as [COI], has distinct advantage over any military or naval agency.[106]

The memorandum was quickly approved by General Marshall, and Donovan informed Roosevelt on 10 October that 'he had assumed the clandestine intelligence function as a result of agreement with the Army and Navy intelligence services.'[107] What Donovan had yet to do was to find someone with experience in organizing spy networks who was acceptable to all interested parties.

Donovan's options were limited, but a logical choice for the job of setting up COI's intelligence gathering capability soon emerged in the form of Wallace Phillips, who was a civilian assistant to the US Director of Naval Intelligence. Phillips managed the Navy's small overseas clandestine collection effort, which consisted principally of a handful of agents in Latin America and twelve diplomatic vice-consuls assigned to US Consulates in Vichy North Africa. He was a successful businessman who before the war had lived in London, where he headed the US Chamber of Commerce.[108] Phillips appeared to be an excellent candidate – he had the military's blessing, practical intelligence experience, and a network of British contacts. He retained control of his former Navy intelligence assets for a time when he moved to Donovan's headquarters in October, and his formal COI appointment came on 17 November.[109]

Phillips held his COI job for just six weeks, however, because he clashed with Donovan over the organization and direction of his component, and he was replaced by David Bruce. In spite of his UK connections, the British distrusted Phillips[110] – whom they believed to be an opportunist – and were disinclined to work closely with him. Their negative view was shared by Roosevelt's close friend Vincent Astor, who described him as indiscreet and charged him with shamefully exaggerating his ties to the White House at social gatherings. SIS's reticence, however, probably had more to do with its desire to retain exclusive control over Allied intelligence-gathering operations than with any personal misgivings about Phillips. Perhaps it was Phillips' potential that was at issue rather than his competence or motives.

According to Menzies' biographer, SIS hoped to use Donovan to control US intelligence activities[111] rather than to include COI as an equal partner. Claude Dansey, who was Britain's most experienced intelligence officer at that time and had been tutor to America's military intelligence chief during the First World War, was chosen by Menzies to impose control. Dansey was respected by Donovan, who referred to him as 'the Master'[112] with regard to espionage, but the Coordinator had no intention of accepting a purely subordinate role to the British in espionage affairs. In time, Donovan pressed inexorably for independent responsibility and authority for his spies – at least partially to justify his organization's worth to a still skeptical Washington – first in North Africa for the coming Allied invasion, then in France and elsewhere. This approach pitted Phillips' successor against the powerful Dansey. Phillips was not around long enough to be affected by the coming clash, but David Bruce found himself at odds with Dansey almost from the moment of his first dealings with him. Once Bruce had the personnel in place to make a substantive intelligence contribution, he found himself continuously obstructed by Dansey, whose biographers have explained:

> [Bruce] found no difficulty in getting on with Menzies, who treated him with his usual smooth and polished charm. But Dansey, it seemed was a different matter . . . Bruce's bewilderment at Dansey's attitude displays a naiveté which was typical of the OSS at that time . . . In his eagerness to get things done and to be in the thick of the action, he overlooked one essential point: although he was the chief of all OSS activities in Europe, he had been in the business for less than a year, and had no practical experience whatever – and neither did his chief. Dansey had been in it for forty-five years, more than half of them at the top, and his practical experience was immeasurable. It is hardly surprising that he was not disposed to treat Bruce as an equal.[113]

Perhaps Menzies and Dansey were skillfully playing the proverbial 'good guy–bad guy' roles often adopted by interrogators to keep their subjects off balance, in this instance, in an effort to further SIS's position in the Anglo-US bureaucratic struggle for control of Allied espionage.

Looking to the Far East

The sudden war with Japan – and Tokyo's military successes in the Far East – prompted Donovan to look to the Pacific theater as a key target area for propaganda, intelligence, and special operations. Even before Pearl Harbor, Donovan had in September 1941 set up a Far Eastern section of his research and analysis branch, which prepared 'strategic surveys for the armed services [and] assisted [COI] in planning propaganda for the Far East.'[114] Bob Sherwood's propaganda arm collaborated with BSC in investigating Japanese propaganda efforts in the Western Hemisphere. In the process, it had obtained 'much intelligence [which] was passed to London, Ottawa, and Washington [from] contacts [who] were later utilized . . . in building up services for the penetration of Japan and Japanese-held territory in the East and the Pacific.'[115]

In December 1941, Donovan set up a Far East secret intelligence branch for operations, first in China, then elsewhere in East Asia. While the leads provided by Sherwood's group and BSC proved helpful in getting started, this branch suffered badly from inexperience and – some have charged – from poor management in the conduct of its early collection operations. According to Norwood Allman, a senior officer in the Far East intelligence branch:

> The Branch was not handicapped so much by starting late as it was by a failure to face and deal with reality and cold facts. There has been an unwillingness . . . to seek or listen to the cumulative experience of Americans from the Far East. There was far too long a time a failure . . . to place a competent experienced person in charge of SI interests, especially in China. [We are] still laboring under the delusion that we can get intelligence by and through interpreters . . . Adequate use has not been made of American personnel with language qualifications [and] there has been too much emphasis on quantity rather than quality.[116]

When exploring his options for special operations, Donovan did solicit the views of some former US Far Eastern expatriates. In a 7 January 1942 paper titled 'Chinese Scheme,' for example, an 'original plan' proposed by a 'Mr. Larsen' and a 'Mr. Underwood' from outside COI 'that a commission of four men be sent to China for the purpose of preventing a decisive Japanese victory by the augmentation of effective guerrilla warfare' is discussed. The COI staffer who wrote the memo stressed the need to 'work closely with British interests' in such action, and proposed additional COI activities, such as organizing 'Mongol guerrillas . . . to operate against the Japanese in Mongolia'; undertaking 'large-scale sabotage' in Manchukuo (Japanese-occupied Manchuria) and Korea; and creating 'a set up to harass the Japanese military convoy route between the China Coast and off-lying islands, particularly Formosa and the Pescadores.'[117] Pointing out that a recent British proposal to Chiang Kai-shek's government in China that SOE undertake similar activities from Chinese territory had been turned down, the staffer went on to criticize the aspiring American operations officers:

> Larsen had no detailed plan prepared. He stated that he had seen the Chinese Military Attaché in Washington who had assured him that the approval and cooperation of the Chinese Government could be obtained, but beyond this, he

had little to say . . . Underwood states he hoped to organize and operate his Manchurian saboteurs from Eastern Russia but submitted no detail of how he proposed to approach the Russian authorities on this matter . . . No useful purpose can be served by having any further meetings from our point of view until a completely comprehensive plan is prepared.[118]

Donovan followed up exploration of the 'Chinese Scheme' with other ideas – some of which were to prove impractical – on how to attack the Japanese quickly and effectively, which aroused the attention of the President who was badly in need of a military success. On 24 January 1942, for example, he sent a memorandum to Roosevelt suggesting the creation of a 10 000–15 000 strong force of Marine volunteers, trained and organized 'on the principles of the British Commandos' to be deployed immediately against the Japanese island of Hokkaido to establish a bombing base for raids on mainland Japan.[119] Three days later, Donovan's staff presented him with a detailed plan called 'Scheme OLIVA' to establish a COI 'Mission' in China for special operations activities. OLIVA was to recruit local agents, train them in sabotage, and deploy them – in close coordination with Chiang Kai-shek's nationalist Chinese government – against Axis targets in occupied areas, such as in Korea, Manchuria, north and south China, Formosa, Indochina, Thailand, the Philippines, and the Dutch East Indies.[120] The document included personnel requests, organization, and funding requirements, taking the 'Chinese Scheme' memorandum of three weeks previous considerably further along. And on 28 February, Donovan gave Roosevelt a memorandum titled 'The Importance of Holding Northern Burma,' in which he made a convincing analytical argument for COI action there. This justified Donovan's recruitment in March of US Army Major Carl Eifler – an extremely tough and charismatic regular soldier – to recruit, train, deploy, and lead what became OSS's first and most effective special operations unit, later designated 'Detachment 101.' Eifler and his men spent much of the war in the jungles of Burma, where they recruited guerrillas and disrupted Japanese activities.

Where the 'Chinese Scheme' illustrated the rudimentary nature of COI's early operational planning, OLIVA demonstrated COI's capacity to act quickly, creatively, and decisively. Both documents, along with Donovan's commando report, capture the essence of his broad ambitions in the Pacific region. Moreover, in the case of 'Chinese Scheme,' we are privy to a very early example of an East Asian representative – in this case, of China – viewing American assistance in the fight against Japanese occupiers as much preferable to British help.

The US and Britain did, in fact, become bitter rivals in the Far East as the war progressed, in stark contrast to the much closer working relationship between them in Europe. Britain soon discovered that the prospect of liberation from British imperialism was in future to be as much a motivator for the peoples of East Asia – and for the guerrilla groups supported by Donovan's operatives – as was liberation from the Japanese. Japan had promoted this concept by seeking to portray its territorial ambitions as an effort to liberate its Asian neighbors from white domination. Historian Maochun Yu has suggested that:'Britain's objective in the war in Asia was to reclaim its colonial empire . . . The raising of the Union Jack over Singapore [was] more important to the British than any victory parade through Tokyo.'[121] The US, in contrast, believed that it was fighting to turn the tide of Axis aggression rather than to return imperial possessions to the British and French Empires. This 'moral high ground' as seen from Washington steadily drove the US and Britain apart – especially in the east – as the war progressed and ultimate victory over Japan became more certain. Moreover, it manifested itself naturally in the fields of intelligence and special operations, where the groundwork was being laid for participation of occupied peoples in their own liberation and postwar governance.

CONCLUSIONS

The COI period can be best described as a formative one for the Americans, and the secret service 'partnership' was heavily one-sided, with the British providing most of the information and instruction. Nonetheless, Stephenson's 'long term investment' was beginning to pay dividends. The US had a centralized intelligence entity, firmly committed to collaboration with the British secret services. This organization was under strong leadership that was favorably inclined toward Britain and was finally firmly rooted in the US bureaucratic soil, with OSS placed beneath the new Joint Chiefs of Staff in Washington's wartime hierarchy from June 1942. Donovan was no longer solely dependent upon Roosevelt's favor for his organization's day-to-day survival, nor was Stephenson's information lifeline the only means by which US intelligence could contribute, although Donovan continued to feel great pressure to prove his worth.

In spite of COI's penchant for trying to be everything to everyone, it was evolving and serving a purpose. Moreover, the lessons it learned served OSS well in its own formative period. COI's propaganda and research elements were functioning well, although Sherwood wrested the former away from Donovan in June 1942, and working arrangements were firmly in place between US and British secret service entities in Washington and London. These arrangements carried over to the OSS period and concerned information sharing and dissemination, joint training, and the basis for joint special operations. At the end of June 1942, however, Donovan concluded a series of detailed operational accords with SOE, which became the real basis for future Allied special operations work. Much still had to be done, but OSS was in a position to make a substantive contribution in intelligence collection, analysis, and special operations, and did so in a dramatic fashion in North Africa during the Allied invasion – code named 'TORCH' – of November 1942.

The appointment by Donovan, and indeed, by the British services, of individuals with personal 'connections' and understanding of each other's respective country and customs is another crucial dimension of the Anglo-US relationship under examination. Such ties created a working environment that was conducive to building mutual confidence and trust, which is perhaps more important in the sphere of intelligence – where informal, back-channel dealings are the accepted norm – than in other walks of life. On the US side, in addition to Bill Whitney and his Anglophile credentials came Solborg, who after the war was rewarded by the British for services rendered to SIS and claimed that 'British intelligence has long arms [and] looked after me well [after the war].'[122] Though his time in COI was short, Wallace Phillips' understanding of the English ran deep with his many years as a London resident and contacts in British business, politics, and society. Donovan continued the practice of appointing well-connected Anglophiles to top posts by dispatching Shepardson, an Oxford-educated Rhodes Scholar who had served as Secretary of the British-American Group at Versailles after the First World War,[123] to London in the spring of 1942. David Bruce's social qualifications assisted him in dealing with 'the social club establishment that ran the British secret services.'[124] According to his diarist:

Bruce . . . moved confidently through the ruling strata of British society, dining with Mayfair's smartest set and conferring with cabinet ministers, military chiefs, and heads of various secret agencies. If some of the influential figures with whom he made easy acquaintance were new faces, many more were old friends from less dangerous times, friends whose names filled the pages of *Debrett's* and the rosters of the poshest clubs in St. James . . . His patrician style and understated air of competence provided just the tone needed to dispel their apprehensions about a ham-fisted, upstart American venture into clandestine operations.[125]

There were many others. Fisher Howe, for example, who served as executive officer to both Whitney and Shepardson, had previously worked for a year in Yorkshire in the 1930s.[126] Norman Holmes Pearson, who was recruited to organize Donovan's research branch in London, owed his appointment in part to the mistaken belief that he had been a Rhodes Scholar. Ray Guest, future head of OSS maritime operations in France and Scandinavia, was a 'polo-playing socialite . . . and a cousin of Winston Churchill.'[127] And Henry Hyde, who worked for OSS in London and Algiers, was a Cambridge graduate who had also attended a noted English preparatory school.[128] Another Oxford Rhodes Scholar, William Arthur Roseborough, was a former US counsel in the British Purchasing Commission in New York, who ran COI's Iberian/Greek section in early 1942,[129] then helped to fill the departed Bruce's shoes at OSS headquarters before moving to OSS Algiers.[130] Donovan's faith in the power of personal relationships is strikingly evident from the background of these men.

The British side also found some benefit in matching those officers with 'American ties' to key positions where regular interaction with Donovan's people was necessary. Stephenson, to start with, was a fellow North American from Canada with an American wife, American business interests and friends. Dansey, for all his supposed anti-Americanism,[131] had once been married to an American and had spent considerable time in the US during the First World War; he kept an eye on the Irish-American business community in New York lest private US funds found their way to Irish republicans. Later, after America entered the war in 1917, Dansey worked in Washington helping the US Army set up its own wartime intelligence organization.[132] His cultural understanding might be described as comprehensive.

Like their American opposites, there are many additional examples. The principal SIS officer assigned to liaise with COI and OSS in London for much of the war was Wilfred Dunderdale, who also had an American wife but was much more well-disposed towards the 'New World'[133] than was his boss Dansey. Rex Benson, Menzies' liaison with the US War Department in Washington, was considered by Donovan to be a good choice for the job as he 'knew and liked Americans' and, like Dunderdale, was married to one.[134] The first SOE commandant of the 'Camp X' covert special operations training facility in Canada was Lt. Colonel Terence Roper-Caldbeck, who also had an American wife and got along famously with Donovan's recruits.[135] And Douglas Dodds-Parker, chief of the SOE organization in Algiers, which was known as 'MASSINGHAM,' was yet another senior officer who was notably well-disposed toward the US, later marrying an American member of Averell Harriman's Lend-Lease operation in London. Two of Dodds-Parker's American friends from his Oxford days stayed in close touch with him and went on to be important wartime contacts in his special operations work.[136] Clearly, the added bonus of 'connections' worked both ways.

The role personal ties and cultural appreciation played in the effectiveness of the Anglo-American intelligence relationship in question is very difficult to quantify. Yet, its importance cannot be overstated. As Dick Ellis explained after the war, 'The whole story may never be told, partly for professional reasons, but chiefly because cooperation was largely a matter of mutual confidence between individuals, and was seldom a matter for official record.'[137]

A great deal of the Anglo-American intelligence story was 'seldom a matter for official record,' but much evidence does exist to suggest that while the partnership might have been unequal in 1941–2, the two sides were to some extent mutually dependent. SIS and SOE would have survived without COI certainly, but with a much reduced role over the whole course of the war if deprived of American resources and future breakthroughs in secret intelligence and special operations roles that were hitherto the domain of the British services. COI, on the other hand, probably would have withered on the vine without the British. With British assistance, however, it created a cadre that rapidly grew in size, skills, and experience, moving Donovan's organization from pupil to full partner by mid-1943.

3 Trial by Fire: London and the Proving Grounds of North Africa and Burma, 1942–43

> Recognition of the individual value of the various components of OSS . . . was not sufficient. The organization was predicated upon their combined effect in support of military strategy and operations. This was a concept, however valid in theory, that could only be proved in action, i.e., in the field. Throughout the summer and fall of 1942, the test was in the making.[1]   (OSS War Report)

INTRODUCTION

The dissolution of the Office of the Coordinator of Information (COI) and its replacement by the more focused Office of Strategic Services (OSS) on 13 June 1942[2] gave Bill Donovan the means to secure his organization's place in the highly competitive wartime bureaucracy in Washington through direct support of military operations in the field. The new OSS had shed its controversial 'foreign information activities,' which had rendered COI so vulnerable to criticism and competition in Washington and London. It was now under the authority of the newly established US Joint Chiefs of Staff (JCS), for which it was to 'a. Collect and analyze such strategic information as may be required, [and] b. Plan and operate such special services as may be directed by the [JCS].'[3] These 'special services' included 'sabotage, espionage in enemy-[controlled] territory, organization and conduct of guerrilla warfare . . . counter-espionage . . . contact with underground [and] foreign nationality groups, [and] intelligence functions.'[4]

The subordination of OSS to the military gave it a certain legitimacy in the Washington hierarchy that COI had never managed to achieve because the latter had been solely answerable to the President, whose attention was divided among the pressing responsibilities of his office. Outside of a direct appeal to Franklin Roosevelt, COI had been powerless to cope with a sustained assault by large and established bureaucratic entities. Despite the new arrangements, however, OSS's legitimacy still had to be earned in a military establishment that in mid-1942 remained skeptical about Donovan's 'amateurs' and had been one of COI's most powerful critics. Donovan now had to convince his new military masters, particularly the American theater commanders and their staffs overseas, that OSS performed a useful function and that its working relationship with the British facilitated rather than complicated military operations.

48

Thus, OSS over the winter of 1942–3 was compelled to cooperate closely with SOE and SIS, while simultaneously demonstrating that it was not simply an arm of the British secret services. OSS needed to prove that it could act effectively and independently when and where the military authorities needed 'special' support. This was particularly important in places such as North Africa, which had been targeted for Allied invasion and in which the US – for political reasons – was better positioned to operate than the UK. OSS also saw the Far East, where the Allies were hard pressed to withstand Japanese advances and where OSS might be better received than its UK counterparts in Axis-occupied (formerly British and French) colonial areas, as a region of opportunity. However, the act of exerting independence from the British, while simultaneously appealing for continued British tutoring and other assistance, proved to be a complex and delicate task. It required diplomacy, compromise, and when necessary hard bargaining, as well as a willingness to face the negative consequences of clashing national and parochial interests.

OSS was established against the backdrop of a rapidly changing military climate for the Allies; a fluid situation that yielded opportunities as well as limitations for the US and British secret services and determined, to a great extent, the nature and scope of the relationship between them. In April 1942, for example, Japan had closed the 'Burma Road' – through which Chinese nationalists and US forces in China were supplied – thereby creating an opportunity for OSS that will be explored further herein. German victories over the Red Army at Kharkov in May, meanwhile, increased the pressure Soviet leader Josef Stalin brought to bear upon Britain and the US to open a second front in Europe, while the stunning success of Erwin Rommel's June offensive against the British in the Western Desert helped to turn the attention of the western Allies to North Africa as a desirable invasion point. By the end of July 1942, Roosevelt and Churchill had committed themselves to invading North Africa in the autumn, thereby creating an opportunity for OSS to prove itself in the field and to lead a joint effort with SOE.

Even as North Africa and Burma were shaping up to be the proving grounds for OSS in 1942, London was where the real battles for the future of the organization were being waged. There the negotiations with SOE were conducted that determined the scope of OSS in 1942–3 to conduct special operations, both jointly with SOE and independently. London was also where OSS confronted SIS for a stake in future operations and for the right to have independent access to the intelligence components of the various Allied governments-in-exile. For OSS, the second half of 1942 and early 1943 was to be the period in which it either defined its future role in the war and secured some form of independence from the British or faded into obscurity.

THE ANGLO-AMERICAN INTELLIGENCE PROTOCOLS OF JUNE 1942

In June 1942, in an atmosphere of uncertainty over the future of America's centralized intelligence experiment, a COI delegation led by Donovan flew to Britain to negotiate the operational protocols that governed the Anglo-OSS partnership in the crucial months to come. Donovan's team, which featured his key subordinates David Bruce and Preston Goodfellow, left the US as members of COI and were advised in London that they now belonged to something called OSS.[5] This timely resolution of his organization's status helped to clarify Donovan's position vis-à-vis his British counterparts in London, enabling him to negotiate what SOE chief Charles Hambro termed the 'integral rationing of British and American [special operations] activities [worldwide]'[6] from a stronger position. The American was determined to secure for OSS a fair and adequate stake in the war, and by extension, in the Washington establishment.

Bruce, who was familiar to the British from his days as a member of the International Red Cross in London in 1940, was dispatched ahead of Donovan. He arrived on 20 May 1942 and set to work preparing for the extensive bilateral talks to come. On his first day he met with SIS chief Menzies at Broadway, dined with Lord Louis Mountbatten, future Supreme Allied Commander in Southeast Asia, saw Oliver Lyttleton of the War Cabinet, and Oliver Stanley, Secretary of State for the Colonies. Bruce's second day was spent at SOE's Baker Street headquarters and with senior members of the Political Warfare Executive, then with COI London's staff, US Ambassador John Winant, and Averell Harriman, head of the US Lend-Lease Commission in the UK, all of whom almost certainly provided him with valuable insights and assistance. Over the next fortnight, Bruce sought out the company of such familiar key figures as Admiral Godfrey, Ian Fleming, General Ismay, Claude Dansey, Charles Hambro, and Colin Gubbins (who succeeded Hambro as SOE chief late in 1943), all of whom OSS needed to win over in the hard negotiations to come. He also met with Lord Selbourne, the new Minister of Economic Warfare, James Munn, head of SOE's most important training facility in Britain and future chief of its North African station, and with various useful SIS interlocutors. These included Richard Gambier-Parry, chief of communications, Gerald Wilkinson, SIS's liaison officer to US General Douglas MacArthur in the Philippines, and Felix Cowgill, chief of counterintelligence.[7]

When Donovan and Preston Goodfellow arrived in London on 12 June, their agenda was practically set. They were whisked into meetings over the next week with Menzies, Dansey, Victor Cavendish-Bentinck, head of the British Joint Intelligence Committee, Bill Stephenson and Dick Ellis from BSC, and many others, including SIS's young rising star Kim Philby.[8] Donovan's team then moved on to the more detailed negotiations – principally with SOE – which were framed in part by an earlier letter from Hambro to Donovan which argued:

> It is essential for us to avoid creation of two field organizations each trying to do the same sort of work [and] getting thoroughly tangled up . . . [In] each area there should be one combined Anglo-American field force [either] predominantly British [with] a large minority of [US] personnel and controlled from London, [or] predominantly American with some British personnel and

controlled from New York . . . Each case [should] be decided according to the circumstances, [i.e.,] whether military authorities [are] British or American, whether one or other of us . . . enjoys some special advantages.[9]

The talks were intense but amicable, as evidenced by Hambro's note to Donovan of 23 June:

> May I take this opportunity of saying how much I have valued your visit and how greatly we have enjoyed meeting your staff. I feel certain that the friendship and understanding that has developed during their stay will prove of the greatest value and will ensure the smooth running of our plans for the future.[10]

The agreements reached between Donovan and Hambro were the cornerstone for future cooperation in special operations. They divided an array of responsibilities and geographic areas. The first part of the accords covered liaison in Washington and London, which was now to include information exchanges (operational, technical, and training-related), coordination of equipment production, prioritization, and supply, management of field disputes, and national policy representation. The second part covered field collaboration, and was designed to 'avoid the confusion resulting from [two] completely independent organizations working in the same field.' Distinct US and British operating areas were defined, with each side permitted to set up a special operations mission in the area run by the other, but under the direction and control of the other. Globally, SOE was given initial preeminence in India, East and West Africa, Gibraltar, the Balkans, the Middle East, Western Europe, Poland, Czechoslovakia, and Scandinavia. OSS was given China, Australia and the Southwest Pacific, North Africa, Finland, and the Atlantic islands (the Azores, Madeira, the Canaries, and the Cape Verdes[11]). Burma, Siam, Indochina, Malaya, Sumatra, Germany, Italy, Sweden, and Switzerland, meanwhile, were considered joint areas, and no agreement was deemed necessary for Spain, Portugal, and the USSR.[12]

  In the European Theater of Operations (ETO), where the bulk of the Anglo-US military effort would most probably be targeted, the two sides took the negotiations a step further. SOE, which recognized that the US military planned to use the British mainland as a jumping off and supply point for an inevitable invasion of mainland Europe, agreed that 'a complete . . . OSS section [should be] attached to the American command to carry out strategic services for it in those areas which [were eventually to be] allocated to American forces.' SOE insisted, however, that the fledgling OSS recognize its limitations and agree to SOE direction, since Baker Street already had organizations on the Continent that were carrying out special operations.[13]

  A compromise was reached whereby both sides created for operational purposes an 'Invasion Sphere,' comprising Norway, Holland, Belgium, and France, where Allied forces planned to reenter Europe. They also identified a 'Non-Invasion Sphere,' which encompassed Germany, Italy, Switzerland, Poland,

Czechoslovakia, and Sweden. Within the Invasion Sphere, SOE was responsible for infiltrating and directing any OSS personnel who wished to participate in operations, thereby limiting the US to what was essentially a supporting role. The exception to this rule was unoccupied France, where OSS could work with some independence, but in coordination with SOE. Invasion Sphere operations were further divided into 'first' and 'second' phase activities; OSS agreed in phase one to concentrate on recruitment and training, leaving the issue of which side directed joint activities during phase two to the Supreme Command's division of control over regular forces, with due consideration given to the progress of the OSS 'trainees.'

In the Non-Invasion Sphere, the agreements reached differed for each country. For example, in Poland and Czechoslovakia, OSS was to render assistance where practical in close coordination with SOE, while in Germany and Italy, both sides retained the right of independent operations and separate organizations (provided OSS 'effectuated control' from its London base and duly informed the appropriate SOE counterparts). OSS acknowledged SOE direction in Sweden and on Sweden-based operations launched against the rest of Scandinavia and Germany. In exchange, SOE agreed that OSS could use Switzerland as a base for operations against Germany, Italy, and France – directed from OSS London – in coordination with Baker Street.[14]

OSS and SOE also agreed on parameters of collaboration in equipment research and development, the pooling of resources for equipment production, and joint training. It was agreed that SOE was to begin training large numbers of OSS officers at its various schools, which started one of the most successful aspects of the OSS-SOE partnership. British and American organizational finances were simplified, as the two sides had come to the conclusion 'that it would be better to wipe out any kind of cash transaction between SOE and [OSS] and that each should supply the other with goods without charge . . . There would [henceforth] merely be a system of recording types and numbers of goods delivered.'[15] This enabled OSS in practice to provide the bulk of material and financial resources as part of the *quid pro quo* for British support in training, information, etc.[16]

In the end, both sides achieved their principal objectives, establishing a useful framework for an operational partnership that enabled each party to pursue its vital interests with less risk of duplication and interference from the other. The British secured 'control' of what were to them the core operational areas of France, the Balkans, the Middle East, and India (where potentially destabilizing US influence was to be strictly avoided). In turn, they partially ceded the lead in the Far East, calculating that regular US forces almost certainly would play the decisive role there and Donovan was, in any event, far from being able to do much. SOE believed that OSS needed British experience and at that time superior organization to operate effectively, and through agreement on joint or otherwise coexisting field units in some areas, hoped to retain control over areas technically ceded to OSS. This was important for SOE because it had been obliged to cede to OSS control of operations in North Africa – where its vital interests were at stake. SOE had argued that all of North Africa 'should be regarded . . . as a British sphere' before agreeing to compromise.[17] In areas where OSS was to have greater independence, such as in Germany, Italy, Switzerland, and Iberia, SOE persuaded OSS to agree to direct its field operations there from its London base – where it was easier for Baker Street and Broadway to monitor and influence the Americans. Moreover, the financial accountability and joint production parts of the accords cleared the way for much needed OSS materiel assistance to SOE.

Donovan, meanwhile, achieved his key goal of securing OSS predominance in North Africa, where it might be able to demonstrate its worth in the near-term. North Africa was where US troops had to prove themselves for the first time in the European war, and was the only place where OSS had its own intelligence and special operations networks in 1942. Donovan also won the right to lead special operations in China, which Washington saw as the most important Far Eastern nation. In addition, he secured a means to participate, albeit in a small fashion, in what were for the British the almost sacrosanct areas of France and the Balkans through the joint or coexisting field teams agreement. In Italy and Germany, the long-term keys to the outcome of the European war, Donovan secured virtually complete freedom of action. Moreover, OSS could only benefit from joint training, and many of the previously difficult issues relating to liaison, supply, and finance had been satisfactorily resolved. Whilst much in the accords remained vague, both sides preferred this because it gave them flexibility for maneuver. Overall, the agreements constituted an important step forward with both sides having much to be pleased about. On 10 August 1942, the US Joint Psychological Warfare Committee recommended that the US Joint Chiefs approve the accords,[18] which the latter did two weeks later.[19]

LONDON, 1942

> [OSS London] made it possible for [us] to gain rapidly from the experience of the British, [but kept us] from pursuing activities independently, free from restraints and interference.[20]
>
> (OSS assessment)

Background

The aforementioned substantive discussions and bilateral agreements reached between OSS and the British in June 1942 proved to be a watershed, not only for the overall partnership, but particularly for Donovan's London base. OSS London was subsequently called upon to spearhead Donovan's quest for the substantial role in the war that he had been working so hard to acquire since his appointment as Coordinator of Information the previous year. The difficult road traveled in London by Bill Whitney and Wallace Phillips soon yielded tangible positive results for their OSS successors. Donovan's new team featured J. Gustav Guenther and Dick Heppner for special operations (backed by Ellery Huntington from Washington), Whitney Shepardson and William Maddox for secret intelligence (backed by Bruce until he took over as chief of OSS Europe and moved to London in early 1943), and the ex-diplomat William Phillips as overall chief of the London station. These men greatly enhanced the effectiveness of OSS activities in and directed from the UK. They oversaw and were aided by the substantial augmentation of the station with personnel, resources, and responsibilities in late 1942 and early 1943.

The fight for equality with the British, however, still proved to be difficult. OSS London took the brunt of the strains in the relationship – as it had when it was called COI – by virtue of its physical proximity to British decision-makers and the intelligence components of the various exiled Allied governments that SIS and SOE guarded jealously. OSS London's increasingly aggressive agenda, moreover, added to British anxieties. As the host country, the UK was able:

> to define to some extent the scope of OSS operations [via] control of transport and communications,[21] and through the information it required on . . . OSS personnel movements to and from [Britain]; it was necessary for OSS to assert its equality with its British counterparts to prevent that limitation.[22]

In asserting itself, OSS London had to overcome the obstructions raised by some in the British establishment who felt that its work threatened their interests of both a parochial and national nature. However, OSS proved to be more capable than had been COI in undertaking this task.

The work of the newly augmented London station encompassed much more than Whitney's '95-percent propaganda support' claim of late 1941. 1942–3 saw redoubled efforts to participate in operations with SOE and SIS, to oversee joint training activities,[23] and to foster strong links to other related British organizations, such as the Political Warfare Executive. It also saw efforts to exchange technical assistance and finished intelligence, and to enhance liaison relationships with the governments-in-exile based in London. In pursuing these varied objectives, however, the various components of OSS London often hampered their own work by competing with each other for ties to British and exile entities. As one OSS report described it:

> Conditions . . . were essentially those of free-for-all pioneering and expansion. Every element . . . was bent on marking out the broadest possible monopoly in a fluid situation, while the central office [was] too busy and insufficiently authoritative to rationalize the competition [for] connections.[24]

While the British probably would have found a coordinated OSS approach to be more efficient, SIS in particular almost certainly used this disunity to increase its influence over OSS London. By picking and choosing the frequency and depth of individual contacts with OSS personnel, skilled interlocutors like Claude Dansey attempted to block unwanted OSS plans and activities, facilitating only those that were more in line with perceived British interests.

In addition to its traditional responsibilities, OSS London was given the task of liaising with the new US military presence, including the commander of US forces in Europe,[25] General Dwight Eisenhower. Eisenhower soon played a critical role in the future direction of OSS in relation to the various British services under his overall direction. Describing his first days as OSS London's new chief to Roosevelt in August 1942, William Phillips commented: 'My first task is to get in touch with our own Command. General Eisenhower ... seems to welcome the closest possible association with us.'[26]

The Eisenhower linkage was deemed by Donovan to be a critical component of his strategy to prove the worth of OSS to the US Joint Chiefs. If OSS was useful to Eisenhower, so the logic went, the Joint Chiefs would give it an important role in operations. Donovan also saw Eisenhower as a potentially key element in his plans to achieve equality with the British. Once William Phillips had made contact with Eisenhower, Donovan cabled the US Command that:

> OSS in the Theater was under the control and direction of General Eisenhower [and will] advise the latter fully concerning any of its representatives operating in the Theater, submit to him any project for execution within the Theater, give him all information gathered [in] the Theater and assist him in all possible ways.[27]

This clear statement stands in stark contrast to the ambiguous character of most of Donovan's other dealings. To further clarify the importance OSS attached to London station's subordination to the military, the following was circulated internally by OSS on 12 August 1942: 'This is *not* a mere arrangement struck with [Eisenhower] whereby we are permitted to "go about our work peaceably." It is a contract of the gravest import ... entailing for [us] a test which can make or break the organization.'[28] This strategy evidently impressed the US Command, with Phillips subsequently reporting: 'With [Eisenhower] we have the pleasantest relations and your message about working with and for him, which I read to him, was ... much appreciated.'[29]

SO London

> SOE is offering SO complete cooperation. To fail to act upon this offer would be nothing short of foolhardy.[30]   (Ellery Huntington, September 1942)

The Donovan-Hambro accords of June 1942 were needed because of the increasingly complex and potentially productive relationship between the special operations (SO) part of OSS London and SOE already being forged on an *ad hoc* basis at the working level. In March, for example, a member of Goodfellow's SO team in London reported that the British had begun:

to make available [their agent] chain through Spain to Gibraltar for 'escaped prisoners of war' ... [They] can see the end of their franc supply approaching and want my help at Vichy in purchasing francs against pound credits ... [SOE] agrees to allot us part of [its radio] bands, to [allow us to] use [its] sending and receiving facilities [and has] agreed to place [its] information at our disposal, to provide faked papers, give us use of [its radio] facilities and send supplies. They ask us for help in raising finances in France and for pouch facilities for long, slow communications and possibly cable [facilities] for occasional urgent message[s]. They see [the] necessity for working out some sort of agreement by which our activities in the field should be prevented from conflicting.[31]

Such linkages were the outgrowth of the hard work of Donovan, Stephenson, Goodfellow, and the many others discussed in previous chapters, which created an opportunity for a significant expansion of OSS's special operations. Goodfellow – probably at the behest of Donovan – ordered his staff to draft a report stating the case for enhancing the SO part of OSS. This expanded upon one of Donovan's earliest wartime priorities, which was the establishment of a significant base in London as the staging point for wide-ranging operations into Europe.

The resulting report of 10 June 1942 helped to focus OSS's negotiating position in those watershed talks Donovan held with Hambro later that month. It concluded generally that:

[OSS] should participate in SO to prepare the way for future [U.S.] military participation [in the war, and] adequate SO representation must be established in Britain to make this participation effective [because]: 1) Britain is the base for military operations against France and Western Europe ... 2) British SO ... has been for a long time and is engaged in operations in [these areas]; 3) [SOE] is giving active support to the underground resistance movements; 4) The de Gaulle movement and all other European fighting movements have their [headquarters] in Britain; 5) European nationals qualified for SO work can be recruited more readily in Britain than in the [U.S.; and] 6) SO equipment, wireless, weapons, demolition and other material must be delivered from Britain.[32]

Goodfellow's proposal was wide in scope, linked firmly to the SOE experience, and OSS London was identified as the core platform for OSS special operations into Europe. In many ways OSS London was envisioned as the future OSS co-headquarters. Hence, Donovan's June visit was aimed principally at securing SOE's agreement to build SO London into a cornerstone of OSS.

The part of the accords pertaining to OSS London was intended to secure the sort of unprecedented access to SOE activities that would greatly accelerate the London station's ability to substantially contribute to military operations. It was also aimed at preserving the independence that would allow OSS as a whole to shed its image of being simply an appendage of the British services. The SO part of OSS London, for example, was permitted to maintain an independent administration, provided that 'all operational matters' were coordinated through Baker Street. OSS and SOE were to assign liaison officers to each other's country sections, and SO London was to attach other officers to SOE 'where such attachment [was] of value and in those sections in which it is considered that SO [had] an interest or [could] render assistance,' although the details of this arrangement remained unresolved for some time. As such rotational officers were to have access to information not otherwise available to OSS, it was agreed that: 'It is essential for the establishment of mutual confidence . . . that such information shall be treated as "privileged" and as being [SOE's] property.'

The agreement also stipulated that 'all supply, operational and training facilities of SOE are at the disposal of OSS for any action undertaken from [Britain],' and that SO London 'would conform to [SOE] security measures.'[33] Never before had the two services cooperated so closely.

In practice, SO London found over the balance of the summer that it had accomplished very little towards fleshing out the London agreements; it was eager to move forward, but the British remained uneasy about the possibility of duplication of effort. Gustav Guenther, who was 'capable [and] evidently acceptable to [US] officials in London and to the British,'[34] had been picked by Donovan to lead the branch on an interim basis and to get things moving. Guenther promised not to try to replicate SOE's organization in London or its networks in the Invasion Sphere, but asked instead to be allowed to contribute 'individual operatives' to SOE-directed operations in France and the Benelux whenever possible. Baker Street, in turn, agreed to 'make every effort to recruit and make available for use [ultimately by both services in the Invasion Sphere, native] language speaking "guerrilla nuclei" or "Auxiliary Operations Groups" intended primarily to supplement the work of invasion forces and sabotage units.' In Norway, Italy, and Iberia, however, SO London explained that it wanted to be more proactive. It proposed to: 'put personnel into [Norway] in collaboration . . . with SOE and the Norwegian Government, [and] to carry out operations in other occupied territories and in Germany under the direction of, and in Germany in collaboration with, SOE.'[35] These discussions helped to further reduce misunderstandings, but one additional arrangement – this time concerning the theater commander – had still to be agreed upon.

Eisenhower, who faced the practical problems of OSS-SOE cohabitation in his theater, insisted in July 1942 upon a 'finite arrangement' between the British and US special operations elements and his headquarters. This understanding had to ensure that all sides knew at all times 'precisely what each [was] doing with regard to placing agents in enemy or occupied territory.' As William Phillips explained to Shepardson on 25 July:

[Eisenhower] thinks that the present situation is not sufficiently controlled. He would like me to be on such terms with [my] British [opposites] that whenever [SOE] plans to send agents in [he] will know in advance and there will be no overlapping. The General [wants] precisely the same reciprocal arrangement between his office, through me, and the British, [and he] attaches considerable importance to a very clear understanding with the British on this point.[36]

A suitable mechanism was soon created to satisfy Eisenhower, which included Guenther 'acting as a Liaison Officer with the Military not only for SO [branch] but for OSS as a whole.'[37] This overcame the final major obstacle to full-fledged collaboration between SO and SOE in and from London. By September, OSS Washington had dispatched Goodfellow's able successor as chief of special operations worldwide,[38] Ellery Huntington, to conduct a detailed survey of SOE facilities and methods that was used to turn the principles of June into more of a reality.

Where the Donovan-Hambro accords had established an overall framework for OSS-SOE cooperation, Huntington's survey codified that relationship and moved it decisively forward. It identified problems in the earlier arrangements and proposed ways around them or formal modifications. His findings were principally derived from extensive visits to SOE facilities and discussions with SOE personnel in the UK in September. After evaluating Baker Street's organization and the problems it had encountered, Huntington recommended that OSS personnel be assigned to various SOE components – as had already been agreed – without further delay to facilitate cooperation and provide hands-on training. OSS London was to be enlarged to include Geographic Desk representatives who could work closely with their SOE opposites, and liaison officers were to be assigned to key members of Hambro's staff, including operations, transport, and communications. Moreover, OSS was to start sending officers to fill training places established for them at SOE schools, with subsequent assignment as instructors.[39]

Huntington began with the assumption that while the SI (secret intelligence) side of OSS had 'already accomplished enough to warrant its existence, this [was] not yet true of SO.' His objectives for 'catching up' with SI were fourfold:

1. Collaboration with the British without reservation . . . and the fullest possible use of existing SOE facilities; 2. The building of man power . . . for action on the North and South wings of Europe; 3. The building of liaison personnel and supplies in the Far East; 4. The formulation of an overall plan [for exploiting] the tremendous possibilities which are open to us in the Balkans and Italy.[40]

Huntington then addressed the five topics most relevant to special operations work – field operations, communications, supply, training, and transport – and identified the way in which SO branch could contribute in the near term and what it had to do to meet future objectives.

In the realm of operations, Gubbins told Huntington that SOE was 'weak' in unoccupied France and in Switzerland, and urged him 'to obtain immediate coverage there.' SOE was much more effective in occupied France and the Low Countries, however, which led Huntington to conclude that OSS could best participate in the near-term via supply 'in the form, principally, of planes, boats and radio sets.' In Scandinavia, Gubbins 'invited [OSS] to participate with [SOE in Norway] and to penetrate Sweden and Finland,' and Huntington reported that SO was 'about to begin a program of special training for [four or five] Norwegian Groups of five men each.' SOE, moreover, 'urged that SO "do something" about Spain and Portugal,'[41] which gave OSS flexibility in an increasingly important area to the coming Allied invasion of North Africa.

Across southern Europe and the Middle and Near East, Huntington observed that OSS was 'stymied by reason of our agreement with the British.' He was presumably referring to SOE's prior insistence that Baker Street control all special operations activities in those areas:

> In Italy and the Balkans 'Patriot Groups' are crying for assistance . . . [In] Italy nothing vital has as yet been proposed [yet it] is highly vulnerable. It is an entrance point to the Southern European flank and we will be overlooking a bet if action in this direction is not implemented at once . . . [We also should develop] Greek and Yugoslav contacts . . . We are stymied in most of these areas by reason of the understandings and misunderstandings which have resulted from the [Donovan-Hambro] Agreement. We have need of reorientation with respect to this document particularly as it relates to . . . the Balkans.

While Huntington placed much of the blame for OSS's special operations difficulties in the summer on certain restrictions in the June accords, he nonetheless recognized that the slowness with which OSS had foreseen the need to organize itself in Cairo was a major contributing factor to the problem. SOE had established a significant presence in Cairo at the start of the war to handle special operations in the Balkans, Middle and Near East regions. SOE Cairo was in some ways a problem for SOE as a whole, as it often had vastly different views about its mission and authority than did its Baker Street superiors – which increasingly confused British policy in Yugoslavia, as will be addressed in Chapter 5 – further complicating its relationship with OSS. 'We should contemplate the building of a sizable operation of our own [in Cairo],' Huntington wrote in his report to Donovan, 'accepting British aid in doing so.'[42]

In the remaining four areas covered by Huntington's survey – communications, supply, transport, and training – the American was more optimistic, both about SOE's willingness to cooperate and OSS's ability to contribute. On communications, for example, he explained:

> SOE has generously offered its facilities to both SI and SO upon the understanding that when sufficient personnel [are] trained, . . . our own OSS stations would be established . . . The only SO contribution for the moment will be in radio sets and components [which] are badly needed and will more than compensate for the assistance the British are willing to give us.

On the matter of supply, Huntington believed that OSS:

> can be of great assistance at the moment in furnishing bulk materials . . . Plastic
> [explosives], fuses, arms, ammunition and radio components should be sup-
> plied by us in exchange for the retail articles we need . . . SOE is urging us to
> develop [a research] department as rapidly as possible . . . The new Research
> Division of OSS will [surely] meet with the hearty approval of the British.

In the biggest problem area for both sides – transport – Huntington acknowledged
that SOE's existing fleet of aircraft was inadequate for its own purposes, let alone
for what he had in mind for OSS. He therefore proposed that OSS try to convince
the US military authorities to allocate sufficient aircraft to OSS to enable it to meet
its planned commitments and to aid the British: 'We should be willing to begin
modestly – three bombers in England, a like number in Cairo, with some reason-
able reserves, would be sufficient to enable us to demonstrate the . . . service
which SO can render with these facilities.'[43]

The British, it must be reemphasized, were protective of what they considered
their right of control in areas where they had key national interests and where SOE
was active. At the same time, however, they remained keen – particularly SOE,
which had neither the pre-war organization nor post-war aspirations of SIS – that
OSS begin to shoulder a much larger share of the practical burdens of operations.
SOE was short of equipment, finance, and manpower, and in Huntington had
found a man who was as eager to provide materiel support as they were to get it.

With Huntington's survey having finally clarified and cleared the way for a
much enhanced special operations role for OSS, principally out of London, the
new OSS-SOE relationship was – on the surface, at least – well positioned to finally begin paying dividends. There were still many difficulties ahead, however,
in getting properly organized for the much more important role envisioned by
Huntington and expected by Donovan. OSS headquarters, the SO staff in London,
and SOE, in fact, all had unrealistic expectations for US special operations in
1942. The 'learning curve' for such work was considerably longer than that of
many other OSS enterprises, such as research and analysis. Few if any at OSS
London had any specialized training prior to their assignment abroad, and had to
learn from SOE by observing. Most had not yet attended British training schools,
yet were expected to begin finding, investigating, training, equipping, and deploying recruits. All of this took a great deal of time, more perhaps than had been anticipated by the impatient Donovan and SOE. OSS London, moreover, had to do
all of this without appearing to threaten SOE's interests. It was a daunting task.

SI London

> It was necessary for [OSS London's SI branch] to establish and carefully cultivate close and
> confident relationships with the officials of each available source of information, and to obtain

an intimate knowledge of how their intelligence was obtained and appraised, so as to weight its credibility and put it in its proper setting in transmitting it to Washington.[44]

At the same time that OSS and SOE finalized their first formal agreements in June 1942, Whitney Shepardson, who had taken over as chief of the secret intelligence component (SI) of OSS London on 1 June – with William Maddox his only assistant – outlined his vision of his branch's future in a memorandum to Donovan. As a result, SI London remained firmly committed to collecting intelligence from an array of British entities to meet OSS's reporting requirements. It sought, however, to avoid duplicating the activities of other US agencies with similar liaison networks. To this effect, Shepardson drew on the negative experience of his predecessors:

> [We] will not trespass unnecessarily on relations already established between [U.S.] and British Service opposites, thereby antagonizing the former when their good will is essential [and duplicating] services already established . . . It will be necessary from time to time . . . to do [this] very thing, [therefore,] arrangements were made with British Military, Naval and Air Intelligence, the British Foreign Office, [Ministry of Economic Warfare, and Political Warfare Executive].[45]

Shepardson also explained how his branch had taken on the substantial added responsibility of acquiring intelligence from the exiled governments in London. He thought these new sources were a valuable resource needing to be fully and independently exploited by OSS:

> Polish, Czech, Norwegian and Dutch services are prepared to communicate [with us] direct. Contact with them has begun . . . Belgian, Free French and possibly [Yugoslav] and Greek sources will doubtless take the same attitude . . . Satisfactory clearance has been made with British authorities who no longer object to our having direct access to and receiving full reports and source material directly from the foreign intelligence sources. On the contrary, the British now seem to think that this would be a good thing, and we have agreed to keep in close touch with them and compare the material we respectively receive.[46]

Shepardson's persistent overtures to SIS about independent OSS contacts and Donovan's intervention with Menzies and Dansey evidently convinced Broadway to concentrate on influencing how the intelligence collected from exile groups was interpreted rather than on blocking the contacts. Elaborating on this 'compromise,' Shepardson wrote on 24 June 1942:

> [We] will collect from British intelligence its selection and evaluation of strategic information received . . . from refugee intelligence services, as well as other secret information received by it from other sources. This arrangement has been confirmed and strengthened by [our] recent direct contacts.[47]

In the spirit of this new 'understanding,' Shepardson established contact in July with Charles de Gaulle's intelligence service, *Bureau Central de Renseignements et d'Action* – or BCRA[48] – headed by André Dewavrin, who was known by his *nom de guerre* 'Colonel Passy.'[49] The first material OSS received from BCRA was 'of uneven value, only part of it falling within the scope of intelligence, [but by] late October the French began to send [to OSS] straight intelligence in some bulk.'[50] The Shepardson-Dewavrin link infuriated SIS, which 'to a peculiar degree regarded de Gaulle and his entourage as the special charge and property of the British Government . . . and in every way except by diplomatic demarche they denied or delayed or postponed the possibility of SI receiving French raw material.'[51]

Menzies summoned Shepardson to Broadway several times in the weeks following the initial contact and attempted to convince him to drop the liaison arrangement. SIS cast aspersions on the quality of French material that was being provided to OSS, arguing that:

> it was in large percentage 'political' and tendentious and that it required [SIS's] own long experience to separate the wheat from the chaff. [SIS argued] that if the French papers were passed on without the most careful screening, [OSS] would only be confused and might [mislead] its own consuming agencies.[52]

Faced with this overt British assault on his sovereignty, Shepardson felt that the future viability of his branch depended on his standing firm. He claimed to have told Menzies that:

> We were new in the business, but [we] were going to try to do it to the best of our ability. I fully appreciated [SIS's] views and would be guided accordingly in the handling of the material, but I wanted to assert . . . that we could not develop a sound secret intelligence service without making mistakes, and that we insisted upon the right, if need be, to make our own mistakes and not to be preserved from them by the processing of our friends.[53]

The otherwise cordial nature of OSS London's relationship with SIS – evident in Shepardson's comment in August 1942 that '[SIS is] immediately responsive to our requests and their officials are always available to us'[54] – masked the increasing tension between the two. Broadway's deeply held suspicions about the wisdom of allowing the American novices a free hand in intelligence matters actually governed its policy throughout the period under examination. While the British were accessible, they were reluctant to include OSS in anything that might embolden it to demand an equal or even participatory role in field operations. An assessment that SI London made in April 1943 about the situation that had existed since Shepardson's initial report the previous summer is particularly revealing:

> Informal suggestions made by us on various occasions that consideration might be given to the development of joint SIS-SI operations in Europe, working from

the London theater, have invariably met with a disinterested and non-committal response. In this respect, our relations with Broadway differ materially from those of SO with Baker Street. The explanation is to be found in the fact that Broadway is a much older and more firmly established organization, operating . . . under conservative leadership within the bounds of its own traditions.[55]

The aforementioned assessment's author – probably William Maddox, who had by then succeeded Shepardson – offered a possible explanation for why SIS's willingness to be forthcoming was in direct proportion to OSS's ability to tangibly contribute to operations:

The suggestion made by us that we might be able to furnish trained personnel for continental work has fallen on stony ground. Broadway has argued that unless a man has been resident in the country in which he is to be dropped within the past year, he would be of little value. If, however, we actually reached the point where we were equipped with our own trained personnel and transportation and communications, [we] would command respect. Broadway itself might then raise the question of joint operations since it would not be keen to see another network established among the already complicated lines of underground organizations . . . Given the enormous difficulties which would face an attempt to establish [a] new network . . . it would seem wiser then to join with Broadway.[56]

The logic of this argument was compelling, and probably was intended to press OSS headquarters for more support. But SI London had a long way to go before it was prepared and equipped to participate in joint operations on anything approaching equal terms, or to try going it alone.

Facing the reality of its own weakness and an unhelpful SIS, SI London focused much of its collective energy in the second half of 1942 and early 1943 on building up its linkages to the exiled governments. These might, if deftly managed, address some of the branch's shortcomings by giving it what had been previously unavailable – privileged access to native recruits, resistance networks, and raw intelligence. These ties helped to boost SI London's prestige and enhanced its position vis-à-vis SIS because it forced the British to take into account the probability that the exiled governments – with their own vested interests – might sometimes prefer dialogue with the US over that with Britain. The first approaches made by Shepardson, Maddox and William Phillips in the summer of 1942 developed into more formal ties by the autumn to the Czechs, Poles, Yugoslavs, Greeks, Dutch, Belgians and Norwegians.[57] 'The British tried mightily to discourage these independent contacts . . . in the same manner and for the same reasons they used in attempting to prevent the SI-French liaison.'[58] Evidently, Broadway's supposed acceptance of the inevitability of these contacts had been a misperception by

Shepardson, or perhaps SI's new link to BCRA prompted SIS to act more aggressively to recoup lost ground.

As the British position hardened and SIS increased its efforts to wean the exile groups away from contact with the Americans on intelligence matters, Shepardson sought out Menzies on several occasions to try to negotiate a bureaucratic truce. For once, OSS's position was a relatively strong one, as the exiled governments were not easily intimidated by SIS and were themselves keen to establish independent ties to Washington. According to Shepardson:

> Each time [Menzies] made it clear to me: a) that these exiled governments were in fact the guests of the British Government on British soil and that it was appropriate that their intelligence relations should therefore be confined to Broadway; and b) that a great deal of this exiled government intelligence was none too good, and that everything valuable in it would be found by us to have been incorporated in the Broadway reports which he had agreed to let us have.[59]

With no real change in SIS policy in sight, SI London decided on yet another new approach – it proposed establishing a tripartite intelligence arrangement with SIS and de Gaulle's BCRA.

Shepardson and Maddox had first proposed tripartite cooperation to SIS in September 1942 and again early in the following month. They urged that 'it would be far better if [SIS and OSS discussed] their problems with the Free French in the presence of each other . . . rather than separately,'[60] but were rebuffed. Once SIS began to sense that it might be excluded from future OSS-BCRA collaboration, however, it relented. But before a tripartite mechanism was established, three incidents occurred which damaged then ended this first tripartite initiative.

The first incident occurred on 2 October 1942, when SIS intercepted an uncoded transatlantic telephone conversation between a member of de Gaulle's staff in London and a Gaullist Frenchman in Washington. Sensitive information about French agents operating from the US was discussed and SIS believed that the Germans had also intercepted the message. Already very fearful about security in general, Broadway believed the incident to be a grievous breach of procedure and so informed Donovan on 12 October.[61]

The second incident was known as the 'Clamorgan Affair,' after the code name of its French protagonist. An aircraft that was carrying a Gaullist agent to Tangier crashed in Spain, also in early October, and materials related to Allied agent networks in North Africa were compromised. SIS used the incident to argue against further tripartite activity on security grounds. 'There was also the possibility, from the viewpoint of SI, that [SIS's] rather inflamed feeling about the whole matter might have [had] the secondary purpose of hamstringing OSS.'[62]

The third event in October was more of a misunderstanding than any lapse of security, but resulted in the suspension of tripartite work entirely. General Strong, the senior Allied officer in charge of security for the invasion of North Africa –

code-named 'TORCH' – ordered OSS to use only the codes of the invasion forces on matters pertaining to TORCH as part of his plan to tighten communications security. Shortly afterwards, Strong received an information copy of an OSS cable on the status of tripartite cooperation and mistakenly believed that OSS was communicating with the British and French about the invasion in its own codes. Immediately and without consultation with OSS, he ordered that all tripartite activity be stopped.[63]

As tensions between SIS and BCRA had increased many-fold as a result of the events of October, OSS decided that its interests were best served by remaining neutral and not backing either the British or Gaullist sides against the other. Shepardson's branch was in a difficult situation and he was eager to limit the damage to his organization's position in a future tripartite scheme. Donovan sent Arthur Roseborough to London to meet with BCRA officials, and he subsequently recommended that ties to the Gaullists be increased regardless of the consequences for OSS London's relationship with SIS.[64] He believed that too much useful information and potential for future collaboration with BCRA in France was at stake to reject de Gaulle. Roosevelt's decision to disengage from the Gaullists in favor of other French factions as a military expedient in the North African campaign, however, caused OSS to disregard this advice.

In the run-up to TORCH, the Allies were faced with the increasingly perplexing problem of deciding which among the many elements seeking to represent France they should support. The urgency of the situation was increased when security for TORCH was seemingly threatened by the incidents involving BCRA in October. De Gaulle had secured military recognition from the US and Britain in the spring of 1942, but craved the political recognition that would give him unquestioned authority as the official leader of the French people in exile or under occupation. In spite of its problems, his remained the most effective French organization from a military standpoint. In recognition of this, SIS had been supplying him with communications, transport, training, and weapons for some time, and the Gaullists were active in occupied France. But Britain's desire to use its hold over the Gaullist logistic train as a means to control the activities of the independent-minded French leader had prompted his courtship of OSS[65] and led – along with the October incidents – to increasing SIS–BCRA tension.

TORCH heralded the arrival of US troops *en masse* into the European war and Washington was acutely aware of the consequences an initial military setback would have on Allied strategic planning and morale. To facilitate military operations and reduce casualties, the Americans – and especially OSS – had begun to build the widest possible web of contacts among the various French factions. These included, in addition to the Gaullists, the Vichy government, officials in Vichy-administered areas of North Africa – where the issue of divided loyalties within the French military and political leadership was of great interest to OSS – and supporters of de Gaulle's new resistance rival, General Henri Giraud. The decision to disengage from de Gaulle[66] stemmed from the belief that these other factions were – with the exception of Giraud – enemies of the Gaullists, who had labeled them traitors to France; their collaboration with the invading forces was, it was thought, more likely with de Gaulle out of sight.[67]

Britain had less flexibility to deal with the Vichy factions because of its unpopularity with them after its attacks on Vichy naval forces at Mers-el-Kebir and Dakar in 1940. Broadway saw the new American policy as an opportunity to increase its leverage over the Gaullists and soon put its immediate security concerns aside once the US had become thoroughly enmeshed with Gaullist arch-enemy, Vichy Admiral Jean Darlan, and General Giraud during TORCH. The 'French factor' was to be a critical element of the Anglo-American secret intelligence and special operations relationship until the Germans were driven from France in 1944.

NORTH AFRICA, 1942–43

North Africa is likely to be regarded by [OSS as] a test case for collaboration.[68]

(SOE Evaluation)

Background

In October 1941, Donovan sent Roosevelt his assessment that North Africa was a suitable proving ground for his organization in intelligence and special operations. He explained his plans to set up a radio station in Tangier and to place a military attaché there to 'stimulate efforts in the selection of local agents of information.' According to the OSS *War Report*:

> North Africa was a perfect target for Donovan's concept. If we were eventually to invade, not only intelligence penetration, but subversive action, organization of resistance groups and guerrilla or commando activities would be of obvious and inestimable value . . . From an intelligence standpoint, French North Africa was a unique situation in which to develop an independent [OSS] network, the British having been denied official status there following the French Armistice and [British] attacks on Mers-el-Kebir and Dakar. From the standpoint of subversive activities, it was an early opportunity to collaborate with SOE [in] Tangier.[69]

By the early autumn of 1942, Donovan was searching for a means to silence his critics in Washington and to enhance OSS's status vis-à-vis the British. To accomplish this he needed to demonstrate through positive action *in the field* that OSS was a viable organization uniquely suited to supporting military operations. 'North Africa presented an easily recognizable example of the manner in which [his] concept of secret intelligence, propaganda, morale, physical subversion and guerrilla action could be used in preparing the way for a large-scale invasion.'[70]

OSS had a functioning clandestine radio network supervised from Tangier by Bill Eddy, a large network of informers, and was assured general operational direction over US and British special operations as a result of the Donovan-Hambro accords. North Africa was, in fact, the only place where OSS was capable of undertaking more than token operations at that time. It had been hotly contested by both sides in the Donovan-Hambro talks in June. SOE had argued that it should lead special operations in support of TORCH because Britain's colony at Gibraltar was 'the natural base for North African operations [as] the point at which all stores would have to be assembled for distribution and [where SOE] would eventually operate all agent [radios] in North Africa.'[71]

Donovan and Goodfellow rejected the British position on the grounds that the US had to spearhead Allied approaches to the Vichy authorities in North Africa because the British were still virtually *persona non grata* there.[72] Since July 1940, 'all British nationals [had been] banned from the area and their diplomatic and intelligence representation evacuated to a perimeter position in the international city of Tangier.'[73] The US Army would command any invasion, they asserted; Eisenhower's staff, in fact, thought it 'essential [that the] operation should be entirely American at first instance . . . assisted by the Royal Navy and Air Force.'[74] Moreover, the US directed Allied economic policy in the region by virtue of the Murphy-Weygand Accord[75] of 10 March 1941, which had opened the way for trade between America and Vichy North Africa. OSS, therefore, proposed that it establish a mission at Gibraltar and that Iberia and North Africa should be kept separate.[76] In the end, a compromise was reached whereby North Africa was provisionally designated an OSS special operations sphere of influence, OSS set up a mission to direct all operations, but the existing SOE organization remained separate – physically, administratively and operationally – 'under the general direction and control of [OSS's Bill Eddy].' Moreover, Gibraltar remained outside of the North African theater and under SOE control, although it served as a base for special operations in North Africa 'from which supplies of arms and equipment, transport [and radio] facilities' came throughout the campaign.[77]

Eddy worked out of the US Consulate at Tangier under the cover title of Naval Attaché. In August 1942, he was appointed 'head of the joint British-US organization [covering] the whole of North Africa,' including French and Spanish Morocco.[78] A colorful figure, he had lost a leg on the Western Front in the First World War, and was once the head of Cairo University's English Department. 'He spoke French and Arabic fluently, was a distinguished author and scholar, and harbored an innate distrust of SIS.'[79]

Broadway and the SI part of OSS were not affected by the Donovan-Hambro accords, which established Eddy's preeminence in joint special operations matters only. They were thus free to operate with complete independence in the region. The fact that Eddy and the SIS representative for North Africa, Toby Ellis, 'loathed each other, [further ensured that] there was precious little on-the-spot coordination between the British and the Americans'[80] on intelligence matters, although there were some notable exceptions. One of Eddy's vice-consuls, for example, acted as an intermediary between SIS and some of its North African agents, paying them as necessary and transmitting their intelligence reports back to SIS in Tangier. From October 1941 until December 1942, another vice-consul, equipped with an SIS radio set, reported enemy ship movements in the Mediterranean to SIS Malta. And from January 1942 until the TORCH landings, an American consul in Casablanca 'handled 193 SIS requests covering agent contacts, transmissions of wireless sets and fuel, and the distribution of salaries and clothing.'[81] For the most part, however, the two organizations kept a respectful distance from one another.

Independently, SIS and OSS[82] both proved useful in North Africa in the months preceding the invasion. SIS provided a great deal of important SIGINT (signals intelligence) to the military planners on Axis intentions and responses to the complex Allied deception plan for TORCH.[83] OSS, meanwhile, provided HUMINT (human intelligence) from chains of informants and used its networks to spread subversive propaganda. Eddy's operatives recruited widely, counting among their collaborators 'Strings,' 'who was the leader of the most powerful religious brotherhood in northern Morocco,' and 'Tassels,' one of the most influential undercover tribal leaders in the Rif (the coastal region transversing Spanish and French Morocco).'[84] OSS recruited local fishermen, traders, Berber adventurers, bureaucrats, French military officers, and virtually anyone who might be of use. In French Morocco alone, Eddy had 190 Spanish Communists on his payroll,[85] while in Algiers the Americans recruited mostly Frenchmen, and in Tunis, Arab natives.[86] Eddy's networks provided useful information on ports, military installations, and political machinations in the months leading to TORCH. Civil uprisings were planned, guides for the invading forces were recruited and organized, and sabotage teams were readied.

To assist him in this vast undertaking, Eddy had been assigned SOE's Brien Clarke as deputy of the 'joint' mission. Clarke controlled SOE's Gibraltar base, 'the [joint] radio network, the supply of equipment, and the existing SOE organizations in North Africa.'[87] He had been chosen somewhat at the behest of British General Mason-MacFarlane, who was distrustful of OSS security and had insisted that 'Eddy should have a British deputy to keep him on the right lines and prevent him from doing anything too outrageous.'[88] Eddy and Clarke were placed under the overall authority of the US State Department's Robert Murphy, who, largely through his and Eddy's network of clandestine contacts with anti-Nazi sympathizers in the Vichy ranks, had conducted secret negotiations with the North African defenders before the invasion in the hope that many could be persuaded to collaborate. According to SOE's post-TORCH evaluation, 'complete reliance [had] to be placed on the network for all the preliminary negotiations.'[89]

In an effort to take full advantage of the work of Murphy and Eddy, Eisenhower dispatched US General Mark Clark, less than three weeks before the first Allied landings, clandestinely to North Africa. There he met with pro-Allied Vichy officials who had requested face-to-face assurances from the US Command that they would receive adequate military support if they changed sides. Clark was landed 75 miles west of Algiers by British submarine on the night of 21/22 October, coming ashore in a canvas canoe escorted by a small group of aides and British commandos. He was met by Murphy and one of Eddy's vice-consuls, Ridgeway Knight,[90] who had helped to arrange Clark's forthcoming meetings with Vichy General Charles Mast[91] in a beachfront cottage. The Frenchman provided Clark with intelligence he later described to Eisenhower as 'extremely valuable' and confirming that the TORCH plan 'appears to be sound.'[92] This included information about likely French resistance to an Allied invasion – which Clark estimated as weak – coastal defenses, the capacities of ports to handle Allied ships, and the length of runways and types of military aircraft at various airfields.[93]

Operation 'TORCH'

The Allied invasion force that came ashore in North Africa on 8 November was divided into three parts: one landing at Algiers and attempting to drive into Tunisia to block any German or Italian countermoves, another landing at Oran, and the third at Port Lyautey, Fedala, and Safi. The 'joint OSS/SOE organization' was ordered to 'assist by subversive action the landing[s] and subsequent operations,'[94] including the advance into Tunisia. Specifically, special operations teams were to illuminate beaches to assist landing forces, neutralize coastal defense batteries, seize and protect dock, bridge, and wireless installations from destruction by the enemy, sabotage enemy aircraft, block key roads and rail links, and provide guides.[95] OSS was expected to accomplish these tasks in and behind the invasion zones without much help from SOE, since the latter did not have the personnel in place for the reasons previously discussed.

OSS participated in TORCH on many levels with varying degrees of usefulness. Confusion reigned at many of the landing beaches, but OSS recruits helped to sort out the military units that had been put ashore at the wrong map coordinates, sometimes in landing-craft that were unsuitable for beach operations, and who faced unexpected resistance; they also acted generally effectively as guides once the troops began moving inland. Other recruits 'assisted in cutting communications [in some areas] and sabotaging coastal artillery,'[96] but sabotage missions further inland proved less effective 'for varying reasons, including French defections and lack of American authorization to carry them out.'[97] OSS, however, concluded after the invasion that:

Secret operations [in support of TORCH] were handled in a wholly satisfactory manner. Our SO people felt that the fullest use was made of this weapon and [US] General Lemnitzer [of Allied Forces Headquarters – 'AFHQ,'] before leaving for the campaign congratulated OSS for their contribution. Actually, the success of our cooperation with AFH[Q] in this field should stand as one of the best evidences of the advantages to the Armed Forces of having OSS represented in the basic planning of any similar campaigns.[98]

Many other activities performed by OSS during TORCH were less successful. Due to the intense secrecy surrounding the operation and invasion date, for example, many of Eddy's operatives – particularly those tasked with sabotage missions – were out of position when they were most needed. OSS wireless operators tasked with dispatching critical intelligence to Eisenhower and his staff via military channels were obliged to switch over to the SOE communications net almost from the outset of the invasion because of technical difficulties, 'with consequent prestige and advantage to [the British].'[99] Detailed data about target areas given by the R & A branch of OSS to Eisenhower and his British deputy General Alexander was used in planning and executing the main attacks. This included 'information on conditions Allied forces could expect to meet in North Africa, from the level of surf at the Casablanca beaches to details about North Africa's roads and railways . . . [and] information on the strengths and dispositions of French forces.'[100] These same materials, however, 'were not available to the [military and intelligence] Services when they needed them . . . in London.'[101] OSS officers played a key propaganda role in the pre- and post-landing phases as part of Eisenhower's AFHQ Psychological Warfare Board – OSS photographers even filmed the invasion – but overall, OSS judged that 'propaganda . . . was not fully utilized because it was not completely integrated with the plans and operations of the armed forces.'[102]

In spite of its secondary role and orders to stand down in the region until the invasion began, Baker Street considered its role in support of TORCH to be 'the most important in which SOE have so far been concerned.'[103] SOE acted with great energy and effort, although like OSS it had mixed results. Its most important contribution was its establishment of secure radio communications between Gibraltar, the invasion forces, and Eddy's operatives during the vital phase of the landings. This link proved crucial when 'the [US] Army's signals [met] with insuperable difficulties' almost from the start of TORCH, and SIS communications proved totally inadequate.[104] As Brien Clarke reported to OSS London's William Phillips on 9 November: 'For you and Donovan's personal information and satisfaction we would like to inform you that the sole channel of communications from Gibraltar to North Africa since . . . TORCH commenced has been [the] OSS/SOE channel.'[105] And as Baker Street later concluded: 'The work carried out by [our radio] network . . . rendered a most effective service to the successful landing of TORCH.'[106] SOE, of course, was wholly responsible for this facet of the 'joint' operation and had provided virtually all of the radio equipment being used in the field. SOE's secure communications link, in fact, remained the Allied Task Force's main communications facility until 11 November.[107]

SOE's role, however, was not restricted to communications. Five SOE signal parties were assigned to the landing forces to help them ashore,[108] and numerous efforts to drop supplies to 'friendly' special operations agents behind the lines by aircraft, submarine, and boat were made throughout the landing phase. Most of these resupply efforts, however, were later judged to have been 'distinctly disappointing' due to reasons ranging from the failure of pilots to identify clear recognition signals on the ground or even to locate drop zones, to the inability to locate reception parties on beaches.[109] SOE did not criticize its field operatives for these difficulties, but instead attributed them to the demands by the mostly French recipients for unrealistic quantities of materiel to be delivered in too short a period of time, and it also blamed OSS:

> There is no doubt about it that if [OSS] had left the arrangements for the dispatch of these consignments entirely in our hands, to be carried out in small quantities over many weeks, a quite useful supply might have been delivered. Our American colleagues, however, felt from the morale and psychological point of view that it was most important to give the French exactly what they asked for without stint, and [we] did not feel that it was up to us to question these decisions.[110]

An additional facet of the operation demonstrated the complexity of the relationship between OSS and its British counterparts in late 1942. The tense relations between SIS and SOE, already simmering almost since the latter's creation in 1940, came to a boil in the weeks preceding TORCH and put OSS in the unusual position of sometimes having closer relations with its British secret intelligence and special operations opposites than the two British organizations had with each other. According to Carleton Coon, who served in OSS during TORCH:

> [SIS] holds itself aloof from the SOE as from us, and it is a question whether the worst enemy of the SOE is the Germans or the SIS. In Tangier the SIS was headed by Colonel [Toby] Ellis, a man of no scruples, universally detested by British, Americans, Arabs and everyone else . . . Our relations with him were formal, aloof, mistrustful. He tried on several occasions to impede our operations, and if he had succeeded he might have completely ruined our preparations for the landing and given the show away.

Coon's poor opinion of SIS in North Africa, however, reveals that OSS had its share of problems with Broadway's representatives in the region. He later named AFHQ's security chief as 'another SIS man who is our enemy [and who] has tried on several occasions to upset our shows.' SIS, wrote Coon, 'is an imperialistic organization [which] we have any reason to mistrust.'[111]

What complicated the SIS–SOE relationship during the preparations for TORCH, however, concerned two specific incidents of SOE operations which put SIS in a difficult position vis-à-vis British Ambassador Sir Samuel Hoare in Madrid. Hoare opposed any operation – covert or otherwise – that might prompt Spain's dictator, General Francisco Franco, to cooperate more closely with the Germans, and he generally made life very difficult for SIS and SOE personnel seeking to work in the area under his authority. The first operation in question – code-named 'FALAISE' – consisted of the successful destruction by SOE saboteurs of a clandestine German radio station near Tangier, which had been set up to transmit information about Allied ship movements in the Gibraltar Straits. The second consisted of a failed effort by SOE to sabotage a French ship, which resulted in the 'premature explosion of its limpet mine on a ferry [which] killed 39, including 8 Britons . . . The SIS Head of Station [in Tangier], Toby Ellis, had to take the blame and experienced a damaging round-up of his local agents.'[112] Both incidents prompted Hoare to take steps to rein in SIS even further, which did not endear SOE to Broadway. SIS-SOE mutual distrust, when taken with Coon's comments, Eddy's supposed personal dislike of Ellis, and the fact that the OSS and SOE elements participating in TORCH were not organizationally integrated, yet were expected to operate as though they were, it is not difficult to imagine why relatively little was accomplished of a truly joint Anglo-American nature in the secret intelligence or special operations aspects of the initial invasion.

The French Dynamic

The French dynamic in the whole TORCH affair was also of great importance, both for the success of the invasion and the ability of OSS and the British to collaborate with the Gaullists in future operations. Having rejected Gaullist participation in TORCH, the American Command had turned to General Giraud as an alternative. Eddy and Murphy had contacts among supporters of the French General in North Africa and they convinced Roosevelt and his advisers in the months leading up to the invasion that he might be of considerable use. Murphy was subsequently assigned to Eisenhower's staff in London 'as "political advisor" in charge of coordinating OSS activities in support of TORCH,'[113] and negotiations were opened with the Giraud group forthwith. 'After [Giraud's] escape from prison in Germany [in April 1942, he contacted] SIS in Switzerland and it was with the help of SIS that he reached Algiers the day after the Allied landings.'[114] The Allies hoped that Giraud's prestige among the Vichy defenders in North Africa might facilitate the invasion and reduce casualties on both sides. However, when the General arrived on the scene, he demanded that *he* be given overall command of the invading force instead of Eisenhower, and when rebuffed proved to be less helpful in persuading the Vichy defenders to lay down their arms than the Allies had hoped.

With unexpected opposition being encountered by Allied forces in some landing areas, and facing Giraud's hesitance, Eisenhower turned for support to the collaborationist Admiral Jean Darlan – the Vichy vice-premier – who was coincidentally visiting Algiers. In October 1942, 'Darlan had approached the US authorities in Algiers to warn them that Germany had got wind of forthcoming assaults on Dakar and/or Casablanca and to tell them that he feared Germany would retaliate with an invasion of French north Africa through Spain.'[115] Nearly taken prisoner in Algiers by anti-Vichy Frenchmen when the invasion began and sensing an imminent collapse of Vichy sovereignty, Darlan agreed to help the Allies and within the week announced that he was taking direct control of the Vichy-administered areas in North Africa with Allied consent. His intervention resulted in a cessation of hostilities in the Algiers area on the evening of 8 November and a more general ceasefire two days later. Darlan then negotiated a 'provisional settlement' with Eisenhower on 13 November,[116] effectively ending French resistance to the invasion.

The use of such a notorious collaborator as Darlan by the Allies as an expedient in military operations outraged the Gaullists, who were already suspicious of the sudden emergence of Giraud in the Allied camp as the new commander of French military forces in North Africa. De Gaulle ordered his intelligence service to break off relations with OSS, which André Dewavrin did, albeit informally, temporarily halting the flow of Gaullist intelligence material to the Americans.[117] Moreover, 'the natural result of the events in North Africa was to tend to unite more closely the French and British behind de Gaulle. With the Americans supporting Giraud,' and working with Darlan, 'there was an alarming possibility of an increasing alignment of forces on each side which would not only have split open the whole French Resistance movement, but also could have seriously injured Anglo-American relations to the extent of interfering with the conduct of war.'[118] Even before TORCH, the British had taken the position that Giraud's arrival in Algiers did not 'supersede the role of the [Gaullists]'[119] in the battle to liberate France, indicating that an intra-Allied struggle on the issue of the French resistance was inevitable.

Once it was clear that TORCH had succeeded, however, de Gaulle softened his position toward Giraud, reducing the potential for added friction between OSS and the British. He indicated that he would attempt to come to an accommodation with his rival – perhaps even accepting Giraud as a military leader once the Allies granted the Gaullists political recognition – provided 'Giraud were able to gain the effective support of the French North African Army.'[120] This compromising attitude actually was first hinted at in a meeting de Gaulle had with Churchill a week before the TORCH landings in which he 'agreed that France came first and that he would equalize himself with any leader bringing equal assets to the Allied cause.'[121]

Darlan, however, remained completely unacceptable to de Gaulle and to most of the other resistance factions. On 24 December 1942, he was assassinated by a Gaullist supporter who had been trained in North Africa by SOE, but evidently acted in this case of his own volition.[122] Darlan's death cleared the way for talks between de Gaulle and Giraud, which occurred at the end of January 1943 and were 'fruitful as to plans for cooperation along certain lines.'[123] Shortly thereafter, 'the de Gaulle–Giraud conflict was gradually resolved into a working arrangement which resulted in the French Committee of National Liberation'[124] under the joint leadership of the two men. By spring 1943, Gaullist–OSS relations had improved, with both sides conceding that they needed each other and agreeing to put their differences over North Africa aside.

The MASSINGHAM Controversy

Even before the first Allied landings in North Africa on 8 November, a significant controversy erupted between OSS and SOE that caused bad feelings between the two and hampered relations in North Africa well into 1943. The problem centered on divergent OSS and SOE plans for establishing the capability to operate from North Africa into the Mediterranean region and southern France after TORCH.

On the US side, Donovan had proposed in late-summer 1942 to set up an independent OSS mission in Algiers for 'out of area' operations as soon as possible following the Allied invasion.[125] He recognized OSS's limitations and expected that it would take some time to get the mission fully staffed and equipped; personnel had still to be recruited and trained. He felt, however, that the best way to silence his critics in Washington was to 'create an impression . . . that he [was] building up and [was] responsible for a big [special operations] organization based in North Africa . . . [which was in] no way dependent upon, or subservient to, the British.'[126] When SOE pressed him in October about its preference for largely integrated activities after TORCH, Donovan 'was extremely emphatic that he intended to set up his own independent mission and that he would not consider anything in the nature of a joint show.'[127]

SOE, meanwhile, believed that it was 'extremely important [to] make a good start' in North Africa after TORCH and made plans to deploy some of its 'best personnel' to Algiers to establish a special operations mission – code-named 'MASSINGHAM' – as soon as practicable.[128] Baker Street had been obliged to accept that its pre-TORCH role was severely limited because of a directive by the Allied Command in September specifying that SOE 'shall not take any overt action in North Africa before zero [the invasion date].'[129] The TORCH planners evidently feared that an increase in activities by SOE in the region might reveal Allied intentions to the Axis. Hambro, therefore, was all the more determined to get established as quickly as possible in Algiers and SOE convinced Eisenhower shortly before the invasion to agree to 'the establishment in North Africa of [an] advanced operational headquarters of SOE to control activities into Europe for which SOE are responsible.'[130]

When Donovan discovered on the day before TORCH that SOE had come to an agreement with Eisenhower and planned to deploy MASSINGHAM immediately, he concluded that this was a ploy by SOE to wrest control of the western Mediterranean from OSS. In meetings with SOE, he left the impression that he had become very wary of British intentions:

> [Donovan] has developed a slight touch of suspicion of the British. He reverted again and again [in our talks] to the British genius for getting their own way and

'nobbling' innocent Americans . . . He made it very clear that he was himself determined not to be 'nobbled' or managed [by SOE in North Africa].[131]

On 10 November, Stephenson warned Hambro that: 'A serious position has arisen in view of the fact that a definite agreement had been made with General Eisenhower without it being arranged that [Donovan] should be informed that such an agreement was to be concluded.'[132] OSS clearly felt slighted by SOE's maneuver and was determined to fight for its perceived rights.

Once the more general ceasefire with the Vichy defenders in North Africa was agreed to on 13 November and Allied forces consolidated their position over the subsequent fortnight, the MASSINGHAM controversy increasingly became a point of contention. OSS's activities during TORCH had secured for it the support of the US military authorities in Eisenhower's theater, and Donovan felt that his position was strong enough to challenge what he thought was SOE's contention that it had exclusive rights to operate into Europe from North Africa.[133] He lost no time in attempting to consolidate and expand the OSS position. Eddy's headquarters was moved from Tangier to Algiers, where he was close to Eisenhower's newly established Allied Forces Headquarters, and OSS built up its training facilities at Djebel Hallouf and Ain Taya. With the meager assets capable of operating in Europe at his disposal, Eddy was instructed to begin building a solid framework for 'out-of-area' secret intelligence and special operations work from Algiers. He started by agreeing to continue to fund OSS's agents in Algeria and Morocco in the hope that they would compensate somewhat for his organization's lack of trained personnel[134] until he could be reinforced. Meanwhile, Eddy retained the leadership of the 'joint OSS-SOE Mission' against targets in North Africa, although the need for such work in Algeria and Morocco had significantly decreased; moreover, OSS also lacked the personnel to participate in what were mostly tactical intelligence operations required in Tunisia, and SOE's 'BRANDON'[135] element had already been attached to the British First Army for that purpose.[136]

Baker Street accepted Eddy's continued preeminent role in local operations and even agreed that he remain as the 'figurehead' leader for all joint special operations in the theater. SOE was confident that Hambro's pre-TORCH agreement with Eisenhower ensured that OSS-SOE 'out-of-area' activities remained merged at MASSINGHAM under SOE's practical direction. Moreover, it was clear that SOE had the trained personnel available for deployment to MASSINGHAM and the equipment stocks at Gibraltar to begin operating into Europe immediately, whereas OSS lacked both. The British were therefore opposed to OSS requests in late November to change this arrangement with Eisenhower in any substantial way:

Believe AFHQ have laid down that all OSS SOE action from Africa is under head MASSINGHAM. Suggest unwise [to] ask AFHQ [to] alter arrangement which is working smoothly.[137]

In addition to OSS's political need to demonstrate its independence, Donovan was also driven by his belief that North Africa was now more critical than ever to future Allied plans to move against Italy and southern France. He was particularly 'anxious for Italy to be allotted to America'[138] and suspected that SOE's 'arrangement' with Eisenhower was an attempt to relegate OSS permanently to a subordinate role. Baker Street had only reluctantly ceded leadership to OSS for TORCH, he remembered, and might now be trying to take advantage of the situation – which included OSS's difficulties arising over the Darlan affair – to take over all of the important operations in the region before OSS was ready. As an SOE report of 22 November explained:

> [There is] deep resentment against SOE [for] attempting to 'beat the gun' [in North Africa.]. They [OSS] still feel . . . that London has rushed in too quickly without making the necessary arrangements, firstly with OSS in Washington and secondly with [Murphy and Eddy], and without taking into full consideration the very difficult political situation which was obviously likely to arise in North Africa with the various French factions.[139]

SOE was bitter about the American attitude, which it attributed to the time spent by OSS 'playing politics' in Washington instead of 'carrying on the war' by expediting deployment of trained personnel and necessary materiel to North Africa. It argued that 'the sole object' of Baker Street's actions had been to 'get first class officers and men on the spot quickly so that they act as an advance party and prepare the ground.'[140] Moreover, the British had qualms about an interim OSS-proposed arrangement whereby MASSINGHAM activities in practice were to be managed more closely by Eddy until a fully independent OSS mission was established: 'It will be a mission with a US chief and all the staff will be SOE as well as the facilities. Is it really necessary to kowtow to [OSS]? So far we have given everything and obtained nothing.'[141] SOE believed that 'until OSS can produce men with experience, the head [of] the North African Joint Mission should be from SOE.'[142] It proposed that OSS attach officers to MASSINGHAM 'to gain experience and form the nucleus of their mission, to be formed as soon as possible . . . Whatever OSS say now they will be forced by events to some form of joint mission.'[143] Britain's objective throughout was to lock OSS into a joint status whereby SOE's superior local manpower and deployed resources gave it a measure of control over whomever was named to lead.

The controversy was further complicated by divergent views about MASSINGHAM within OSS itself. For example, OSS London's Dick Heppner – who had been temporarily assigned to Algiers to assess the special operations environment – held discussions on the subject in November with SOE in London during which he hinted at internal discord:

> [Heppner] feels that in spite of several long telegrams from the London office, OSS Washington have not yet grasped the object of MASSINGHAM. As an in-

stance, he mentioned that Eddy appears to be taking charge of the OSS side of MASSINGHAM, whereas what is required is an officer who is an expert on, say Italy or France, not North Africa . . . [Heppner] feels that the position regarding MASSINGHAM will be straightened out, but he pointed out that there are many interpretations of the word 'joint.'[144]

William Phillips in London, meanwhile, believed that MASSINGHAM talks 'should take place exclusively in London' and was described as 'distressed at the course events have taken,' in reference to OSS Washington's interference in policy discussions.[145] In Washington, Donovan remained committed to handle the MASSINGHAM controversy himself.

By December, difficulties over MASSINGHAM persisted, but both sides had become more flexible. Hambro instructed MASSINGHAM to 'collaborate fully with Colonel Eddy on all [special operations] into Europe' and suggested that 'the details of cooperation and coordination' had to be worked out 'on the spot between Colonel Munn and Colonel Eddy.'[146] It was agreed that there would be two missions: MASSINGHAM was headquartered at the Club de Pins in Sidi Ferruch whilst OSS continued to work out of a building in Algiers, with the two training facilities previously mentioned located outside the city. All essential services, however, were to be pooled: this included 'transportation, communications, supplies, training and any other services required, [and] joint geographical desks by countries for work into Europe.'[147] The joint geographical desks put OSS Algiers and MASSINGHAM in much closer contact, satisfying SOE's desire for some integration. By February, the two sides had agreed further that 'all joint operations from the theater [into Europe were to] be directed locally by a Policy Committee composed of the Chiefs of SOE and SO and their respective regional heads.'[148] Moreover, a measure of equality was achieved when SOE recognized that while MASSINGHAM had 'practically no men at all suitable for infiltration . . . into Sardinia, Italy or Sicily, [OSS had] a considerable number of both Italians and Sicilians under training in the [US].'[149]

Back in London, OSS was still faced with the political side effects of America's dealings with Darlan. There was very real concern among the OSS leadership in the aftermath of TORCH that the 'Darlan deal' had jeopardized OSS London's liaison relationships with all of the exiled governments, not least of which included its important work with the Gaullists. 'The Darlan affair is deplorable,' wrote James Grafton Rogers at OSS headquarters on 4 December 1942. 'The world will soon see us as opportunist Yankees, with no standards but security for ourselves. We will lose the war if so.'[150] And again on 20 December: 'Darlan has bought our souls – a dreadful error.'[151] The German occupation of Vichy France in response to the Allied move in November had created new and exciting opportunities for OSS, SIS, and SOE by 'further [extending] the meaning of the war to the French nation – in other words, it stirred up . . . an 'asleep' area and forced people to take a position for or against resistance';[152] OSS was keen not to be left behind. If the US could switch allegiance so quickly from the 'real' resistance forces to Quislings[153] for short-term military expedience, the argument went, the exiled governments might all rethink their relationship with OSS at the very moment when it could be of most use.

SIS could have attempted to use the Darlan affair to foster distrust between the exiled governments and OSS, which could conceivably have satisfied its policy objectives in 1942. With the US contributing troops, military leadership, and ever increasing quantities of materiel, however, Menzies chose instead to respond positively to OSS's plea for support in December:

> In a conversation with a Broadway Colonel, [OSS's] Maddox expressed concern over the anti-Darlan tone of the British [media]. As if in answer to this, two days later Brendan Bracken . . . called a meeting of newsreel commentators urging them to eliminate controversial political comment from films for the duration.[154]

SIS showed itself to be capable in this small but not insignificant way of putting aside parochial considerations in order to help OSS to recover its political position. Perhaps the British also realized that while the exiled governments could afford to be morally indignant over the Darlan matter, these groups understood that they still needed the Americans over the longer term, and would continue to deal with them independently, the Darlan affair notwithstanding. Dewavrin's earlier decision not to break relations formally with OSS – just to temporarily suspend the provision of raw intelligence – might also have been seen by Broadway as an indication that even the party most offended by the Darlan matter had chosen to leave its options open.

Darlan's death altered the equation somewhat for OSS in Britain and North Africa. In London, the most visible irritant to OSS London's intelligence liaison activities with the exiled governments had been removed – albeit in an embarrassing fashion – and the way was at least partially cleared for an OSS rapprochement with the Gaullists. Giraud's appointment to succeed Darlan as the French High Commissioner for North Africa, however, continued to complicate US relations with the Gaullists, but also gave the Allies some additional leverage over de Gaulle, who as previously discussed, soon found it necessary to begin a rapprochement of his own with Giraud.[155] The belief of many Frenchmen in North Africa that the Allies had been complicit in Darlan's murder, meanwhile, caused a popular outcry among former Vichy supporters, and for a time OSS and SOE were concerned that their activities in the region might be restricted by the Allied Military Command at the behest of the French. OSS, in fact, suspended operations at the joint facility where Darlan's assassin had been trained by SOE for other work.

Against this turbulent backdrop, Donovan visited Algiers just after Christmas to assess the damage done by Darlan's assassination to his and SOE's ability to operate in the area and to plot his organization's strategy of how to proceed in North Africa. During the first week of January 1943, a meeting was chaired by Eisenhower with Donovan, Gubbins, and Douglas Dodds-Parker – who had been nominated to succeed James Munn[156] as head of MASSINGHAM. It was at this gathering that Eisenhower ordered OSS and SOE to 'work together 100 percent' in all special operations in his theater and at which Dodds-Parker's appointment was approved.[157] When Donovan returned to North Africa a fortnight later, he dined privately with Dodds-Parker and explained that in spite of Eisenhower's orders, OSS still needed to have independent operations in the region to establish its viability with the President. According to Dodds-Parker:

> Donovan told me that if he went to the President and told him that he was merely supporting another half a dozen British operations he wouldn't get the support that he would have to get . . . I fully agreed with that and said that I would do my best to help him to find methods of having wholly supported American operations . . . although I realized that I would have to 'carry the can' [with Eisenhower and Gubbins] if things went wrong.[158]

Donovan was determined to capitalize on the goodwill of Dodds-Parker and others at MASSINGHAM to achieve maximum positive effect for both organizations, even while he recognized the political need for OSS to pursue independent activities. From a practical standpoint, Donovan had also to consider that the well-provisioned SOE base at Gibraltar greatly facilitated MASSINGHAM's communications capability, whereas OSS Algiers was still experiencing considerable difficulty in this area. Moreover, SOE Gibraltar provided Dodds-Parker's mission with some air transport – a capability Eddy's organization had not yet acquired from the US military. OSS Algiers, therefore, was reorganized by Donovan before he departed:

> No hard and fast distinction had been made [by OSS] between SI and SO work [in Algiers. Donovan decided that] there should be a distinct SO set-up, and approved a suggestion that its pattern conform rather closely to the British SOE set-up . . . The hope [was] that the SO set-up, after some two or three months of work, would be in a position to run its own independent show.[159]

With OSS Algiers thus established, Donovan believed the next logical step to be the renegotiation of the accord with SOE that he had worked out in London with Hambro during the previous June. In fact, he had already dispatched his trusted special operations chief Huntington to London earlier in January to lead the renegotiations with Hambro and his staff at Baker Street. The proving grounds of North Africa had taken OSS to the next level of participation in the war; this level required greater flexibility to pursue independent activities on a global scale.

THE SO-SOE OPERATIONAL REVISIONS OF JANUARY 1943

The intensive OSS-SOE discussions held at Baker Street during 9–14 January 1943 resulted in a number of revisions to the June 1942 accords which, like those original understandings, were the product of compromises that left both sides generally satisfied. While SOE's leaders in London and North Africa were willing to allow OSS certain latitudes in meeting its political need for independent action, these same individuals were determined that this independence be confined when at all possible to areas outside of the 'Invasion Sphere' as was agreed in June 1942. Therefore, they were pleased to have secured from Huntington a pledge in January 'not to set up in London a wholly separate operational base [and only to] . . . offer limited assistance to SOE in France, Holland and Belgium.'[160] Moreover, they were satisfied that OSS's additional promise to 'endeavor to form "guerrilla nuclei" or "auxiliary operations groups" to supplement the work of the forces invading these areas, [also making] available sabotage units before the invasion for "*coup de main*" projects,'[161] did not threaten SOE's preeminent position in the sphere. Such activities might even prove useful when the time came for action, it was thought, as long as OSS was properly coordinated and controlled.

Reinforcing promises made in June 1942, OSS and SOE formally agreed on rules for 'the conduct of operations from London' by the SO branch of OSS. Bowing to their host's continued wishes, the Americans promised to coordinate all operations 'through SOE,' to set up more reciprocal liaison exchanges between geographical desks, and to attach additional officers to 'various SOE sections . . . where such attachment will be of value and in those sections in which [SO] has an interest or can render assistance.' For its part, SOE promised to continue to place its 'supply, operational and training facilities . . . at the disposal of OSS for any action undertaken from [Britain].'[162] In this way, SOE felt reasonably certain that OSS – in London at least – did not pose a threat to its leadership or operations via uncoordinated action.

Having yielded to SOE on British territory and as yet organizationally unprepared to operate independently in regions of primary importance to SOE, Huntington pressed instead for more latitude in Norway. This was meant to supplement what OSS believed were excellent operational opportunities in Italy and Iberia in 1943.[163] The OSS plan was to use Norway as a means to establish itself within the 'Invasion Sphere,' albeit on the outer edge. Moreover, Huntington was driven by the US military's desire after TORCH to participate in Norway:

> The [US] Command was very anxious to participate in operations against Norway, as being one of the flanks from which the German main defenses might be turned. They already had a Naval Base in Iceland, from which operations by submarine or flying boats might be suitably launched against Norway, particularly the northern part of the country. Finally, America had in the Middle West a large population of Norwegian origin, who were anxious to take part in the liberation of Norway and were clamoring to be used in this theater.[164]

Specifically, it was agreed that OSS:

> will recruit and train for guerrilla warfare two groups of 10 to 25 Norwegian speaking men . . . SO will set up a Norwegian desk in London . . . All supplies

and training facilities available to the Norwegian Collaboration Committee and SO will be pooled to the benefit of both, but in particular SO will normally service operations which take place north of parallel 65.[165]

The Norwegian portion of the new accord further specified that recruits were to come from the US and training was to take place in the UK, where the candidates were to be absorbed eventually into a joint OSS-SOE Norwegian network.[166]

Other important operating areas, such as the Balkans and Middle East, were discussed in January, but it was agreed that the June accords sufficiently covered operations there for the time being, or at least no mutually agreeable revisions related to the regions were reached. North Africa was also addressed, but Donovan's meetings with Gubbins and Dodds-Parker in Algiers, together with Eisenhower's '100 percent' cooperation edict, had already largely determined the future character of the relationship there, at least as far as Huntington and Hambro were concerned. As for Germany and the other occupied territories in Europe, OSS agreed to 'collaborate with and rely on the direction of SOE,'[167] which suited the British.

Even as Donovan was preparing for his meeting in Algiers and Huntington was traveling to London to meet with Hambro, special operations planners at OSS headquarters in Washington were busily devising a worldwide SO strategy for 1943. Taking into account 'all possible areas in which [OSS] might conceivably be asked to or permitted to engage in [special] operations during the calendar year,'[168] they drew up a list of activities that was so ambitious as to suggest that Huntington's negotiating position in London may have hidden a much wider OSS agenda. Perhaps Huntington's real purpose was to secure from SOE enough flexibility for OSS to expand to the point that it was able to withstand any British objection to future American demands that SO be permitted to work as an equal in areas that were hitherto 'off-limits' to it and under British authority. The OSS drafters of the plan, for example, envisaged establishing or building upon existing OSS special operations bases in Iceland, Scandinavia, Baltic Europe, North Africa, Italy, and the Middle East. They included in their plans Egypt, Turkey, Syria, Palestine, Lebanon, Jordan, Saudi Arabia, Iran, and Iraq, the Balkans, Hungary, India, Afghanistan, Eritrea, Abyssinia, China, Manchukuo, Korea, Indochina, Thailand, Burma, Malaya, and 'reachable islands' in the Far East, the Aleutians, and Australia. They proposed 'to offer formal projects as rapidly as possible, to request the sending of advance-survey parties into the areas not already covered by previous proposals,'[169] and concluded their report to Donovan with the following unambiguous statement of intent:

Please note that operations everywhere – though coordinated – are independent. It will be disastrous to both [sides] if any other program is ever accepted.[170]

This presumption was more certain than SOE was prepared to concede in January 1943, although American confidence and ambition continued to grow without hindrance.

By March 1943, OSS felt that SOE's leadership in London was not only resigned to the fact that SO required independence from strict British control, but had even come around to supporting OSS in such an endeavor. As Huntington explained to Donovan:

> Hambro and General Gubbins have agreed with us on the practical necessity for an independent operational status everywhere for our organization. Without this we would be an adjunct of SOE and as such would not only not receive the facilities and aid we need from our own military services but would be compelled, for political reasons, to confine our dealings with National groups to those who are not willing to 'play' with the British. This would result in no good to SOE or ourselves and would certainly not increase the joint contribution of our organizations to the war effort.[171]

However, OSS also discovered that the 'cooperative' tone adopted by SOE's leadership in London on the matter of independent special operations was not always shared by those in the field – or even among Baker Street staffers, for that matter – whose cooperation was essential in implementing OSS's new policies of independence. Even as Huntington praised SOE's leadership to Donovan, he complained about those who were obstructing his activities:

> In all fairness I must say that the broad and generous approach of [Hambro] and [Gubbins] is not shared by all of their subordinates. This is notably true of Major Robin Brook (Western Europe, London) and Lord Glenconner and Colonel Keble (Cairo). I am hopeful that we have softened Brook somewhat and that he will without the necessity of more pressure, accede to our desires to establish a small organization of our own in Central France to 'tie up,' indirectly, with his own and those we now have in Southern and Southwestern portions of the same country. In Cairo, Glenconner would probably be all right if he were not influenced too much by Keble. The latter is keen but terribly pompous and 'stuffy' and is so considered by his own people. [Hambro] will, I am sure, see that we are independent in the Mid East.[172]

Unfortunately for OSS, Huntington's confidence about his ability to overcome the objections of Brook, Glenconner, and Keble to independent OSS action in France and the Middle East, respectively, proved throughout most of 1943 to be unrealistic. Even in August 1943, OSS continued to complain that 'no [special operations] work may at present be done in France without preliminary agreement with Massingham.'[173] Huntington also encountered no end of trouble with SOE Cairo – which controlled all Allied special operations in the Balkans – over OSS activities in Yugoslavia, which will be further explored in Chapter 5.

BURMA AND INDIA: SUCCESS AND MISTRUST

There was no experience in clandestine operations available to OSS in the Far East, such as had been to OSS in Europe. The liaison established with SIS and SOE in London and the lessons learned . . . saved OSS in Europe many trials and errors. Operations such as OSS contemplated in the Far East, however, were unprecedented for the British as well as for the US[174]

On 26 May 1942, Carl Eifler – a charismatic US Army Major recruited by Preston Goodfellow into COI – led a handful of fellow officers and enlisted men he had, in turn, recruited on the first independent special operations mission by Donovan's organization in the Far East. Eifler and his key subordinates had been trained for special operations and intelligence work by the British at the 'Camp X' facility in Canada in April 1942,[175] and the 'Eifler unit' – later code named 'Detachment 101' – was soon thereafter dispatched to India without a specific assignment. During the course of the next year, Eifler's unit proved both militarily successful and a major source of political irritation for the British. It paved the way for greater OSS activity in the Far East, and at the same time helped to expose what became a major rift in OSS-British relations in the entire region. This rift concerned the future of British and French colonialism throughout Southeast Asia and turned the OSS-British partnership in 'secret warfare' into more of a rivalry as the war moved into its decisive phases in 1944 and 1945.

In the spring of 1942, however, Donovan had modest short-term ambitions and almost certainly did not see British colonialism as an obstacle to his endeavors; he had much else with which to be concerned. He had hoped only that Eifler could convince General Joseph Stilwell, commander of US forces in East Asia, to give Detachment 101 a chance to prove its worth in China, where OSS soon secured a mandate from SOE to lead all special operations activities. Stilwell had rejected previous requests by Goodfellow to allow COI to operate in China because he had not liked the officer selected to lead the detachment and feared that the nationalist Chinese leader Chiang Kai-shek would reject such activity on his territory. Goodfellow had offered Stilwell the chance to recommend anyone he preferred, and Eifler's name was forwarded as one possibility.[176] Goodfellow jumped at what he saw as an opportunity to change Stilwell's mind, and without further contact with him, moved the Detachment 101 project forward.

Eifler hoped to find Stilwell in Delhi, where he was last headquartered, but after arriving there on 16 June 1942 discovered that Stilwell had moved his command to Chunking, China. Eifler finally arrived at Chunking on 31 July, having left behind the rest of his unit – which had arrived in India by boat on 4 July – in Karachi.[177] Stilwell remained very skeptical about Eifler's ability to assist his forces in China,[178] but agreed to authorize him to operate in Burma, within which lay 'the only overland route by which the United States could supply China and the American air bases and training centers in China.'[179] Japan had closed the 'Burma Road,' upon which the bulk of Stilwell's and Chiang's supplies traveled, and the Allies were resolved to reopen it.[180] Eifler was ordered to 'disrupt

Japanese communications, shipping, and to bring about . . . reprisals on [the] native population [to discourage] native aid to Japanese.' He was also given specific targets – an aerodrome, railway line, bridge, and fuel-carrying river vessels – and was directed to 'establish liaison with British authorities so no mutual interference will arise.'[181] Eifler dutifully contacted the British Governor General of Burma, Sir Reginald Dorman-Smith, and prevailed upon him to assign someone to his team as 'permanent' liaison officer.[182] Dorman-Smith chose a former member of his staff, Lieutenant-Colonel Wally Richmond, who subsequently became Eifler's close friend and partner, working diligently to ensure that friction between the OSS unit and British forces in Burma was kept to a minimum. Richmond was also responsible for maintaining smooth relations between Detachment 101 and SOE.[183]

Detachment 101 set up its headquarters at a remote tea plantation in Nazira, India – leaving a support element in Calcutta – and began to recruit native Burmese in September 1942. Initial recruiting efforts were disappointing, but 'Richmond aided in securing some Anglo-Burmese, and the program was launched,'[184] with training in 'radio operation, cryptography, security, unarmed combat, weapons, demolitions, junglecraft, and techniques of ambush and roadblock'[185] beginning in mid-October and including 16 SOE recruits. Dorman-Smith proved again to be helpful, providing 100 000 Burmese rupees *gratis* to Eifler to get him started.[186] By February 1943, Eifler's new teams had started to become operational: inserted behind Japanese lines by parachute or on foot through the jungle, they mined rail lines and roads, destroyed bridges, attacked Japanese convoys, disrupted communications, and otherwise made a nuisance of themselves. Yet, SOE and OSS continued to operate virtually independently in Burma,[187] prompting Hambro at Baker Street to write as late as summer 1943 that since Eifler's arrival: 'there has been no true coordination [because] Eifler is responsible to General Stilwell, and General Stilwell and the [British] Commander-in-Chief, India, have not yet been able to define clearly where their interests divide.'[188]

The Eifler-led presence in India, however, and a request by OSS in February 1943 to establish a branch in Delhi to liaise with SIS and SOE, raised concerns in London and Delhi about the larger question of US activities in India. India and Burma, it had been agreed, fell within the British sphere of control, while America retained control of operations in China. Under the provisions of the Donovan-Hambro accords of June 1942, furthermore, OSS was permitted to operate into Burma from China, but SOE was to control all Burmese operations from India. Eifler's headquarters in Nazira technically violated this agreement, yet SOE evidently did not object at first, probably because the Japanese were advancing unchecked and Allied resources in the theater were very limited. Hambro, in fact, went as far as to note in late-1942 that with regard to Burma, he had agreed with Donovan that 'a hard and fast delineation of spheres or responsibility was undesirable.'[189] The British Commander-in-Chief in India, Field Marshal Wavell, had in September 1942 personally approved Eifler's efforts to coordinate Detachment

101's activities with his British opposites.[190] In October, Eifler had promised that 'his group [was] to be separate from but be operated with fullest cooperation between it and SOE India, [undertaking] only such operations as [were] previously approved by [Wavell] and the head of SOE in India [Colin MacKenzie].'[191] Eifler further soothed British sensitivities by issuing a general directive to his unit in October that 'liaison with British authorities should be initiated to the end that no possible cause for complications should arise.'[192]

Hambro, who at Baker Street was far from the scene, probably was satisfied that the Eifler situation was well in hand, but MacKenzie required further confirmation of Eifler's intentions. The latter was concerned enough in December about Detachment 101 to describe 'the position of Major Eifler' as 'not altogether satisfactory.' MacKenzie acknowledged that Eifler had 'received instructions, both from General Stilwell and from Washington, to do nothing to cause embarrassment to the British Authorities,' but observed that SOE India had 'no effective control' over him 'as long as he could appeal direct to Stilwell.'[193] He drew up an agreement that Eifler evidently signed which specified that (a) Eifler's mission was a separate entity, 'although there will be the fullest cooperation between it and . . . SOE India'; (b) Eifler's activities required the approval of Wavell and MacKenzie; (c) liaison between Eifler and the British authorities 'will be effected through SOE India'; and (d) OSS and SOE will 'avoid competition for agents.'[194] Nonetheless, MacKenzie continued to observe that Eifler had ignored the understanding and was not submitting his plans for British approval or even coordination.[195] By February 1943, in fact, the British War Office felt obliged to warn Wavell that 'SOE [had been] unable to obtain the agreement of OSS Washington that Eifler be responsible to MacKenzie.'[196]

The British Foreign Office, SIS, and the governing authorities in India, meanwhile, remained even more wary than had been MacKenzie of OSS intentions. In February 1943, Whitehall confirmed to the British authorities in Delhi – who 'wanted very much to counteract American influence [in India]'[197] – that Eifler was 'allowed to work Burma from India *subject to British control*,' but acknowledged that it would be 'difficult to retain British control over [him] in practice.'[198] The Foreign Office went on to suggest that it was 'highly undesirable to allow OSS . . . to work in or from within [the] India Command [because of] overlap and duplication,'[199] presumably with the US War Department Observer Group. This group had been working in Delhi since mid-1941 'with full access to all types of service intelligence including that obtained through SIS channels,'[200] and through SOE. While it had 'no objection to close liaison,' the Foreign Office thought it 'undesirable for [OSS] liaison officers to be in positions to obtain full details regarding British agents [and] their connected matters,'[201] a key obstruction almost certainly added at the behest of SIS. The Foreign Office concluded that: 'Cooperation should be limited to liaison [and] there should be no operations from within [the] India command by OSS Burma . . . We think it essential that [Eifler's] activities be under [the] control and direction of SOE in India.'[202]

In addition to their concern about duplication of effort, the British attitude reflected a deeper wariness about American anti-imperialist sentiment. Through the uncontrolled actions of OSS and other US agencies in India, many in London and Delhi feared, local passions might be inflamed against British rule in India and, indeed, throughout the Far East. There was already a belief in British diplomatic circles that the US intended to undermine British and French imperial 'rights' in North Africa and the Middle East – 'The British are thinking . . . of Arab independence we might encourage,'[203] wrote James Grafton Rogers in January 1943 – so why not elsewhere? In the autumn of 1942, Roosevelt had gone as far as to dispatch OSS's William Phillips as his personal emissary to Delhi – with subsequent meetings in London with Churchill, other senior British leaders, and prominent Indians – to explore the possibility of Britain granting India the 'principle of self-determination.'[204] Throughout the spring of 1943, OSS and personnel from the US Office of War Information (OWI) in India were accused by the British of everything from 'issuing invitations to members of the Indian press to visit China' without first obtaining permission, to collecting and reporting intelligence from American missionaries in India about the local situation without consideration for Britain's censorship privileges.[205] Concern was even expressed about a thesis written by an OWI student at a training facility in India, 'which was based on the idea that propaganda to Burma should be anti-Imperialist.'[206]

The request by Phillips that OSS be permitted to set up an independent mission in Delhi and Eifler's continued uncoordinated activities further exacerbated British anxieties. In February, the British civil authorities in India and Wavell reluctantly agreed to the OSS mission, provided that it was limited to liaison activities and did not undertake special operations or secret intelligence missions.[207] They also exacted a promise from Phillips to use his influence in Washington to facilitate a mutually agreeable solution on matters concerning Eifler's special operations work and any other plans Donovan had for independent SI missions in or from India.[208] Shortly thereafter, the British Director of Military Intelligence in India, Major-General W. J. Cawthorn, appealed directly to Stilwell, protesting that Eifler was already subordinate to Wavell by virtue of his presence in a British sphere – a proposition that Stilwell rejected. This led the British to characterize the Eifler situation as a 'crisis,' as the British Chiefs of Staff backed Wavell and the US Joint Chiefs were reluctant to countermand Stilwell.[209] To all intents and purposes, the two sides were deadlocked in early 1943; OSS escaped much of the blame, however, as the British saw Stilwell as the major problem.[210]

The flurry of British messages that followed the Cawthorn–Stilwell exchange lasted through the spring and indicated clearly that the Anglo-US relationship in the China-Burma-India (CBI) theater was becoming increasingly strained. The minutes of one of Wavell's internal meetings held in May, for example, were full of suspicion and concern:

US [still] silent on question of control of Eifler and full coordination of all intelligence from India and no independent US activity in India . . . Greatly increased activities in India by US [OWI] in direction of both blatant US publicity and propaganda and collection of economic intelligence regarding India . . . Censorship has confirmed anti-British tendencies and activities on part of subordinate staff of OWI India . . . OSS collection by agents in India (US missionaries) of reports on internal political and security situation . . . causing disquiet to Viceroy and General Staff – India.[211]

In another May message, Wavell suggested that higher US authorities should mediate:

Penetration by OSS [within the] India Command under discussion for some time likely to be source of mutual irritation and friction if not resolved soon . . . Suggest meeting in Washington.[212]

A further telegram from Wavell indicates his increasing frustration:

Uncoordinated US activities or proposed activities regarding propaganda, publicity in India leading to mutual distrust and dangerous potentialities . . . US trying to set up parallel organizations resulting in overlap and waste . . . helping to produce unsettled situation in India . . . undermining Indian loyalty to Britain.[213]

Wavell's motivation, however, was driven much more by his concern about the impact of uncontrolled American activities in the region than it was by any assistance he hoped to render to SOE and SIS. Interestingly, his writings earlier in 1942 indicate that the British secret services were faced with the same skepticism about their usefulness from the British military authorities in Asia that OSS had to contend with in Europe and North Africa from the US military. Before Eifler had even arrived in India, for example, Wavell described SOE as 'expensive, and from [the] aspect of practical results to date in the Mideast and Far East, [it is a] wasteful and ineffective organization leading to duplication and competition for personnel, material and agents.' He cited mutual recriminations by SOE and SIS over their failures as a case in point. 'Situation should not be tolerated whereby SIS can dictate policy,' he wrote, 'and can sustain objections to economic proposals.' Criticizing Broadway even more harshly, he blamed SIS mistakes in 1939–40 for preventing the General Staff in India from 'developing an intelligence service covering Persia, where so far SIS have failed to produce adequate results even under peace conditions.'[214] Thus, some of the sensitivity to OSS activities in the Far and Near East on the part of SIS and SOE may be partially explained by the atmosphere in which all of the concerned secret services were fighting an uphill battle to carve out a niche for themselves.

Regarding the Americans, however, communications from all quarters in London during this period generally echoed Wavell's fears. The India Office, for example, restated Wavell's comments about 'mutual irritation and friction . . .

leading to mutual distrust [with] dangerous potentialities'[215] nearly verbatim in its own correspondence. Furthermore, it blamed OSS for leaving the British and US military staffs with 'divergent intelligence and views,' and for playing into the hands of the Japanese by helping to create 'unsettled conditions in India . . . aimed at undermining the loyalty of [the] Indian population in general and [the] Indian Army in particular.'[216] Baker Street was still convinced in mid-May that OSS was 'playing the game' in India, although it continued to worry about Eifler's apparent reluctance to work under MacKenzie. It blamed Stilwell for the 'Eifler problem,' however, complaining that the General's uncompromising attitude 'is typical of the American way of going about things in this area . . . [He] has of course nothing to do with SOE but he insists on being a law unto himself.' Baker Street also observed with some trepidation that not only was OSS/SI 'making a definite effort to establish a very strong organization in India and China,' but the British Indian authorities were not 'being sufficiently active or taking the necessary steps to counteract this penetration.' SIS, meanwhile, continued to oppose any 'US penetration of enemy countries based on India.'[217]

In the aftermath of Britain's strongly worded complaints, an effort was undertaken to come to a negotiated settlement on Allied differences. Responding to a note from the British Chiefs of Staff, the US JCS proposed that 'a joint intelligence center [be established] in Delhi.' Wavell countered with a more specific proposal to integrate 'all intelligence or quasi-intelligence organizations' in areas under his authority.[218] Senior British and US officials met subsequently in London to discuss their differences, and soon reached an understanding on coordinating 'all activities in India and India-China-Burma Commands to ensure commanders and Joint Staffs in London and Washington get a coordinated, common intelligence picture and remove competition, friction, and waste of resources.'[219] Specifically, the understanding called for the creation of an 'inter-Allied organization' covering what was thereafter known as the CBI (China-Burma-India) theater, which included 'Naval, military and air intelligence . . . SOE-SIS-OSS activities . . . PWE activities in enemy [and] occupied areas . . . United Nations propaganda in non-enemy territory, . . . monitoring [and] radio security.' The agreement was, as a member of Wavell's staff explained, 'a unique opportunity to settle rivalries and differences of functions between the US and British.'[220]

Understandings reached in London, however, proved much more difficult to implement in the field and were greatly complicated by evidently contradictory positions within both the British and American camps. On the British side, Cawthorn went to Washington to secure further clarification for Wavell of the OSS role in India and Burma. The India Office was confident that both SIS and SOE were prepared to accept 'unified control of integrated British-American' organizations and had so informed Wavell on 14 May.[221] Cawthorn, however, evidently was of the opinion that SIS and SOE were not desirous of full integration in India as proposed by Wavell. After being informed by Donovan that OSS 'did not like the idea of integration' but supported some form of 'coordination,' Cawthorn reported that he had agreed to a 'modification' of Wavell's plan,[222] which resulted in promises of closer collaboration within the general framework of so-called 'inter-Allied organization' outlined in the previous paragraph.

Following these discussions, SOE began to complain more vociferously that OSS was '[ignoring] the existence of the SOE/OSS agreement'[223] as it pertained to India. Growing increasingly frustrated in June, it charged that Eifler still 'refused to submit his operational plans in advance to MacKenzie for coordination . . . although personal relations between MacKenzie and Eifler are good.'[224] BSC defended Donovan by explaining that his personal efforts to subordinate Eifler to MacKenzie had been overridden by Stilwell's continuing reticence to yield overall authority over Eifler to Wavell.[225] Baker Street, however, began to suspect that Donovan's expansionist agenda in North Africa had spread eastward and that OSS was only using Stilwell as a convenient means to claim that it had no choice but to act on its own. SOE also wondered whether Donovan was circumventing his longstanding agreement with Hambro by redesignating OSS/SO personnel deployed to India as dedicated solely to espionage, which he continued to pursue against all SIS objections and apparently in violation of the understanding reached with Wavell about the function of the OSS Delhi mission: 'It is open to [Donovan] to say that [everyone] he proposes introducing into India are really for his SI and are therefore excluded from the [OSS-SOE] Treaty.'[226]

At this point, the British began to consider what implications their dispute with OSS over India and Burma might have on their secondary position vis-à-vis America in China and vice versa. The US certainly dominated the Allied position in China – SIS and SOE were very restricted by the Chinese and US authorities – yet many of Britain's colonial interests were at stake, particularly the status of Hong Kong and Shanghai. 'The Americans have full liaison with the sabotage organization of the Chinese Government,'[227] SOE complained in June, '[yet] we are excluded from this by order of [Chiang Kai-shek].' Donovan had given the British additional fodder for their arguments by asking 'as a matter of grace' that the small SIS/SOE liaison mission in Chunking 'be withdrawn, and liaison on Chinese matters [be] carried out in London and Washington,' evidently to strengthen OSS's role in China and limit Chiang's ability to play the US off of the British.[228] With OSS adopting a double standard in China and India, Baker Street felt justified in posing the question in mid-1943: 'If OSS needs a liaison mission in India, why should we not have one in China?'[229] And when SOE decided concurrently to back the French in Indochina – initially from bases in China – in an effort both to end Japanese occupation and to reassert French colonial authority, yet another point of contention arose;[230] OSS later chose to back indigenous Indochinese in their quest for independence from any sort of occupation. The stage was set for a further deterioration of relations in the Far East.

In 1943, however, both sides agreed to disagree for the time being about the role of OSS in India and that of SIS and SOE in China. Eifler continued to go about his business in Burma relatively unfettered by SOE interference, but a face-saving arrangement was worked out in the latter part of 1943 with the creation of the Southeast Asian Command (SEAC), under the direction of British Admiral Lord Louis Mountbatten. SEAC imposed a modicum of order on the Allied command structure in Southeast Asia by unifying authority over British and American forces operating in all parts of Burma, *inter alia*. Following Donovan's visit to the Far East in November–December 1943, a separate OSS unit was established to support directly the Southeast Asia Command. Eifler retained the 'protection' of Stilwell, who was now theoretically required to clear Detachment 101's operations with Mountbatten, but in practice rarely did so. As events soon proved, however, the clash between American anti-colonialism and British imperialism – not just in India, but in China, Indochina, and the Middle East – had only just begun. Over time, it turned the hitherto generally positive collaboration between OSS and the British secret services into something more resembling a rivalry in many areas of the world.

CONCLUSIONS

The period under examination in this chapter was characterized predominantly by energetic efforts by OSS – particularly in London, North Africa, Burma, and India – to assert its independence from the British in field operations and liaison, while preserving access to British training, field support, and operations. On the surface, these objectives – on the one hand operational disengagement and independence, and on the other operational integration principally through joint training and shared support functions – appear hopelessly contradictory. Yet, both were important elements of Donovan's program to demonstrate to the US military and to Roosevelt that OSS was an important component of America's warfighting capability. This objective could be reached only by creating as effective an American intelligence and sabotage organization as was humanly possible, which meant that Donovan was obliged out of good sense to secure the continued cooperation, guidance, and support of the British secret services.

OSS intentions in this regard are manifestly evident in the many seemingly contradictory, yet in reality complementary activities discussed herein. The efforts by Shepardson, Maddox, and William Phillips to secure independent intelligence links to the exiled governments, while simultaneously seeking joint training and operations with SIS, stand as one notable example. The willingness of Donovan, Goodfellow, and Huntington to subordinate SO London to SOE and to promise not to operate independently within the British-controlled 'Invasion Sphere,' while OSS simultaneously operated largely independently elsewhere, particularly in North Africa and Burma, is another. The controversy over MASSINGHAM, which resurfaced later in 1943, stands as a clear example of the contradictory tactics used by OSS in pursuit of a separate identity. Detachment 101's largely independent operations into Burma from India – whilst its leader professed coordination with and subordination to SOE – might be considered a fourth example, although the difficult conditions in Burma at the time which made field collaboration difficult must also be considered when making this judgment. Huntington's consistent willingness to accept joint or subordinate status for his special operations personnel in Britain, Western Europe, and elsewhere in his discussions with SOE in September 1942 and again in January 1943, whilst his staff simultaneously prepared plans for 'coordinated but completely independent' special operations worldwide, stands as a fifth and final noteworthy observation. The analogy of a child growing up with a corresponding desire for independence, yet still dependent upon his parents for shelter, guidance, and sustenance might be an appropriate one for helping to explain the relationship between OSS and the British during the period under examination.

The British, for their part, reacted in a mixed fashion to the steady encroachment by OSS on what had hitherto been their operational domain, be it in the realm of intelligence or special operations. SOE, by all accounts, proved more willing than did SIS to engage OSS in the sort of substantive dialogue that led to a modicum of integrated action in the field during and after TORCH in North Africa, and in the substantial joint training activities throughout the period. Perhaps the leadership of SOE – an organization without a pre-war history and with a relatively short wartime mandate – was more capable of identifying and utilizing expedients that ultimately facilitated operations with the Americans than was SIS. Yet, SOE – which had its own problems with SIS that had prevented Baker Street's saboteurs from operating in certain parts of France, Iberia, and elsewhere – aggressively sought in the negotiations with OSS of June 1942 and January 1943 to exclude independent OSS activities wherever possible and particularly in regions where British interests were thought to be most at stake, such as within the 'Invasion Sphere,' the Middle East, and in other areas within the Empire, particularly India. Perhaps SOE's 'overprotective' nature in defending its rights in the Invasion Sphere not only reflected its concern about duplication of effort with OSS, but also was related to Britain's grand strategy of keeping the war in Europe to the periphery of the Continent, lest American enthusiasm for an early cross-Channel invasion of France bring the Western Allies precipitously to grips with the full might of the German war machine. Donovan, after all, had considerable influence with Roosevelt, and widespread and 'uncontrolled' activities by OSS on the Continent might have resulted in the US pressing even harder for that cross-Channel attack than it had done previously.

SIS, meanwhile, proved more concerned than SOE about parochial interests vis-à-vis OSS. Broadway's strongly negative reaction to OSS contacts in 1942 with the exiled governments – and particularly with the Gaullist intelligence service – and its reticence to include the Americans in joint operations of almost any sort, including tripartite activities with the French that might lead to joint operations, clearly illustrates that it began in mid-1942 to see OSS encroachment as a threat as well as an opportunity. The French dynamic in both North Africa and elsewhere was generally played by SIS to its parochial advantage – with the notable exception of Broadway's help for OSS after the Darlan affair – most probably in anticipation by Menzies and Dansey of the important role to be played by the Gaullists in laying the groundwork for the inevitable cross-Channel invasion of France. If SIS alone had control over the Gaullists, Broadway's leadership probably believed, London would be in a position to exert considerably more influence over the strategic and tactical decisions of any cross-Channel operation, particularly regarding timing. It then might be fair to conclude that another secret service of the British government was acting in its relations with its American counterpart as an instrument to help implement and protect Churchill's grand strategy during the period where it was most vulnerable to changes due to American pressure.

Like the Donovan-Hambro and Huntington-Hambro accords, the development of the Anglo-OSS relationship at this time ultimately consisted of a series of compromises which left both sides somewhat free to pursue their respective agendas, but unable to act with disregard for the other, except perhaps in Burma. SIS made it more difficult for OSS to position itself for independent or joint operations in 1943, but OSS succeeded in doing just that. SOE, in large part, kept its preeminence in the key areas of Europe, but OSS secured important concessions on Norway and Italy. While OSS was forced – both by British demands and its own weaknesses – to subordinate itself to the British in many areas, Donovan achieved his major goal. OSS demonstrated through field operations in North Africa and Burma that it was a partner as well as a pupil of the British, and that it had considerable growth potential. While the determination of OSS to break free of its British-imposed restrictions governed the relationship during the period, it also dominated the balance of 1943 as shall be further explored in the next chapter.

4 Coming of Age: London, Norway, and the Jedburgh-Sussex Negotiations, 1943

The Americans generally have two ideas steadily growing in their minds. The first is that as they are by far the strongest element in the United Nations, they ought to be the senior partner in the alliance and take a leading part in the direction of the war. The second is that they are not doing this . . . I think [that] these two convictions [will] cause difficulties in all spheres. The best insurance we can take out now [is] close collaboration with OSS. It will be easy now when we can be of great help to them whilst they are still floundering . . . It may be very difficult indeed later on when they have got the bit between their teeth.[1]   (SOE assessment)

The year 1943 [was] a formative period for the London headquarters of [OSS] in the sense that questions of policy, plans and the organization itself were settled and defined but not yet tested in the field . . . Projects that [were] devised during 1943 were put into effect [in 1944].[2]
                                                                            (OSS assessment)

INTRODUCTION

In many ways, 1943 was a watershed year for relations between OSS and the British secret services, and it was in London that the parameters for the future development of the relationship as a whole were determined. Donovan's organization had proven in North Africa and Burma that it was capable of playing a leading role in operations and intended in 1943 to capitalize on its new-found influence with the US Command. It was determined to achieve equality of status with SOE and SIS – whatever the cost to the relationship – in time for the decisive invasion of occupied Europe from the United Kingdom. This was true in spite of the fact that OSS realized that many of its practical shortcomings could only be overcome through continued cooperation with the British, and even integration in certain circumstances under SOE or SIS direction. The British, meanwhile, were to varying degrees in 1943 intent upon retaining as much control over OSS activities as possible. They came to realize, however, that some concessions had to be made if OSS was to be persuaded to contribute the materiel and personnel necessary to realize the ambitious special operations and secret intelligence plans for the coming year. Added to this mix was the propensity of the British and American military establishments to interfere in what had hitherto been largely bilateral OSS-SOE and OSS-SIS negotiations.

During 1943, the situation in London as it concerned the secret services was complex and dynamic, sometimes characterized by threats and bluff, but ultimately was resolved to the general satisfaction of all parties largely through reason and self interest.[3] OSS London and SOE steadily built upon the Donovan-Hambro accords of June 1942 and the Huntington-Hambro revisions of January 1943. By April 1943, yet another working agreement was negotiated, this time establishing a basis for truly joint operations. The centerpiece of joint OSS-SOE work through the balance of the year was the development of the 'Jedburgh' program – the three-man joint special operations teams deployed behind enemy lines in France in 1944 to support the Allied invasion. Much of the latter half of 1943 was spent recruiting, training, and equipping personnel for Jedburgh operations. OSS London, meanwhile, battled throughout the same period both with SIS and the US Joint Chiefs for authority to act more independently, succeeding in the end by securing a directive to do just that as well as a place in the joint intelligence-gathering operation – the 'Sussex' program – being prepared for the coming cross-Channel invasion.

OSS-SOE, NORWEGIAN OPERATIONS, AND THE JEDBURGH PLAN

The relationship between the special operations component of OSS London and SOE throughout 1943 was characterized overall by a steadily growing mutual confidence and trust. This positive atmosphere prevailed even as OSS wrangled with the issue of just how much control over its personnel it had to cede to SOE in activities related to the coming invasion of France, and SOE saw its power to direct the relationship exclusively ebb. Recognizing that it would not be allowed to 'absorb' the special operations part of OSS London *en masse*, SOE's leaders – particularly Charles Hambro – embarked on an incremental program to include select American personnel in the more practical aspects of SOE's field work. This was intended to help to prepare OSS to work in a more integrated fashion with SOE on actual operations – albeit as a junior rather than equal partner – or in the worst case, to limit any mistakes OSS might make if it chose to strike out independently. In February, for example, Hambro invited Bruce and some of his staff 'to witness a typical moon operation'[4] being launched from a secret SOE airfield in the United Kingdom. Participation by OSS London in SOE propaganda and other training activities, meanwhile, including the assignment of the first OSS instructor to a major SOE training facility,[5] continued from February into the spring at an increased pace. 'Instruction was offered to prospective OSS agents on such matters as printing and engraving, photography and reproduction, [and] radio.'[6] In March, 'SOE invited OSS . . . to participate in an operation [code named "MIDHURST"] against two factories in Norway – the first suggested realization of their [joint] operational agreements' - but the mission was canceled before serious preparatory steps were taken.[7] Gubbins blamed the cancellation of MIDHURST on a bureaucratic difficulty concerning the reluctance of the US Joint Chiefs to give OSS operational approval for Norwegian activities without clear authorization by the British Chiefs who controlled the theater.[8]

MIDHURST, in fact, was an abortive effort by Baker Street to respond to the increasing desire of OSS to play a serious role in Scandinavia. The understandings reached in January between the two organizations included a very specific 'Provisional Agreement' on collaboration in Norway;[9] on 12 March, OSS London attempted to move the accord forward by formally proposing the start of Norwegian activities. SOE immediately registered its support for the initiative and agreed to allow OSS to set up a base for Norwegian work in either northern Britain or Ireland.[10] British sensitivities about the potential for 'overlap' of OSS and SIS activities in Norway, however, prompted the Admiralty on 15 March to insist on 'a clear and tactful definition' of OSS work.[11] Five days later, the War Office declared that SIS must have a veto over OSS activities in Norway, which emboldened the Admiralty to demand that OSS should only work in the country through SOE.[12] The Chiefs of Staff advised Hambro on 23 March that 'they cannot agree to yet another independent organization operating in Norway.'[13]

Thus, SOE found itself in the difficult position of having made promises to OSS in January that it might not be able to keep in March. Fearful of the implications for SOE's overall collaborative strategy with OSS – which included securing greatly increased US supply in 1943–4 – Hambro told a subordinate that 'it would be fatal to turn [OSS] down at this point.'[14] On 24 March, he appealed to General Ismay to reconsider the position of the British Chiefs:

> The proposal put forward by OSS is the first offer of concrete cooperation which has been made by them and I consider that it would be a mistake to turn it down flat . . . I have been most careful to impress on OSS the fact that all operations must be submitted to Admiralty requirements. I am confident that if the [OSS] proposals were to be accepted on the terms of SOE's draft reply, there could be no danger of any overlapping of activities on the Norwegian coast.[15]

This intervention resulted in a compromise allowing OSS to work in Norway – north of 65° latitude[16] – but 'subject to the approval and under the control of SOE.'[17] Furthermore, as Hambro wrote to Bruce on 26 March, 'SIS activities in Norway are of paramount importance and any operations undertaken by OSS and SOE must be subject to agreement with SIS.'[18]

Another major influence on SOE's thinking about OSS and Norway at this time was a decision taken by the British earlier in March which implied that OSS London was expected to make a much more substantial materiel and personnel contribution than had hitherto been realized. On 4 March, the 'British Committee on Equipment for Patriot Forces,' which had been set up to determine and prioritize SOE aid to anti-Axis groups in occupied areas, recommended that ' "resistance groups" to a total of 300 000 men and "patriot forces" to a total of 800 000 men be fully equipped for military action' as soon as practicable. The committee defined 'resistance groups' as 'irregular organized bodies operating behind enemy lines, such as the forces of [Royalist General Draza] Mihailovic in Yugoslavia and the

Polish Secret Army; "patriot forces" were defined as "forces which may be organized in areas liberated by the Allies." '[19] As it was inconceivable at that time in the
war that SOE would be able to equip and train these cadres on such an enormous
scale, it was clear that OSS had to shoulder a substantial share of the burden.

Yet, nowhere in the committee's report was mention made of OSS participation
in the 'planning for equipping [operatives in] France, the Low Countries, Norway,
Yugoslavia, and Greece . . . Nor did the report mention any provision for supplying the western Mediterranean area, in which OSS was active,' as Ellery Huntington was quick to point out to SOE. OSS, instead, was to provide – in addition to
equipment – foreign language proficient personnel, which were to form into units
called 'auxiliary operations groups.' These groups were to be used:

> a. As focal points around which to rally local patriot units with the aid of OSS
> and SOE . . . b. As an organized military 'cadre' into which may be inducted a
> limited number of members of resistance groups . . . c. As skilled instructors of
> local units and as centers of distribution of supplies of equipment . . . and d. In
> cooperation with paratroops or . . . as combat units operating (alone or with
> organized and trained resistance groups) against military objectives behind
> enemy lines and in collaboration with the spearheads of invasion units.[20]

All of this was presumably to take place under SOE direction, and Huntington
countered with the suggestion that a 'more modest program aimed at the selective
arming of limited numbers of strategically important resistance groups'[21] be developed instead.

Caught between increasing requirements from its political overlords and still
desiring to retain as much direction as possible over any joint activities with the
Americans, SOE began in March to redouble efforts to secure enhanced materiel
support from OSS. It was hoped that OSS would agree to make its principal contribution to joint activities in the form of materiel. On 18 March 1943, Hambro
turned to North Africa, where SOE had been technically subordinated to OSS, and
asked Bruce to provide aircraft for MASSINGHAM's operations:

> I am very exercised [about] the aircraft situation in North-West Africa . . . As
> we are working under the control of OSS in this area, [you should] supply the
> aircraft necessary for our operations . . . It would seem an admirable oppor-
> tunity for OSS to show the authorities that they are in a position to operate.[22]

North Africa was an interesting case where SOE – having reluctantly ceded
leadership to OSS in 1942 – sought to regain its independence in 1943. In late
March, Huntington reported:

> As [SOE's] 'show' in North Africa grew in size, [it] wanted independence with
> coordination at the top rather than a 'joint venture.' Accordingly, on my first
> visit to Algiers we scrapped the elaborate document prepared in London and

signed a paper of a few lines stating that we would carry on operations independently but would coordinate them through a 'Policy Committee.'[23]

This situation suited OSS, which also wanted to use North Africa to demonstrate its ability to operate independently. Gubbins had agreed with Huntington that operations should be independent, but resources and facilities should be pooled 'to the greatest possible extent.'[24]

Meanwhile, OSS's leaders realized that an enhanced US materiel contribution to joint special operations, far from restricting OSS to the role of supplier rather than participant, actually gave it increased justification to demand a role with SOE in future field operations launched from Britain. Thinking ahead to the campaign to liberate France and responding to the increasing pressure from SOE for materiel, OSS began to explore ways in which to interest General Frank Andrews – the US European theater commander – and his successor from May 1943,[25] Lieutenant-General Jacob Devers, in special operations work, as it was they who had the power to shift resources to OSS in Europe. On 20 March, Bruce took Andrews and his staff on a visit to a secret British airfield 'from which teams and equipment for resistance groups were dispatched to the Continent.' Bruce spent a great deal of time explaining OSS's capabilities and mandate, first to Andrews then to Devers, and especially to Devers' Assistant Chief of Staff (G-2), General Crockett. When Donovan traveled to London in June, he too spent time with Devers and his staff, explaining further the potential of OSS to support military activities.[26]

OSS also began to look at the implications of a British-led cross-channel invasion in 1944. It was only natural, OSS London thought, that the British would demand control over an invasion launched from their soil. Therefore, 'all the subsidiary operations in connection with it, such as the Jedburgh Plan, necessarily would be subject to British control.' As Bruce explained:

> We can scarcely hope to maintain an independent status vis-à-vis the British, if the other [US] agencies and units are subordinated to their policy, but must assume a secondary position in actual field operations . . . If, on the other hand, we become integrated with SOE, take advantage of their experience and their evident desire to have us participate in whatever measure of credit may evolve from their operations, we will . . . develop much faster than we could without [SOE].[27]

SOE had invited OSS to participate – in an undefined way – in its 'Jedburgh plan,' 'in accordance with the operational arrangements concluded in January [1943],' in the belief that US materiel and personnel were required to meet ambitious Jedburgh objectives. By the middle of March, Bruce had developed a plan for 'getting in on the ground floor with the British on this proposed Jedburgh operation' by securing a specific agreement, and convinced SOE to begin providing detailed bi-monthly 'sabotage summaries.' These summaries were useful in that they showed the Allied military authorities 'an accumulating body of evidence of the military destruction carried out in various countries on the Continent' by operatives of the 'special' services. They were just the sort of thing that Bruce needed to win over Devers and Crockett.

SOE outlined its Jedburgh plan on 6 April 1943 in a paper titled 'Coordination of Activities Behind the Enemy Lines with the Actions of Allied Military Forces Invading Northwest Europe.' Baker Street drew from the experience gained in a large-scale military exercise involving Jedburgh teams, which was code-named 'Spartan.'[28] A week later, Donovan began to have second thoughts about ceding too much control to SOE. He instructed Bruce to inform Hambro that OSS 'will completely join with [the British] in their operations, but warned':

> If [they] mean by complete integration of [SO London] and SOE that we should be merged and our identity thus lost, then I think it would be better to have no participation. If by complete integration [they] mean to accept a position of authority under British leadership by maintaining our organization in a secondary position, although subject to British orders, I have no objection whatever.[29]

OSS London then drafted its own Jedburgh paper under the same title as SOE's document and passed it to Baker Street on 23 April. 'The two treatments of the subject were roughly parallel with the exception that the OSS paper requested permission to conduct the operation in collaboration with [SOE] and the [British] omitted any mention of [OSS].'[30]

During the discussion about OSS's role, Hambro and Bruce drafted a bilateral accord clarifying OSS London's position in the Jedburgh plan. Hambro conceded in the document that:

> [OSS] was to function autonomously and take complete charge of – and responsibility for – all of its agents, although it was to be under the operational control of SOE. This stipulation was to apply whether or not [OSS] operations were to be conducted 'independently' or in conjunction with SOE . . . Provision was made for free consultation . . . to ensure that the activities of both could be properly coordinated [and] would meet with the approval of both.[31]

Moreover, OSS London was to assign a representative to SOE's Planning Staff, who was to:

> be consulted on all matters affecting . . . Norway, Denmark, the Low Countries and France. [He] will also be represented on such other Planning and Operational Staffs as is necessary to enable joint operations or operations carried out by [OSS] to be properly coordinated with operations carried out by SOE.[32]

With this understanding in place, Bruce approached the US Command, formally requesting airlift for the first time on 5 May 1943: '[If] OSS is to participate jointly with SOE as is at present proposed, it requires to have placed at its disposal as soon as possible one squadron of heavy bomber aircraft complete with all necessary personnel.'[33]

SOE at this time had only sixteen modified light bombers and occasionally had access to six additional aircraft under SIS control. With this meager airlift capacity, SOE was required to service all of the occupied areas of Western Europe, including France.[34] The acute situation OSS and SOE faced in this regard had – it was feared – already lowered the morale of the resistance fighters in France and elsewhere who were urgently requesting more arms and ammunition, *inter alia*. At this critical juncture, the two services saw as their primary duty the 'continued support of all resistance groups' at a minimum level, 'so that they will not be left in the cold, deprived of funds and equipment.'[35] Clearly, OSS had to secure more aircraft if the Jedburgh plan was to be realized, and OSS London believed that it could greatly enhance its role and status by doing so.

It did not take long for OSS to begin to come through with the much needed transport, but some requirements proved easier to meet than others. On 5 June, for example, SOE asked OSS London to provide air transport from the UK to Egypt for parachutes that were to be used in joint operations in the Middle East. Within two weeks, Bruce had secured the needed transport through the offices of OSS Cairo and had so informed Hambro. In August, SOE requested OSS assistance in acquiring three small US Navy ships for joint operations in the North Sea to be launched from a secret base in the Shetland Islands. OSS helped to persuade the US Navy to release the vessels, and by October, three 110-foot 'sub-chasers' were operational and in SOE's hands.[36] The US European Command, however, was slower to respond to Bruce's request for the much needed aircraft, prompting OSS to restate its requirements formally to General Devers on 12 October. A week thereafter, Devers approved the request, but it was not until January 1944 that the aircraft were fully operational.[37]

Regarding personnel for joint activities, SOE notified OSS on 3 August of what it believed were realistic estimates of OSS London's expected human contribution to operations in France and the Low Countries. 'Including personnel for 35 Jedburgh teams and the staffs to be attached to armies in the field, SOE considered that OSS would need a grand total of 278 men,' a many-fold increase over what OSS had previously projected for its London staff. SOE also asked that OSS establish its own schools and handle its own security and administration, which also required a substantial augmentation of OSS London's resources, human and otherwise.[38]

Faced with such high British expectations and believing that his flexibility was limited due to the likelihood that Britain would command the invasion of France, Huntington returned to the view that OSS London had to cede more control to SOE. He decided at the end of August to incorporate OSS personnel sent to London directly into SOE. These operatives, he wrote: 'will be dealt with by SOE as if they were members of that organization, and they will be largely used [to support] British military operations. This is the . . . result of British domination of military operations based on the United Kingdom.'[39]

Huntington remained concerned, however, that under such circumstances of integrated subordination, SOE was in a position to take most if not all of the credit for American special operations work on the Continent. 'Our American commanders, when the day for action comes,' Huntington said on 28 August, 'are not going to be interested in what we have done for the British, but in what we are able to do for them.' He suggested, therefore, that some American personnel be diverted to North Africa for independent OSS operations into southern France.[40]

Once the 'Combined Operations Staff Supreme Allied Commander' (COSSAC) was established as the command center for the planning of the Allied cross-Channel invasion,[41] it was decided that operational control of the invasion forces would be equally divided between the British and Americans, under the overall command of General Eisenhower. This had immediate implications for OSS and SOE, and for Huntington's previous decision on integration. 'Preliminary directives were issued in September placing both SOE and OSS activities in northwest Europe under COSSAC control [which] assured OSS's equality with [SOE] in all tasks that they might jointly perform . . . [This] constituted a change in emphasis in the SO/SOE relationship that prevailed during the first half of the year 1943.'[42] No longer did OSS London feel obliged to cede the nearly complete control envisioned as necessary by Huntington in August. And when Hambro was replaced by Gubbins as 'CD' (Chief) of SOE in September, a smooth transition in OSS London's relationship with SOE was assured. As Bruce explained: 'The standing of our [special operations] people with SOE is highly gratifying. The retirement of Charles Hambro from his position was a great disappointment to us, but the relationship with his organization will remain unimpaired.'[43]

OSS-SIS, JOINT CHIEFS' DIRECTIVES, AND OPERATION SUSSEX

Relations between the secret intelligence component of OSS London and SIS evolved significantly over the course of 1943. In some ways, the association was stormy, as the Americans sought to move from what had hitherto been almost exclusively an intelligence liaison function in London through the end of 1942 to a role that included independent or joint field operations. The British had consistently opposed any intelligence work by OSS London that might compromise their existing agent networks on the Continent, but began to show some flexibility in 1943 in the face of implied threats by OSS to 'go it alone' if necessary in France and the Low Countries. OSS London's position, however, was weakened by its lack of agents and experience, and complicated for much of the year by the unwillingness of the US European theater commander's staff to back OSS's Continental ambitions and to counter interference by the British Chiefs of Staff. Indeed, both the US and British military authorities had qualms about the implications of parallel OSS and SIS spy networks that might work at cross purposes in Europe, which put OSS in the awkward position of having to ask SIS for help in this regard in a situation reminiscent of a similar OSS appeal over the Darlan affair discussed in Chapter 3.

Yet, throughout 1943, the OSS-SIS relationship continued to be productive in terms of intelligence shared and realized a breakthrough in the matter of joint operations. Due to the dramatic increase in the number of intelligence reports being exchanged with SIS in 1943 – on something approximating equal terms in volume if not quality for the first time from July [44] – OSS London's Research and Analysis (R & A) branch had to be significantly upgraded to handle processing and targeting requirements. Tripartite relations between OSS, SIS, and the Gaullists – which had been suspended since TORCH – were resumed in 1943 and served as the cornerstone of the joint intelligence gathering operation, code-named 'Sussex,' that played an important role in the Allied invasion of France. Perhaps most importantly, OSS London was able to secure from the US Joint Chiefs before the end of the year a directive that established beyond all doubt its right to conduct intelligence activities – independently or jointly – over any British objections.

At the start of 1943, OSS London was able to shed many of the responsibilities that had previously taxed its overworked staff. Of particular significance was the enhancement of liaison ties to SIS. These had developed to such an extent over 1942 that OSS London was no longer obliged to acquire intelligence from all of the various offices of the British military and civilian authorities through separate liaison arrangements. Instead, all pertinent material was now passed through SIS to OSS London directly.[45] This freed substantial human resources to pursue other endeavors, which included first and foremost securing a role in Continental operations.

In the early spring, Bill Maddox, who had replaced Whitney Shepardson as chief of OSS's secret intelligence component in London in December 1942, began to look for ways in which his branch could redefine its relationship with SIS. A staff member – Stacey Lloyd – drafted a plan that envisioned 'the organization of a number of two-man intelligence teams, equipped with [clandestine radio sets], to be dropped well behind the lines at the time a Continental bridgehead was being established.'[46] This was to be an independent OSS operation, staffed and led by OSS London. The plan was discussed in greater detail in OSS London's SI branch report of 16 April: '50 parties of observers and reporters [would be inserted] behind enemy lines at the time of Continental invasion . . . [They] would be recruited from and attached to airborne units of the invading armies as reconnaissance intelligence groups.'[47]

The 'Lloyd plan,' as it was generally known, had developed out of a new strategy adopted by Maddox that was intended – in his own words – 'to pry open Broadway's exclusiveness' in field operations by '[creating] facilities, human and technical, in [the European theater] for the development of [an OSS] network.'[48] According to an OSS assessment of the situation:

[OSS London] met the opposition of the British whenever it suggested that OSS and SIS should conduct a joint intelligence operation on the Continent in conjunction with the invasion. Although through both lack of qualified personnel and experience [OSS] did not at that time consider itself adequately equipped to participate equally in such an operation, it nevertheless wished to assert its equality as an intelligence agency and towards that end make at least some contribution to a joint intelligence effort.[49]

Broadway's reticence was principally based upon the fear that OSS would compromise its complex agent networks on the Continent. OSS London, it was thought, was not capable of sufficiently training recruits, nor did it have access to a pool of potential recruits with the local knowledge necessary to meet Broadway's strict cover criteria for field operations.[50] Thus, OSS agents were considered a potential menace in the dangerous operating environments of occupied Europe because they would be easy prey for the German security services. 'Since [SIS] controlled the transportation and communications on which [OSS] would have to rely as long as England remained the base of operations, [it was] in a position to make [its] will felt.'[51]

Maddox wrote to Bruce on 1 April offering the 'Lloyd plan' as his preferred course of action from what he believed were three possible options. Recognizing that 'it would be impractical for [him] to attempt to build . . . a new and independent network of agents in Western Europe,' he suggested that the only other realistic alternatives were either to find anti-Axis groups that were not working with SIS, or to continue to foster contacts with the British-sponsored groups in an incremental fashion, 'abandoning thought of any grand plan.'[52] In effect, Maddox sought to bluff SIS into being more cooperative by threatening to establish his own spy network, regardless of his ability to properly recruit, train, and equip his operatives.

Bruce had reservations about the 'Lloyd plan,' but forwarded it in May to OSS Washington for consideration. Donovan was also skeptical and rejected the plan on 6 June:

Lloyd was to be commended for his foresight and effort, [but] the consensus of opinion was that reconnaissance intelligence groups constituted a combat intelligence function more appropriate to orthodox military organization and personnel than to [OSS]; that as a general rule [OSS] should operate behind enemy lines out of uniform, although it had some responsibility for securing combat intelligence along with other intelligence; and that [OSS London] should think in terms of individuals rather than of groups.[53]

Donovan's decision almost certainly was also influenced by US JCS directive 155/7/D issued on 4 April, which authorized OSS:

to conduct espionage in enemy occupied territory and to maintain contact with underground groups, [but restricted it to those functions] necessary for the planning and execution of the military program for psychological warfare, and for the preparation of assigned portions of intelligence digests and such other data and visual presentation as may be requested.[54]

Instead of providing OSS London with the flexibility it wanted to facilitate field work, JCS 155/7/D raised questions about whether OSS was even permitted to conduct independent intelligence collection activities, particularly in the realm of military information. It also cast doubt on whether OSS could deviate in any way from the military's political warfare (propaganda) program. Until Donovan could find a way around the directive or force a revision, a high-profile move by OSS London to assert its independence – that probably would draw the ire of both SIS and the US Command, and possibly violate JCS 155/7/D – was deemed inadvisable and vetoed. The issue of the military's involvement in OSS London's plight became a more significant problem in the summer and autumn and will be further addressed later in this section.

While the 'Lloyd plan' was still pending in May, however, there were indications that SIS had begun to rethink its opposition to any participation by OSS London in field operations within the 'Invasion Sphere.' OSS attributed this change of attitude largely to Maddox's implicit 'blackmail' strategy, using the 'Lloyd plan' as a sign of OSS London's determination:

> In spite of their early reluctance to accept [OSS] as an equal partner and in part because of OSS's determination, as the Lloyd plan illustrated, to establish itself as an independent and if necessary autonomous intelligence organization, the British [began to recognize] the need to include [OSS London] in SIS operational planning and to accept the theory, already embodied in the Jedburgh Plan, of joint participation under British control.[55]

Because it had no trained agents at that time and lacked experience, however, OSS London was poorly positioned to *demand* that SIS relent; it chose instead to negotiate. Bilateral working level talks were held throughout May, and culminated in a meeting between Menzies and Bruce at which the former tentatively suggested that OSS London be included in renewed tripartite activity with SIS and the Gaullists that would include field operations.

The resumption of tripartite activity, however, was a concept that originated in Washington rather than in the bowels of Broadway or OSS London. A month before Menzies' overture to Bruce, Shepardson – who had become the overall chief of secret intelligence in Washington – had instructed OSS London to 'renew conversations with the French and British with regard to [the resumption of tripartite activities] and to expedite with all possible rapidity the formulation of collective plans.'[56] OSS Washington had evidently decided that General Strong's prohibition of tripartite activities during the TORCH operation was no longer valid because it applied to circumstances that no longer existed. Tripartite work, moreover, might be a low-profile means to achieve OSS London's principal objectives and to circumvent JCS 155/7/D.

Bruce was reluctant to reopen tripartite discussions at first, because he believed the almost certain opposition by SIS to this activity might disrupt other aspects of the relationship that were running relatively smoothly. He suggested that Shepardson should concentrate instead on augmenting OSS London's staff to better position it to participate in activities directly related to the Continental invasion. Bruce had, in fact, actually become an obstacle to the efforts of both Shepardson and Maddox to transform OSS London into a field-capable organization from one which was concerned only with liaison. This was in complete contrast to the pro-active operational role he played in 1944–5 and for which he is remembered. Bruce had opposed Maddox's 'Lloyd plan' initiative and had refused Shepardson's request on 4 April to detach Maddox for 'field operations training' in North Africa in preparation for Europe becoming an active theater. Shepardson had argued that Maddox's additional training would enable him to return to London after a relatively short period to manage the '5 or 6 individuals' OSS Washington planned to train in the interim for future operations in Europe.[57] Bruce replied that he 'had reluctantly abandoned hope of recruiting agents in the UK, since all prospects were absorbed by Broadway and allied agencies, and had abandoned hope of recruiting American agents because of Broadway's opposition to the idea.' He did, in fact, make it clear to Shepardson that he believed SIS might cut off the flow of intelligence to OSS London if the Americans challenged it in this way.[58] Maddox's views of Shepardson's proposal are not known, but it is probable that he would have welcomed the additional training and the new recruits.

In the end, Bruce's fears were unfounded and Donovan was resolved to press ahead with the expansion of OSS London's secret intelligence role. The OSS director settled the matter for Bruce after a flurry of cables between London and Washington. He concluded on 15 May that:

> an independent [U.S.] intelligence service must be available to the Theater Commander wherever [his] forces operate . . . The best way to obtain this objective [is] to work out a series of tripartite agreements with the British and French, the British and Dutch, the British and Belgians, and the British and Norwegians. These agreements would provide for [our] participation in committees which would plan and supervise intelligence operations in any sub-theater on the Continent which would include [U.S.] forces, and would be implemented at such time as [U.S.] participation in any one of these sub-theaters was indicated.[59]

Donovan ordered OSS London to 'reopen negotiations with representatives of the five services concerned, [with] the aim [being] to supply at least a few under cover agents, whose recruitment in the Theater should be started immediately.' He believed that 'the joint introduction and supervision of such agents would provide invaluable experience to [OSS London's] SI [Branch].'[60] As in 1942, when SIS felt obliged to yield to OSS's independent contacts with the exiled governments, Broadway opted to include OSS, but on its own terms as much as possible.

The resumption of tripartite activity quickly became dominated by the planning for the invasion of France, and therefore largely took the form of what was thereafter known as Sussex.[61] Sussex was a plan by which – like the Jedburgh operation – joint SIS-OSS-French teams would be recruited, trained, and deployed into France to support the Allied invasion. While the Jedburghs were to undertake sabotage activities and organize resistance cells, the Sussex teams were tasked with collecting intelligence. Sussex proved as important to the OSS-SIS relationship as the Jedburgh plan was to OSS's relationship with SOE, and it required a degree of integration never previously or subsequently achieved between British and US secret intelligence personnel. Before OSS participation in Sussex could be formalized, however, obstacles had to be overcome.

As previously discussed, OSS London was woefully short of qualified agent personnel in the spring of 1943 – a situation further complicated by SIS's insistence that 'a successful agent should have a thorough and recent knowledge of the territory into which he was to be sent.'[62] Those agents OSS might recruit in North America, therefore, were disqualified. Moreover, OSS had hitherto been excluded from recruiting agents in the UK who might meet SIS's stringent cover requirements. Bruce met with Menzies on 28 May and was promised access to 'a common pool of about a thousand Frenchmen' from which OSS, SIS, and the French 'could draw their agent personnel'[63] for Sussex. By mid-June, Bruce was able to report that 'the present idea is to have about twenty-five teams, each consisting of a radio operator and an agent,' and that 'some of [the new] French recruits . . . have already been ear-marked and others are being examined.'[64]

SIS's change of heart about sharing its recruitment pool can be attributed directly to the reversal of its previous assumption that a parallel Allied agent network in France was dangerous and unnecessary. While the previous threats by Maddox to go it alone almost certainly laid some of the groundwork for Broadway's 'U-turn,' it took sound logic to move SIS to open up its prized Sussex operation to OSS London. By mid-June, Menzies had determined that:

a new agent system superimposed on the existing one is necessary [because] the Germans would tighten their security measures in occupied France [when] they felt an Allied invasion was growing imminent . . . Existing Allied sources of intelligence information would be discovered and liquidated.[65]

Moreover, the military requirement for tactical and strategic information about all parts of France before and during the invasion would in all probability quickly overwhelm the existing networks and traditional military collection assets. According to Bruce, 'At the present time, the Allied secret intelligence network is said to have reached saturation point, especially as regards to wireless operators.'[66] Sussex – with American participation and support – was therefore in many ways the ideal solution to the challenges posed by the invasion plan for 1944.

On 5 July, the plan for OSS participation in Sussex was submitted to the US Command for approval, which was granted three months later. Specifically, Sussex was to provide:

> strategic and tactical military intelligence to the Allied armies upon their invasion of Northern France through a group of some 96 agents organized in two-man teams, each team consisting of an observer and a radio operator, who were recruited from French army personnel, trained in England in joint [OSS]/SIS schools and dispatched into France by parachute.[67]

OSS was to provide five instructors to supplement the SIS instructor contingent for Sussex, and a share of the 96 agents.[68] On 13 November, the joint Sussex school was made operational.

Before Donovan's aspiring spymasters could concentrate their energies on recruitment, training, and joint planning for Sussex, however, they had to overcome another important obstacle back in the spring. Even as SIS was first warming to OSS London's overtures, OSS was faced with a skeptical and obstructive American European theater commander and British Chiefs of Staff. These individuals had yet to be convinced that OSS collection operations launched from the UK into Europe were desirable and not disruptive. When examining this circumstance, it is important to understand that communication among and between the various national military elements, their secret services, and political masters was often convoluted, contradictory, and incomplete. In this case, both the American Command's views and those of the British Chiefs were heavily influenced by the earlier arguments against OSS work voiced by SIS. Even when SIS's views changed, theirs did not; at least not at the same rate. Donovan explained OSS's problem with the US Command in an appeal in the summer to the US War Department for intervention:

> General Crockett's office (G-2 to Devers) [believes] that 'two separate secret intelligence agencies cannot work the same territory.' We think this is a grievous error. Since the inception of our conduct of espionage, we have always insisted . . . on our right to maintain and operate an independent American service, while cooperating to the fullest extent with the British and the other Allied Services. I need not emphasize to you the importance, from the point of view of the American theater commander and the [Joint Chiefs], of maintaining an independent American [spy] Agency. This is particularly true of the [European theater] with its wealth of opportunity for [secret intelligence] work.[69]

The view of the US Command was also not always consistent, and it was somewhat driven by their perception that as host nation the British had considerable rights and practical leverage over activities on their territory. In an effort to test the resolve of the British Chiefs to obstruct OSS, General Devers – without first consulting OSS – formally approached his British counterpart on 14 July for permission to use OSS in secret intelligence and special operations activities managed from London against targets throughout Europe. By placing this sensitive issue

before the British military authorities instead of allowing OSS and SIS to negotiate bilaterally, OSS was put in the awkward position of having to go to SIS and
SOE to plead for leniency in their answers to the British Chiefs, who in turn had to
reply to Devers' formal query. This unusual situation later prompted Bruce to
complain bitterly that:

> it is remarkable that we enjoy any independence whatsoever . . . In fact, to date,
> we have obtained our strongest support, not from an American authority, but
> from our English competitors, which is a set and undeniable fact.[70]

The preliminary response by the British Chiefs to Devers on 31 August recognized that OSS had a legitimate interest in SI work in Iberia and Germany, but objected to any independent espionage activity directed against targets in France, the
Low Countries, and Scandinavia. In spite of SIS's revised position, the Chiefs
continued to cite the potential risks to existing SIS networks. They approved the
request for an OSS communications capability in the UK, however, and with regard
to counter-subversion and counter-intelligence, they accepted OSS's proposals:

> on condition that it is clearly understood that central coordination will be exer-
> cised by SIS in London . . . In the COSSAC theaters of operations the Supreme
> Allied Commander will direct policy. OSS personnel in the field will be under
> command of the Army groups to which they are attached. Channels of commun-
> ications from those theaters by OSS personnel will be strictly limited to those
> controlled through SIS in London.

On 16 September, the British issued a more formal reply, reiterating that while the
relevant special operations work could continue – subject to prior OSS-SOE understandings – 'independent OSS intelligence activities' remained inadvisable.[71]

The reaction from OSS was predictably harsh. Concerned that the British
Chiefs were seeking to relegate OSS London to a permanently subservient status,
Donovan appealed to the US Joint Chiefs on 18 October. He began by pointing out
that OSS already had 'existing and well-functioning organizations in Sweden,
Switzerland, Spain and Portugal [which were] American made and controlled.'
From Sweden, he explained, OSS had penetrated Germany, while from Switzerland, OSS had begun to penetrate Germany and Italy 'with secret radio communication with Algiers and radio telephone from Washington.' Donovan told how
OSS operatives based in Spain and Africa had infiltrated southern France, 'despite
the handicap of having no planes,' and he argued that while OSS did not operate in
the UK and did not seek to do so, it needed to use Britain 'as a base from which to
operate in certain enemy or enemy-occupied countries.' Donovan complained vociferously about the British in this communication and he clearly suspected SIS
duplicity, concluding that:

> Physical circumstances permit [them] to exercise complete control over
> the United States intelligence . . . The habit of control has grown up with

them . . . through their relations with refugee Governments and intelligence services . . . We are not a refugee government . . . SIS would reduce the OSS Secret Intelligence Service to a subordinate and subservient status.[72]

Donovan's ire did not stop there. In discussing Sussex, he told the US Chiefs that 'the British retain the right to carry on this long range [espionage] service, grant a considerable measure of that right to the [Gaullists] but deny it to us.' On counter-intelligence, he wrote: 'It is directed that OSS shall not only be coordinated by SIS but will be limited to SIS communications; [a situation] tantamount to regulating the OSS communications activities to those of a basic training depot and supply dump.'[73] Donovan's proposal was specific and challenged the premise of JCS 155/7/D:

> OSS should be permitted to use the [UK] as a base for the penetration by its intelligence agents of Scandinavia and the Low Countries and France, with the status of an independent [US espionage] organization, and that the good faith and common sense of the intelligence agencies of both countries should be relied upon to cooperate in the use of base facilities and to avoid any crossing of lines and danger to security . . . An American evaluation service should be set up in London [to process and appraise] all intelligence material gathered by American agencies . . . Coordination of counter-intelligence should not rest with SIS but in the Theater Commander. Coordination should not be controlled by one of the parties to be coordinated . . . In all communications stations [US] units should be allocated their own positions, their own channels, and their own frequencies.[74]

Donovan's appeal fell on sympathetic ears this time in the US Joint Chiefs of Staff, which – with the appointment of Eisenhower as Supreme Commander – was determined to enhance America's leading role in the liberation of France. Acting swiftly and decisively, the US planners issued directive JCS 155/11/D on 27 October 1943, which affirmed OSS's right to conduct 'SI' activities – collecting intelligence 'without restriction as to type'[75] – over any British objections. Specifically, the directive authorized OSS:

> to collect secret intelligence in all areas other than the Western Hemisphere by means of espionage and counter-espionage, . . . evaluate and disseminate such intelligence to authorized agencies, . . . transmit [intelligence from agents] through facilities of the Military Intelligence Service and of the Office of Naval Intelligence, . . . [and] obtain information from underground groups by direct contact or other means.[76]

Having secured for the first time the unreserved backing of the Joint Chiefs for independent espionage, OSS was positioned at the close of 1943 to assert its independence from SIS control.

CONCLUSIONS

The increasing and persistent assertiveness on the part of OSS in London throughout 1943 achieved for Donovan his principal goals without unduly upsetting the overall relationship with SOE and SIS. The Americans now had a truly joint stake in both special operations and human intelligence collection efforts in support of the coming invasion of France, and the British saved face by retaining overall direction of these activities within a loosely integrated framework. The bickering in London over OSS participation in Norwegian special operations ended positively, with the Americans securing the right to work in northern Norway, which they exercised freely in 1944–5. OSS was expected in 1943 to begin making a more substantial materiel contribution to joint efforts and promoted this expectation in the belief that greater leverage with SOE and SIS would result; this proved to be a sound assumption. The combination of Bruce's caution and Maddox's barely veiled threats, moreover, succeeded in maintaining the less controversial exchange of intelligence with SIS whilst nudging Menzies ever closer to a constructive compromise on operations. It is interesting that Bruce began in September to refer to SIS as a 'competitor' in internal OSS communications, which demonstrates his appreciation of the evolving nature of the relationship at that time.

The US Command's decision to back OSS in its quest for more autonomy from the British – after having helped to undermine this objective earlier in the year – proved to be a decisive factor for Donovan. Concurrent with the military's change of attitude came the release of the greater quantities of transport assets and materiel long sought by OSS for its covert contribution. This in turn strengthened Donovan's hand considerably with the British in 1944, enabling him to act with ever greater independence, especially in such areas as the Balkans and the Far East. The US Command's positive attitude reflected not only its new confidence in the utility of OSS after TORCH, Burma, and to a lesser extent Yugoslavia, but perhaps more importantly, its confidence in itself and increasing assertiveness directed towards securing a leadership role commensurate with America's ever growing contribution to the Allied war effort. The timing of JCS 155/11/D just two months before Eisenhower was officially named Supreme Allied Commander for the cross-Channel invasion was certainly not a coincidence. As long as it was believed that Britain would command the cross-Channel invasion – a notion dispelled within the Allied camp certainly by October – the American Command felt obliged to concede certain points to the British Chiefs of Staff; OSS was in many ways an easy target. Once Eisenhower was in place, however, the US Joint Chiefs could afford both to back Donovan and to placate the British by leaving the leadership of special operations and secret intelligence work to them within the agreed upon joint framework in circumstances reminiscent of the Allied arrangements for TORCH, but with the benefit of considerable experience.

5 The Yugoslav Morass: A Case Study in Anglo-OSS Divergence, 1942–44

We've got hundreds of mugs / Who've been trained like thugs / And now they're at the mercy of / The Greeks and the Jugs / And the man at the helm's / A peer of the realm / And nobody's using us now, oh no / Nobody's using us now // We've got a partisan itch / And there's Mihailovitch / And the Foreign Office never seems / To know which is which / We're the talk of the town / We'd better close down' Cos nobody's using us now, oh no / Nobody's using us now.[1]
(Song about SOE Cairo)

Liaison with the Americans [is] like having an affair with an elephant: it is extremely difficult, you are apt to get badly trampled on, and you get no results for eight years.[2]
(Bickham Sweet-Escott, SOE)

INTRODUCTION

Yugoslavia from 1942–4 was the setting for what was perhaps the clearest example of diverging Anglo-US subversive policy in the European war. This divergence transformed the relationship between OSS and its British counterparts in this occupied country – as well as in Cairo, from where Balkan operations were directed – from a generally cooperative wartime arrangement to something characterized more by competition, suspicion, and rivalry. The Yugoslav campaign saw traditional standards of trust and transparency between OSS and SOE disintegrate over time, only to be replaced in some instances by obstruction, deceit, and efforts to undermine the other's position. It was a far cry from the integrated framework for cooperation in the coming French campaign that was being created in London and Algiers, despite the many differences encountered in both places along the way. This is not to say that all activities connected with Yugoslavia drove the OSS and the British apart – Allied materiel support to the Partisans, in fact, was often collaborative. Nonetheless, Yugoslavia proved in many ways to be a battleground for Donovan and the British, where the question of OSS independence threatened to tear the partnership apart and where the Byzantine politics of the region greatly complicated the intelligence picture upon which both sides based their activities.

As in London in 1943, the British and US military establishments played an increasingly important role in the activities of the secret services. The British Chiefs of Staff, in particular, intervened more frequently over Yugoslavia to arbitrate or protect what were perceived to be national and parochial interests. Yugoslavia fell into a mutually recognized British sphere of influence, as did India and Burma; perhaps Britain's dissatisfaction with the activities of OSS Colonel Eifler in India and Burma – discussed in Chapter 3 – made it wary of Donovan's intentions and even encouraged confrontation rather than compromise. The Balkans represented a considerable opportunity and offered status to the British, who increasingly saw their leadership within the alliance challenged. Moreover, Yugoslavia was chosen to be the first and foremost Allied-supported guerrilla campaign on the European continent, eclipsed in relative importance only by the work of the secret services in the liberation of France. The difficulties encountered by the British and American operatives in and concerning Yugoslavia illustrate perhaps better than any other wartime case study the multifaceted challenges – military, political, economic, and ideological – that often confronted the secret services and policymaking community.

BACKGROUND

When the Germans invaded Yugoslavia on 6 April 1941 and forced the Royalist Army to capitulate in less than two weeks, Colonel Draza Mihailovic of the 4th Yugoslav Army refused to surrender. He chose instead to organize a resistance group[3] that took the name *Chetnik* after a Serbian nationalist group active in the First World War. Shortly thereafter – following the German invasion of Russia – Josip Broz 'Tito,' a Moscow-trained Croatian communist, began to organize the *Partisan* movement to resist the occupation forces. Mihailovic broadcast an appeal for assistance that was picked up by the British in September 1941. A month later, he established a radio link with the Yugoslav government-in-exile, which had been formed by King Peter, and announced that he was 'launching a national revolt as head of "The Royal Yugoslav Army in the field." ' [4] Peter recognized the Chetnik movement as his sole legitimate army of resistance and promoted Mihailovic from Colonel to General, naming him Minister of War in January 1942.

The British seized upon this opportunity to work with the Chetniks in the hope that with Allied assistance, a viable large-scale subversive movement in the Balkans could be created to harass and impede the enemy in a strategically important region of occupied Europe.[5] The Yugoslav resistance – about which precious little was known in the autumn of 1941 – rapidly became a crucial component of Britain's peripheral grand strategy in the European war. SOE had dispatched William Hudson to Yugoslavia by submarine in September 1941 with orders 'to contact all groups opposing the enemy and report on them by [radio].' He initially came upon a group of Partisans, then was instructed in October to find Mihailovic,[6] who was soon recognized by Britain as 'the leading insurgent' in the country, in the hope that all resistance elements could be unified under the Chetnik umbrella. Hudson subsequently facilitated the clandestine delivery by SOE of a small quantity of arms and ammunition to Chetnik forces as a sign of goodwill.[7] Simultaneously, the British and American propaganda organizations embraced

Mihailovic and in a matter of weeks had transformed him from virtual obscurity into one of the foremost heroes of popular resistance to the Nazis on the continent of Europe. The stage was set for the first important Allied program of assistance to a subversive movement; a program, however, which was soon beset by difficulties and became a source of divisiveness within the Allied camp.

In many respects, Yugoslavia was ideally suited for insurgent operations. It was a large country with an underdeveloped infrastructure and rugged terrain, which made it difficult to occupy and control. In theory, which later proved true in practice, relatively few guerrillas could force the Axis and its proxies to commit a disproportionately large number of troops to protect lines of supply and communications within Yugoslavia, and more importantly, through the country to Greece, the Soviet Front, and the eastern Mediterranean.[8] This fact proved especially significant when Yugoslav insurgents kept the Axis from deploying many badly needed troops from occupation duties to the Italian and Russian fronts in 1943–4. Yugoslavia, moreover, was populated by hardy people who had struggled for centuries against foreign occupiers and had succeeded in maintaining their ethnic, religious, and cultural identities despite often brutal efforts to suppress them. Perhaps most importantly for the Allies, the country had at the end of 1941 a legitimate if embryonic insurgent movement – the largely Serbian Chetniks – a military leader, Draza Mihailovic, and a *bona fide* government-in-exile led by King Peter.

Whilst appealing to Allied strategists in many ways, Yugoslavia was nonetheless beset by a variety of internal problems and natural circumstances which impeded the Allied effort to foment organized rebellion. First, its diverse ethnic composition and history of internal strife left it vulnerable to outside manipulation. The Germans were able to establish a strong Quisling regime in Croatia and an important if weaker one in Serbia. The Croatian fascist movement – the Ustashi – began to commit acts of ethnic genocide shortly after the occupation, mostly against ethnic Serbs in Croatia and Bosnia, as did other groups against Muslims, further dividing a nation that had only been politically unified since the end of the First World War. Moreover, Yugoslavia was seriously divided by ethnicity, cultural practices, language, and religious beliefs not only among its principally Serb and Croat inhabitants, but also within and between its large indigenous groupings of ethnic Bosnians, Slovenes, Macedonians, and Montenegrins, and minority communities of Hungarians, Turks, Albanians, Greeks, Bulgars, and Romanians. Added to this volatile mix was the stark divide between the rural peasant and the urban worker, and between monarchist, communist, and the indifferent. Mihailovic's Chetniks were comprised mostly of Serbian peasants and supported the King, whilst Tito's Partisans at first attracted mostly displaced urban dwellers throughout the country – including Serbians fleeing the Ustashi – using communist ideology both as a unifying force and later as an alternative to the monarchy.

The divisions among the Yugoslavs in outlook and motivation, combined with the country's other complex interrelationships, made it exceedingly difficult for the Allies to identify friend from foe. Internecine conflict and the looming threat of an all out civil war between Partisans, Chetniks, and collaborators also greatly complicated and degraded Allied insurgent efforts. Many of the same factors that made Yugoslavia so appealing for insurgent operations – its remoteness, troublesome terrain, large size, diverse composition, etc. – also made it very difficult to obtain reliable information on the activities, strength, and intentions of the Chetnik and Partisan forces. The followers of Mihailovic and Tito competed fiercely for Allied favor and engaged from the outset in propaganda against each other that was difficult for the Allies to corroborate or refute. The Chetniks, for example, charged that Partisans helped the Ustashi to murder ethnic Serbs, whilst Tito's supporters accused the Chetniks of collaboration with the Axis and its proxies; 'There was some truth in both allegations [but] in British thinking, the charges against the Chetniks were considered to be of greater import'[9] because collaboration undermined the Allies' principal objectives. Britain and America often had to rely on dubious sources and were themselves divided on the reliability of information, its relevance, the significance of ideology, and the motivation and potential of many of the protagonists. This problem was compounded by the fact that OSS and SOE personnel in Yugoslavia were trained for special operations, yet were asked to become 'in effect intelligence officers and were instructed to send in enemy battle order, economic information, and political and military intelligence on the resistance . . . Lack of SI training was evident on political and economic reporting, [especially from the Americans].'[10]

EARLY MANEUVERING

In early 1942, as the Allied propaganda campaign in support of the Chetniks was elevating Mihailovic to exalted status, several events occurred that began to put US and British subversive policy in Yugoslavia on divergent tracks. In February, concurrent with SOE's wider decision to involve Donovan's organization in some practical joint activities, Baker Street requested that the Americans begin to recruit Yugoslavs and other Eastern Europeans for use in special operations. Specifically, as Donovan reported to US General George Marshall:

> The British have asked us to recruit . . . 450 Yugoslavs . . . to be sent, under American leadership, to the British Schools in the Near East to be trained for subversive activities . . . These men would be paid by [my] organization, their leaders chosen by us, and they would be assigned to their respective tasks as America's obligation in the joint effort.[11]

Donovan, whose interest in Yugoslavia dated from his mission to Belgrade in January 1941, almost certainly interpreted this request as an invitation to begin direct support to Mihailovic. He dispatched an envoy, Frank Morand, to Cairo to meet with General Mirkovic, who represented the Yugoslav army-in-exile.[12] The two met in March and negotiated an agreement providing for:

> the allocation of four American bombers to the Yugoslav Air Force in addition to supplies which would be transported to the Cetniks by parachute drops. Plans were also made for direct US contact with Mihailovic through the infiltration of American officers into the country.[13]

Mirkovic, however, was soon dismissed from his post by King Peter's government and nothing further was heard of his agreement with Morand.

In conjunction with the Morand initiative, the US Command formulated a plan to use Mihailovic's forces to keep Axis troops in Yugoslavia from deploying to support the German effort in Russia. The plan's specific objectives were threefold: 'a. To interfere with supply lines and communications . . . b. To aid the Russian front by immobilizing Nazi divisions. c. To prevent [Mihailovic's] collapse.'[14] On 26 March, US General Walter Bedell Smith instructed Donovan to 'make representations through [his] agent in Cairo to the commanding officers of the Yugoslav forces in the Middle East proposing that General Mihailovic be requested to carry out this plan.'[15] As Yugoslavia fell within an agreed British-led theater, however, the US Joint Staff ruled four days later that 'the [US] should not initiate this plan nor assume primary responsibility for it.'[16] Instead, Donovan was to 'offer to the British, if they accept the plan, such assistance as may be practicable.'[17] This was a fine but important distinction, since the Joint Staff was in effect indicating that it was not prepared to press the British on this issue if any resistance whatsoever was encountered.

It is interesting that no mention of the Morand initiative can be found in OSS's official war report or in Sir Harry Hinsley's seminal work on British intelligence in World War II. Indeed, it is absent from the major works on wartime Yugoslavia by Mark Wheeler, Nora Beloff, Bill Deakin, Michael Lees, and Kirk Ford, among others. Very little declassified information, in fact, has as yet surfaced to shed light on the true dynamics of this abortive arrangement. Morand's promise to provide aircraft and supplies to the Chetniks, however, probably was linked to a promise by Mirkovic to get Mihailovic to comply with the objectives of the plan. Perhaps Mirkovic overstepped his authority by committing Mihailovic to offensive operations that he was not yet prepared to undertake. Mirkovic's credibility almost certainly suffered further from the US decision to defer to the British, which might have hastened his dismissal. Morand promised more than he could deliver, given the US military's decision, and the British probably were keen to keep strict control over all Balkan operations, and thus rejected the US version of the plan, even though they separately pursued its overarching objectives.

Some British officials at this time were already beginning to question the wisdom of having given unreserved political support to Mihailovic without the benefit of adequate intelligence on resistance activities throughout occupied Yugoslavia. Hudson's first reports in November 1941 claimed that Chetniks and

Partisans had begun to attack each other indiscriminately. Instances of collaboration by Chetnik elements with the Quisling Serbian government of General Milan Nedic[18] against Partisan formations were also mentioned. Hudson felt that the Chetnik–Partisan conflict was a potentially disastrous development for Allied policy, and he threatened to suspend supply efforts to the Chetniks while they were fighting the Partisans. Mihailovic and Tito had begun a dialogue in September 1941 that Britain hoped would unify the resistance elements. Meetings between the two, however, actually exacerbated tensions, and following a short truce, Chetnik–Partisan clashes increased.[19] German moves against Chetnik groups over the winter forced Hudson to break contact with London for several months. He ultimately chose to leave Mihailovic in the spring of 1942 to observe Tito's forces, and soon 'became quite impressed with the military effectiveness of the Partisans, just as he had grown impatient with Mihailovic's reluctance to take vigorous military action against the enemy for fear of large-scale German reprisals against the civilian population.'[20] As Hudson later explained: 'By spring 1942 this Cetnik non-combatant attitude, aggressively anti-[Partisan], had spread . . . The indiscriminate BBC moral backing [for Mihailovic] at that time was regarded by [the Chetniks] as carte blanche.'[21]

The most striking element of Allied subversive policy in 1941–2 is the extent to which it was supported by meager and incomplete intelligence on the operations and composition of the Chetnik and Partisan movements.[22] The dispersed activities of both groups over wide geographical areas and the almost certainly biased nature of most information acquired from local sources – vice personal observation by Allied personnel – would have made the collection task difficult even for large and well-staffed missions, as was later proved. Hudson's accounts were relevant, of course, mostly because little other first-hand information was readily available, but should have been of marginal use due to the relatively short time he spent with both movements and his difficulty in moving about on foot. Basil Davidson, who served both at SOE Cairo and with Partisan forces in the field, commented after the war that Hudson's reports were 'highly inefficient and misleading . . . all through the late months of 1942, [and] were a major cause of the muddle of that time.' According to Davidson, Hudson 'completely failed to do his duty by telling us the facts we ought to have known.'[23] Some SIGINT from German units in Yugoslavia was available to selective British consumers, but it painted an equally incomplete picture. It did, however, reveal that some Chetnik units were coordinating their activities with Italian forces in operations against the Partisans, although the Foreign Office – still excluded from this source of information – judged most collaboration charges at this time to be fabrications.[24]

The intelligence situation was badly muddled, as Davidson observed, which helps to explain why SOE London continued to back Mihailovic even after SOE Cairo had begun to favor Tito. According to SOE London's Bickham Sweet-Escott, '[We] put up remarkably stiff resistance to contacting the Partisans, even during early 1943.'[25] He later explained to Davidson:

I did not say [that] you in Cairo didn't know about Mihailovic's [problems], but that we in London didn't . . . We in London were put on the spot because as the result of persistent lobbying, . . . we had just persuaded the [Foreign Office] to give Mihailovic one more chance at the very moment at which you in Cairo had rightly decided to put your/our shirt on Tito.[26]

Efforts by SOE to ameliorate the intelligence situation in 1942 met with failure. Terrence Atherton was dispatched to Yugoslavia early in the year and joined a Partisan group for a short time, but died in mysterious circumstances in April before he could play much of a role. To make matters worse, Hudson left the Partisans and rejoined the Chetniks in late spring, but had his radio set confiscated by order of Mihailovic.[27] The Chetniks had greeted him with hostility and suspicion because of his contacts with the Partisans, and resented the paucity of British supplies that had reached them.[28] Hudson was confined in uncomfortable circumstances until the official British mission reached Mihailovic in December 1942,[29] which both removed him from the scene at a critical moment and probably made him more subjective. In fact, he was considered by SOE London in late 1942 to be 'so antipathetic to Mihailovic that he would be driven before long to recommend that all support should be directed to the Partisans.' The Chetniks allowed him to contact Cairo in the autumn, and he used the opportunity to accuse some of Mihailovic's top subordinates of collaborating with the Italians;[30] what Hudson omitted was that the Chetniks were increasingly desperate for arms as the year wore on since British supplies continued to be meager and irregular when they came at all. The Americans were in no position to help to clarify the intelligence picture. Donovan had not yet dispatched anyone to Yugoslavia and would not do so until the summer of 1943. The net result of this intelligence shortfall was that the Allied covert supply program was virtually blind in 1942, which made it difficult to justify allocating the resources necessary to make the policy of supporting Mihailovic an effective one.

In spite of the difficulties, America and Britain had become committed politically by mid-1942 to large-scale subversion in Yugoslavia, but both remained unable to move forward decisively and in unison. King Peter visited Washington in June and met with both Roosevelt and Donovan. The latter promised on behalf of the President to provide materiel assistance to Mihailovic as soon as practicable. Donovan's organization, however, was frustrated at its inability to meet its new obligations and placed much of the blame on SOE, which it believed was procrastinating and obstructing America's Balkan plans. A report drafted for Preston Goodfellow by his staff on 10 June best describes the growing antagonism within the Allied camp:

In my opinion the project of aiding the . . . Yugoslavs with arms, ammunition, food, materiel, etc. has reached the point where we must fish or cut bait . . . [The Chetniks] have received nothing from us and practically nothing from the British, [who have] admitted that their SO operations have had practically no result . . . They were unable to obtain the materiel asked for and even if they had [done so], they would have been unable to transport it . . . I think we should emphasize strongly [to the British] that up to now the project has been a complete failure.[31]

SOE Cairo, which was charged with overseeing all Allied special operations in the Balkans, was identified by Goodfellow's staff as being a principal obstacle. A passage in the aforementioned report outlining the role that Donovan's special operations branch envisioned for itself in the Balkans and the extent to which SOE Cairo was thought to be a problem is particularly illuminating:

Our participation in SO activities was for the purpose of making up [for British] deficiencies. In return we were to participate jointly in the management. As the situation now stands [the] head of [SOE] in Cairo seems to be shying away from any real American participation in management of SO affairs . . . It will not be possible to reach any satisfactory agreement as to the definite form of our participation except by a direct order from [SOE] London.[32]

The report's author probably was referring in his comments about 'SO activities in the Balkans' to the request by Hambro in February that Donovan begin recruiting Yugoslav-Americans for training and future operations.[33] Evidently, SOE Cairo considered that particular initiative either to have been unrealistic or undesirable, and Baker Street was not prepared to press the matter.

SOE London, in fact, had focused its energies in June on the job of securing OSS recognition that Yugoslavia was within the British sphere for special operations. Given Britain's keen interest in the Balkans and SOE Cairo's hard line against ceding any control over Balkan operations to the Americans, this course was a logical one. The Donovan-Hambro accords – covered in detail in previous chapters – explicitly recognized SOE's operational preeminence throughout the Balkans, but with the proviso that the British were to be 'assisted by an American Mission . . . under the command of the Controller of the existing British Mission.'[34] This latter concession was a necessary one because at that time SOE, above all else, desired US materiel support – especially transport – for many of its operational objectives, as has been discussed. US-supplied air and sea craft, in fact, were considered crucial in establishing any sustainable subversive aid program in Yugoslavia. The Donovan-Hambro negotiations covered this in detail:

If the American SO can become possessed of aircraft, seacraft, etc., it might be possible for them to send them to their own Mission [in] the Middle East and place them at the disposal of the British SOE . . . It would not be necessary for the American SO to send their own crews and spares, etc., so that the aircraft could be serviced as an independent unit . . . It was agreed that SOE London should make up a list of equipment in this category of which they stand in need and supply it to [OSS] . . . SOE London should [also] make up a list of their requirements [for radio sets and other equipment] . . . There could be no objection to the [OSS] either (a) detaching it to their American Mission in the Mid East; or; (b) supplying it direct to SOE Mid East.[35]

Inflated expectations regarding OSS capabilities in 1942, as discussed previously, led to disappointment on both sides, especially regarding failed promises about transport. Hence, SOE for all practical purposes was left on its own in Yugoslavia throughout 1942, and indeed through much of 1943, as OSS could not even manage to establish a viable mission in Cairo – where Balkan policy was being directed – much less to deploy trained personnel to Yugoslavia.

By autumn 1942, it was clear that mutual suspicions between OSS and SOE about the future direction of the Yugoslav effort had, if anything, increased since the June accords. OSS regretted acknowledging SOE's 'operational preeminence' in the Balkans and challenged the agreement's relevance, largely because of frustration about missed opportunities. Ellery Huntington reiterated some of the same arguments that Goodfellow's staff had raised in June when he wrote in September of the 'tremendous opportunities open to [OSS] in . . . the Balkans [where] Patriot groups are crying out for assistance' which were being consistently blocked by SOE Cairo.[36] An internal SOE memorandum from November 1942 indicates that the desire to govern and limit independent OSS action in the Balkans was indeed SOE policy at that time, even in London. 'We can effectively control OSS activities in the Balkans,' wrote a senior SOE officer, 'without ever having a head on collision.'[37] The strategy for 'avoiding collision' evidently rested largely upon SOE's plan to absorb the special operations element of OSS Cairo – once it was fully established there – much like SOE's plan to absorb SO London, as was discussed in the previous chapter. SOE's talking points for an October meeting with Huntington indicate a clear preference for integration as a means both to avoid disputes and to control OSS:

> We cannot afford to have two quite separate organizations working independently in [Yugoslavia and in Cairo]. If we do, we will inevitably be played off against each other, confusion and misunderstanding will arise, and in time serious friction and a spirit of antagonism will develop . . . Something approaching the integration of the SO and SOE organizations covering [these areas] must be secured . . . The Yugoslav sections of SOE and SO should actually work together in Cairo as permanent standing Executive Committees . . . There would then be a single field force [under British direction] in each country.[38]

A month after this proposition was made, SOE London reiterated its concern about OSS's steadfast determination to have 'an independent role in the Balkans and particularly in Yugoslavia, [which] we [SOE] will somehow have to prevent.' Acknowledging that part of the problem was OSS's suspicion that SOE 'may try to keep them from taking any very active part' on the basis of the Donovan-Hambro agreement, Baker Street continued to argue that parallel Allied efforts 'would . . . lead to a great deal of confusion;'[39] this, it was thought, would find resonance within Allied decision-making establishments and ensure Britain's leading role.

Thus, the pattern of divergence in the OSS-British relationship – which featured inconsistency and increasing mutual suspicions – continued relatively unchecked. Yet, Baker Street's appreciation of America's future potential to 'go it alone' in the Balkans – combined with its near desperation for US transport – prompted moderation from some quarters of SOE London on the OSS role. While Baker Street on the one hand saw OSS as 'extremely embryonic and not yet . . . capable of any serious work,' some within the organization clung to the hope that Donovan 'might be prepared to supply equipment now to SOE before [OSS is] in a position to operate [in the Balkans].' Specifically, SOE continued to press for aircraft, radio sets, and fast surface craft. The more farsighted at Baker Street, meanwhile, concluded that: 'However much of a mess [OSS] may be in now, and however useless they are likely to be for the next six months or so, they will eventually get themselves straightened out and then they will be a very important factor indeed in our [Balkan] sphere.'[40]

In November, SOE's George Taylor went as far as to declare:

I think it would be disastrous merely to stand pat on the [Donovan-Hambro] agreement and simply say they must not do this and they must not do that and make it quite clear that we expect them simply to help us and work entirely under our control. If we take that line they will simply break out and get the agreement modified by the Chiefs of Staff.[41]

Such practical thinking helped to reconcile immediate Anglo-US interests by facilitating greater OSS involvement in 1943. Greater involvement, however, meant greater independence, access to information, and freedom of interpretation in a highly complex and politicized environment.

Donovan's position on Yugoslavia had remained consistently pro-Mihailovic during 1942, even as he became increasingly dissatisfied with the Yugoslav government-in-exile and Britain began to flirt with Tito. In October, Donovan reassured King Peter's representative of America's continuing commitment to the Chetniks. Behind closed doors, however, OSS criticized his government for being 'unbelievably stupid [in sewing] the seeds of strife for many years to come' by disseminating anti-Partisan propaganda and charging that the British were pro-Croat and anti-Serb.[42] 'They have fanned the flames of [internecine] revolt,'[43] OSS complained, but at the same time came to a different conclusion about Mihailovic's usefulness than did the British.

OSS rejected growing British doubts about Mihailovic's reliability and SOE's increasingly conservative estimates of the size and potential of the Chetnik movement. OSS's assessment in the autumn of 1942, in fact, was as follows:

[Mihailovic's] following has grown to such an extent that he has not . . . been able to give arms and equipment to them all and has instead organized them in order that they may combat the Axis when the time comes and at the same time be under his control to avoid them being implicated in inimical political parties.[44]

This strategy was deemed logical given the supply constraints, and OSS saw Mihailovic as 'the most influential figure in Yugoslavia,' concluding that with proper direction and support he 'is the person who can be of most use to the war effort.' OSS analysts concluded that it was dangerous folly to think that more than one resistance element could be adequately backed in Yugoslavia at this time, whilst SOE Cairo had begun to look for ways to contact the Partisans ever since Hudson had crossed over to Partisan lines in the spring. Donovan was willing to give the Chetniks more of the benefit of the doubt, as is clear from the following OSS assessment:

The mere fact that Mihailovic has a large, if latent, organization in the country requires the Axis to keep considerable forces to avoid the possibility of this latent force becoming more active . . . It is surely necessary to have some central figure around which all resistance can be gathered and there would appear to be no other figure on the Yugoslav horizon greater than General Mihailovic.[45]

British SIGINT in Yugoslavia – still available to few on the British side, and almost certainly to none in OSS – indicated in late 1942, meanwhile, that the seizure of a key town by Chetniks in Bosnia had been erroneously credited by the Allies to the Partisans. More significantly, SIGINT also revealed that the Germans were determined to crush Mihailovic and were unhappy about the effect Italian-Chetnik collaboration was having on Italian forces.[46] Yet, disagreements within the British camp and especially between SOE Cairo and OSS about the situation on the ground persisted, which helps to explain the former's reluctance to give OSS more freedom of action. If one subscribes to the more recent theory that a strong British pro-Partisan clique based upon ideological grounds was already at work on influential levels at this time, the reasons for this reluctance are clearer.[47] It is also important, however, to consider that SOE's desire to absorb and control OSS efforts in other regions was very strong at this time, which made the Balkan situation not entirely inconsistent with the overall mood and objectives of Baker Street.

As 1942 came to a close, several more separate but related developments occurred that influenced Anglo-OSS considerations about the situation and demonstrate the increasing complexity of the whole Yugoslav subversion issue. First, the Political Warfare Executive – which directed the British propaganda effort – and the Foreign Office approved a Yugoslav government broadcast via the BBC advising Mihailovic to 'conserve his forces and energy.'[48] This was consistent with SOE's advice earlier in the year, but contrasted markedly with the BBC's (PWE's) decision at this time to focus more upon Partisan effectiveness, downplaying the

Chetniks,[49] and SOE's renewed determination to encourage more rather than less Chetnik action. Donovan, meanwhile, opted to cease sending OSS officers *ad hoc* to Cairo – where they were to help to coordinate American operations into Yugoslavia – until such time that OSS was ready to deploy a complete mission. Qualified American personnel were simply not yet available and distractions of other work temporarily sidelined Donovan's Balkan ambitions. Acknowledging OSS's immediate shortcomings, Huntington, moreover, suggested that for the time being, 'control should be in British hands [and OSS would try] to make a substantial contribution in the form of explosives, arms and stores.'[50] SOE was pleased with these developments:

> We have, of course, encouraged [OSS] in this idea which is perfectly sound and which, if adhered to, will save us from any further arrivals in Cairo of OSS people with no . . . instructions and no idea of what they have been sent to do.[51]

OSS's decision also gave SOE Cairo time to deploy a full mission to Mihailovic in December to evaluate more fully the Chetnik movement. The initial reports from this mission, which was led by Colonel Bill Bailey,[52] were to influence the British authorities greatly, particularly the Foreign Office and SOE Cairo, turning them gradually away from Mihailovic and toward Tito.

DOWN THE SLIPPERY SLOPE IN 1943

The British mission that was sent to Mihailovic in December 1942 was directed to 'report on the military value of the Chetnik movement as a whole and to persuade Mihailovic to undertake active sabotage.'[53] The mission's first reports early in 1943 noted 'Cetnik military ineffectiveness, and [some] did not believe that Mihailovic's genuine fear of continued German reprisals justified his policy of passivity.' Bailey also noted 'the friendly relations between Italian troops and some of Mihailovic's lieutenants.' In March, he wrote about the fateful speech of 28 February in which Mihailovic severely criticized the British for not sending enough supplies and allegedly threatened that 'as long as the Italians remained his sole adequate source of benefit and assurance generally, nothing the Allies could do would make him change his attitude towards them.'[54] Bailey said Mihailovic was 'willing to compromise himself in order to defeat the Partisans'[55] and temporarily suspended all British supplies to the Chetniks, which led to a general deterioration of relations between the mission and Mihailovic. This rift was only partially relieved through lengthy diplomatic negotiations involving the Foreign Office, Mihailovic, and the Yugoslav government-in-exile lasting several months.[56]

In some ways, it is not surprising that the Chetniks fared so poorly in Bailey's *prima facie* evaluation. He arrived at the onset of winter and made his key judgments before spring. Treacherous weather conditions during this short period forced the suspension of most military operations, as well as British resupply efforts, which were minimal anyway. Thus, Bailey is unlikely to have witnessed much Chetnik activity of any kind and saw the Chetniks at their worst, when inactivity and cold had sapped their morale, a sense of isolation due to the lack of Allied materiel support had set in, and British contact with the 'hated Partisans' had added to their suspicions. Moreover, Mihailovic was a notoriously poor administrator who failed throughout the war to document his operations[57] – he had 'no practical means of public relations'[58] – which must have left Bailey bewildered about what to believe and skeptical that much at all had been accomplished. Taken with the fact that Hudson was the first to brief Bailey in December, and that the former probably was somewhat predisposed against Mihailovic after his long and uncomfortable 'incarceration' at the hands of the Chetniks,[59] and it is not surprising that Bailey stopped the Chetnik's supply and thought the worst about Mihailovic's remarks about the Italians.

Bailey and Hudson, however, had correctly assessed that the majority of Chetniks were more concerned with fighting the Partisans than they were with fighting the Germans or Italians, which was Britain's main objection. According to Mihailo Protic, a veteran of Mihailovic's Field Headquarters 501, 'Our primary problem was the communist [movement] not the Germans ... We primarily fought the communists since 1941.'[60] A message from Mihailovic's headquarters[61] to a Chetnik field unit in 1942 was more explicit: 'The most important thing at the moment,' concluded a senior Chetnik officer, 'is to exterminate the communists.'[62] Protic attributes the animosity he and his fellow Chetniks had for the British solely to Britain's decision to help the Partisans.[63] Dusan Marinkovic, a veteran of the Chetnik underground in Belgrade, however, attributes the problems between Mihailovic and Hudson, and between the former and Bailey, to British pressure on the Chetniks to undertake 'more intensive attacks on German military communications in Yugoslavia, especially along the Belgrade–Skopje railway line.' According to Marinkovic, this pressure began to increase after Bailey first arrived at Chetnik headquarters in December 1942,[64] and Mihailovic was simply not willing to be managed in this way.

Bailey's decision to halt supplies to Mihailovic temporarily also coincided with the Allied preparations to invade Italy. Roosevelt and Churchill had given the final approval for the first phase of this endeavor – the invasion of Sicily – at the Casablanca Conference in January 1943. The success of the Italian campaign, it was believed, could be greatly facilitated by the Yugoslav resistance, which was expected to engage Axis forces and thus prevent them from reinforcing Italy's defenses. Baker Street dispatched Sweet-Escott in July to brief Allied Forces Headquarters about 'the importance of keeping as many Axis troops as possible out of Italy but in the Balkans instead.'[65] ENIGMA decryptions over the first half of 1943 supported the growing British belief that 'the fighting value of the Cetniks was greatly inferior to that of Tito's Partisans [but] contained no evidence of Cetnik collaboration with the Germans. On the contrary, they [indicated] that the Cetniks were playing off Germany against Italy and [that the Germans had] instructed their own forces that no Chetnik formations whose leaders were [in] touch with Mihailovic [were] to be spared.'[66] Nedic's collaborationist regime, moreover, had ordered that: 'All the mayors of the municipalities [in Serbia will] organize a search and capture [operation against] Draza Mihailovic and his men, otherwise armed units will be put in charge of this throughout the municipalities concerned.'[67]

Nonetheless, as Tito's forces were geographically better placed than were Chetnik formations to disrupt Axis supply and reinforcement to Italy with attacks in western Bosnia, Croatia, and Slovenia, the British Chiefs of Staff approved a plan in March 1943 to have SOE recontact the Partisans. On 20 April, ethnic-Croat SOE agents from Canada[68] were dropped into Yugoslavia by parachute and reached Partisan forces; on 27–28 May, SOE's Bill Deakin and two other British officers were infiltrated by parachute and soon reached Tito's headquarters. Deakin, who served under Basil Davidson at SOE Cairo, began immediately to report that the Partisans were a force to be reckoned with and were worth supporting.[69]

Donovan soon began again to agitate for a role in the Balkans, prompted in part by Roosevelt's decision in May that OSS should be represented alongside the British at both Tito's and Mihailovic's headquarters. SOE Cairo, however, continued to raise obstacles. Back in February, Huntington had moved to stop SOE Cairo from usurping OSS authority as a result of his deferential posture the month before. He advised Lord Glenconner[70] that:

> We will be compelled to recognize that our primary responsibility is to our Theater Commander . . . This would indicate that policy control must emanate from Washington so far as we are concerned . . . I firmly believe [that] our sections and our operations should be separately maintained.[71]

Glenconner had even tried to prevent OSS Cairo from independently meeting with representatives of the Yugoslav government in Cairo, to which Huntington replied: '[OSS] has, for a considerable period of time, been dealing with foreign and Allied governments and groups. To discontinue this would be impolitic if not dangerous.'[72]

OSS then stepped up efforts to find suitable officers to deploy to Yugoslavia, and even tried to designate them as intelligence rather than special operations officers to avoid SOE's control.[73] Two Yugoslav-Americans, George Musulin and George Wuchinich, were the first chosen. They went to Cairo on 23 May with orders to join Mihailovic as soon as possible. OSS Cairo pressed for the two to have independent communications or, at a minimum, to use their own ciphers via 'existing British communication channels.'[74] SOE Cairo's refusal to budge on the communications issue and SOE London's repeated objections to the initiative on the grounds that it violated previous OSS-SOE agreements on Yugoslavia, resulted in the postponement of this operation until mid-October, when Musulin finally joined the Chetniks in the field.[75]

Shortly thereafter, OSS tried to go around SOE on this and other matters by proposing that OSS Cairo be placed under the auspices of the US Command in the Mediterranean, rather than under the British theater commander where it was subject to the whims of SOE Cairo. The British Chiefs of Staff quickly moved to quash any such thoughts of OSS independence:

> We consider that the establishment of an independent OSS mission in Cairo . . . is most unacceptable since it is clear that in due course we would be confronted with the same difficulties which now prevail in India . . . The sphere of influence [in the Middle East] has been accepted completely as a British responsibility . . . A separate mission . . . must result in separate control and uncoordinated effort.[76]

Mention of India as a problem is interesting in that the British Chiefs had evidently become increasingly suspicious about OSS and US intentions in general, and were determined to exercise as much control as possible in British-led theaters. Thus, OSS activities in Yugoslavia were vulnerable to such pressure, so long as operations were directed solely from Cairo.

The failure of OSS's May initiatives led to talks with SOE in London in July that resulted in a partial compromise over communications. The Americans were to be given free access to British radio sets and operators for their messages, but all field communications were to continue to go through SOE Cairo, although they were to be uncensored. OSS Captain Melvin 'Benny' Benson, who was in Cairo undergoing British special operations training, was subsequently ordered to await preparations to join Deakin's mission to Tito. As Benson waited, James Grafton Rogers of OSS Washington wrote in his journal that the Partisans were 'a typical Russian subversion and agitation series of groups,'[77] which is an interesting insight coming from near the top of the OSS hierarchy, and suggests that Donovan's pro-Mihailovic stance had remained unchanged. Being pro-Mihailovic, however, did not stop OSS from seeking to use the Partisans in the Allied cause, as is evident in Rogers' entry on 8 September: 'We can penetrate with irregulars helping Mihailovic and the Partisans in the northern Adriatic.'[78]

Benson had volunteered for the Yugoslav assignment, and Donovan's decision to send him to Tito was consistent with the theme first discussed in Chapter 2 whereby OSS appointed officers with British ties to key positions requiring close Anglo-American cooperation, finesse, and mutual trust. According to Deakin, Benson received British training:

> in the delicate months before the Japanese attack on Pearl Harbor . . . then [was] drafted to join an Anglo-American party to be sent to the Burma Road from a base in Java. He escaped from the Japanese invading forces [and arrived] in Egypt in December 1942. Benson was sent on a British parachute training course and to another specialist establishment dealing with explosives.

Deakin claims to have encouraged SOE Cairo in early July to expedite the deployment of someone from OSS to his mission because this would 'emphasize Anglo-American solidarity in our policy towards Yugoslav resistance.'[79] Benson arrived on 22 August[80] and stayed for four months. Deakin's view of this early collaborative effort is worthy of full quotation:

> We worked as one mission, and shared without reserve our impressions and information . . . It was agreed that [Benson] should use our radio link rather than set up separate [radio] communications [because] we were operating in mobile and uncertain conditions. The natural hesitation at OSS Headquarters that the lack of an American [radio] set, operating independently, would lead to undue absorption of their representative by the existing British mission and a mere repetition of identical reporting was quickly dispelled by Benson himself. His independence in regard to the British mission never became an issue.

Deakin acknowledged that Benson thought his dependence upon the British radio and operator 'was not entirely satisfactory,' but noted that Benson was not overly bothered.[81] Nonetheless, as had been the case in London for much of 1942, OSS dependence upon SOE communications meant that the British exercised considerable control over what was reported from the field and could manipulate the timing of dissemination. This 'manipulation' was done on at least one important occasion by SOE Cairo in autumn 1943, which will be discussed later in this section.

Four days before Benson's arrival in Yugoslavia, a young US Marine lieutenant, Walter Mansfield, parachuted into Chetnik territory and became OSS's first representative to Mihailovic. He was placed under the auspices of Bailey's SOE mission and soon complained about the communications arrangements, noting the 'long ciphering delays in Cairo'[82] and requesting that OSS dispatch 'a [radio] set and operator here as soon as possible . . . Use of [our] own code here [would be] a big step.'[83] Mansfield's first reports revealed divisions within the British ranks. He told of 'much friction between [the] British here and at Cairo, due to Cairo's refusal to learn the facts . . . and [to] give Colonel Bailey something in the way of supplies to help enforce such a policy [of offensive action].'[84] Mansfield discovered the contradiction in SOE's policy, which on the one hand required Bailey to press Mihailovic to undertake more operations, while on the other denied the Chetniks the supply necessary to do the job and to fend off Axis reprisals. This became a counterproductive cycle whereby British complaints prompted Chetnik suspicions and mistrust rather than increased activities, and perceived Chetnik inaction fostered more British complaints and mistrust. OSS took a diametrically opposed approach to that of SOE, pressing first for supply that would give Mihailovic the confidence to proceed with more useful activities.

Mansfield initially felt obliged to 'show a united front to Mihailovic' and wrote of his 'complete cooperation' with Bailey.[85] Other messages, however, revealed an unease about his position and were highly critical of British policy. First, his comparatively low rank made it difficult for him to work as an equal with the mission's more senior British officers:

> British Mission here comprises 2 Colonels and 1 Major . . . Brigadier [Charles] Armstrong [who will replace Bailey] is bringing one Lieutenant Colonel and one more Major, so I hope something can be done on [my] request for promotion. [The] fact that I took a British [parachute] course may impress.[86]

Mansfield's preliminary assessment of the situation in the field diverged greatly from the Titoist line then being aggressively pursued by SOE Cairo:

> You must not fall into the mistake the British at Cairo make . . . They would think that Mihailovic was not a good boy. Too, the British would give all their support to the Partisans. This straight simple military approach sounds OK [until] you get here and find that Mihailovic virtually controls all the operations in Serbia proper, Sanjak and part of Montenegro. The Allies cannot ditch Mihailovic here, because they would not find a substitute.[87]

A summary of Mansfield's four subsequent messages in early September continue the pro-Mihailovic theme and imply an increasing wariness about British intentions:

> The Serbs look to Mihailovic and will follow no other . . . If the British drop [him] they will have no resistance group at all in this vital area. The first fallacy in the British position is that they cannot treat the problem as one of choosing between the Partisans and Mihailovic. It still remains one of trying to get Mihailovic to devote less attention to the Partisans and more to the Axis . . . He knows he depends on the British for supplies . . . [The British] have failed to use political as well as military pressure, whereas Mihailovic has adroitly used political means to delay action.[88]

Shortly thereafter, Mansfield appealed to his OSS superiors to: 'Cease thinking of the problem as one of choosing between Mihailovic and the Partisans. Mihailovic is supreme in his own sphere.'[89] OSS Washington responded by making Mansfield a Captain and by dispatching a more senior officer, Lieutenant-Colonel Albert Seitz, to join him before the end of September.

Throughout September, in fact, the Allied missions to Mihailovic and Tito were substantially upgraded. British Brigadier Fitzroy MacLean replaced Deakin as head of an enlarged 'joint' Anglo-US mission to Tito. Deakin, like Bailey, stayed on as 'political advisor' whilst OSS Major Lyn Farish joined MacLean and became one of the Brigadier's joint chiefs of staff along with British Colonel Vivian Street. The Americans were soon allowed to use their own radios, but all information was still sent to SOE Cairo where it was processed for retransmission to London, Washington, and wherever else it was required. The arrival of MacLean represented a formalization of the Allied relationship with Tito and put him for the first time on something approaching an equal footing with Mihailovic politically, although the Allies had not yet officially recognized his National Liberation movement.

Before MacLean and Armstrong took over the two principal missions, however, Italy's surrender thrust Bailey and Deakin into the middle of a fierce competition between Chetnik and Partisan forces for the arms of the Italians in Yugoslavia. SOE Cairo evidently either withheld or otherwise failed to report to the Cetniks the news of the Italian armistice concluded with the Allies on 3 September. Mihailovic did not learn of it until 8 September when it was announced publicly. This 'allowed the [Germans] to beat [him] to the punch in taking over Italian garrisons, whereas some advance notice would have strengthened Mihailovic's position.'[90] Already disadvantaged, Mihailovic nonetheless moved quickly to seize a strategic town[91] in Montenegro from the Germans that lay between his forces and the well-armed Italian Venezia Division. After defeating the small German garrison, the Chetniks drove down the Lim valley where 'the Italians greeted them as Allies as they were accompanied by Colonel Bailey.'[92] The Chetniks wanted to disarm the division immediately, but Bailey persuaded them to allow him to negotiate with the Italian commander on their behalf. A deal was struck in accordance with earlier instructions from SOE Cairo allowing the Italians to retain their arms[93] and to fight alongside the Chetniks, which was reluctantly accepted by the Chetnik commander. Whilst the details were being finalized, however, a strong Partisan force – which soon grew to 20 000 – arrived on the scene accompanied by its own British liaison officer. The Partisans demanded that the Italians surrender their arms to them, then attacked the Chetnik-Italian position. Facing a growing Partisan presence and hearing BBC broadcasts denunciating the Chetniks, the Italians soon complied with Partisan demands, leaving the Chetniks to flee Montenegro with nothing to show for their effort. 'It was a major disaster [for Mihailovic], the turning point [in] Yugoslavia.'[94]

Bailey's actions almost certainly were largely responsible for this Chetnik debacle and contributed greatly to the subsequently rapid deterioration of relations between Mihailovic and the British.[95] He may have been motivated by a desire to forestall further use of arms by the Chetniks against the Partisans, but may also have acted as an instrument of SOE Cairo's pro-Tito policy. It is interesting that SOE Cairo appears to have ignored Mansfield's repeated requests to accompany Bailey on this trip. In any event, SOE Cairo, MacLean, and elements of the Foreign Office spared no effort in the aftermath of these events to convince Churchill formally to abandon Mihailovic in favor of Tito, whilst SOE London continued to back SOE Cairo's right to 'remain in day-to-day executive control of the Balkans.'[96] They were aided in their endeavor by the fact that the Partisans – in addition to acquiring the Venezia Division's sizeable arsenal – seized the arms of the Italian Bergamo Division in Split with the help of Deakin under the observation of Benson.[97] The balance of military power had clearly shifted inexorably in Tito's favor.

The two key OSS personalities with MacLean and Armstrong, respectively, were Farish and Seitz. The two OSS men were remarkably similar, yet had different experiences in their new assignments. Both had close ties to the British that made them desirable emissaries from Donovan's point of view and should have eased their transition into the joint Anglo-OSS missions; it did so in Farish's case. An oil engineer by profession, Farish joined the Canadian Army when the war began and was sent to Persia as a member of the Royal Engineers; he soon transferred to a British commando unit and was subsequently recruited by OSS.[98] MacLean's comments about Farish indicate the high personal regard that he felt for this officer and the extent to which Farish's choice had been a useful one for promoting closer Anglo-US working-level ties:

> We were even more pleased when we met Farish . . . He was wearing [the] uniform of a Major in the Royal Engineers. We asked him how this had happened. 'Why,' he said, as if it had been the most natural thing in the world, 'Why, when the war started over in Europe, I felt I just had to get into it, so I joined the British Army; and I've never got around to quitting it . . . Now I'm coming on this job, I guess I'll need to join the [US] Army,' and the next day appeared resplendent in the uniform of a Major in the [US] Engineering Corps, but with British parachute wings still on his shoulder . . . From then on 'Slim' Farish was one of us, and Anglo-American cooperation was of the closest.[99]

Farish was as impressed with the Partisans as was MacLean, at least partially because the recent acquisition of Italian arms made it possible for Tito to increase his activities. His report was enthusiastic about Partisan capabilities and critical of Britain's previous policy of supporting Mihailovic out of 'attachment to monarchist principles' rather than military realities.[100]

Seitz was also an engineer and had been involved with the Canadian authorities, but as a member of the Royal Canadian Mounted Police.[101] Unlike Farish, however, Seitz became embroiled from the outset in the increasingly contentious atmosphere of the Anglo-Chetnik relationship, presaged by Mansfield in his reports. Seitz and Mansfield were approached in October by Mihailovic, who beseeched them to send more US observers to confirm that he was indeed fighting the Axis, contrary to British charges.[102] This led Seitz to conclude:

> The Serbs were never quite sure what was in the mind of the British; they felt that the British politicians would not hesitate to throw the Balkans to the Communists if by so doing [they] could retain their hold on Greece and the eastern Mediterranean. With the Americans, the Serbs believed there was no purpose except to win the war by fighting the Axis; no political or territorial aspirations, and that we meant what we said without qualification.[103]

Moreover, the two OSS liaison officers were in agreement from their personal observations that the Chetniks were indeed fighting the enemy under extremely difficult conditions and that charges of collaboration leveled by the British and the Partisans against them were greatly exaggerated. Mihailovic was said by the two to be 'a modest man without any dictatorial ambitions, a popular leader enjoying tremendous prestige and wide popularity among the Serbs.'[104]

The 'unauthorized' contact between the Americans and Mihailovic, however, not only further strained personal relations between Armstrong and Mihailovic,[105] but promoted distrust between Armstrong and Seitz. Armstrong and SOE Cairo almost certainly feared that Mihailovic intended to play the Americans off against them, and chose to prevent this by undermining the work of Seitz and Mansfield. Hudson later reported that the British mission believed that Mihailovic 'wanted the Americans in charge of the Italian sphere [to] take over Balkan activities,'[106] which probably incited Armstrong to make further obstructions. Seitz, meanwhile, had become increasingly critical not just of British policy, but of what he believed were blatant efforts by Armstrong – whom he disliked personally – to undermine the American contingent:

> [We] are relegated to the position of doing practically nothing. [We] have no supplies or operations to administer and have either been ruled out of conferences with Mihailovic by the British or have not been invited. [Our] only function is to transmit to Cairo daily intelligence which cannot be confirmed.'[107]

Seitz later recalled:

> The Mission was British and the whole show would remain a British show. I would be permitted to see or talk to Mihailovic only at [Armstrong's] discretion. [Mansfield was] not permitted near the Headquarters . . . I was even forbidden to address Mihailovic directly in French. Further, any message destined for my people in Cairo would be subject to the Brigadier's censorship.[108]

Fearing continued marginalization by Armstrong and sensing that a decisive moment for Allied policy on Yugoslavia was approaching, Seitz requested permission from Cairo in late October to leave the mission with Mansfield to conduct an extensive survey of Chetnik forces in the field.[109] SOE Cairo evidently did not respond, so the two Americans struck out on their own on 6 November, having first declared their intention to make their observations then to proceed overland to the Adriatic for exfiltration. Presumably, Seitz felt that he and Mansfield should report their findings in person, perhaps distrusting SOE Cairo's handling of their reports and chafing at Armstrong's violation of the previous OSS-British understanding that American communications would not be censored. Prior to leaving Mihailovic's camp, Seitz submitted a detailed assessment of the situation at the urgent request of OSS Washington – which also expected the future direction of Allied policy on Yugoslavia to be decided at the upcoming Tehran Conference. This interim report appears to be both balanced and filled with thoughtful analysis of the composition, history, strengths, and weaknesses of the Mihailovic movement and the pros and cons of British policy. It concluded, however, that

Mihailovic should get more supplies and that his motive for holding back his maximum effort until he received them was generally sound. Moreover, it detailed British efforts to undermine his position, criticized SOE's desire to establish mutually exclusive zones of operation for Chetnik and Partisan forces,[110] and attacked erroneous and biased BBC reporting on Yugoslavia in general.[111] These judgments must have been very badly received by SOE Cairo, which helps to explain its otherwise indefensible subsequent actions that were certainly not in the spirit of Anglo-OSS collaboration and might even be seen as the hostile acts of a rival service rather than those of a wartime ally.

The matter of SOE Cairo's 'mishandling' of Seitz's interim report and the arbitrary restrictions placed upon the Americans serving with the Chetniks raise the most serious questions to date about SOE's intentions and the future course of OSS-British collaboration in Yugoslavia and elsewhere. The preface to the report indicates that it was completed and transmitted to SOE Cairo on 25 October, which meant that even after allowing adequate time for deciphering and retransmission, it could have been expected to arrive in the hands of decison-makers in Washington and London in time to have an impact on intra-Allied deliberations on Yugoslavia in preparation for Tehran. SOE Cairo's 'In Message Operational Log' for Yugoslavia, however, shows that it was only logged in on 17 November, some twenty-three days after transmission.[112] This delay seems excessive, even when the shortage of communications personnel at SOE Cairo during this time is taken into account.[113] It ensured that Seitz's report arrived late, and Brigadier C.M. Keble, head of SOE Cairo, appears to have been deliberately responsible. Three days *before* Seitz's report was logged in as having been received, Keble wrote a letter to his OSS counterpart in Cairo, Lieutenant Colonel Paul West, in a blatant attempt to undermine Seitz's arguments. Referring explicitly to Seitz's key points one by one – in a report that he supposedly did not yet receive from the field – Keble claimed that he had new information on Axis dispositions that rendered Seitz's observations moot. He refuted point-by-point Seitz's views on Mihailovic's motivation for delaying offensive action in some places and his criticism of erroneous BBC reports, all to an officer (West) who had not yet been privy to Seitz's report. Moreover, Keble attempted to block Seitz's plan of exfiltration via the Adriatic by arguing that: 'It is our firm rule that no officers with the Partisans or Cetniks shall ever . . . visit the opposite side. Were this to happen, distrust would immediately be sown.'[114] This so-called rule ignored the fact that SOE Cairo – from the time of Hudson's initial movements – regularly approved such activities on the part of British officers whenever it suited.

On the same day that Seitz's report was finally logged in by Keble's team, Donovan arrived at SOE Cairo for a contentious meeting. Perhaps the two events were not unrelated and were it not for Donovan's visit, Keble might have buried Seitz's report for longer. SOE's minutes of the meeting indicate clearly that OSS's difficulties with the British were not only related to the activities of Seitz and Mansfield, but like them were tied to the question of information gathering:

Donovan said that he was considerably disturbed in the matter of Intelligence (SI) and had found that SOE were causing considerable obstruction in the implementation of his SI development. He acknowledged the leadership of SOE in [the] Middle East in respect of OSS/SO but not in respect of OSS/SI. He felt that there was considerable misunderstanding and mistrust between OSS and SOE in this matter and he wanted to have it cleared up, with special reference to the position of Yugoslavia where, he said, his organization do not recognize . . . MacLean as representing any form of Intelligence authority, British or [OSS].[115]

At this same meeting, Turner McBaine of OSS Cairo complained that Tito had on a recent occasion approved the infiltration of OSS intelligence officers into Partisan territory, only to have the operation vetoed by MacLean. Since the British controlled all transport to and from Yugoslavia, they were in a position to block OSS indefinitely and clearly intended to do so. Donovan picked up on this point as well as on previous difficulties with the British over the issue of independent OSS communications and threatened to 'go it alone' if necessary:

> Donovan [said] that it was essential [that he] have independence and secret lines of communication with his intelligence workers, and since OSS were in no way concerned with the British Foreign Office, [which objected to any form of OSS independence in Yugoslavia], he intended to install such channels of intelligence as he chose, preferably with the goodwill of SOE but failing this, without.[116]

Colin Gubbins, who had come to Cairo from London, argued that MacLean would be placed in an impossible position if he did not have full access to information (i.e. control) from and about all Allied personnel in Yugoslavia. Donovan rejected this and Gubbins finally agreed to allow OSS to increase its presence in Yugoslavia up to a maximum of fifteen officers with the Chetniks and fifteen with the Partisans, and to use its own radios. In turn, Donovan reconfirmed that he considered the Armstrong and MacLean missions to be integrated SOE-OSS entities under British leadership.[117] The meeting adjourned with both sides promising to meet more often.[118]

While SOE Cairo was undermining Seitz and Mansfield and working to block OSS intelligence activities, MacLean was simultaneously expediting his own report – dubbed 'Blockbuster' – which was to influence Churchill decisively at Tehran. MacLean had arrived at Tito's headquarters on 17 September and had quickly come to appreciate the capabilities of the Partisans – which had been substantially augmented with the captured Italian arms – and Tito's dynamic leadership. MacLean's memoirs are full of praise for both the man and the movement. He recognized that the decisive moment for Allied policy on Yugoslavia was nearing and, like Seitz, made arrangements to leave the country to make a personal report. Unlike Seitz, however, MacLean reached Cairo in time personally to hand over his written version of events to Foreign Secretary Anthony Eden, who was *en route* to Tehran, and to back up his findings with force of personality. In sum, Blockbuster explained that the Partisans were led by communists and were pro-Soviet, but praised their effectiveness and potential, which he suggested could be significantly augmented with Allied materiel assistance. Perhaps his most compelling assessment was that the Partisan movement was much larger and better organized than the Chetniks and would undoubtedly play a decisive role in post-liberation Yugoslavia, with or without Allied help.[119]

MacLean based Blockbuster upon his three-week stay at Tito's headquarters (17 September–5 October), along with Deakin's input; a paltry collection effort for so important a decision. Thus, Partisan sources rather than personal observations formed the basis of most of his findings, even when Deakin's limited time in the field is considered.[120] Lees, who was deployed with the Chetniks at this time, has attacked Blockbuster as being an exercise in Partisan propaganda based on unprovable and even outlandish claims. His rationale is insightful:

> [MacLean said Tito lost] one man killed for five of the enemy against Germans and ten against Ustasi or Cetniks [and] received the wholehearted support of the civil population . . . This is sheer rubbish . . . I was [in] touch with the population for a year without minders brainwashing me, and I spoke their language. MacLean was not in Serbia. He was just writing down what Partisan headquarters told him . . . [He] said that the Partisans had 26 divisions and a total of 220,000 men . . . The divisions were much smaller in November 1943 than they were in the summer of 1944 [when] each division counted only 1,700 to 2,500 . . . Thus a generous figure would be 60,000 . . . [He said] 30,000 Partisans [were] in Serbia and Macedonia [yet only] 1,700 [were reported by our officer] in Serbia in January 1944 . . . The Partisans were [supposedly] ten to twenty times more numerous [than the Cetniks, which meant] that Mihailovic had [just] 10,000 to 20,000 men, [which is an absurdly low estimate].[121]

Nonetheless, 'Comrade Fitz,' as he was nicknamed by Armstrong for allegedly contributing to BBC 'disinformation' about the Chetniks,[122] aired his views to Churchill before Tehran, whilst those who were favorable to Mihailovic were excluded. BBC, meanwhile, continued to carry:

> Tito's communiqués accusing Mihailovic of treason and almost every other crime in the catalogue of crimes. When Mihailovic issued denials, the denials were ignored; when he issued communiqués, the communiqués were ignored; when the Axis press attacked him, or when Axis communiqués spoke of actions against the Cetniks, the Axis communiqués were ignored.[123]

Donovan at this time based his impressions upon both Farish's report,[124] which reflected much of Blockbuster, and on the earlier messages of Seitz and Mansfield. He almost certainly was aware of Seitz's interim report, but as it was only logged into SOE Cairo on 17 November, as was previously discussed, he probably did not see it in its entirety before meeting Roosevelt in Cairo. At that meeting, Donovan proposed that the Allies should back both Tito and Mihailovic, dividing Yugoslavia into Chetnik and Partisan operational areas along a rough east–west divide. He suggested that the Allied Supreme Commander in Italy, rather than in Cairo, should control the support operation, and that neither side should receive any arms unless they agreed to the proposal. Roosevelt evidently left Cairo intent upon pursuing this course of action at Tehran.[125]

THE HUOT AFFAIR AND OSS BARI

Donovan's decision in November 1943 to support inclusion of the Partisans in Allied plans was certainly influenced by Farish's report and Tito's acquisition of Italian arms. It also, however, almost certainly dates back to September and was related to an OSS operation to resupply the Partisans from Bari, Italy, organized by a member of OSS Cairo, Louis Huot, with the help of Hans Tofte and Robert Thompson of OSS. The generally accepted premise about Huot is that he decided in September, after reading Deakin's glowing reports about Tito and a resupply plan drafted by Tofte and Thompson, that OSS should do more to support the Partisans. On his own initiative, he, Tofte, and Thompson transferred themselves to Bari – after meeting with Partisan representatives in Algiers – and proceeded to organize an unauthorized supply operation across the Adriatic. They secured 'a fleet of small ships which would ferry clothes and ammunition to the Yugoslav mainland' and Huot briefly slipped into Yugoslavia in October – without the knowledge or permission of the Allied military authorities or Brigadier MacLean – and met with Tito, soon becoming 'charmed by the Tito personality.'[126]

Documentary evidence, however, suggests that far from the mission being unauthorized, Donovan himself formally approved a plan for an endeavor of this sort in mid-September[127] and SOE was fully complicit. It was thus only unauthorized from MacLean's perspective and that of the British Mediterranean (Middle East) Command. Both 'aggrieved' parties lodged strong protests as soon as the operation was uncovered, Huot and his team were briefly placed under house arrest, and the 'errant' Huot was sent back to Cairo and replaced by Tofte. Deakin attributes MacLean's objections to the fact that no decision had as yet been made by the Allies to grant formal recognition to Tito's National Liberation movement, and thus Huot's operation 'confused' the situation.[128] More likely, MacLean was concerned that he would lose control over Allied dealings with Tito, who was already complaining that the British were not delivering enough supplies. Either reason would explain Donovan's refusal to discipline Huot and his men, as had been requested by the British authorities. Tofte wrote the following about the operation:

[Donovan] approved a plan concerning aid to Tito's Partisan forces. The plan was placed before [him] by OSS officers of the [SO] Branch, M[iddle] E[ast]., during a meeting in Algiers the 16th September 1943. The plan was roughly to establish an advanced OSS base on the Adriatic Coast of Italy by having officers of SO, M.E. follow the British Eighth Army, then fighting its way up the 'Heel' of Italy, and select a suitable site from which contact could be made with [Tito's] Army in Dalmatia with a view to organizing a supply line across the Adriatic . . . In the first days of October 1943, OSS officers proceeded to Italy via Algiers.[129]

The party traveling to Italy via Algiers was surely Huot's group. Tofte also explained: 'Details with regard to Anglo-American cooperation were to be worked out at Cairo upon the return of a British survey party, which was to follow the OSS officers to Italy during the first half of October.'[130] The suggestion that the British – presumably SOE Cairo's 'Force 133' in Italy – provided a survey party for Huot's team casts doubt on the charge that the British were not properly informed. On 29 October, Tofte reported that Gubbins 'recognizes OSS initiative in regard to organizing the supply line Italy-Yugoslavia. Promise British cooperation.'[131] Moreover, SOE's Dodds-Parker recalls that Huot came to him in Italy with little more than finance, and that SOE arranged for the acquisition of arms and supply by the OSS team on his instructions.[132] Thus, MacLean and the British Command were the only ones not properly advised, which was the fault of SOE not OSS.[133] The subsequent British protests probably were directed more at regaining control over all activities related to Yugoslavia rather than at ending this useful means to support Tito. Prior behavior of both MacLean and the British Chiefs is consistent with this explanation.

The OSS mission, whether authorized or not, succeeded in giving Donovan the measure of independence that he had been unable to secure through the work of Seitz, Mansfield, Farish, and Benson. He acceded to British demands in November that the operation be deemed 'a joint Allied undertaking' rather than an independent OSS activity, probably as a face-saving gesture. Brigadier W.A.M. Stawell, who had replaced Lord Glenconner as head of SOE Cairo, was dutifully advised by the British Mediterranean Command that 'the activities of OSS/SO in the Balkans are under [your] control . . . [You] will coordinate their potentialities as regards stores, personnel, etc. with those of Force 133 to the best advantage of the common effort.'[134] Nonetheless, 'all movements of supplies on the sea transport route to Yugoslavia and the immediate liaison with the Partisan delegation at Bari [remained] exclusively an OSS responsibility,'[135] according to Tofte. Possibly as part of this 'compromise,' OSS 'loaned' SOE $2.5 million, 'stipulating that the currency [was] to be used only in Yugoslavia;'[136] these funds probably were designated to 'offset' SOE expenditures related to the training, insertion, and maintenance of OSS personnel in Yugoslavia (i.e. the loan became a grant). Even with the pay-off, the British – not surprisingly – 'tried in many subtle ways to gain control over the sailings and thus over the Partisan fleet and the deliveries of supplies to Yugoslavia.'[137]

The performance of the OSS team supporting the Partisans from Italy between October and December 1943 was a testament to the American's ingenuity and energy in moving huge quantities of captured Italian materiel in combat conditions to Yugoslavia. Indeed, it was in the best 'can-do' traditions of Donovan's organization. When OSS dispatched Sterling Hayden in November to Bari, he quickly established a base on behalf of Allied Forces Headquarters at the Italian port of Monopoli, which lay some 30 miles to the south, which became the principal operating base when Bari was bombed by the Germans soon thereafter. With 400 Partisans, 14 schooners, and assorted other vessels, Hayden directed the resupply of the Partisan-held island of Vis, mostly using Italian arms prized away from the British Command.[138] OSS Bari, meanwhile, delivered 6500 tons of uniforms, food, medicine, weapons, and ammunition to the Partisans via a motley assortment of some 60 seagoing vessels between 15 October and 31 December. The Americans provided 150 000 gallons of petrol to a British torpedo boat facility in the Dalmatian islands that had been established at OSS Bari's request to protect the supply fleet, and delivered large amounts of diesel oil, kerosene, petrol, and lubricating oil to Tito's forces. In conjunction with SOE's Force 133, OSS organized, equipped, and transported to Dalmatia a 'brigade' of 2000 fighters who had been recruited from among Yugoslavs interned in Italy. OSS assigned an officer to manage the Partisan supply facility on Vis and organized a shipping line between Bari and the three major Sicilian ports 'to assist in transporting 7000 tons of captured enemy material to Bari for trans-shipment to Yugoslavia . . . By the end of December 1943 four Partisan bases at Bari, Monopoli, Molfetta, and Manfredonia were in full operation under the command of OSS officers with a staff of some 600 Partisans.'[139] All told, in less than three and a half months, OSS had delivered more than the sum total of materiel supplied by SOE to all resistance forces in Yugoslavia since Hudson's first shipment to Mihailovic in late 1941.

SOE'S FORMAL BREAK WITH MIHAILOVIC

The Tehran Conference (28 November–1 December 1943) presented an opportunity for Roosevelt, Churchill, and Stalin to discuss Yugoslavia amidst their other pressing business. Buoyed by MacLean's Blockbuster report, Churchill was determined to secure nothing short of full Allied support for Tito and was supported in this endeavor by Stalin. Perhaps through the force of Churchill's personality and the fact that OSS Bari was already pressing ahead with aid to the Partisans, Roosevelt was persuaded to drop the plan proposed to him by Donovan, whereby Yugoslavia would be divided for operations, and aid would be used to enforce compliance. The three leaders agreed 'to give maximum support to Tito'[140] virtually without preconditions.

Roosevelt may also have been willing to accede to Churchill's wishes as a means to steer him away from larger-scale Allied 'strategic diversions into

South-Eastern Europe and away from Northern France.'[141] The US Chiefs of Staff were wholeheartedly committed to a 'France first' policy and had fought their British counterparts long and hard over Churchill's persistent efforts to shift the main Allied push to the Balkans.[142] If more fully supported, Tito might also prove helpful by keeping additional German forces away from France. Moreover, Roosevelt was keen to mollify Stalin – who insisted at Tehran on a firm Allied timetable for the long-awaited cross-Channel invasion of France – in the belief that Soviet cooperation was necessary both to defeat Japan and to forge a stable post-war order in Europe. Stalin secretly promised at Tehran that he would enter the war against Japan as soon as Germany was defeated, which fulfilled Roosevelt's primary goal. And the Americans almost certainly felt that aiding Tito in no way precluded continued assistance to Mihailovic; a fact borne out by Donovan's efforts in 1944 to do just that.

British actions during and immediately after Tehran, however, indicate that they were not simply pressing to shift the Allied effort away from Mihailovic, but were looking for a pretext to break with him entirely. This divergent policy put OSS and the British on another collision course in 1944. Evidence of anti-Mihailovic maneuvering on the part of the British came not just from the machinations of SOE Cairo, the BBC's distorted press coverage, or the actions of MacLean's mission, but were clearly evident in a Foreign Office-SOE Cairo plot in December 1943 to manufacture an incident to facilitate the break. Four days after an internal Foreign Office message on 4 December claimed to have 'reliable evidence of cooperation between certain Mihailovic forces and the [Quisling] Nedic authorities [in Serbia],'[143] the British 'Special Operations Committee' in Cairo devised a 'final test' in which Mihailovic was ordered to conduct a specific set of operations, and if he failed to do so, Britain would have its pretext. According to Ralph Stevenson, Britain's Ambassador to the Yugoslav Government-in-Exile:

> These operations involve simultaneous attacks on two definite points on railway lines . . . Mihailovic's compliance has been requested by December 29th . . . Armstrong is being separately instructed that he must not admit to Mihailovic that the operation is intended as a test. But it is being explained to [Armstrong] for his own information that a final decision as to future policy towards Mihailovic may in fact depend upon the extent to which Mihailovic complies.[144]

The Foreign Office advised the British Embassy in Washington of its plan in preparation for informing the Americans, but ordered that no action be taken until further notice,[145] which effectively cut the US out of the scenario entirely.

The role of Ambassador Stevenson – a principal player in the orchestration of the so-called test – is an interesting one in that his actions were clearly intended to discredit Mihailovic before the Chetniks had a chance to meet Britain's requirements. On 29 November, for example, the Ambassador reported to Anthony Eden that Mihailovic had ordered one of his field commanders to mobilize against the Partisans,[146] and Stevenson subsequently lent his weight to the paltry evidence of Chetnik collaboration with Nedic in a message to the Foreign Office on 6 December.[147] On the very same day that the test was authorized, moreover, Stevenson advised the Foreign Office that 'It has been represented to me that it is possible that Mihailovic may stage some kind of ineffective action perhaps even with the knowledge of the enemy.'[148] This 'representation' probably came from SOE Cairo, with which the Ambassador was almost certainly in constant contact at this time, and is indicative of its concern that Mihailovic might succeed. Stevenson's overtures had a definite impact on the Mihailovic-Tito debate within the Foreign Office, elements of which were also scheming against Mihailovic's position:

> We discussed the Yugoslav problem [with] Stevenson . . . We should probably be forced to withdraw our support of [Mihailovic] . . . It was felt, however, that our case with King Peter would be greatly strengthened if we could say that Mihailovic had failed [his test].[149]

Thus, the test results were already rigged against the Cetniks and their fate was all but sealed. Churchill, in fact, met with King Peter in Cairo on 11 December on his way back from Tehran and told him that the British had 'irrefutable proof' that Mihailovic was collaborating and warned that he might have to be dropped from Peter's Cabinet.[150] Three days later – a full two weeks before Mihailovic's test deadline – the Foreign Office discussed how it might lure Mihailovic out of Yugoslavia, presumably to facilitate the dissolution of his movement by perhaps detaining him in Cairo.[151] Stevenson, meanwhile, had already prepared a note for King Peter on 12 December explaining that Britain was withdrawing its support for Mihailovic because, *inter alia*, he had failed the test.[152] Stevenson wrote on 15 December of his worry that if Mihailovic somehow passed his test, it would be impossible to convince King Peter to drop him. He recommended, therefore, that the Foreign Office allow him to approach Peter immediately to discuss dropping Mihailovic rather than wait for the 29 December test deadline to pass;[153] such panic may also have been stoked by SOE Cairo, which wanted to hedge its bets.

A review of the reporting from British liaison officers serving with Chetnik groups during the latter half of 1943 does indeed indicate that some of Mihailovic's forces were performing poorly and were suspected of collaboration with the enemy. Typical examples include:

> [The Chetniks were] not willing to do sabotage or let [us] have complete control of the [Chetnik] Commando [unit] as had been promised by Mihailovic.[154]

> The [Chetniks] say 'We are not helping the Germans . . . the Germans are for the moment helping us.'[155]

> With 700 Chetniks [we] set off to do this [sabotage] job . . . and got within half an hour's march of the job, when we hung about, excuse after excuse, and so on.

After the excuses got petty, we realized it was again bluff, and all 700 of us returned to the hills.[156]

Mihailovic approved [the] sabotage mission [but Chetnik General] Djuric raised [inexplicable] obstacles until it was dropped.[157]

Many of these observations were certainly above question, but some might be explained by the Chetniks' chronic lack of training, weapons, ammunition, etc., as was previously discussed. Such reports, however, almost certainly were given precedence by SOE Cairo over the equally many positive reports on Chetnik military accomplishments filed by other British liaison personnel.

These positive reports on Mihailovic indicate that the Chetniks were undertaking important acts of sabotage at the very time SOE Cairo, the MacLean mission, and the Foreign Office were successfully portraying them as virtually completely inactive and worthless. Even Hudson reported that on 6 October 1943 Chetniks destroyed 'the four bridges on the Uzica–Visegrad line . . . prior to their successful attack on Visegrad, and [this was] after a similar demolition of the big bridge over the Drina at Medjedja.'[158] Another British liaison officer wrote that 'the train I did derail [with the Chetniks in December along the main north–south route] was only a goods train, but it blocked the line for two days.'[159] Yet another SOE officer in Serbia reported that he observed significant sabotage activity by Mihailovic's forces as follows:

1. Attack on rail line near Gurdelica (end of September [1943]); 2. Train blown near Grabonica (middle of October); 3. Train blown by Serb personnel alone, across Bulgarian border in October; 4. Train blown South Gurdelica (October); 5. Line blown . . . near Brabonica (October); 6. Train blown by Serbs alone, north of Lescovac; 7 and 8. Trains blown across Bulgarian border (early December); . . . Each time the line was blown, it was held up from working about 5 or 6 days.[160]

The record is full of such evidence of Chetnik activity, which again raises questions about the motives and actions of SOE Cairo. One SOE officer in Serbia even accused SOE Cairo of ordering him to lead specific Chetnik operations then canceling them at the last moment for no apparent reason:

The difficulties here were . . . increased by Cairo's apparent lack of confidence in [us] . . . Orders and counter orders regarding the commencement of operations and [the] extraordinary replies, if any, received to our cables [were perplexing].[161]

On his way back to London from Tehran, Churchill took a last decisive step – without consulting Roosevelt – to force a break with the Chetniks. In Cairo, he met with MacLean, who reemphasized the key points from Blockbuster, especially his belief that Tito would rule Yugoslavia after liberation with or without Allied support and that he was pro-Soviet. Interestingly, MacLean did not approach the

Prime Minister 'until after all of [Churchill's] professional staff and top commanders had departed.'[162] MacLean has claimed that Churchill asked him at this meeting whether he planned to make Yugoslavia his home after the war. When he replied negatively, the Prime Minister is alleged to have said: 'Neither do I . . . And, that being so, the less you and I worry about the form of Government they set up, the better. That is for them to decide. What interests us is, which of them is doing most harm to the Germans?'[163]

Churchill decided to write to Tito, who had just been forced by a German attack to flee his headquarters, and pledged both to increase aid and to break off relations with Mihailovic.[164]

Churchill's promise to Tito must have come as a relief to SOE Cairo, but posed significant new challenges for the British. Armstrong's mission had to be withdrawn safely from Chetnik territory and OSS had to be convinced to follow suit. Eden advised Churchill on 22 December that any British liaison officer 'who could be withdrawn unobtrusively' should do so immediately.[165] From SOE's perspective, it 'need have no further direct involvement in Yugoslav politics, thus removing a continual source of friction between Baker Street and the Foreign Office. [Moreover,] a decision to cease giving military support to the Cetniks greatly simplified the supply arrangements both by air and sea.'[166]

DEEPENING DIVISIONS IN 1944

SOE's hope that its tense relations with OSS over Yugoslavia would be assuaged by Churchill's unilateral decision to break with Mihailovic was soon disappointed by Donovan's continued belief that the Chetniks were worth supporting. SOE had moved swiftly in December 1943 to shift its resources to Tito, and managed to deliver some 6000 tons of supplies to him by the end of January 1944 – an astounding figure when compared with the paltry total of 300 tons delivered to Mihailovic from 1941 through 1943. As the massive British airlift began to have effect and committed the Allies more and more to the Partisans, Donovan continued to suffer from a lack of first-hand intelligence from Chetnik-held territory. Seitz and Mansfield had returned to Mihailovic's headquarters in late December from their extended survey, but both had difficulty leaving the country. Mansfield finally reached Cairo by sea in mid-January 1944, but Seitz's efforts to cross Montenegro to the Adriatic were complicated by unexpected encounters with German troops and unfriendly Partisans – he did not reach Italy until 15 March and it took another month for him and Mansfield to reach Washington.[167] Their reports, however, were very favorable to the Chetniks and recommended increasing rather than suspending Allied assistance.

Donovan did not wait for Seitz and Mansfield to return before deciding to defy the British by increasing support to the Chetniks. In January, he pushed again for OSS Bari to be released from Cairo's authority, and in February authorized the deployment of forty OSS officers to Mihailovic's headquarters; his promise three months earlier to limit this contingent to fifteen had been rendered moot by SOE's decision to abandon the Chetniks. In the first instance, the British Chiefs of Staff again intervened to block Donovan's wishes, advising the new Supreme Allied Commander Mediterranean, General Henry Maitland Wilson, as follows: '[Foreign Office] urge and we agree that SOE and OSS must be integrated and that your control over special operations would be severely handicapped if American special operations were controlled under separate arrangements.'[168]

Wilson was inclined toward integration as a solution to continuing SOE-OSS difficulties, but Gubbins convinced him that OSS would reject any such proposals.[169] Wilson decided that the command arrangements should remain unaltered for the time being.

Donovan's second initiative – to deploy the 40 officers – was frustrated by the British decision to withdraw the Armstrong mission from Serbia. The withdrawal began on 21 February and Wilson stopped additional OSS deployments by ordering that all Allied personnel be withdrawn from Chetnik territory as soon as was safely possible.[170] OSS did, however, initially attempt to keep George Musulin on at Mihailovic's headquarters, informing SOE Cairo that: 'Musulin should remain, not as a liaison officer, but in order to collect needed intelligence . . . A "purely and confessedly intelligence mission" should remain . . . regardless of whether [Mihailovic] would be given future Allied assistance.'[171] The British saw this request simply as a ploy to redesignate Musulin as a secret intelligence rather than special operations officer to circumvent their control, but when Armstrong encountered delays in evacuating his officers from Serbia, OSS used the additional time to press its case further. In March, Donovan appealed to the US Joint Chiefs, Eisenhower, and Roosevelt for permission to keep Musulin in Serbia; Roosevelt backed Donovan's plan to attach an officer to Mihailovic for intelligence collection purposes only,[172] and the US military authorities were told that Musulin would be there simply to facilitate the infiltration of OSS agents into Austria and Germany via Yugoslavia.[173] Churchill, however, intervened personally with Roosevelt on 1 April, arguing that the presence of an American with Mihailovic would indicate to Stalin that Britain and the US were at odds in Yugoslavia. A week later, the President changed his mind and Donovan was forced to abandon his plans.[174]

'It seemed strange that the Prime Minister would himself intervene in such a seemingly minor matter, but it was becoming evident that Mihailovic's unequivocal departure from the political scene was an essential part of Britain's foreign policy in Yugoslavia.'[175] In fact, Bill Bailey suggested even more drastic means to deal with Mihailovic than had hitherto been contemplated, possibly to deny OSS independent access to the Chetniks:

Mihailovic [should] be disposed of [by] his own followers . . . Before [we] withdraw from Mihailovic's headquarters, dissident officers [should] be unofficially encouraged to take the law into their own hands . . . It is believed there is an even chance of eliminating Mihailovic without disturbing his movement.[176]

This was a remarkable proposition, especially given that most British charges of collaboration and general criticism singled out Mihailovic's key subordinates – especially General's Djuric,[177] Jevdjevic,[178] and Markovitch[179] – rather than Mihailovic himself. Bailey recognized that his scheme to do away with Mihailovic could rupture relations with OSS, however, and therefore cautioned that 'there must be complete identity of policy and action in this matter between [Britain] and the [US],'[180] which made his proposal a non-starter.

OSS relations with and concerning the Partisans, meanwhile, continued to be constructive, mostly as a result of the sealift operation from Bari and Monopoli; intelligence officers were also working closely with Partisan field units from early 1944.[181] The sealift was soon phased out, however, because of the threat posed by German naval and air forces in the Adriatic, but was more than adequately replaced by the British-led airlift, which had been substantially augmented. OSS sent some sixty special operations officers to Yugoslavia in 1944, Farish was named commander of the OSS contingent at MacLean's headquarters, and OSS Colonel Richard Weil was dispatched to Tito's headquarters to make an independent assessment. Weil characterized Tito as a nationalist first and a communist second, and said that 'Tito . . . expressed a desire for wider political contacts with the Americans,' which Weil favored.[182]

The rapidly increasing size and scope of OSS participation in Partisan affairs made the British more malleable in dealing with OSS where Tito was concerned. The British recognized early in 1944 that 'full American participation . . . in Balkan relief [was now] essential'[183] because of the increasing demand for personnel, transport, and supply. In April, Cairo relinquished control of OSS operations in Yugoslavia to Allied Forces Headquarters (AFHQ), Mediterranean Theater of Operations, and by June SOE was even complaining that OSS had not met 'the numbers promised for [radio] operators' and that 'the situation is rapidly becoming critical . . . our manpower stringency is very great and trained signals staff are simply unobtainable.'[184] Thus, while SOE–OSS relations were severely strained over Mihailovic, the Americans and British were now locked into a mutually dependent relationship of sorts in the Partisan camp.

In the summer of 1944, OSS found a pretext to reestablish a mission to the Chetniks which revolved around the evacuation of downed US airmen from Chetnik territory. Musulin had been urging since the first Allied airmen found their way to the Cetniks in February 1944 – and especially after his forced departure from Chetnik territory in May – that OSS deploy a team to Mihailovic's headquarters to facilitate their evacuation.[185] Tito had been approached by Farish in January about helping to exfiltrate airmen from territory controlled by the Partisans, and when the British showed no signs of moving to assist those in Mihailovic's territory,

Donovan saw an opportunity and moved swiftly. On 14 July, the Air Crew Rescue Unit (ACRU) was established by the Mediterranean Allied Air Force (MAAF) at OSS's behest and was staffed principally by OSS men.[186] Donovan advised OSS Bari on 19 July that it should use the chance afforded by the ACRU as a proverbial 'foot in the door' to establish a secret intelligence mission to Mihailovic.[187] Musulin was chosen to lead the first OSS team into Chetnik territory and interestingly, he failed in four attempts to locate a suitable drop zone, finally succeeding on 3 August; the American suspected that SOE Cairo – which was responsible for briefing the pilots used to transport his team – was deliberately sabotaging his mission and attempting to drop him into Partisan-controlled territory.[188] SOE Cairo's behavior throughout 1942 and 1943 suggests that Musulin's suspicions might well have had some validity, but in SOE's defense, radio contact had been broken for some time with the Chetniks and was only just reestablished as Musulin was making his attempted entry. This fact almost certainly complicated the already difficult task of parachuting men into hostile and rugged territory at night.

Once Musulin's team was established, OSS turned to the next task – deploying a suitable secret intelligence team to Mihailovic's headquarters. Lieutenant-Colonel Robert McDowell, who was one of the forty OSS officers denied permission by the British in the spring to enter Chetnik territory, was chosen to lead this mission. Like Seitz and Farish before him, McDowell was well-connected in British circles; he had even served for a time in British military intelligence during the First World War.[189] In July, he had been secretly moved from Cairo to Caserta, Italy, in anticipation of recontacting Mihailovic – *without* British knowledge – if a suitable opportunity presented itself.[190] On 5 August, however, Roosevelt approved his deployment to Mihailovic's headquarters with concurrence from General Wilson and the British Foreign Office.[191] McDowell was directed to assist the ACRU and to collect intelligence on Axis, Chetnik, and Partisan forces and activities. He was not to act as a liaison officer, therefore ensuring that he would not become involved in internecine political questions.[192] This was an obvious gesture to the British, who had been outflanked by Donovan. Nonetheless, McDowell was seen by the Chetniks as their 'savior,'[193] and claims by them that McDowell was there in a liaison capacity reached Tito, who reacted by raising obstacles to Allied movement. These obstacles hampered American activities in Dalmatia for the balance of the war.

The McDowell Mission arrived in Serbia on 26 August and stayed until 1 November, when it was withdrawn along with the ACRU. During this time, McDowell conducted an extensive personal survey of Chetnik forces and operations, reported on a wide variety of issues related to Axis and Cetnik activities, and assisted in the evacuation of over 400 Allied airmen. He also met twice with the Germans through an intermediary to discuss surrender terms, although no agreement was reached.[194] In September, Mihailovic had mobilized the Serbian population in a last effort to win back Allied favor, but Churchill had already convinced Roosevelt to recall the American mission – against all objections by Donovan and McDowell[195] – ostensibly as a demonstration of Allied unity and almost certainly in response to Tito's non-cooperation. This decision was also made at a time when Soviet forces were invading Romania and Bulgaria. Tito's invasion of Serbia that same month crippled the Chetniks and coincided with the arrival of the first Soviet forces in Yugoslavia. For all practical purposes, the Allies conceded Yugoslavia to Tito, and King Peter was prevailed upon to lend his diminished political support to the Partisan leader.

Perhaps as a *quid pro quo* for withdrawing McDowell's team, the OSS contingent with the Partisans was designated an independent mission in September and became operational as such on 9 October. The US presence was also substantially augmented to include OSS Operational Groups (OGs)[196] – which worked with Partisans and British Commandos to harass enemy forces throughout Dalmatia – and some forty additional intelligence officers to run fifteen collection teams. The OSS and British paramilitary units, *inter alia*, conducted various joint operations against German forces on many of the Dalmatian islands and the mainland, and undertook extensive reconnaissance. The intelligence contingent, meanwhile, collected order of battle information, helped to coordinate Allied air attacks with Partisan operations, and established clandestine meteorological stations, although OSS continued to be hampered by Partisan restrictions placed on them in retaliation for the McDowell mission. Evacuation of airmen continued from Partisan areas; some 1600 were rescued in total by the end of the war.[197]

CONCLUSIONS

The differences between OSS and the British over Yugoslavia did not prove fatal to OSS's relationship with SOE and SIS, but did accelerate Donovan's drive toward full independence for his organization. In many ways, the Yugoslav morass and British actions there and in Cairo during 1942–4 removed any vestige of naivety within OSS about the nature of special warfare and of the organization's relationship with the British. The Huot affair, in particular, demonstrated again that OSS could organize and run a large-scale special operation on its own, which encouraged OSS to seek out such opportunities elsewhere. Cooperation continued, of course, where it was mutually beneficial, such as in the OVERLORD and ANVIL / DRAGOON campaigns in France during 1944. This demonstrated again the determination of both sides to keep difficulties in one area from significantly damaging relations elsewhere, which was the real strength of the Anglo-American 'special relationship' and remains so today. Where national interests collided during the war, however, so thereafter did the secret services. OSS no longer gave the British the benefit of the doubt on matters that had previously been beyond its control, such as communications or 'joint' missions under British leadership; the latter experiment had failed miserably. More than partially as a result of its experiences in Yugoslavia, for example, OSS never again – with few exceptions – permitted SOE or SIS to handle its field communications.

Why did the same combination of American aggressiveness and British recalcitrance in London during this period have such different results in the Yugoslav case? The above parallel between British perceptions of OSS activities in India/ Burma and in Yugoslavia was certainly partially responsible. The fact that OSS lost faith in the objectivity and intentions of its British counterparts in Cairo and Yugoslavia in the autumn of 1943 was another important factor. When this occurred, OSS began to oppose SOE on most matters related to Mihailovic and collaborated on resupplying the Partisans more out of the imperatives of mutual dependence rather than from a sense of partnership. SOE Cairo's possible ideological bias towards Tito and disregard for intelligence from Serbia almost certainly provoked OSS's negative attitude to some extent.

Whether SOE Cairo's 'biased' attitude was more a perception on the part of the Americans than a reality, however, remains controversial. The conditions under which SOE Cairo had to operate were far from ideal. Not only was Brigadier Keble's organization chronically understaffed, but it was unable to review the background of many operational matters in the Balkans after the partial evacuation of the British from Cairo to Jerusalem in the summer of 1942.[198] SOE Cairo had been forced to burn many of its case files, which left it in a distinctly disadvantageous position and might help to explain some of the inconsistencies in its behavior in 1943. Moreover, SOE Cairo almost certainly acted as it did in Yugoslavia at least partially because it had been ordered by the British Middle East Command to prepare the resistance forces to support a major Allied military campaign in the Balkans as a contingency. If SOE Cairo genuinely believed that Tito could better support this contingency than Mihailovic – substantial evidence supports the premise that it did – then its strenuous effort to shift what were insufficient resources for both the Chetnik and Partisan movements to Tito's forces alone was rooted in logic, even if its means were somewhat Machiavellian. As Sweet-Escott has explained:

> We know now that, long before [the Italian collapse], Churchill had reluctantly agreed with the [US] that there would be no major campaign in the Balkans. But at the time this was not so clear to the [Chiefs of Staff] in the Middle East. For one thing, plans might change. If so, [we] had to be ready . . . If anybody thinks this is of no importance, I would ask what would have been expected of SOE in the Balkans if Salerno had been a pushover [or] if we had had landing craft to use in the Eastern Mediterranean?[199]

Donovan's desire to build upon OSS's success in North Africa by demonstrating that his organization was independent and effective in the Balkans also probably contributed to Anglo-OSS confrontation. Like Sweet-Escott's comment about feeling as though he had been trampled by an elephant when dealing with OSS, the British almost certainly felt that OSS was seeking in Yugoslavia blatantly to violate what Donovan had agreed to in June 1942 concerning the

Balkans, i.e. that Britain was in charge. Stopping the OSS 'elephant' almost certainly became an obsession of many in the British establishment, who saw encroachments by the Americans at nearly every level in the war effort. Many British also feared that America would encourage the break-up of the British Empire after the war through the promotion of self-determination, and perhaps acted where and when they could to stem the 'American tide.'

OSS policy in Yugoslavia, unlike that of the British, has been demonstrated to have been generally consistent throughout the war. Whilst SOE, the Foreign Office, the Political Warfare Executive, and the British military fought among themselves over which side to support, Donovan and his analysts backed the proposition from the outset that Mihailovic was a valuable commodity and should be the principal focus of support right through 1944, although America's Office of War Information switched sides to Tito in the propaganda war when its British opposite did. OSS's commitment to the Chetniks was not shaken by British charges of Chetnik collaboration with the enemy or by questions about Mihailovic's inactivity. Donovan did, however, decide to aid the Partisans when he believed it would help the war effort, or perhaps in an effort to demonstrate that OSS was innovative and useful. OSS's inability to staff its Cairo office adequately towards the end of 1942, and its failure to put Americans into the field before late-summer 1943, however, left Donovan in a relatively weak position to make his will felt. By the time OSS was in Yugoslavia in force, Britain's pro-Tito, anti-Mihailovic policy was a foregone conclusion and had helped to change unalterably the balance of forces in the country in Tito's favor. Thus, OSS was struggling to keep up with events rather than driving them. This might help to explain why Donovan chose to authorize the Huot operation to resupply Tito even when he was seeking to expand OSS ties to Mihailovic. It was another means to get OSS more involved in the Balkans and to create linkages that were somewhat independent of the British. Similarly, OSS's decision to try to back the Chetniks after Britain had broken off contact with them might be seen as part of the same strategy, rather than as a purely objective exercise.

6 The Liberation of France: A Case Study in Anglo-OSS Convergence, 1943–44

In England it was realized that in [France] there lay a great potential force which, if controlled and armed, could be used [to] to harass and strike at the German [occupiers] . . . The organization entrusted with this task started from small beginnings, which gradually developed into the vast network of Resistance that has played so great a part in driving the Germans out of France.[1]

(OSS Assessment)

What was in 1942 a purely British operation and in 1943 a joint British-American headquarters eventually evolved in practice into a predominately Franco-American operation [after D-Day], a fact which no doubt dismayed some of our British counterparts.[2]

(Paul van der Stricht, OSS London)

INTRODUCTION

Whereas Anglo-OSS relations in Yugoslavia evolved from close collaboration in the early stages of the war to competition and rivalry by 1944, the reverse proved true in France. British and OSS intelligence and special operations in support of the French resistance developed from what were essentially divergent subversive efforts at the start, to something approaching integration in time for the invasion of France in June 1944. The truly joint nature of secret activities in France, however, turned into parallel but complementary field operations once Allied troops came ashore in Normandy. Nonetheless, the apex of the Anglo-OSS partnership was reached in France in 1943–4. Never before had both sides cooperated so closely and on such a large scale, and never again did this occur during the war.

As happened simultaneously in Balkan affairs, the Allied political and military leadership played a key role in the development of Anglo-OSS ties as they pertained to France. It was Roosevelt who initially set OSS on a divergent course from the British in French affairs by pressing for General Henri Giraud as an alternative leader to Charles de Gaulle. Eisenhower's arrangement with Vichy Admiral Jean Darlan during the TORCH invasion, moreover, strained OSS-Gaullist relations at a time when the British were pursuing an opposite course. Because France – like Yugoslavia – initially fell into a mutually recognized British sphere of interest, the British Chiefs of Staff worked tirelessly to ensure SOE and SIS predominance there. When Allied military arrangements changed at the end of 1943, however, leaving Eisenhower as Supreme Commander in Europe with all French subversive efforts under his control, Anglo-OSS convergence followed. And

146

while the US European theater commander's support for independent OSS activities late in 1943 helped to convince the British to include the Americans in their French operations, it took Churchill's personal intervention at the start of 1944 to secure the resources necessary to make these operations meaningful to Allied victory. Thus, OSS, SOE, and SIS remained, as always, hostage to the workings of the greater Anglo-US relationship.

BACKGROUND, 1940–43

The unexpected collapse of France in the spring of 1940 posed enormous problems for the British secret services, and soon thereafter for those Frenchmen who began to rally behind General de Gaulle in London. The speed with which the Allied armies were defeated by the German Blitzkrieg left SIS – and SOE when it was created in July 1940 – without a cadre of local contacts and other indigenous 'stay behind' personnel that normally would have been in place in any defeated country of such strategic importance. As a member of SIS's 'Section D' – the forerunner to SOE – explained, 'We did not possess one single agent between the Balkans and the English Channel [following France's collapse].'[3] The Gaullists, meanwhile, 'were as bereft of knowledge of the country from which they were exiled as were the British,'[4] and thus were denied full recognition by London, and later by Washington. Recognizing the importance of all French resistance elements, SIS and SOE established separate sections in 1940 to deal with Gaullist and 'independent' French groups. Lacking the means by which to contact and organize such groups inside France, however, both the British and the London-based Gaullist movement were forced to start virtually from the beginning.

After the Franco-German armistice was signed in June 1940, France was divided by the Germans into three zones – occupied, unoccupied, and a north coastal exclusion area. A quasi-independent French regime was established at Vichy whose very existence helped to undermine the resistance of Frenchmen by dividing their loyalties. Nonetheless, opponents of the occupation and of Vichy collaboration began to surface almost immediately, but in an uncoordinated and largely unorganized fashion. It was not until late-1940 that resistance began to coalesce into roughly organized entities, and these focused largely on drafting and circulating nationalist papers, and on holding discussion meetings. 'Gradually some of these groups – estimated at the end of 1940 to number approximately eighty – merged into larger organizations; those in the non-occupied zone organized branches in the other zones and vice versa.'[5]

These nascent French entities formed the basis of British, Gaullist, and later OSS subversive strategy in France for much of the next four years. For London, they represented a means by which intelligence on the enemy could be gathered and large-scale anti-Nazi subversion could be pursued – as was concurrently the case in Yugoslavia – at a time when Britain was less capable of mounting effective conventional military action. It was thus imperative for SIS and SOE to begin establishing links with the resistance leaders, including with the Gaullists, who were making their own contacts. For de Gaulle, 'the Resistance was to form the basis of his legitimacy, a popular mandate which symbolized the rejection of the armistice, of the occupation, of Vichy. The Resistance was to play a military role, certainly, one which included intelligence gathering. But that role was subordinated to the ultimate political purpose of the achievement of postwar power by Free France.'[6] De Gaulle's political motivations meant that Britain felt it 'had to look very hard at reports from Free French sources . . . Secondly, it provided further justification for the existence of two French sections,'[7] even in the face of stiff Gaullist opposition. 'This duplication of secret services,' de Gaulle's intelligence chief, André Dewavrin, wrote after the war, 'risked to provoke anxiety and tragedy.'[8] The political nature of the subversive war in France proved time and again to be a seriously contentious issue complicating relations between all sides of the Anglo-OSS-French triangle. 'The American perspective, to get the war over with as soon as possible with the least possible losses, gave [even] less weight to political considerations than the British, who, after the war, would still be living next to postwar France.'[9]

SIS and SOE spent much of 1941 laying the foundations for future resistance networks, mostly among those opposed to Vichy, while the still neutral Americans built up their contacts within the Vichy regime and among its adherents in North Africa. The first British agents deployed to France were Frenchmen who were dispatched by clandestine means to the occupied zone on 10 May 1941; agents of British nationality were first deployed a month later, on 9 June.[10] When these and others succeeded in making contact with indigenous resistance groups, men and women were recruited, outfitted with radio sets or employed as clandestine couriers in operations throughout France.[11] 'The delivery of supplies to France began very modestly in 1941 and 1942, with an occasional Halifax which would drop an agent or two plus some containers or packages of radio equipment and explosives.'[12] SOE's influence with de Gaulle's intelligence apparatus – the BCRA – was largely predicated upon its control over the organization's communications with resisters in France. This proved to be the single most important factor in Britain's ability to manage and often direct the development of pro-Gaullist resistance from mid-1941 onwards.[13] SOE and SIS, moreover, soon established schools in Britain to train new agents in intelligence collection, radio communication, sabotage, parachuting, close combat, weapons, etc. Identity documents were forged, local currency was acquired or counterfeited, and SOE's 'Station IX' (Research and Development) produced a range of radios and other equipment.[14]

Over time, trained and equipped field operatives were deployed by the British to France, usually by parachute at night, and their activities were supported by a cadre of French experts at Baker Street and Broadway. 'Complicated arrangements had to be made for the people on the other side to receive [agents] and to assist them . . . Escape routes had to be made available for those who required to be brought out from France.'[15] SOE's 'DF Section' handled exfiltration:

> A network of clandestine lines was built up, running through Portugal and Spain to eastern France and Switzerland, to northern France, Belgium and Holland . . . Operations [involved] the clandestine crossing of frontiers, housing of the travelers [and] production of [identity] papers . . . Transport [was acquired], circuitous routes studied and the timing of the journey carefully planned . . . Other activities included transport of messages and payment of money . . . The delicate negotiations required to bring such operations to fruition were carried out with the help of [clandestine radio] and often BBC messages.[16]

In 1941–2, a number of readily identifiable resistance groups, varying greatly in size, allegiance, and political objectives, were contacted by the British secret services. *Combat* was the largest in unoccupied France and was one of de Gaulle's most important backers from the spring of 1942. It had been organized shortly after the armistice by Henri Frenay, who resigned his army commission to lead 'a group of general staff and Deuxième Bureau[17] officers . . . in what was called *Libération Nationale*.'[18] Frenay had ties to Vichy, but abandoned these and combined his organization with a Catholic group to form the socialist-leaning *Combat*. In 1943, *Combat* joined with the centrist group *Libération*, led by Emmanuel d'Astier de la Vigerie, and the smaller radical socialist organization *Franc-Tireur* in a union renamed *Mouvements Unis de Résistance* (MUR). MUR proved to be 'fairly successful in [coordinating] paramilitary activities in [southern France].'[19] Prior to the establishment of these formal linkages, Frenay's *Libération Nationale* and d'Astier's *Libération* forged a loose interim alliance with the anti-communist group *Liberté* on 5 September 1941. This was accomplished with the help of the charismatic Gaullist Jean Moulin, the former Mayor of Chartres, who became the triumvirate's accredited representative in London and soon thereafter returned to France as de Gaulle's principal organizer and an agent of SOE.[20] The French Communist Party, meanwhile, organized *Front National* following Germany's invasion of the Soviet Union in June 1941 as an umbrella for both communist and non-communist resisters. The military arm of *Front National – France Tireurs et Partisans* (FTP) – proved to be one of the most well organized and formidable resistance groups. *Armée Secrète* (AS) was the loose amalgamation of the various *Maquis*[21] groups, *Sédentaires*,[22] and later the FTP, while on the purely military side was the *Organisation de Résistance de l'Armée de l'Armistice* (ORA), which recruited from Vichy's 100 000-man armistice army that had been disbanded as a result of TORCH. ORA backed General Henri Giraud. *Forces Unies de la Jeunesse* (FUJ), meanwhile, focused on organizing the French youth, and smaller groups included *Organisation Civile et Militaire* (OCM), which was centered around ex-army officers, *Ceux de la Résistance*, and *Ceux de la Libération*.[23]

Stimulated largely by Anglo-US and Gaullist overtures, efforts were made from the outset to coordinate the resistance groups to increase their effectiveness. This task took on an increasing urgency as the planning for OVERLORD – the code name for the Allied invasion of Normandy – began. The most significant positive outcome was the establishment – by order of de Gaulle – of the *Conseil National de la Résistance* (CNR) between autumn 1942 and May 1943,[24] which attempted to organize and control all resistance elements inside France. From the time of its establishment, the resistance council theoretically answered to the *Comité Français de la Libération Nationale* (CFLN), which was created at Algiers in February 1943,[25] and co-chaired by de Gaulle and Giraud from June until the latter was ousted by the former in the autumn. The CNR had representatives from the principal resistance groups, political parties, and trade unions, and it formed sub-committees to deal with key issues. France was divided into 12 regions and numerous sub-regions by the resistance council to facilitate organizing efforts, and two parallel groups were set up – *Bureau d'Opérations Aëriennes* in the north and *Section d'Atterrissages et Parachutages* in the south – to facilitate Allied parachute supply operations to the French resistance, including distribution of arms and other materiel.[26]

In the first half of 1942, Jean Moulin's organizational successes and the expanded activities of many of the various resistance groups 'made it possible to contemplate carrying out sabotage activity throughout France on a wide scale and in accordance with a coordinated policy.'[27] Baker Street entered immediately into detailed discussions with the *Bureau de Renseignements et d'Action Londres* (BRAL) – the London-based office of de Gaulle's BCRA – and concluded an agreement in early 1942 empowering SOE to coordinate all joint subversive activities with the British and American military staffs.[28] On 2 June, the new British Chief of the Imperial General Staff, General Sir Alan Brooke, empowered SOE further by detailing formally 'the part which SOE should play in the building up of resistance and the relations with exiled Governments in London.'[29] De Gaulle's ceding of military liaison authority to Baker Street and Brooke's recognition of SOE's role put Hambro in a strong position on French matters when he met with Donovan later in June to negotiate the parameters of the SOE-OSS relationship in France and elsewhere, which is discussed in detail in Chapter 3.

It was during the Donovan-Hambro negotiations of June 1942 that OSS and SOE formally recognized the obvious – that the French resistance had great potential and needed to be thoroughly exploited. It was also where the two sides first sought to coordinate their approach to France's many disparate resistance elements. Most significantly, SOE and OSS agreed for the first time in writing to back the French with arms and training.[30] Moreover, 'it was provided that support from England of resistance organizations in France should be carried on through the SOE services, and that OSS should cooperate in this activity by supplying whatever additional material and personnel might be available.'[31] While the agreements reached in London temporarily resolved the problem of leadership within the SOE-OSS partnership in France, it left much room for disagreement about whom specifically to support within the French camp.

Anglo-US dissension on this fundamental matter of whom to support plagued OSS's relations with SOE and SIS on French affairs through much of 1942–3. It also put the Americans at a comparative disadvantage vis-à-vis the Gaullists, who were gradually growing in strength. The dispute was rooted in the deep disagreement between Roosevelt and Churchill about the future of post-war France. Indeed, the two leaders of the Western Alliance were at odds about the future of the world imperial system in which France was still a key player:

> Roosevelt was skeptical concerning the French need for a strong central government on liberation. His plans for the post-war world did not include restoration of the French colonial empire. They did envision the establishment of bases at Dakar and other French colonial possessions as part of a global UN security system. In contrast, Churchill and the British foreign office envisioned a strong post-war France to whom her colonies would be restored.[32]

In America's view, General Giraud soon became a far more palatable leadership figure than the independent-minded de Gaulle, who was dedicated to restoring France's empire and had greatly antagonized Washington's many Vichy contacts. Britain, despite its own serious difficulties with the Gaullists – especially concerning various notable security lapses[33] – found in de Gaulle an ally in its quest to restore the British Empire and a charismatic figure to whom many in France were expected to rally. For his part, de Gaulle had a similar agenda, fearing at this time that America 'had entered a stage of imperialism and colonial expansion [whilst] the French empire, under control of Vichy, was like a ripe cheese, a constant temptation to a hungry appetite.'[34] In a meeting with senior members of the British Foreign Office in June 1942, de Gaulle indicated that:

> he had very little suspicion of [Britain] but deep suspicion of the Americans . . . The [US] Government did not even regard the free French as belligerents . . . Their policy was to disintegrate and neutralize the French Empire.[35]

De Gaulle's growing suspicion of America and his rapprochement with his British hosts in 1942 was in marked contrast to his efforts throughout the previous year to play the Americans off against the British in an effort to gain some independence from British control. Less than a year before de Gaulle's return to the British fold in mid-1942, he had greatly antagonized London by stating publicly that the US rather than Britain would win the war.[36] This impolitic but calculated move resulted in the degradation of Anglo-Gaullist relations that hampered the work of SOE's RF (Gaullist) Section inside France during the year. To show his displeasure, Churchill had even issued the following instructions upon de Gaulle's arrival in the UK on 31 August 1941:

(i) No one is to meet General de Gaulle on arrival; (ii) No British Authority is to see him after he has arrived or have any contact with him or with any of his subordinates; (iii) If he asks to see any official, his request is to be refused.[37]

This nadir in relations between the British and the Gaullists was further evidenced in September 1941 when the British Commander-in-Chief Middle East complained that:

> So evident is [the] anti-British attitude of the [Free French] leaders that natives have discovered [that the] best means of getting a man into trouble is to denounce him as [British]. A secret note has been issued forbidding French and native officials from having anything to do with the British.[38]

When de Gaulle began to see that America was actively seeking alternatives to his leadership, however, he took steps to smooth relations with the British, later recounting in his memoirs that:

> It was not without concern that I watched [the British] being taken in tow by the newcomers [from America] . . . Should France be unable to play her traditional leading role on the Continent, this obliteration of England, who had hitherto been so directly involved with that leadership . . . was a distinctly evil omen.[39]

While the most senior levels of both Allied governments agreed to disagree in 1942 about the future of France, SOE renewed its efforts to consolidate its position vis-à-vis the Gaullists. Baker Street negotiated an agreement with de Gaulle's staff – 'which aimed at fostering the organization of secret resistance for intelligence purposes within France'[40] – that was approved by the British Chiefs on 12 August 1942.[41] On 31 August, a supplementary accord was signed stating that 'in addition to supporting French resistance for intelligence purposes, plans would be made for specific sabotage and other subversive activities in France.'[42] Operations prior to D-Day to be conducted in conjunction with resistance groups inside France included the following:

> 1. General sabotage designed to damage the overall enemy war effort [to force] the enemy to disperse its forces throughout occupied Europe; 2. Guerrilla warfare . . . ; 3. Sabotage aimed [principally at] the German air force [including] attacks against aircraft factories, ballbearing factories, precision instrument factories, gasoline and oil dumps; 4. Sabotage designed to lower the morale of German military forces, such as derailment of German troop and leave trains, destruction by explosives of German headquarters buildings, etc.[43]

For both the British and the US, the issue of French leadership surfaced again in November 1942, when the TORCH landings directly involved the Americans in large-scale military operations in which OSS played an important role. As has been discussed in Chapter 3, '[America's] arrangements with Darlan and Giraud shocked most of the resistance elements in France, and the events in North Africa dealt a severe blow to OSS cooperation with the British in SOE and other intelligence agencies.' Whilst on the one hand, Donovan now had some of the legitimacy and independence from the British that he had been desperately seeking, he was still at a great operational disadvantage with regard to activities directed at France due to organizational shortcomings and a lack of field experience and resistance contacts. This circumstance was, of course, exacerbated by the souring of OSS-Gaullist relations. Thus, Donovan had to choose between pursuing a wholly independent course by infiltrating France as best he could through Giraudist elements, focusing instead upon building ties with both Giraudists and Gaullists independent of the British, or joining with SIS and SOE as a distinctly junior partner in French operations from the UK in which Gaullists were the leading players.[44]

The responsibility for exploring these options fell in large part to Arthur Roseborough, Bill Eddy's new deputy at OSS Algiers, who had failed to convince his superiors prior to TORCH that the Gaullists should be aggressively engaged.[45] Roseborough concluded that 'the considerable volume of primary intelligence' coming from the Gaullists since his pre-TORCH talks with André Dewavrin's BCRA remained very important to OSS. Thus, OSS's intelligence arm, especially, should '[maintain] a discreet temporization on future North African intelligence relations,'[46] and the organization as a whole must find a way to deal with de Gaulle, lest it be left even further behind the British in supporting the invasion forces. At the same time, the liberation of North Africa created exciting new opportunities for French operations by enabling OSS, SOE, and SIS 'to establish a base where agents could be recruited, from which air and sea operations for the supply of Resistance could be carried out, and, finally, where plans could be made for the support of the Allied invasion of Southern France.'[47] This required exploiting both Giraudist *and* Gaullist resources, although it still took some time before OSS special operations and BCRA forged the lasting ties that carried them both through the OVERLORD invasion.

OSS London, in fact, remained an observer when in early 1943, SOE undertook to conduct an extensive field survey of the resistance elements in the northern half of France. Baker Street was responding to a perceived need to develop a more coherent strategy for infiltrating agents into France and organizing the rapidly expanding resistance forces, especially now that a cross-Channel invasion was only a matter of time. An SOE officer and a Gaullist agent were dispatched together to the occupied zone[48] in February 1943.[49] Their mission – code-named 'Sea Horse' – was to contact as many resistance leaders as possible in the occupied zone and to: 'investigate and report on the various elements of the resistance movements in the [north]: Their strength . . . training, morale, the state and distribution of their armament; in general, their effectiveness for the activities envisaged by SOE.'[50] A second Sea Horse mission was deployed in September,[51] and the two missions together made possible 'the coordination of the responsible elements of resistance with SOE . . . It was primarily due to Sea Horse's reports that the true functions of [the] resistance [groups] were clarified.'[52]

During the first half of 1943, SOE and the Gaullists solidified their working relationship. The British supplied increasing quantities of arms, ammunition, and other supplies to resistance elements inside France and received increasing assistance from Gaullist supporters in return. Moreover, 'personnel for the field – organizers, agents, [radio] operators, etc. – were often recruited by SOE on behalf of [Gaullist intelligence]. All field personnel were trained, equipped, dispatched to the field and exfiltrated when occasion demanded by SOE acting in the interests of [the Gaullists].'[53] Thus, de Gaulle got much of the credit with resisters in France for what SOE was able to provide, all at a time when he was working hard to consolidate his authority.

OSS lagged far behind SOE in London during this period for the usual reasons of inexperience and lack of personnel. Estrangement from the Gaullists – despite Roseborough's efforts – was also a factor, as was the fact that OSS still had only 'limited dealings with the key groups that comprised the "non-Gaullist French," who in fact were close to being a British network.'[54] In December 1942, Donovan sought to improve OSS's standing in French affairs by dispatching a group of special operations officers to London. Their primary task was to explore how OSS could meaningfully support the French resistance. Franklin Canfield arrived first and was followed on 18 January 1943 by Paul van der Stricht.[55] van der Stricht's orders, back-dated to 8 December 1942, authorized him to 'set up a French desk for [OSS special operations in] London [and to serve as] Chief of the Western European Section, [Special Operations] Branch, OSS European Theater of Operations.' He held this position until 1 September 1944 and spent his first year, in his own words, 'working in practice under British tutelage.'[56]

From the outset, the van der Stricht-Canfield group 'realized that the most practical solution to the [French] problem was to work closely with [SOE, and the Gaullists where possible].'[57] The group backed Baker Street's concept of organizing resistance 'along paramilitary lines, [and] fought for a substantial increase in the quantity of arms, ammunition and other supplies sent to France to increase participation in the resistance and generate maximum support for the invading armies.'[58] The Western Europe Section began working closely with its Baker Street opposite, the so-called 'London Group' under the leadership of Eisenhower's G-2 [military intelligence chief] for TORCH, Brigadier E.E. Mockler-Ferryman, creating the basis for the joint entity that was formally established in January 1944.

While van der Stricht's section was technically independent throughout 1943, OSS personnel were attached to the RF (Gaullist) and F (Independent French) Sections at Baker Street beginning in mid-1943.[59] The Americans, in fact, accounted for approximately 10 percent[60] of what was – to all intents and purposes – a joint staff. OSS documents clearly indicate that 'close touch was maintained . . . between SOE and [the van der Stricht-Canfield group] in regard to all SOE activities and planning.'[61] From March through September, regular meetings were held 'by the SOE Planning Section, with the active participation of [OSS] personnel and [the] Free French, to discuss and draw up plans for the employment of French patriots before, on and after D-Day.'[62] These arrangements ensured that SOE controlled operations in France that originated in the UK, and the physical presence of OSS personnel at Baker Street's French desks provided the van der Stricht-Canfield group with the practical experience and contacts it had hitherto lacked. van der Stricht later observed that he could recall no serious disagreements with his SOE counterparts, but he and his staff nonetheless felt that:

> the relationship was never very close [because our] small . . . contingent was a latecomer [and] our British counterparts considered us as novices – and quite rightly so – at this sort of activity. After a few months, however, the latecomers had become increasingly important contributors to the joint operations, probably more as a result of the availability of American equipment, particularly aircraft, than ability or experience.[63]

By mid-1943, OSS London was prepared to begin sending its own agents into France. The first OSS special operations officer deployed was E.F. Floege – codenamed 'Alfred' – who parachuted into the Tours area on 13 June 1943 and operated successfully near Angers, where he had lived before the war.[64] Floege was followed in August by Victor Soscice, who sabotaged a synthetic oil plant before being captured and executed. In October, an OSS officer attached to SOE's DF-Section entered France and exfiltrated a downed US pilot and an SOE agent.[65] Other OSS personnel in the field included 'members of Inter-allied Maquis Missions,' which will soon be discussed in detail, 'organizers of networks, instructors, and about twenty radio operators . . . Their jobs were essentially of a paramilitary or sabotage nature, or one of liaison with French resistance leaders.'[66] OSS staffed 'positions throughout all echelons of the joint [SOE-OSS] headquarters as well as [for] field operations . . . Large stocks of American weapons and equipment were procured and a station to pack equipment for air delivery was established.'[67] With SOE's French sections leading, OSS began to help to organize the resistance: 'into small, secret, self-contained cells directed from London by [radio] . . . These cells would build and husband their strength until called into action for specific assignments as their territory became significant to the invading armies.'[68]

Moreover, OSS Switzerland involved itself increasingly in French resistance activities in 1943, but in so doing, ran afoul of SOE. Baker Street claimed that this work violated previous bilateral agreements providing for 'SOE's control of activities [in] the occupied countries of Europe.' Charles Hambro explained to OSS's David Bruce on 19 May 1943 that:

> Resistance movements in the unoccupied zone, [whose] directives are subject to [SOE] control, seem each to have appointed an individual representative in Switzerland to make contact with the British and American authorities. The result is that these [groups] have set up in Berne a new committee [that is seeking]

to negotiate for financial support and materials, deliveries, etc., with [OSS]. There are in addition a number of other emissaries self-appointed or otherwise who are naturally drawn towards Switzerland in the hopes of financial aid. The resultant situation must be utterly confusing and the security position deplorable. It can only lead sooner or later to a disaster inside France.[69]

Hambro felt that he was in the untenable position of having to make good on promises made by OSS Switzerland to which he had not been privy. He asked Bruce to tell OSS Switzerland that:

Control of the French resistance movements comes within the sphere of British influence as [previously agreed] . . . The French resistance must be kept together at all costs to avoid their disintegration into independent units . . . A single emissary should be appointed to maintain contact with the British and American representatives in Switzerland [and] no directives on policy or operational matters should in any circumstance be initiated from Switzerland or North Africa, as they must first submit to the test of whether or not they fit into the military plan which is laid down in London.[70]

Bruce agreed, but refused to limit OSS Switzerland to one contact with the French. He informed Hambro that he had instructed Allen Dulles in Bern that he was not to discontinue contacts: 'provided that (1) the policy is well coordinated and (2) the requirements of security are fully safeguarded.'[71] OSS's Swiss activities – while achieving some success in France[72] – nonetheless continued to be a source of irritation in OSS-SOE relations for some time to come. They did, however, give the British an additional incentive to involve OSS London in their French operations.

The progress that SOE and OSS had made in France, meanwhile, was jeopardized by a series of operational failures by the British in 1942–3, and by opposition from SIS and the Allied Air Forces. The set-backs in the field complicated efforts to convince Allied military planners that the French resistance could play a key role in the coming invasion. Claude Dansey of SIS, moreover, was 'concerned primarily about the security of [Broadway's] intelligence networks and ever fearful that the activist resistance would blow them, and the Air Marshals [Arthur Harris and Carl Spaatz], anxious to keep their planes for bombing operations, would minimize the size and the potential value of resistance forces.'[73] As van der Stricht observed:

The German penetration of resistance networks had certainly shaken confidence in the value of resistance forces. During the last half of 1943, despite the impending invasion, arms deliveries to France had a lower priority than deliveries to Italy and Yugoslavia.[74]

Specifically, SOE's position was first compromised in 1942 when the *Abwehr*[75] in Holland captured one of its radio operators and turned him into a double agent. The subsequent false messages sent to Baker Street resulted in the capture of 52

SOE agents over the next year. The Gestapo's intensive countersubversive campaign in 1943, meanwhile, resulted in the loss of 'virtually all of SOE's principal agents [and] subagents around Paris together with many tons of hidden weapons.' German penetrations of SOE networks in France continued over the winter of 1943–4, resulting in the loss of 18 more agents.[76] This bolstered the arguments of those in the US and British military establishments 'who felt that the resistance was insecure, that it could not be controlled, that no one could be sure that arms dropped to them would be effectively used.'[77] It was the growing strength and success of the *Maquis* in the second half of 1943, however, that convinced Allied planners to include the resistance forces in their invasion plans and to establish and place a 'joint' SOE-OSS component under the direct control of the Combined Operations Staff (COSSAC) from September or November, depending on the source.[78]

THE MAQUIS AND THE SPECIAL INTER-ALLIED MISSIONS

> The real Maquis, the patriotic French people who risked everything to aid in the liberation of France, were tremendous. They lived without adequate food, shelter or clothing and were continually being hunted down. Many of them carried on the fight for three or four years, operating as individuals or in small bands. They made the occupation of France a continuous hell for the Germans.[79]

The *Maquis* posed perhaps the greatest organizational challenge for the Anglo-OSS teams working with the French, but they also held the most potential of any of the resistance elements for large-scale subversion. Facing deportation by the Germans for forced labor, the men of the disparate groups of *Maquis* were from all walks of life. They had fled to the mountains and forests throughout the country to wage largely disorganized guerrilla warfare against the Germans and their collaborationist French proxies. They called themselves *Maquis* after the Corsican word for a parcel of wild, bushy land[80] and loosely organized themselves into small bands; they lacked effective leadership, training, arms, food, and clothing.[81]

As the *Maquis* expanded significantly in number during 1943 – largely as a result of increased German labor demands – their activities came more and more to the attention of the SOE-OSS element in London. In spite of the many hardships they endured, some *Maquis* bands had, by the autumn of 1943, become so strong that they were 'able to prevent any German from entering their territories [and] were a serious threat to the strong German armies surrounding them.'[82] SOE-OSS estimated in January 1944 that there were some 40–50 000 *Maquis*[83] – a number that was expected to rise significantly in the time left before the invasion – yet serious efforts to coordinate their activities and to provide them with adequate supply had not yet been undertaken. van der Stricht blamed 'the Air Force generals [who] were eager to use every available plane to bomb German industry [and] were not sympathetic to diverting planes to the supply of Frenchmen who did not figure in their military plans.'[84] While this was certainly true – the total commitment of 'Bomber' Harris and Carl Spaatz to their strategic bombing strat egy and unwillingness to part with aircraft is well documented – SOE and OSS had other problems. The two clandestine organizations, along with the Gaullist movement, lacked the necessary instructor personnel to train the *Maquis* properly provide a reliable means of communicating with the numerous guerrilla bands and gather specific information about each group.[85]

The Allies sought to remedy these shortcomings by deploying 'Special Inter-Allied Missions' to liaise with the *Maquis* bands. These missions differed from other resistance aid programs in France in that they were 'the first attempt to organize the *Maquis* as a paramilitary force on a tripartite basis coming under direct command of Allied headquarters in London.' SOE's David Keswick is often credited with establishing the tripartite structure of the *Maquis* missions, but OSS documents indicate that van der Stricht's Western Europe Section was in fact responsible. OSS London 'had long felt that the French should have their full share, and should finally assume complete control of their own resistance subject to the requirements of the theater commander.'[86] Such an important organizational contribution by OSS at that time indicates that the Americans were functioning as partners with SOE's French sections, albeit still junior ones.

The Special Inter-Allied Missions – also called the Special *Maquis* Missions – were comprised of SOE, OSS, and Gaullist operations officers.[87] Their objective was:

> to put at the disposal of the Allied High Command, London, for D-Day operations, a number of self contained units, located in appropriate sub-regions of the *Maquis*. Such units were comparable to military formations introduced into the country by parachute and hidden until the day when directed to cooperate with an invasion of the Continent by Allied military forces.[88]

It was deemed imperative that the *Maquis* conserve their strength and not rise prematurely. In London, SOE and OSS agreed that a system of rigid centralization of resistance forces in France might actually impede their ability to react rapidly to the unfolding military situation during the invasion. As the situation was apt to be fluid and different in every area, the *Maquis* missions – in conjunction with the *Comité d'Action* of the resistance – would seek to:

> decentralize the [*Maquis*] into a number of autonomous districts, each comprising two or three departments, separately linked with the Allied High Command through the representative of the *Comité d'Action* in London acting as the executive agent of the French High Command. The links were provided by having separate [radio] communications between each district and London.[89]

The first of many *Maquis* missions was called 'Cantinier-Xavier' and was successfully deployed to France on 18 October 1943.[90] It was handled jointly by Baker Street's F and RF Sections, presumably in full consultation with the van der Stricht-Canfield group from OSS. Cantinier-Xavier was instructed to make contact with the *Maquis* near Lyons, and – like all future missions – to seek to create 'a more effective integration of the *Maquis* activities with the operations of the Allied military forces [arriving on D-Day].' It was in no way to command the *Maquis* groups,[91] although some Allied officers did play a leadership role. It was only to provide periodic progress reports, function as liaison between the *Maquis* and the Allied High Command, and give advice to the *Maquis* military chiefs 'in matters of security, organization, day-to-day sabotage, and D-Day plans.' Moreover, like all future missions, Cantinier-Xavier was to stress quality over quantity with regards to *Maquis* recruitment. It was also to focus the mission's energies and resources only upon those groups that could be used 'directly against the enemy' in attacks against 'morale, causing the maximum degree of dispersal of German occupying troops, and disrupting and destroying the German Air Force.' The *Maquis* – supported first by the missions, then later by Jedburghs and Allied special forces units – were to 'carry out specific tasks [when called upon] either of demolition or preservation of essential communications or installations . . . foment[ing] and support[ing] uprisings by the civilian population.'[92]

Cantinier-Xavier confirmed that the *Maquis* had great potential, but also revealed that much needed to be done if the groups were to play a meaningful role in the coming invasion. While the *Maquis* with whom the mission was in contact had weapons, for example, they had little ammunition, lacked funds, and needed false documents. The countersubversive efforts of the Germans in 1943 had robbed the *Maquis* of their most effective leaders, and many *agents provocateurs* had penetrated the groups. Transportation was another area where the *Maquis* had shortages, and *Maquis* estimates of the strength of collaborationist French militia – the *Milice* – operating against them were everywhere exaggerated. These were problems common to many if not all of the *Maquis* groups, and the inter-Allied mission succeeded in righting some of them by first fusing together three local resistance organizations, then insisting that more rigorous recruitment procedures be followed.[93] The missions began to have a positive effect almost immediately, with successful *Maquis* attacks on a ballbearing factory being reported on 13 November and a total of 81 enemy locomotives being disabled between October and December in just one regional department.[94] The effectiveness of resisters of all stripes, in fact, was up significantly in the second half of 1943, largely as a result of the efforts of SOE.[95]

One of the first truly tripartite *Maquis* missions was code-named 'Union' and was deployed in January 1944. Union succeeded in making contact with *Maquis* near Lyons and found an 'extremely confused administrative situation in the area, where several resistance organizations with divergent political views and loyalties were working independently and often at cross purposes.' It was soon discovered that these groups suffered from many of the same problems as those previously contacted by Cantinier-Xavier, such as lack of transportation, weapons, finance, morale, etc. In a relatively short period of time, Union succeeded in coordinating the activities of the resistance groups in the region and establishing an effective radio net and clandestine courier service, but failed to provide adequate supply due to the chronic shortage of aircraft available for clandestine operations. Nonetheless, Union was deemed a success and with increased support after D-Day, accomplished much in the way of guerrilla action and sabotage.[96]

At about the same time that Union was deployed, the joint SOE-OSS *Maquis* strategy found an important ally in the person of Winston Churchill, who was seeking a means to re-energize his plans for a drive into Germany and Austria from Italy. The Italian campaign by this time was stalled south of Rome, leaving Churchill less able to argue against the strong desire of Roosevelt and his military advisors to accelerate and strengthen the forces that were to invade France, drawing troops and equipment from the Mediterranean theater to do so. The US had also devised a plan to invade southern France – code named 'ANVIL' – involving the redeployment of some Allied forces from Italy, which would impede the Italian effort. ANVIL – whose code name was later changed to 'DRAGOON' – had been approved at Tehran in November 1943,[97] but Churchill almost certainly hoped that the plan might be shelved. The *Maquis*, if properly supported, might force Germany to draw down some of its own forces in Italy to meet the guerrilla threat in France, and thus open the way for an Allied advance in Italy before ANVIL could be properly organized. 'The more the French Resistance could accomplish the less need there might be for landing craft to be employed in southern France.'[98] Churchill's vociferous championing of Tito's Partisans in Yugoslavia at this time had much the same intent.

When Churchill's interests were identified by SOE, Baker Street devised a means to focus his attention on its needs in France, principally as a means to break the deadlock with the Air Ministry over aircraft required for clandestine activities. De Gaulle and resistance leader d'Astier had already lobbied the Prime Minister in Marrakech – shortly after Christmas – for more materiel support,[99] and Churchill had subsequently met in London with SOE's Mockler-Ferryman, Minister of Economic Warfare Lord Selborne, and d'Astier on 17 January to explore the issue. The British leader was clearly warming to the idea of increasing support to the resistance – he ordered Selborne on 31 January to double materiel deliveries in March over those planned for February[100] – and it was believed that a first-hand report of the situation in France might add significantly to the momentum. SOE's F.F.E. Yeo-Thomas, recently returned from a survey trip in France for RF (Gaullist) Section,[101] was sent to the Prime Minister on 1 February:

> Moved by Yeo-Thomas' account of the *Maquis*, and their organization, their will to fight and their needs for arms and clothing, Churchill dictated a memo on the spot directing the Air Ministry to put 100 serviceable aircraft, capable of making 250 sorties during a moon period, at the disposal of the RF section of SOE. Within 48 hours, 22 Halifaxes, 12 Liberators, 36 Sterlings, 6 Albemarles and a number of smaller aircraft were made available.[102]

If Churchill needed any more reassurances, he got them on 10 February when his Defence Committee reported that it was 'much impressed with the results which might be expected from a larger scale of operations in [support of] French *Maquis*.'[103]

Churchill's intervention came at a time when OSS was still able to contribute only a small number of aircraft for French operations – US General Spaatz refused yet another request for planes by OSS and SOE on 12 February[104] – and inexorably changed the fortunes of the *Maquis*. The further tilt in favor of SOE in the amount of resources committed to French operations, however, had the practical effect of reinforcing the second-class status of OSS London and amounted to 10 air sorties by SOE for every 1 by the Americans.[105] This 'frustrating period,' as van der Stricht later described it, made it appear to the resistance forces that the British were doing everything and the Americans nothing, and that this circumstance was related to US hostility to de Gaulle, and thus was an inexcusable interference in French politics: 'At every opportunity, [Donovan and Bruce] urged that more [US] sorties were needed not only to support the forthcoming landings but also to dispel any idea that the [US] had political motivations in not helping the French . . . more fully.'[106] As OSS was finding out in Yugoslavia, only a measure of equality in contributions could secure for it equality of status with the British and a measure of independence.

SEMI-INTEGRATED ORGANIZATIONAL COLLABORATION

The relationship between [OSS and the British secret services in France] – a relationship perhaps unique in the history of warfare – finally became so close that at the beginning of 1944 it was considered advisable to substitute partnership for liaison. There was constituted therefore a Joint Headquarters which subsequently operated as a single unit.[107] (Internal OSS Assessment)

On 10 January 1944, SOE's 'London Group' and the special operations element of OSS London were combined and subordinated to the newly created Supreme Headquarters Allied Expeditionary Force (SHAEF) under General Eisenhower.[108] SOE's Mockler-Ferryman and OSS's Colonel Joseph Haskell, the latter a former operational planner on the Combined Operations Staff Supreme Allied Command (COSSAC), were jointly named to lead what was later officially designated 'Special Forces Headquarters' or 'SFHQ.'[109] At the same time, van der Stricht and Baker Street's Robin Brook, who as a regional controller had supervised the work of SOE's two French sections, were jointly named to lead the Western European Directorate of the new combined staff. Thereafter, SFHQ was empowered by SHAEF as 'the agency qualified to handle all resistance in enemy occupied territory,'[110] and the latter had to approve all special operations prior to their execution.[111] Thus, for the first time, all approved special operations activities in France had full military authority, as well as the personal backing of the Prime Minister, which greatly improved their efficiency in the six-month run-up to the invasion.[112] This authority was further extended in May, when Supreme Headquarters took control of special operations in southern France which had hitherto been under the authority of the British-led Allied Mediterranean Command.[113] Perhaps of equal importance for OSS, the creation of Special Forces Headquarters placed Americans for the first time 'in a position of joint responsibility for the activities of all sections of the former 'London Group' of SOE,'[114] even though OSS's still paltry contribution of aircraft made it less than an equal partner in the endeavor.

Haskell's recruitment by OSS as joint chief of Special Forces Headquarters proved to be inspired. As a West Point graduate and former Combined Operations staff officer, he had an 'impeccable military standing to deal with American and British generals, [as well as] connections in the Allied Planning Staff and in the US Army Air Force which were to be immensely helpful.' Not only was he of the stature and rank to deal with Mockler-Ferryman more or less on equal terms, he brought to the operational level of OSS a legitimacy with the military that it had hitherto lacked. Moreover, van der Stricht described him as 'sensitive to the complexity of his relations with the British and patient, considerate and perceptive in his dealings with his own staff.'[115] Haskell's 'intimate knowledge' of the closely guarded plan for OVERLORD – acquired at Combined Operations – also allowed him to make truly informed decisions about the employment of resistance groups acting in support of the invasion forces.

Before the activities of the new Special Forces Headquarters are examined, however, three significant developments, which had a lasting impact on the dynamics of the tripartite Anglo-OSS-Gaullist relationship, must first be explained. These took place towards the end of 1943 and laid the groundwork for the establishment of a much closer working arrangement between OSS and the Gaullists, which gradually marginalized SOE's work in France – *vis-à-vis* OSS – during and after the invasion. The first occurred in November, when de Gaulle ousted his rival Giraud from the *Comité Français de la Libération Nationale* (CFLN) in Algiers. Giraud remained in name as Commander-in-Chief of the French Army until April 1944,[116] but to all intents and purposes, was no longer a force to be reckoned with in French affairs. Giraud's fall prompted the US to pursue both a *rapprochement* with de Gaulle at the strategic level, and a strengthening of ties at the working level, particularly between OSS and Dewavrin's BCRA. The Gaullists were amenable to these overtures, particularly since they had little time to consolidate their control over the still largely disparate French resistance forces.

The second major development was somewhat related to the first in that it concerned an attempt by de Gaulle – in the wake of his victory over Giraud – to subordinate to his organization all military directives by the Allied Command to the resistance forces. His demands divided SOE and OSS on how to respond and left both more willing to deal bilaterally with the French – even within the trilateral arrangement – than had been the case since 1941. The trouble began when SOE sent an *aide mémoire* to OSS London on 25 November recommending that both organizations act together to thwart de Gaulle's initiative. SOE argued that the French should be told in no uncertain terms that the Allies intended to communicate directly with the resistance groups, and if the Gaullists refused, aid should be withheld from them all and the Gaullists held to account.[117] Baker Street believed that only in this way could de Gaulle be brought into line, and was willing to risk a break in relations, although it thought this to be unlikely.[118]

OSS demurred, arguing that the question was not one of whether or not the resistance forces should continue to be supported, but 'one of selecting which portions [should] on account of their immunity to political consideration continue to receive [aid].' OSS recommended that rather than threatening the French, the Gaullists should be reassured that Giraud's ouster did not affect Allied plans to conduct the paramilitary program as previously agreed.[119] The Americans felt that this approach was more constructive and was justified because most resistance groups were prepared to fight, regardless of politics. As van der Stricht wrote on 14 December: 'The plans of a few politically minded Resistance leaders outside of France may not constitute a sufficient justification for our no longer sending deliveries of stores to the [French] patriots whose sole purpose is to fight the common enemy . . . SOE appears to be more hasty and uncompromising [than us].'[120]

In explaining his rationale to Donovan, van der Stricht revealed much about the standing of OSS within the tripartite arrangement at this time, and he was consistent with OSS's policy elsewhere of seeking independent arrangements whenever possible. Specifically, he noted that:

> (a) [OSS London] is barely starting activities in France, has had fewer dealings with the French Special Services, and as a result, has fewer grievances against them than SOE . . . and (b) there would seem to exist a tendency on SOE's part to rely on its separate network (F Section) and to disregard rather easily the [Gaullist] French networks (RF Section) whenever difficulties arise between SOE and the French Special Services.[121]

Thus, OSS sided with the weaker tripartite partner (the Gaullists) against the stronger one (SOE), much as it was doing at the same time in Yugoslavia with the Chetniks, perhaps also as a means to exert independence from the British. SOE backed down in this instance, and OSS advised that:

> '[We are] not in a position to take any drastic course with the [Gaullists, because the Allies have not yet] approached the French with an equitable overall plan providing a set up in which they would have a rightful share in the organization of Resistance among their own compatriots.'[122]

Even as the structures to promote greater Anglo-OSS ties were being created, the seeds were being sown for separate if parallel relations with the French within the tripartite arrangement.

The third occurrence of particular significance in late-1943 involved the deterioration of relations between SOE and the Gaullists over the latter's 'abuse' of communications facilities for political purposes. The primary dispute evidently arose from a seemingly trivial incident – but one probably symptomatic of a trend – that nearly caused relations between Baker Street and the BCRA to 'break down' in the late autumn, according to van der Stricht. At issue was a case in which an SOE officer refused to transmit a long Gaullist political message to the field, only to have it resubmitted in encrypted form. Baker Street decided to break the French code to check the content of the message and discovered that the political material had not been edited out as the French had claimed. When SOE objected, the Gaullists accused Baker Street of spying on them and seeking to interfere in their internal political affairs.[123] When combined with the significant operational failures being experienced by F and RF Sections in France at the time,[124] it is not surprising that bilateral relations were strained. While clamouring for moderation in dealing with the French, van der Stricht nonetheless admitted in a December 1943 message to OSS Washington that 'there is no doubt that some of the incidents which have occurred between SOE and the French might have led us, under similar conditions, to [be] less tolerant.'[125]

Even as the tripartite partners bickered and the nature of their relationships with each other evolved, a specific strategy was being developed for the use of resistance forces in invasion-support activities. Between March and September 1943,[126] SOE, OSS, and the Gaullists together drafted and refined nine separate plans for D-Day operations. These were for action largely meant to delay enemy troop movements; they targeted railway communications (Plan *Vert*) and turntables (Plan *Grenouille*), armored formations (Plan *Tortue*), headquarters units (Plan *Noir*), telecommunications (Plan *Violet*), ammunition dumps (Plan *Jaune*), petrol dumps (Plan *Rouge*), counter-demolition to save essential services and equipment (Plan *Momie*), and protection of Allied mines (Plan *Gris*).[127] Supplementary activities included misdirection of traffic, placement of road blocks, derailment of trains, the conduct of ambushes, and sabotage of factories aimed at reducing the flow of war materiel to the Germans. Planning was complicated by the fact that the French, for security reasons, were not to be given any details about the invasion plan. 'This made for an awkward relationship in that the French were under considerable pressure to develop specific capabilities for contingencies of which they were deliberately kept in ignorance.'[128] After study, SOE and OSS decided that 'the resistance movement would be most effective if it limited its operations to those traditionally associated with guerrilla warfare.'[129] It was agreed that only the plans dealing with railways, armored units, and telecommunications were practicable, and the other plans were subordinated to *Vert*, *Tortue*, and *Violet* in autumn 1943.[130]

During the first half of 1944, SOE and OSS strongly discouraged their French partners from undertaking large-scale armed uprisings. Small-scale sabotage, however, continued apace, resulting in the degradation of some 100 factories producing war materiel.[131] According to OSS:

[London] kept repeating its instructions to those who had received arms to remain quiet until such time as action on their part could be coordinated with an Allied landing or advance. Premature actions invariably brought severe reprisals from the Germans, bitter criticisms of the resistance activities and a sense of frustration to those involved in such well meant but inadvisable actions.[132]

It is interesting that SOE so clearly recognized that the realities of reprisals, morale problems, etc., applied to the French, but not equally to the Chetniks in Yugoslavia. This double standard was, perhaps, due to the fact that France was about to be invaded by Allied troops, whilst Yugoslavia was where the Allies wanted to draw Axis forces.[133] Nonetheless, this inconsistency helps to explain some of the rifts in Anglo-OSS relations in the Balkans examined in the preceding chapter, but which did not apply to that relationship in France.

Once SOE and OSS London were combined in January 1944, the pace of resistance planning, training, and organizational work accelerated markedly. The Jedburgh and Sussex programs, which will later be covered in detail, were well under way, and the inter-Allied missions succeeded in supporting many of the *Maquis* groups. Another attempt by the British Chiefs of Staff in January to prevent any 'independent' special operations by OSS in what they considered to be their 'spheres of strategic responsibility' was thwarted by the US Chiefs, who argued that SOE and OSS were in full accord and were supervised in France by Supreme Headquarters.[134] By February, van der Stricht and SOE's Brook, together with the head of Gaullist intelligence in London – P.E.J. Manuel[135] – were named to chair jointly a committee to handle all *Maquis*-related affairs,[136] marking another milestone in tripartite cooperation. A month later, de Gaulle felt strong enough to announce that all of the resistance groups in France were henceforth to be considered as one entity for military operations under the umbrella of the *Forces Françaises de l'Intérieur* (FFI).[137] De Gaulle benefited personally from the substantial increase in materiel support air-dropped to the resistance by SOE and OSS in February and particularly during the first half of March.[138] America's manpower contribution for special operations, moreover, began to be an important factor in the spring, both in filling the gaps left by German countersubversive successes the previous year and fulfilling new requirements:

Passy and [SOE's Maurice] Buckmaster, [head of F-Section], with [OSS's] van der Stricht and [William] Grell now able to provide American bodies and working actively with them, sent in [50] of the most experienced and field tested operators they still had to fill the gaps . . . and to strengthen the circuits established and still functioning in the south, east and center of France.[139]

As spring wore on and the pressures on the combined SOE-OSS organization increased, special operations gradually became more closely integrated into the work being done at Supreme Headquarters. On 23 March, SHAEF was ready to assume full control of Special Forces Headquarters and began to designate target-ing priorities and direct other activities. Three weeks later, SHAEF dictated a long-term policy to SFHQ by ordering that French 'patriot forces' be organized and equipped up to a maximum of 172 000 by D-Day + 300 [days] 'for the purpose of garrisoning liberated areas and for internal security.'[140] This increased the workload of SOE-OSS substantially. Meanwhile, the 'integration' of OSS special operations with SOE's 'London Group,' which had been accomplished on 10 January and officially completed when SFHQ received its mandate from Supreme Headquarters on 1 May, was deemed 'satisfactory' by OSS, which described it as 'the most effective method of making full use of resistance groups in support of military operations.'[141] The British Chiefs had noted in April that the 'closest co-ordination is said to exist between [OSS] and SOE, and any concerns Donovan may have had about OSS's 'second class status' were partially allayed by Britain's acceptance of the principle of 'continuing independent OSS operations under the control and direction of [Eisenhower].'[142]

Nonetheless, the OSS contingent at SFHQ continued to appeal to Washington for more officers to redress the imbalance in OSS-SOE staffers. Pleas for an in-crease in US airlift for special operations were redoubled, as such a contribution was believed to be the only way 'to achieve parity [with the British] in support of resistance groups.'[143] The attention of the Supreme Commander was focused on these problems by de Gaulle's public statement on 30 April crediting the British exclusively for the substantial increase in arms deliveries over the February–April period to the French resistance. General Marshall in Washington advised Eisenhower that same day of the interest of 'high authorities [in] the relative US and British efforts in furnishing supplies to the French.' Eisenhower was ordered to provide a breakdown of all OSS and SOE supplies delivered to the French in the February–April period so that ratios could be established and corrected if neces-sary.[144] As early as 17 April, Marshall had warned Eisenhower that: 'The question of arming the resistance groups has become an important political issue and the impression has spread that the British are doing [everything].' The Supreme Com-mander was requested to 'effect equalization of effort between the [US and UK].'[145] Eisenhower's report to Marshall on 6 May identified the disparities shown in the Table.

On the basis of this obvious imbalance, Eisenhower ordered that two additional squadrons of US aircraft be allotted to OSS-SOE for French operations.[146] Crew shortages and training requirements meant that many of these planes did not be-come fully operational until late June.[147] By D-Day, however, Special Forces Headquarters had the following available aircraft:

(a) Based in the UK – 22 Halifaxes [and] 57 Liberators; (b) Based in North Af-rica – 18 Halifaxes, 15 Liberators, 3 Fortresses . . . Total: 115 aircraft.[148]

All aircraft and materiel destined for the French were pooled. Deliveries were made 'indiscriminately to groups in the field based on operational requirements.'[149] The increasing OSS contribution 'gave added weight to American views on [special operations] policy.'[150]

Tonnage of supplies procured in the US and furnished to the French:		
	OSS	*SOE*
February 1944	0	277.75
March	1.5	564.75
April	20.25	439.5
Tonnage of supplies delivered:		
	OSS	*SOE*
February	26	251.75
March	56.75	509.5
April	107.25	352.5
Number of air sorties:		
	OSS	*SOE*
February	57	337
March	62	584
April	90	371
Aircraft available:		
	OSS	*SOE*
February	14	50
March	12	85
April	28	56

This 'added weight' allowed OSS to realize several important objectives before the end of May. First, SOE-acquired intelligence from Western Europe – which had hitherto reached OSS only after it had been vetted by SIS – began to be disseminated directly to OSS London, which reported that 'efforts to extend this arrangement to global SOE intelligence are now in progress.' Second, the relationship between OSS and Britain's Political Warfare Executive improved substantially, resulting in OSS London's Morale Branch – which dealt with covert propaganda, *inter alia* – 'steadily achieving greater parity of contribution to 'black' operations.'[151] Perhaps most importantly, the British finally agreed in May to OSS's proposal to give the French 'not only an equal voice in the direction of resistance in France, but [also] administrative control.'[152] In theory, this was to be achieved through the establishment of *Etat-Major Forces Françaises de l'Intérieur* (EMFFI) – a headquarters element under the command of Gaullist General Pierre Koenig and staffed on a tripartite basis.[153] EMFFI was to relieve Special Forces Headquarters of responsibility for France,[154] but in effect, SFHQ became part of *Etat-Major*.

Similarly, Allied Forces Headquarters (AFHQ) in North Africa established on 23 May a tripartite SOE-OSS-Gaullist unit called the Special Projects Operations Center (SPOC) in Algiers. SPOC was to mirror Special Forces Headquarters in London, but for the direction of resistance in support of the ANVIL / DRAGOON invasion of southern France.[155] Gaullist General Couchet was named commander at Allied Forces Headquarters of all SPOC-directed resistance, although in practice – as was the case at SFHQ – SOE and OSS continued to direct operations.[156] Anglo-American relations at SPOC were considered by OSS participants to be 'extremely cordial;' the Americans were advised that their activities constituted a truly 'joint operation, [with OSS] authority and responsibility in no sense subordinate to the British.' The OSS contingent at SPOC, however, continued to be plagued by a 'lack of experienced and trained personnel, [and] depended a great deal on the British due to their long experience and thorough knowledge of the situation.' As late as mid-June, OSS observed that 'only slowly are we able to exert a positive and equal voice in operations [at SPOC].'[157]

Koenig's EMFFI was an effort by Supreme Headquarters to unify all aspects of French special operations in advance of the Normandy invasion. It amounted to the 'practical merger' of SOE's F (Independent) and RF (Gaullist) sections, and its joining together with the joint Jedburgh Section and OSS [special operations].[158] Structurally, *Etat-Major* consisted of six sections, covering personnel and administration (*Premier Bureau*), tactical intelligence, counterintelligence, and false documents (*Deuxième Bureau*), operations and air transport (*Troisième Bureau*), planning, arms, and supplies (*Quatrième Bureau*), communications (*Cinquième Bureau*), training, Jedburghs, special forces, and the inter-Allied missions (*Sixième Bureau*). According to van der Stricht, who was named with SOE's Buckmaster and Koenig's assistant, Colonel A. Ziegler, to jointly run the EMFFI staff after D-Day:

> The purpose of EMFFI was not merely to end the lack of coordination between the Passy [RF-Section] and Buckmaster [F-Section] forces . . . In the mind of the French, this was an instrument to control fully the [resistance] after the landing, and it is fair to assume that some Gaullists had other purposes in mind than paramilitary operations.[159]

Eisenhower probably was also concerned that in the event OVERLORD had to be canceled at the last moment – after the resistance forces had been called to arms – the French command would share accountability with Supreme Headquarters for the subsequent resistance casualties.

The fact that Special Forces Headquarters continued to control all of the essential elements of operations in France during OVERLORD makes it clear that *Etat-Major* was indeed a means by which SHAEF could control the French. Though it technically came under Koenig's authority from D-Day onward, SFHQ in reality continued to be run by SOE and OSS, in consultation with the Gaullists, and its actions drove Koenig's headquarters. On 26 May, Anglo-OSS intentions were made clear in an OSS report titled, 'Command and Control of Resistance':

> The French recognize that [EMFFI] does not amount necessarily to a total merger of all personnel and services. In fact personnel would continue to come under the jurisdiction of their own authorities and all matters connected therewith would continue to be handled in Baker Street, [by OSS London or BCRA] . . . Packing stations and airfields would remain under [Mockler-Ferryman] and [Haskell]. In short, the component parts of SFHQ which are [service-related] would remain . . . under the direct command of [Mockler-Ferryman] and [Haskell], whereas at the [staff] level . . . Koenig's views would find their full expression not only through the representatives he will appoint but also through his authority to veto any action of which he does not approve.[160]

To add credence to the charade of French command, Mockler-Ferryman and Haskell were designated as Koenig's deputies, and Buckmaster (SOE), van der Stricht (OSS), and Koenig's Chief of Staff jointly ran EMFFI, within which Gaullist, SOE, and OSS officers were assigned. The most critical jobs, moreover, went to either British or US officers, including the operations and special missions sections, which were assigned to SOE. As Arthur Funk has noted:

> [SHAEF] made the decisions and presented de Gaulle and Koenig with a *fait accompli* . . . Even when Koenig's command was confirmed on June 6, he was informed that orders from SHAEF would be transmitted to him via SFHQ, in other words, through his own deputies. It was clear that for the time being he would simply be a figurehead so far as the Allied command was concerned. Not until June 17 did he receive a specific directive from SHAEF . . . SFHQ really ran the show . . . In July [orders] were given to the effect that SFHQ would in fact as well as theory come under Koenig . . . But this separation was not carried out until August 21, by which time three-quarters of France had been liberated.[161]

Dewavrin, who was appointed as Koenig's Chief of Staff, said after the war that he and Koenig were not even consulted – only informed by SOE's Gubbins and OSS's Bruce – about the decision on the eve of OVERLORD to issue the orders to the French resistance forces to set in motion all 'destruction and sabotage operations.'[162] So much for Koenig's 'veto' rights.

Nonetheless, the establishment of Koenig's command created a framework for what later became the actual as well as figurative control by Frenchmen over Frenchmen, and was largely a result of American persuasion. OSS in great measure made EMFFI possible, and the creation of the French headquarters proved to be another milestone in the coming together of Franco-American interests. With OVERLORD under American command and US troops soon engaged in a break-out from the Normandy beaches, French and OSS interests naturally coincided. The fact that British forces became bogged down at Caen after encountering the main German armored forces only reinforced the Franco-US bond because OSS and the Gaullists had to work so closely together to support the American drive. 'Circumstances,' van der Stricht later recounted, 'and not any policy decision, had made the paramilitary operations of French Resistance a Franco-American affair.'[163] Van der Stricht's close personal relationship with his Gaullist opposites at EMFFI, especially Ziegler and de Gaulle's somewhat Anglophobic[164] aide Jean Millet, moreover, also 'helped make the Americans prominent in the tripartite staff after the landing.'[165] And when SOE began to express its fear that the Gaullists would try to use the weapons being dropped to their loyalists to consolidate power over non-Gaullist resisters, OSS gained further favor with Koenig by choosing to play down such concerns.[166]

THE JEDBURGH PLAN

> The function of Jedburghs will be strategic in that they will operate some distance behind the lines, and their role in the field is likely to be one of some duration. But the actual tasks carried out will be of a tactical nature. They will harass and hinder the enemy's movement in the rear . . . working in conjunction with their resistance groups.[167]   (OSS paper)

The inclusion of OSS by SOE in the Jedburgh Plan from spring 1943 – discussed in Chapter 4 – was predicated upon an apparently contradictory set of assumptions, yet in practice functioned logically and with notable success. While Baker Street had been forced to concede at the start that OSS could operate autonomously within the Jedburgh structure, running its own agents if it chose, the Americans agreed in exchange to SOE's 'operational direction.' This murky situation was made less so when the integration of OSS personnel into SOE's two French sections was accomplished later in the year. The SOE-OSS coordinating committee that followed this largely informal integration clarified the situation further, and once the committee set up a 'Jedburgh Section' to 'handle all aspects of Jedburgh training and field deployment [from] April 1944 onwards,' genuine integration was achieved.[168] The subordination of SOE and OSS work in northwest Europe to the Combined Operations Staff (COSSAC) in September/November 1943, moreover, facilitated this process by ensuring that the two sides could coexist on roughly equal terms under military direction.

By all accounts, working level cooperation and division of responsibilities between SOE and OSS on the Jedburgh Plan occurred naturally and almost always conformed to practical considerations. For example, when the task of recruiting 'Jed' personnel proved difficult, largely because the best candidates were usefully employed elsewhere, SOE and OSS agreed to recruit separately from their respective military services. Similar but distinctly parallel efforts were pursued in this regard, with both sides administering their own examinations and undertaking other assessment procedures to identify unsuitable volunteers.[169] The British tended to recruit tank crewmen as Jedburgh radio operators because they were used to working in a team environment and already had infantry-type training; some 55 officers were taken from first-line British regiments in the UK. OSS, meanwhile, recruited radio operators from US Army signals schools, and 55 officers from various airborne, infantry, and artillery units.[170] These groups were later pared down, first during separate then via joint assessment and training programs.

When circumstances dictated a possible benefit to joint activities, SOE and OSS explored collaborative endeavors fully and evidently without much regard for parochial interests. This was almost certainly due in part to the mounting pressure to prepare fully a Jedburgh force in the short time left before D-Day, but reflected other integrative moves, such as the Sussex program, and later the creation of Special Forces Headquarters and the Special Projects Operations Center. In December 1943, for example, a joint SOE-OSS recruiting team visited French regiments in northwest Africa, returning with approximately 100 French volunteers. Three hundred Jedburgh field operatives were needed in all, along with 300 additional personnel to liaise with Supreme Headquarters and with Army and Army Group commands, and to staff the Special Jedburgh Signals Section that handled all communications. In the end, the British provided 200 and the Americans 100 of these support personnel.[171] Thus, independent identities were maintained – in accordance with Donovan's decrees – but within the integrated framework.

Jedburgh training was perhaps the area in which integrated collaboration was most apparent. The jointly administered training program lasted twelve weeks and took place mostly at Milton Hall,[172] an estate property near Peterborough, England, but also at various other locations throughout Britain. There were 17 British and 8 OSS instructors on Milton Hall's staff; these were led by a British officer with an American deputy.[173] Recruits were instructed in:

> demolitions, physical training, map reading, fieldcraft, weapons training, field orders, guerrilla tactics, aerial resupply and reception committee work, anti-tank mine warfare, street fighting, [silent killing], motorcycle and car driving, and intelligence training . . . Language study continued at Milton Hall [and trainees learned] what life was like in occupied France, Holland, and Belgium.[174]

As Arthur Brown, a British Jedburgh veteran, has explained:

> All forms of segregation by nationality were deliberately avoided if not actually banned . . . [We] were quartered together, trained and messed together and, in all matters of food, equipment and privileges, were treated identically . . . There was a strong suspicion that the only reason the British [radio] operators were one day [promoted] to lance sergeants, *en masse*, was to put them on an equal footing with their American opposite numbers.[175]

American Jedburghs, such as William Colby, have made similar observations: 'We ate together, talked together, drank together . . . They encouraged [us] to form ourselves into teams. It was a courtship then marriage sort of thing.'[176] The intent, *inter alia*, was to promote bonding between the recruits, and this was definitely accomplished.[177] Building upon the joint structure, SOE and OSS set up another integrated Jedburgh staff in February 1944 to facilitate communications between Milton Hall and SFHQ.

The British and OSS Jedburgh evaluators and instructors generally worked well together, although cultural differences sometimes affected the Jedburgh selection process. OSS psychiatric evaluator and Jedburgh veteran, William Morgan, was assigned to SOE's Special Training School No. 7, where pre-training assessments were conducted. He was the only OSS officer on the evaluation board and has noted that the British at first failed an inordinate number of Americans:

> The [British] wanted to pass Americans, but just could not understand their ideas . . . In the beginning, [we] were sending people through who were too egotistical, too boastful . . . It quickly became apparent that some of [the problems concerned] the American language . . . I had to explain these things to [the British and] we got along very, very well. Most Americans were [ultimately] passed.[178]

Morgan has also noted that while the Americans preferred for leaders to emerge naturally, the British were more comfortable with assigned leaders. This caused some differences of opinion, none serious.[179] Colby, meanwhile, has explained away the few difficulties he observed during Jedburgh training by reference to the different personalities and backgrounds of the recruits:

> The American [Jedburghs] were young and brash . . . The old cliché applied: 'over-paid, over-sexed, and over-here,' [and they were] without a strong military background . . . The [British] were a little bit older and more serious, while the French had a lot of people who had been regular soldiers.[180]

Such differences notwithstanding, the Jedburghs by and large worked well together and any Anglo-OSS conflicts during the evaluation and training phases were remarkably few and minor.

When complete, the Jedburgh program yielded 101 three-man teams, 92 of which were ultimately deployed to France.[181] Each of these comprised two officers and a radio operator,[182] and they were indeed largely established by the trainees themselves – during the last two weeks of March 1944[183] – almost certainly as a means to improve teamwork and efficiency. One of the two officers in every team was a native of the country into which his unit was later dropped by parachute – French, Belgian, or Dutch – and the other was either British or American; radio operators could be any nationality. This meant that there were [considerably] more Frenchmen in total than there were British or Americans.[184] Specifically, 109 Frenchmen, 88 British, and 78 Americans were used for Jedburgh operations in France during June–September 1944.[185] It is commonly believed that the majority of the Jedburgh teams had tripartite representation, but in actual fact, only 10 of the original 101 teams were configured this way; 18 had two to three Frenchmen, 32 had two Americans, and 41 had two British.[186] Thus, while it is fair to say that the Jedburgh program was fully integrated – on a tripartite basis – SOE and OSS Jedburgh officers rarely served together in the field.

The mission of the Jedburghs was varied and required a great deal of teamwork, self-motivation, and flexibility. The teams were, first and foremost, to liaise with the resistance, operating 'at least 40 miles' behind the German front lines. They were to:

> provide a strategic reserve for creating and controlling offensive action behind the enemy lines on and after D-day where existing communications, leadership, organization, or supplies are inadequate, and for carrying out additional specific tasks demanded by the military situation.[187]

In accordance with the various resistance plans devised on a tripartite basis in 1943–4, the Jedburghs were to 'coordinate and synchronize' resistance activities with regular military operations connected with OVERLORD and ANVIL/DRAGOON.[188] Special operations officers assigned to the various commands were to provide 'speedy two-way links direct with SOE headquarters, which [was to be] in radio contact with Jedburghs in the field.'[189] The teams brought with them 'arms, explosives, and stores,' and were expected to:

> a. Organize [resistance] for guerrilla activity; b. Equip [units] with arms and stores; c. Give instruction . . . in the use of arms; d. Provide [radio] communication, and pass along orders received from London; e. Lead, giving technical advice, or assist . . . in operations against the enemy.[190]

The Jedburghs, together with resistance forces, were to destroy rail lines and bridges, attack vehicles and trains, misdirect, delay, and otherwise harass the enemy, especially German armored units. They were to sabotage telecommunications, power stations, and aircraft, attack Command and Staff, and prevent destruction of vital points required by the Allied armies.[191]

While the inter-Allied missions and other means of liaison prior to D-Day had been quite effective in organizing the resistance forces to accomplish many important tasks, the Jedburghs were to provide 'last-minute stiffening, reinforcement, and support.' They did not function as intelligence collectors – that was left to the Sussex teams – although Jedburghs were advised to 'keep their eyes open and pass back to [SFHQ] any information of military value . . . They [were to] report what they [saw], but [not to] draw deductions.' In the end, SOE and OSS convinced the Allied Command to back the Jedburgh concept on the premise that 'if allotted suitable tasks, Jedburghs working with resistance groups [could] achieve a really considerable effect, out of all proportion to the small expenditure of men and equipment involved.'[192]

All told, this unprecedented exercise in Anglo-OSS, and indeed, tripartite cooperation achieved an important measure of success, in support of the OVERLORD and ANVIL / DRAGOON campaigns. A significant number of resistance groups throughout France were successfully contacted, motivated, and in some instances guided by the Jedburghs in guerrilla, sabotage, and other special operations which were later deemed of much use by the Allied Command.[193] General George Patton, commander of the US Third Army, which broke out from Normandy and swept through Brittany, 'credited resistance with providing appreciable aid in . . . the early days of his campaign . . . [Jedburgh-assisted] resistance on many other occasions gave specified aid by way of sabotage, intelligence or guidance to Allied troops.'[194] In fact, evidence strongly suggests that the Jedburghs were limited only by the relatively short amount of time that they had to prepare themselves, and the much shorter period in which they had to work with the resistance groups in the field. As Arthur Brown has noted: 'If there was any complaint from the Jedburghs it was that they had been sent in far too late to do a really effective job and their greatest burden was not the brutality of the enemy but the timidity of the Supreme Command.'[195]

OPERATION SUSSEX

As well as being the first, Sussex represents also the greatest contribution made by [the secret intelligence component of OSS] London to the military operations involved in the invasion of the continent and the liberation of France.[196]

The inclusion of OSS by SIS in Operation Sussex from May to June 1943 – examined briefly in Chapter 4 – marked a decisive turning point in relations between Britain and America in the realm of secret intelligence collection. Intelligence operations in support of the Allied invasion of France – hitherto considered by SIS to be its exclusive domain – were to become integrated through the Sussex program, on a level not reached before or after in France, or any other area of operations. For OSS London, Sussex became the principal means by which it became an intelligence collector in its own right, rather than just an intelligence consumer. 'Prior to the Sussex operation, essentially all intelligence disseminated by [OSS] London was obtained from Allied services or contacts, or from other OSS outposts.'[197]

OSS and SIS interests in France began to converge from the time Broadway first submitted its draft for 'Plan Sussex' to OSS London on 19 June 1943.[198] The immense military requirements for intelligence in France that were expected to precede, accompany, and follow the Allied invasion in 1944, as well as the almost certain increase in German countermeasures,[199] left SIS amenable to OSS participation. From the outset:

[OSS] officers charged with the development of Sussex worked closely with their opposite numbers in SIS. Meetings started even before the arrival from

Washington of the staff members who later took charge of Sussex. These meetings became increasingly frequent.[200]

Nonetheless, difficulties characterized the initial phase of Sussex planning through the summer of 1943, delaying implementation of the program:

> Among these may be listed the long delay before the plan received the approval of the Theater Commander;[201] some reluctance on the part of SIS to accept [OSS] as a full partner; inadequacy of [OSS's] staff . . . and delay in agreement by the French authorities in Algiers to French participation in the plan.'[202]

Perhaps the most challenging part of the Sussex program was in meeting the requirements for suitable personnel. As Sussex was to provide the Allied Command with important tactical intelligence from behind enemy lines, a large number of Frenchmen 'with knowledge of particular areas and localities, and preferably with military experience,'[203] were needed. Some 96 agents had to be selected from a much larger group of recruits. Those chosen were 'organized in two-man teams, each consisting of an observer and a radio operator, trained in England in joint British-American schools, and dispatched into France by parachute over a period extending from early-April to early-September 1944.'[204] Some of the agents were to operate in rear areas, others near enemy-occupied coastal areas where enemy countermeasures would be most intensive and the intelligence targets most critical.[205] It was highly dangerous work, requiring skills and personality attributes which proved to be in short supply.

Much like the Jedburgh program, recruitment for Sussex often involved parallel but distinctly separate efforts on the part of OSS and SIS, with joint endeavors taking place when mutually beneficial. While Broadway focused its recruiting efforts on those who had escaped from France to Britain, OSS initially wanted to recruit from 'among such personnel as may be available in the United States, refugees, prisoners of war, and labor groups, although it was anticipated that the cooperation of [OSS] in Algiers and Madrid would be enlisted.'[206] Some French officers receiving military training in the US were initially chosen by OSS Washington for Sussex, but were soon rejected, mostly because they had been out of France for too long a period, but also because the Gaullists were concerned that they were too closely associated with Vichy. The joint OSS-SOE 'Sussex Committee' determined in September 1943 that French recruits must have a military background and have left France after 1941; half should be officers, the other half non-commissioned officers (NCOs) to serve as radio operators.[207] Further efforts by OSS to recruit in the US met with failure and were abandoned in mid-October.[208] OSS next looked to North Africa, dispatching a recruiting officer from London to Algiers in August 1943.[209] Delays were encountered, however, when it was discovered that OSS Algiers had not been properly briefed on Sussex and its requirements, nor were personnel on hand to focus on the recruiting drive.[210] The Gaullist intelligence service in London provided some 'agent candidates' in late October, and these were jointly interviewed by SIS and OSS.[211] The joint 'Sussex Selection Board' was established in London shortly thereafter, and by the end of October, OSS London was able to report to Donovan that 'the Sussex Plan is definitely underway.'[212]

Anglo-OSS preparations for Sussex increased significantly in November 1943. An initial tranche of French recruits had been selected and on 13 November a joint SIS-OSS Sussex training school was opened in the UK. The Selection Board, meanwhile, passed another 10 Gaullist candidates during the month, and chose an additional 11 on 6 December to fill out the third Sussex training class.[213] Six more trainees were added by the Board on 18 December, which was enough to fill a fourth class,[214] and OSS Casablanca's D.W. King's first recruits from North Africa finally arrived in England shortly thereafter. The North African French, however, had not been fully briefed about Sussex by King for security reasons, and all of them dropped out as soon as they were informed of the considerable personal risks involved in Sussex work.[215] This setback caused recruiting to fall 'seriously in arrears,' and OSS London felt obliged to dispatch another officer to North Africa just before Christmas 'to accelerate recruiting [and] straighten out this confusion.'[216] Difficulties notwithstanding, the level of cooperation achieved by Christmas 1943 between SIS and OSS in London on the Sussex program is an impressive indicator of just how far Broadway had come from its previously uncooperative position on working with the American 'upstarts' in field operations. Like the Jedburgh program, time and resource constraints – when combined with greatly increased military requirements and opportunities – evidently drove the two sides together naturally.

The level of Anglo-OSS cooperation on Sussex in London, however, was not matched in Algiers, which helps to explain why recruiting there proved difficult. The officer assigned by SIS to handle Sussex recruiting in Algiers, in fact, 'had not even met any of the OSS staff in Algiers [by the end of 1943], much less having discussed Sussex with any one of them.' Moreover, the head of Gaullist intelligence in Algiers – Commandant Pelabon – thought that the US was anti-Gaullist and was unable to cooperate effectively with the aforementioned SIS officer because of personal differences. According to OSS reports, there was a 'complete lack of understanding of the Sussex plan [in Algiers] . . . and [a] complete absence of any feeling of urgency in connection with preparation to make the plan operative.'[217] This was further complicated by the fact that the regular French Army, which was still commanded from Algiers by Giraud until April 1944, drafted all eligible French males and was not inclined to part with recruits for what it perceived to be a Gaullist operation. De Gaulle and Giraud were, after all, locked in a power struggle in the autumn of 1943, and the former had just ousted the latter from the *Comité Français de la Libération Nationale*. When the constraints of secrecy are added, as well as the fact that the Algiers-based representatives of OSS, SIS, and BCRA were fully occupied with operations in their region, it is not surprising that little was achieved for Sussex in North Africa.[218]

Nonetheless, OSS London and Broadway continued to pursue recruits in North Africa into 1944, establishing a tripartite commission in Algiers on 4 January to screen Sussex candidates who were to be provided by the Gaullists. Forty-two recruits were immediately chosen by this authority, but it was discovered on 12 January that a group of 162 Frenchmen sent by previous recruiters to England from North Africa had arrived and had been deemed 'very inferior' by the Sussex Selection Board. On 29 January, several officers from the London Board arrived in Algiers to take over recruitment, and on a tripartite basis established a school for pre-selection evaluation. 'Rejection amounted to between 60 and 70%.'[219] Nonetheless, this program marked the high point in Anglo-OSS-Gaullist collaboration on Sussex in North Africa.

Back in London, Sussex collaboration continued apace. On 4 January, at the suggestion of OSS's Francis Miller, two tripartite committees were formed; a main 'Sussex Coordinating Committee' to deal with policy issues, and a sub-committee to handle other matters.[220] In February, the Coordinating Committee formally asked Supreme Headquarters to designate 50 key points throughout France 'for coverage by Sussex teams, equally divided between the zone of operations assigned to the [US] armies and that assigned to the British.' This was done forthwith, with a focus on enemy communications, railway centers, armored unit facilities, major river crossings, headquarters, airfields, and repair centers.[221] At Sussex training facilities, meanwhile, British, American, and French officers worked together to establish suitable cover stories[222] and to provide documentation for agents.[223] The British, however, actually manufactured most agent documents in the end because OSS did not set up its printing operation in time to be of much use.[224] OSS London regularly pressed Washington for additional instructor personnel to achieve a '50–50 equilibrium' with the British, but failed to achieve such a balance, while the French were content to provide recruits along with some policy direction.[225]

There were many examples of the growing intimacy between SIS and OSS on Sussex in the UK in early 1944, although both sides managed to retain their separate identities. It was decided, for example, that the 'Brissex' (British-run Sussex teams) and 'Ossex' (American-run teams) should use the same codes.[226] Separate radio stations were established, however, for SIS and OSS to communicate with their respective agents once they arrived in France.[227] A joint parachute and equipment packing station, moreover, was established in London:[228]

Parachutes . . . were supplied by the British, packed by [OSS], and functioned perfectly . . . SIS supplied cylindrical compartmented [supply] containers, which were soon replaced by containers from [OSS] made of pressed cardboard [that] were easier to dispose of . . . SIS quickly followed this lead.

Parachute training took place at a British-run facility, where instruction was also given in 'how to choose proper terrain for receptions, the arrangement of lights, and disposal of parachutes, containers, and any other incriminating evidence.'[229]

Brissex and Ossex teams were dispatched from different airfields and were billeted separately, with all of the American agents housed and briefed at Grendon Hall near Harrington, where the OSS aircraft were assigned.[230] The methods by which agents were dispatched, however, were worked out in close coordination, and with the US 8th Air Force, which provided the bulk of the aircraft used for Sussex dispatch.[231]

SIS and OSS also assigned Sussex personnel to the various Army and Army Group headquarters that participated in the OVERLORD and ANVIL / DRAGOON operations. These officers were organized into what were called 'Field Detachments':

> The Field Detachments were to maintain close liaison with the G-2s of the [headquarters] to which they were attached, to transmit to them all intelligence received from the Sussex agents and other sources via [OSS and SIS in] London, and to receive and send back to [Sussex] Headquarters . . . for transmission to agents in the field, all requisitions for intelligence received from the G-2s.[232]

OSS staffed the detachments sent to the US commands and SIS those sent to the British. It was a natural division of responsibilities that generally worked efficiently and ensured that both sides received credit from their national military authorities for the activities of their respective teams.

Prior to the deployment of the Brissex and Ossex teams, a number of special units called 'Pathfinders' were sent to France. Their mission was to 'make advance arrangements for safe parachuting fields, hideouts, and reception committees, which would receive [Sussex] agents and [help] them [to get started. They were also to] recruit a network of local informants.' The first Pathfinders were deployed on 8 February 1944, and others followed shortly thereafter.[233] From the start, the Pathfinders were hampered by the short time they were given to accomplish their many difficult tasks. Most failed to find suitable informants and struggled on their own to meet the assigned objectives. Delays in deploying the Brissex and Ossex teams resulted, but the Pathfinders did manage to find enough landing sites and to arrange for the safe reception of the Sussex teams,[234] which was no small feat.

The mechanics of deploying Sussex personnel reveals a further level of integration achieved between the various tripartite participants. When a Pathfinder, for example, advised London of a suitable drop zone for a Sussex team, the message was decoded by either OSS or SIS personnel, then given a code name. It was sent to the joint SOE-OSS conference room at Baker Street, as all aircraft for special operations and intelligence collection were pooled and this was the repository for useful tactical information. The SOE-OSS team checked the coordinates of the site against up-to-date information on enemy activity along the suitable air routes, including the location of ground-based anti-aircraft and Luftwaffe airfields. If approved, the site information was forwarded to the Air Ministry, which subsequently reviewed the request against moon cycles, weather reports, and availability of aircraft. If the Ministry approved, the 801st Bomb Group (the OSS squadrons), or the appropriate British air dispatch unit, received notification and all of the pertinent details (i.e., number of agents, containers, date of the operation, ground signaling, etc.). Reception committees received coded messages via BBC broadcasts about the scheduled drop, once the Sussex Committee and the various other aforementioned elements had signed off. 'Sometimes one sortie would have both [special operations] and [secret intelligence] agents aboard, in which case the [intelligence] operation was always carried out first.'[235] Anglo-US distinctions were definitely blurred during this phase of operations.

The Sussex teams, once deployed, were extremely active. Due to the delays associated with the Pathfinders, the first teams did not arrive in France until 9 April, several weeks behind schedule. These consisted of 1 Ossex and 2 Brissex units. A day later, two more Ossex teams and another Brissex one were dispatched,[236] and by the end of May, 13 teams (seven Ossex and six Brissex) – along with five Pathfinders – were operational.[237] The first Sussex message was received on 10 May, and the first intelligence report arrived six days later, which consisted of map references for three munitions dumps and a report on the evacuation of a town.[238] In total, 77 Americans, 157 British, 401 French, and 30 agents of other nationalities were successfully deployed during the French campaign as part of Sussex.[239] About half of the teams were sent to the US sector of military operations under OSS direction, and the other half to the British sector under SIS's control.[240] The dispatch of personnel and receipt of intelligence messages steadily increased through D-Day and the campaign,[241] particularly in the American sectors because US units broke out from Normandy more quickly than did the British. In all, the Ossex teams alone dispatched some 800 messages containing almost 1200 separate items of intelligence, covering 'battle order, airfields, bombing targets, bombing results, secret weapons, etc.'[242]

There is much evidence to indicate that Sussex intelligence was very well received and contributed significantly to the success of military operations. According to OSS accounts:

> An officer of SHAEF called to thank [OSS London] for [Sussex information], stating that some had proved most useful. An officer at 21st Army Group [told OSS] that a Sussex agent was the first to identify the movements of the Lehr Panzer Division, and that the value of this piece of information alone was sufficient to justify all the work that had been put into the Sussex project, even if nothing else were accomplished.[243]

OSS's Haskell was informed on 27 July by the US G-2 at Supreme Headquarters that:

> The results obtained [from] the Sussex operation have been very helpful. Not only was the information useful, but compared with the great volume of [British

SIS reports] received, the level of accuracy has been gratifyingly high. The manner in which the operation has been carried out reflects the obviously excellent training which the intelligence teams had been given.[244]

Sussex reports were also praised in July by the US First Army, and were once identified as having 'inspired . . . 4 out of 6 recent air operations.'[245] General Strong, Eisenhower's G-2, reported to OSS on 19 August that: 'The series of reports transmitted to G-2-SHAEF by OSS from Chartres in the early stages of operation OVERLORD were exceptionally able and useful.'[246] The nearly uniform praise for Sussex is a testament to the viability of joint Anglo-OSS field operations. As OSS determined in its final evaluation of the program:

> Without question, Sussex succeeded in its purpose of supplying strategic and tactical intelligence which was of substantial assistance to the Allied military command . . . Despite difficulties which delayed [implementation], most of the teams successfully reached their destinations and sent in useful intelligence . . . The Sussex operation also provided valuable experience for future operations as OSS turned the focus of attention from France to Germany.[247]

OSS OPERATIONAL GROUPS AND BRITISH SPECIAL FORCES

In addition to the Jedburgh and Sussex programs, there were other OSS and British units that participated in the liberation of France which are relevant to this study. These special forces teams were organized to support *Maquis* and other resistance groups in the conduct of guerrilla and sabotage activities behind enemy lines. They did not operate jointly, but occasionally collaborated in the field. On the OSS side, these units were called 'Operational Groups' (OGs), whilst the British deployed the 1st and 2nd Special Air Service (SAS) Regiments, which were part of the British military rather than SOE or SIS. The French equivalent of the OGs and the SAS regiments were the 3rd and 4th Parachute Battalions of the regular French Army.[248]

A typical OSS Operational Group comprised four officers and 30 non-commissioned officers (NCOs) divided into two sections.[249] OSS organized 11 such Groups comprising a total of 356 Americans, as well as 14 foreign Operational Group sections, each with two officers and 13 NCOs. Eight of the foreign sections were French, 3 Italian, 2 German, and one mixed French and Italian.[250] OG members wore military uniforms and functioned essentially as commandos: 'They were dropped in some twenty different places behind the lines after D-Day with the assignment either of protecting an important installation from destruction at the hands of the retreating Germans, or of executing special coups of guerrilla warfare.'[251] Operational Groups were ordered to cut and harass enemy communications, attack vital installations, organize and train local resistance elements, boost the morale and effect of resistance groups encountered, and provide as much intelligence as possible.[252]

There were a number of essential differences between the Operational Groups and the Jedburgh teams. OGs were, first and foremost, combat troops with specific tactical missions that allowed them to 'attack targets not permitted to the [Jedburgh] teams.' They were also, of course, much larger than the three-man Jedburgh units and had a much lower ratio of officers to enlisted personnel. While the priority mission for the OGs was to fight, the first responsibility of the Jedburghs was to organize, then to act as liaison between Special Forces Headquarters or the Special Projects Operations Center and the resistance forces. The only real similarity between the two was that both OGs and Jedburghs worked with resistance groups behind enemy lines, attacking the enemy and impeding his movements whenever possible.[253]

The Operational Groups resembled the British SAS regiments more than the Jedburghs, although there were also notable differences between the two unit types. The strength of the SAS regiments used in France, for example, totaled 773 officers and men, which was about a third more than the total compliment of the OGs.[254] The training regime of the OSS units was similar to that of SAS, but was conducted independently of the British. The course of instruction included basic infantry training, guerrilla warfare, mountain and amphibious operations, radio communications, skiing, and demolitions, all done mostly at night. Parachute training was also provided, with most OG personnel attending the OSS-run parachute school near Algiers.[255] Local language skills were stressed more by OSS than by SAS – 'at least one man in each [OG] squad was familiar with the language of the region in which it was designated to operate.' OSS units also had a larger number of qualified radio operators per unit than their British counterparts. While the Operational Groups answered directly either to SFHQ in London or SPOC in Algiers,[256] SAS had its own headquarters staff and was under the authority of the 21st Army Group. Whilst the details of SAS's work are outside the scope of this book, it should be noted that SAS troops in France often worked together with SOE 'to a greater or lesser degree, depending on the circumstances,' and were later praised for boosting the morale and activities of the resistance groups to which they attached themselves.[257]

The actions of the Operational Groups deployed to France in support of OVER-LORD and ANVIL / DRAGOON were later judged by OSS to be satisfactory. Units participated in the destruction of bridges, railways, and roads, and the rescue of downed Allied airmen. They ambushed enemy units, helped to defend *Maquis* bases, destroyed communications and power lines, organized and trained some local *Maquis* units, and prepared landing strips for aerial resupply operations. They provided useful intelligence, especially in southern France, and boosted the morale of the resistance forces they encountered. According to one OG unit report: 'Many French leaders have said that even if the men had not carried out a single tactical operation, their presence alone was of enormous value.'[258] Like the

Jedburghs, however, it was concluded after France was liberated that the earlier deployment of the teams almost certainly would have significantly increased their effectiveness, which suffered from the rapid pace of events and a lack of mobility:[259]

> Every day spent in training the Maquis brought increased dividends in their combat effectiveness. After the Debarkation from the South, the advance of the Army was so rapid that the Sections sent in after D-Day barely had a chance to get started on Operations before being over-run.[260]

CONCLUSIONS

The important role played by the British and US secret services in the liberation of France is indisputable, and the level of OSS-SOE-SIS collaboration achieved in related field operations was unprecedented for these organizations. The foundation for the covert successes in France lay first in the coming together of OSS's 'van der Stricht-Canfield' group with Baker Street's two French sections over the course of 1943. This, in turn, made possible the tripartite Jedburgh program and inter-Allied *Maquis* missions, and ultimately resulted in the establishment of a truly joint command apparatus – Special Forces Headquarters. On the secret intelligence side, the Sussex team concept did for OSS-SIS relations what the Jedburghs and *Maquis* missions accomplished for OSS-SOE integration. These 'convergences,' however, evolved out of discord among Allies rather than agreement, which makes them all the more remarkable.

This discord, of course, stemmed from what was one of the most important and dynamic elements in the Anglo-OSS relationship – the struggle between de Gaulle and Giraud for leadership of the French resistance movement as a whole. Not surprisingly, Anglo-US differences over the future of the world imperial system – which contributed to Roosevelt's initial rejection of de Gaulle – complicated Anglo-OSS relations in France, just as they had done in India, Burma, the Middle East, the Balkans, China, and elsewhere. This argument persisted beyond the liberation of France, driving a wedge between OSS and its British counterparts in other theaters where Britain was seeking to recover colonial possessions. In the French case, America found by 1943 that it had clearly backed the losing side in the form of Vichy then Giraud, but not before OSS had been greatly disadvantaged *vis-à-vis* SOE and SIS. Whilst OSS gained a measure of independence from British tutelage and control as a result of the TORCH invasion, Donovan was afterwards forced to choose how he would approach the French situation from a definite position of weakness.

SOE and SIS, in fact, held a dominant position with regard to French operations in the aftermath of TORCH, right through mid-1943, at least. This was largely the result of their continuing close relations with the Gaullists in London, which grew even closer because of escalating Gaullist ambitions and continued OSS-Gaullist estrangement. It also came from the considerable experience the British were garnering from their non-Gaullist French networks. The mere existence of this independent channel to various resistance elements encouraged the Gaullists to cooperate out of fear of competition and the Americans to do likewise out of need. Britain's hand was further strengthened by the fact that the vast majority of French operations were launched from the United Kingdom, and the military forces that were assembling to invade France did so on British soil. Thus, Donovan's choice in the aftermath of TORCH was a stark one – he could either strike out on his own in France with little hope of success or he could join forces with the British, take advantage of their experience and contacts, then use what OSS learned and accomplished to further its drive for full independence.

Donovan chose collaboration over divorce, and Britain proved receptive, largely as a result of three important developments in 1943. The first was the realization by SOE and SIS that they lacked the resources necessary to meet the immense military requirements for intelligence and resistance activities that would surely precede and accompany the Allied invasion. OSS was, in their view, well positioned to fill the void, and this attitude was wholly consistent with Britain's policy on collaborating with Donovan dating back to the very beginning of the war. Second, there was concern that if spurned, OSS would indeed attempt to strike out on its own in France, which might jeopardize existing British networks and foster a competitive environment that would degrade Allied clandestine activities generally. Third, and perhaps most important, was the realization that America rather than Britain would lead the invasion of Normandy, and later of southern France. This new command arrangement greatly enhanced OSS's position and necessitated a more equal role for Donovan's spies and saboteurs.

A review of the joint activities that took place during 1943 indicates clearly that both sides had early on grasped fully the need for very close collaboration in support of the coming invasion. The inter-allied *Maquis* missions had begun in earnest long before the end of the year, whilst OSS officers sat together with their British counterparts in Baker Street from the early spring. Within the Jedburgh framework, OSS and Baker Street worked together when it was useful to do so, and somewhat independently when it was not, but achieved nearly complete functional integration for French activities once the training of Jedburgh recruits began. Sussex marked a complete departure in SIS's exclusionary policy, moving relations from mere liaison to something quite different. Sussex required the participants to work together – often side by side – in the planning and conduct of field activities. OSS and SIS managed to retain some independence within the Sussex framework via the Ossex and Brissex team concept, but were still privy to most of each other's secrets, which was remarkable given the derision in which the Americans were still regarded by powerful men like Claude Dansey at Broadway. Agents communicated with separate OSS and SIS radio facilities, but used the same codes. They were dispatched separately, but using methods that had been jointly agreed upon and means that were pooled for common use. OSS staffed the Field Detachments that liaised with the American military authorities on Sussex and Jedburgh, and SIS or SOE did likewise with British military authorities, but all information derived from these arrangements was shared. Any parallel functions inside the Sussex and Jedburgh frameworks were largely indistinguishable to outsiders because they were jointly managed internally and controlled by a joint military headquarters.

The subordination of Special Forces Headquarters, and indeed of all secret operations supporting Allied military action in France, to Supreme Headquarters was perhaps the most critical factor driving OSS, SOE, and SIS towards one another. With the full backing and control of the military, the three organizations had little choice but to work together, integrating their organizations to the extent of maximum utility for operations. Once SHAEF really began to take charge in March 1944, setting targeting priorities for the resistance forces, joint planning accelerated, leaving little time for anything but cooperation on the working level. In the case of Sussex, deployment of personnel to the field had by that time already begun. The high regard in which Supreme Headquarters held key figures like OSS's Haskell and SOE's Mockler-Ferryman, moreover, and the willingness of these men to work with one another without fear of inefficient parochialism, served as yet another powerful incentive to integrate.

No level of integration, however, could ensure that OSS had a truly equal say. This had to be accomplished by other means, first and foremost being the provision by OSS of large numbers of American aircraft for joint clandestine operations, which did not take place until approximately a month before D-Day. Churchill's intervention in January 1944 had brought SOE the aircraft and corresponding prestige that in turn magnified the disparities between the British and OSS. Donovan's subordinates tried to compensate for their shortcomings through various other means, with mixed success. One method used was the courtship of the Gaullists during a time when Anglo-Gaullist relations were strained, yet this development almost certainly would have taken place had de Gaulle's relationship with the British not been in doubt. Another involved the provision by OSS of additional personnel for staff and field positions, which took place in the months leading up to the invasion. OSS operations into France from Switzerland, moreover, helped to keep the British honest, as such activities were beyond their control. In the end, however, the aircraft played the key role, with the number of American air sorties counting for more than all of the other aforementioned activities combined, save perhaps for the American-led military command arrangements. When equilibrium in aircraft was achieved, so too was it reached at Special Forces Headquarters and elsewhere. Having moved from the role of lesser partner to equal one with the British by invasion day, OSS had positioned itself well to become the dominant partner in the relationship once American forces broke out from their beachhead at Normandy. This, in fact, proved to be the case.

7 Key Findings

INTRODUCTION: A RELATIONSHIP OF FOUR THEMES

The relationship between the British and American secret services during the Second World War was characterized by four distinct themes. For the purpose of analysis, they shall be called *indirect mutual dependence, direct mutual dependence, restricted independence,* and *unrestricted independence.* These themes appeared at various times and to varying degrees in different countries or regions, yet had basic characteristics that surfaced in the behavior of both sides of the bilateral equation. The transatlantic 'partners,' who finished the war more as rivals in much of the world, were driven both by national imperatives and narrow organizational interests. They alternated between selflessness and selfishness, trust and mistrust, aggressiveness and passivity, ambition and restraint, strategic vision and tactical preoccupation, possessiveness and independence. In some ways, the relationship can be said to have progressed from the first theme through the next three, although there were many exceptions to this pattern, especially regarding the two forms of independence; in the 1942–4 period, especially, the relationship was characterized at times by direct mutual dependence, restricted or unrestricted independence, depending upon the area of operations in question. The themes discussed herein are used to interpret in a broad fashion the development of the Anglo-US secret service relationship during 1940–45 and are not intended to judge the effectiveness of various activities with regard to the war effort. They are general parameters within which the relationship may be studied further.

Indirect Mutual Dependence

For the purpose of this analysis, the term *indirect mutual dependence* might be best described as follows:

> A relationship whereby both sides of the bilateral association – in this case, COI / OSS on one side, SIS, SOE, and BSC on the other – were dependent upon each other for practical requirements and / or aspirations which often fell outside the realm of more traditional organizational collaboration for relatively narrow operational ends.

Thus, in 1940–41, for example, the British secret services sought to use Bill Donovan to facilitate the acquisition of military equipment and other supply to stave off Britain's imminent defeat. Britain was therefore somewhat dependent upon Donovan, even though it remained capable of conducting independent secret service activities. In exchange for Donovan's help in this particular instance, the British provided intelligence material, guidance, and other related support, including political backing, whilst leaving the issue of a *quid pro quo* in kind to a future date. As Donovan required this support to proceed with his work, he was also in a dependent relationship, but of a different kind. While British dependence upon the Americans extended far beyond anything identifiable with intelligence, Donovan's dependence upon the British for all kinds of intelligence-related support was shared by the President, the FBI, and the military services. The British were motivated by desperation born of military catastrophe and impending national defeat, and Donovan was motivated by a longer-term need, with all recognizing that intelligence was a key component of the much broader Anglo-US relationship.

The theme of *indirect mutual dependence* is most clearly evident in a generally definable period, roughly from 1940 through the short lifespan of COI. During the 1940–42 period, individual associations and mutual trust, more than at any other time in the war, played a crucial role in the expansion of secret service cooperation. This trust was one of the principal reasons why, with British support, the Americans became an important contributing partner in human intelligence and special operations activities in just two short years. In many ways, men such as Donovan, Bill Stephenson, and John Godfrey were kindred spirits, in that they shared goals and motives that they believed were in the best interests of their respective countries. They saw that the outcome of their joint enterprise – getting America into the war with a useful mechanism for collaborative intelligence and special operations – would to some degree determine the outcome of the war itself, and they capitalized on the benefits of their indirect mutual dependence. To this interplay was initially added the weight of linkages between such influential figures as David Bruce, Bill Whitney, Whitney Shepardson, Wallace Phillips, and Bob Solborg on the American side, and Stewart Menzies, Claude Dansey, Charles Hambro, Ian Fleming, Dick Ellis, and others on the British side.

Another key factor making the relationship one of broadly indirect mutual dependence at this time was the wide scope of authority wielded by both sides, particularly by Stephenson's BSC and Donovan's COI. This authority, even though it was not always recognized by competing bureaucracies, nonetheless gave both sides the flexibility required to operate sometimes far outside the traditional mandate of the secret services. Donovan's multifaceted role of presidential advisor, intelligence collector, liaison officer, covert diplomat, sometime propagandist, and principal US disseminator of finished and raw intelligence is one clear example. BSC's hemispheric mandate for all forms of intelligence collection, dissemination, counterespionage, liaison, propaganda, sabotage, etc., is another.

The British 'guiding hand' in US clandestine matters was evident every step of the way during the era of indirect mutual dependence. It was evident in the way in which Donovan's two special missions were managed by the British, and in Godfrey's actions during his own trip to America in the spring of 1941 to assess the state of US intelligence. Godfrey's scheme to influence Roosevelt to create a coordinated intelligence entity led by Donovan, and his and Ian Fleming's advice to Donovan about the formulation of the COI concept are two other significant examples. Britain's influence was also apparent in the close personal relationship Stephenson forged with Donovan, his efforts to provide as much practical advice to him as possible, and the utilization of men like Dick Ellis and Barty Pleydell-Bouverie to monitor and influence COI in Washington. Stephenson's remark in July 1941 that he had placed 'his man' in the top COI job, Desmond Morton's comments at the same time about Britain having taken control of American intelligence, and Fleming's claims to have, in effect, drafted COI's charter are particularly revealing in that they demonstrate the extent to which the British sought to facilitate and influence the creation of a competing US service. Moreover, Britain's decision to funnel key intelligence to Roosevelt through Donovan to boost the latter's standing when he was the most vulnerable bureaucratically indicates the premeditated means by which London was prepared to manipulate internal matters in Washington to its advantage; the 'advantage,' in this case, being what it thought to be the overriding requirements of the war effort.

Yet, there were limits to how far and fast the British were willing to go with their American 'pupils.' The barriers raised by various official British entities, including the secret services, to the London activities of COI in 1941–2 indicate the limits of indirect mutual dependence. Despite there being a tangible if different form of dependence on both sides, the British services were certainly capable of operating without COI, and intended to continue to do so. In the instance of COI London, many British saw this organization as a threat to their parochial and bureaucratic interests. SIS felt threatened, for example, by COI London's attempts to forge independent links with the exiled governments which it had hitherto considered to be exclusively British dependents. General Ismay, meanwhile, feared that COI would acquire too many of Britain's secrets in 1941–2 and directed that it be monitored closely and excluded when he felt it was in Britain's interest to do so. Early bureaucratic opposition to COI from the US State Department, military services, and FBI, moreover, compelled the British to tread carefully in relations with COI lest they unduly offend the non-COI counterparts upon whom they also relied for close transatlantic cooperation.

Above all, however, Britain clearly sought a measure of control over COI, even as it energetically endeavored to make that entity both effective and in the image of its own related organizations. This remained a prime British motivation far beyond the 1940–42 period, and it was the steady erosion of this control over the course of the war which remains the one consistently identifiable element of the relationship in the aggregate. The British secret services exercised control in numerous ways during the indirect interdependence period, not the least of which was via COI's reliance on BSC, SOE, and SIS for secure communications. Interestingly, communication was also the means by which SIS sought to control SOE, and by which Broadway and Baker Street sought to control the Gaullists. SIS also controlled what intelligence was disseminated to COI – from all British and exiled government sources – and determined what form that intelligence took (i.e. finished or raw, selective or *en masse*). When SOE felt that COI was moving too slowly towards acquiring a capability in special operations, BSC stepped in and convinced Donovan to appoint a former SIS agent, Bob Solborg, to lead COI's new special operations branch. And once SIS realized that Wallace Phillips wanted to include COI directly in Broadway's secret intelligence activities, it simply refused to work with him, leaving the Americans to founder until they found the means to convince SIS to act otherwise. Donovan's subordinates could do little to alter these circumstances in 1940–42 because they still had too much to learn from the British and little tangible to offer in the form of intelligence, trained personnel, or other practical assistance.

Two key regions where COI did have considerable freedom of action early on to pursue activities largely independent of the British – North Africa and the Far East – found Donovan's organization lacking the ability to exploit fully the myriad of opportunities which were available. This was less apparent in North Africa, where the British had been effectively excluded by the Vichy French, and Robert Murphy's twelve vice-consuls with their own radio net gave COI a foundation of sorts for its clandestine efforts. Yet, COI personnel there were largely inexperienced, limited in their ability to communicate securely, and were lacking in numbers. The situation was much worse in the Far East, however, where Donovan had great ambitions, but little means to conduct operations of any kind until late 1942.

Difficulties notwithstanding, the British and Americans generally got what they wanted out of the 'unequal partnership' in the era of indirect mutual dependence. First, a close and easy relationship was established at all levels between COI and its British counterparts, which later naturally facilitated joint endeavors. America received a functional service for intelligence collection, analysis, and dissemination, as well as for future special operations, and with British backing Donovan weathered the assaults of his bureaucratic opponents. Americans were for the first time participating in British-led training programs for clandestine activities, and tested mechanisms were in place for exchanging privileged information. For its part, Britain received the lend-lease aid that its military so desperately needed and believed that it had secured the means – COI / OSS – by which its secret services could acquire significant US resources for use in large-scale clandestine work under British direction. While Britain may have had unrealistic expectations about how fast Donovan could contribute, and the control issue became increasingly divisive, the British secret services were well positioned by spring 1942, and had done much of what they had set out to do in 1940 *vis-à-vis* the US. BSC and SOE, moreover, had a first taste of the fruits of their labors in the form of monetary transfers via COI offices in London and New York in 1941–2.

Direct Mutual Dependence

The term *direct mutual dependence* might be best described as follows:

A relationship whereby both sides of the bilateral equation were dependent upon one another for the practical means to conduct human intelligence collection or special operations. This might include elements such as access to funds, special equipment, documentation, transport, training, personnel, experience, or relations with national military authorities, political leaders, indigenous resistance groups, key persons, etc.

Thus, OSS, SOE, and SIS were faced with a situation in 1943 through mid-1944, whereby their assigned tasks in support of OVERLORD were so great that they had to collaborate closely via programs such as Jedburgh and Sussex, and to integrate some functions.

As a disproportionate amount of Allied resources for intelligence and special operations was ultimately dedicated to liberating France, the *direct mutual dependence* theme somewhat mirrors that effort. Thus, this theme falls into a roughly definable period of time – 1943 through mid-1944 – despite the fact that its characteristics are sometimes evident outside of this chronological confine and in non-French matters. In French affairs, however, direct mutual dependence was most clearly evident in Jedburgh and Sussex due to the integrated command, planning, training, and logistics involved up until the end of the first phases of OVERLORD, and to a lesser extent, ANVIL / DRAGOON. Once the American breakout in Normandy began in earnest, Jedburgh and Sussex work soon resembled the theme of restricted independence due to the existence of parallel British and American organizations within the 'integrated' programs that proved capable of largely independent action in support of US and Commonwealth military units, respectively.

OVERLORD imperatives, however, were also the catalyst behind additional instances of direct mutual dependence, especially in the UK. These resulted from many factors, including the existence of British agent networks run by SOE's F and RF Sections – and by SIS – as well as from the ambitious military support requirements which were beyond the capabilities of any one secret service. The political dynamics of US and British relations with de Gaulle and Giraud also played a role, as did the need for parallel agent networks in France following German counterintelligence successes in 1942–3, and the uneven availability of materiel, personnel, and transport. The resumption of tripartite planning and operations with the Gaullists from early 1943 created a foundation for what could only become increasing direct interdependence, as was soon demonstrated by the Special Inter-Allied missions and Pathfinder operations, along with the programs already discussed.

OSS London used the Donovan-Hambro accords of June 1942, the augmentation of its staff, independent communications, and its physical proximity to SIS, SOE, and the exiled governments, to foster a sense of direct mutual dependence. Interestingly, interdependence in London benefited both from the US Command's lack of support for independent OSS work during most of 1943 and a reversal of this position by the end of the year. In the first instance, OSS London was driven to seek common ground with the British at a time when SIS and SOE faced the prospect of overwhelming new operational requirements. In the latter case, the British were forced to accept the Americans more as equals at a time when OSS London had finally acquired the means to make a substantial contribution and the US role in Europe had been greatly enhanced by Eisenhower's appointment as Supreme Allied Commander.

While OSS London proved to be much more dependent upon the British than vice versa throughout 1942–3, a foundation was established for much of what was jointly achieved there in 1943–4. The deployment of the van der Stricht-Canfield Group to London and its de facto integration with SOE for 'Invasion Sphere' activities was a harbinger – if not the full realization – of direct mutual dependence in London. When Eisenhower's '100 percent cooperation' edict of January 1943 in North Africa was followed in July by his insistence that OSS and SOE set up mechanisms in London for full coordination to avoid duplication, a greater degree of interdependence resulted. It was not by mere coincidence that OSS London managed to secure a full role in the Jedburgh and Sussex programs during this period. The creation of Special Forces Headquarters in London and the Special Project Operations Center in Algiers in spring 1944, moreover, exemplified interdependence in its fullest form. It was the allocation of large numbers of aircraft to OSS in May–June 1944, however, that allowed Donovan to achieve some equality of dependence, and gave him the means to seek a greater form of independence thereafter.

While the Donovan-Hambro accords are remembered more for their division of the world for special operations and the independence they fostered, they also created circumstances which proved conducive to direct mutual dependence in some cases. This was due to the considerable flexibility afforded to both sides to establish an operational presence in areas that were under the administrative leadership of the other. Moreover, by simplifying and making less restrictive the accounting procedures for dealings between OSS and SOE, the Americans were better able to provide a larger proportion of the funding for joint activities as a direct *quid pro quo* for British training, intelligence, experience, transport, etc. This removed some of the imbalances in the relationship and fostered interdependence.

The controversial American effort to resupply Tito across the Adriatic from Bari starting in late-1943 is a particularly noteworthy example of direct mutual dependence. What began at OSS's initiative had, in fact, evolved into a virtually integrated OSS-SOE operation by early 1944, with both sides dependent upon one another for contributions ranging from the provision of seaworthy craft, air transport, and air cover, to administrative support, resupply, etc. According to Douglas Dodds-Parker, who was in overall command of SOE in Italy at the time of the Bari operation, this activity was actually somewhat of a joint one from the outset in that OSS brought the finance and management whilst SOE secured access to much of the supply that was subsequently shipped to the Partisans and credited to Louis Huot's innovation. 'We were not worried then,' noted Dodds-Parker a half a century later, 'about whether we or OSS would get the credit later on.'[1] Command, communications, and transport arrangements, moreover, certainly put OSS in a position of direct dependence upon the British almost from the outset of US involvement in Yugoslavia until 1944, even though dependence was in no way mutual, save for Donovan's substantial loans to SOE for Yugoslav work in late-1943. By early-1944, however, SOE Cairo and the Allied missions in Yugoslavia began to rely heavily on OSS for personnel and supply, which equalized the relationship.

A less clear example of direct mutual dependence concerned SOE-OSS relations in Algiers in early 1943, where disputes between the two organizations were somewhat resolved via the creation of separate headquarters and the pooling of resources. While there was little sign of interdependence in the clandestine support for TORCH – nor in the immediate post-TORCH consolidation phase – it appeared somewhat in the working arrangements forged between OSS Algiers and MASSINGHAM in early 1943. Whilst OSS Algiers had a mandate from Donovan to seek independent operations wherever possible, in reality it was chronically short of personnel, transport, and experience. Training and many material assets were therefore pooled, which made both organizations more effective. While the British certainly were more capable of independent action at this time due to MASSINGHAM's easy access to supply via SOE Gibraltar, Dodds-Parker's arrival on the scene in January 1943 and his sympathy for OSS's political imperatives allowed interdependence to mature. In exchange, he achieved partial integration, though not in name, which gave OSS access to British support without appearing to be dependent on it. Collaboration between MASSINGHAM and OSS Algiers in ANVIL / DRAGOON preparations, moreover, almost certainly increased the level of direct mutual dependence through to the summer of 1944.

All in all, the direct mutual dependence era came about largely as a result of two factors. The first was the desire of Britain to get OSS to contribute more – whether this be supply, transport, personnel, or field work – in the face of increasing demands for support from the military. The second was OSS's increasing desire to play an equal if not leading role in the relationship, mirroring that of the US military in the Alliance. Donovan knew that he could not do this without engaging the British more directly in places like London, even while distancing his organization from SOE and SIS in other areas, especially in the Far East, where he hoped to capitalize on the distaste of indigenous resistance elements for British colonial aspirations. The British, meanwhile, came to realize that they risked losing what control they had over OSS by refusing to accept OSS's relative equality.

Restricted Independence

The term *restricted independence* might be best described as follows:

A relationship whereby one or both sides of the bilateral equation was able to act independently of the other in significant operational endeavors, but nonetheless relied on the other for tangible or intangible support necessary to see such activities through to their logical conclusions, or were otherwise limited by political-military considerations.

Thus, OSS and SOE operated largely independently of one another in support of the Allied invasion of North Africa, but were both somewhat confined to the parameters of their 'joint' regional command structure and that of the Allied military command, even though the former existed more in name than deed.

Unlike the previous two themes, *restricted independence* cannot be easily confined to a particular period, but appeared instead in different places and degrees throughout the war. Perhaps the clearest example of this theme concerns the Allied special operations in support of TORCH noted above. In North Africa in 1942, OSS and SOE were able to conduct their activities with little interference from each other because of somewhat unique circumstances. First, Britain had been largely excluded from Vichy-controlled areas, whilst OSS could operate with much greater freedom. Second, OSS intended to use TORCH to showcase its capabilities and independence, and had secured the right in the Donovan-Hambro accords to lead Allied special operations in the region. Clandestine strategy, however, was coordinated under the umbrella of the combined OSS-SOE command structure under OSS's Bill Eddy and his SOE deputy Brien Clarke. While in reality there was little actual integration, the existence of the joint structure placed some limitations upon both sides. Nonetheless, the implementation of the 'semi-coordinated' strategy was left strictly to the separate OSS and SOE field elements, and the physical separation of the joint commanders – Eddy was mostly in Tangier and Clarke worked from Gibraltar – was conducive to this arrangement. With the exception of OSS's unexpected need for SOE communications during the Allied landings, and Clarke's use of OSS tactical information, there was little sign of interdependence.

OSS sought to use its newfound confidence and standing after TORCH to establish a more independent role for itself in key areas, such as France, Yugoslavia, Norway, and Italy, and succeeded to some extent in all four. In French operations, as has been discussed, OSS and the British found increased collaboration to be more mutually beneficial than independence, which resulted in interdependence in 1943–4. OSS Switzerland's activities were an exception to this development, in that the Americans there proved capable of conducting some independent French operations, although these were of a limited scope. Such work was also somewhat restricted both by British objections and the exigencies of tripartite working arrangements in London which governed the vast majority of clandestine work in France. Once Allied forces had landed in France and were driving to liberate the country, however, OSS, SOE, and SIS transitioned rapidly to restricted independence in operations. And as the war moved beyond France to its final stages in Europe, OSS continued to grow more capable and independent-minded. It was not long before the relationship evolved into one characterized predominantly by unrestricted independence.

In Yugoslavia, OSS and SOE achieved a degree of restricted independence at various times, the latter more so than the former, mostly due to its preeminent position in the Balkans that had been reaffirmed in the Donovan-Hambro accords. Before mid-1943, SOE operated with unrestricted independence in the region – whereas OSS remained largely dependent upon the British – then was somewhat restricted by OSS participation in their missions to the Chetniks and Partisans. Britain's increasing reliance on OSS finance in 1944, and later on OSS personnel, also served to restrict SOE's independence in the Balkans. The fact that Anglo-OSS policy on the Tito-Mihailovic dispute diverged and became competitive made independence more of a mutual goal. OSS operations in mid-1944 to rescue downed airmen in Chetnik territory and to reestablish contact with Mihailovic would be an example of unrestricted rather than restricted independence were it not for the fact that intense British pressure limited the scope of this work and forced OSS to withdraw its mission in September.

In Norway during 1944–5, meanwhile, OSS and SOE functioned largely independently of one another, but also faced some restrictions. Special operations, for example, were coordinated at the planning level in a tripartite fashion with the Norwegian government-in-exile. Moreover, most transport assets were pooled, and Norway fell within a recognized British-controlled sphere. Nonetheless, both sides recruited and operated separately; OSS was permitted only to work north of latitude 65 to ensure that there was no conflict or duplication of effort with British operations.

In Italian operations, which were not covered in detail in this study, OSS and SOE functioned both with restricted and unrestricted independence. The Donovan-Hambro accords and their revision in January 1943 provided for what was termed the 'integral rationing' of special operations capabilities worldwide, but left Italy under the leadership of neither side. OSS and SOE, therefore, undertook independent operations and were free from the confines of joint structures. Restricted independence was generally prevalent from the invasion of Sicily until Italy changed sides in the war, and unrestricted independence emerged thereafter. This division of themes occurred principally because of the necessary rationing of resources for operations in 1943, but also was related to the initially fluid nature of the military campaign, which required OSS and SOE to be innovative, to temporary pool equipment and transport, etc. When the Italian campaign bogged down, both sides were more free to pursue separate agendas. With OSS having access to the large Italian-American communities in the US, and SOE focused upon its work with Italian partisan groups in the north, it is not surprising that increased separation resulted. The principal exception was, of course, the resupplying of Tito across the Adriatic, which became a joint affair in 1944.

Where restricted rather than unrestricted independence resulted, this was principally due to the continuing imperatives of limited resources and what were largely politically motivated military and clandestine command arrangements. Practical exigencies included coping with mutual shortages of personnel, training facilities, experienced instructors, agent cadres, false documentation, special equipment, finance, and most importantly, transport. With the US and British militaries carefully negotiating equitable command arrangements, the secret services were often held captive to delicate political machinations to which they were not privy or were powerless to influence. Therefore, in such places as France and North Africa, the independence of OSS, SOE, and SIS was more restricted that it might have been had the military and political authorities not insisted upon a higher degree of cooperation that reflected their own arrangements. In other places, such as Burma and much of the rest of the Far East, political-military competition was more fierce within the alliance, which left the secret services largely to their own devices, especially after 1943.

Unrestricted Independence

The term *unrestricted independence* might be best described as follows:

> A relationship whereby one or both sides of the bilateral equation had the ability to operate largely independently of the other – in areas where both had a meaningful presence – without suffering a significant degradation in effectiveness.

Thus, OSS Detachment 101, for example, did not feel obliged to seek SOE's permission for its Burma operations, nor did it require British assistance to carry them out.

Like the previous theme, *unrestricted independence* appeared to varying degrees in different areas throughout the war, and therefore cannot be easily confined to a particular period. This is especially the case for special operations, although unrestricted independence proved to be dominant in such work from late 1944 onward in key places, such as Germany,[2] Italy,[3] and much of the Far East.[4] The secret intelligence relationship, however, was generally characterized by unrestricted independence through much of the war, with the notable exceptions of intelligence sharing and the Sussex program. There were also some instances of joint training, pooling of transport, equipment sharing, and financial transfers.

SOE acted with much greater independence than did its American counterpart in the early stages of the war, which was the natural consequence of the latter having few deployed assets and virtually no experience. SOE's two French sections, in particular, were functioning independently long before OSS was ready to deploy its first agent into France. So too were the more incipient SOE networks in Latin America, where Donovan lacked a mandate to operate at all, and in places like the Low Countries, Scandinavia, the Balkans, Poland, the Mideast, and in parts of the Far East. It was not until Carl Eifler's Detachment 101 began its operations in Burma that Donovan could claim any significant form of unrestricted independence in special operations anywhere in the world. Eifler achieved this feat for several reasons, the first being that he secured his mandate to work in Burma from General Stilwell in China. Even though Eifler's headquarters was in India, and operations conducted into Burma from India fell clearly within a recognized British sphere, he used the independence of Stilwell's command to justify his own. The fact that Burma was remote and covered with dense jungle – which complicated movement and communications – made coordination in the field generally meaningless in any event. Eifler's arrival, moreover, coincided with the rapid deterioration of the Allied military position in Burma, which increased the urgency of his operations and afforded him additional latitude.

The intense rivalry that developed between the British and American secret services in the Far East during the second half of the war created circumstances which were conducive to unrestricted independence. OSS, SOE, and SIS found themselves not only to be instruments of Allied military policy to defeat Japan, but of national political imperatives born of the wider disagreement between Roosevelt and Churchill over the future of colonialism in the post-war world. As America was the dominant Allied military power in the Far East, and British and French colonial possessions there were mostly under occupation, the region was a natural intra-Allied political battleground. In addition to Burma, the American and British secret services soon found themselves competing – sometimes at cross purposes – in China, Indochina, and Thailand,[5] whilst SOE succeeded in blocking most OSS initiatives in Malaya and the Dutch East Indies.[6] SOE's Far East director had clashed repeatedly with OSS over Eifler's activities and was 'enthusiastic . . . on the subject of [using] SOE as an instrument for the covert re-establishment of British influence in post-war Asia.'[7]

The relationship became so tense in the Far East, in fact, that OSS tried first in 1943, then with more vigor in early 1945 to persuade SOE to remove its small presence in China. This prompted Churchill to write in a note to Anthony Eden in April 1945 that, 'I incline against another SOE-OSS duel, on ground too favorable for that dirty Donovan.'[8] In Indochina, meanwhile, OSS had decided to back the native Vietnamese led by Ho Chi Minh against French forces who were seeking to restore colonial rule with SOE's support. Thus, instances were reported in 1945 of clashes between Viet Minh units backed by OSS and French units backed by SOE,[9] which could not be further from the spirit of partnership and common purpose that had characterized OSS-SOE relations during much of the war. This was more indicative of a full-fledged rivalry, which was the perfect catalyst for unrestricted independence. The complexity of the rivalry and how it was played out in the Far East could easily be the subject of a full book, if not several, and has therefore not been covered in depth herein. Richard Aldrich's 1988 article, 'Imperial Rivalry: British and American Intelligence in Asia, 1942–46,' is an excellent introduction to this issue.

Returning to the realm of secret intelligence, the unrestricted independence theme was indeed prevalent in SIS-OSS relations throughout 1941–5. Broadway had a long history of intelligence operations before the war, and had many well-developed and independently run agent networks in place long before Donovan acquired a similar capability. Senior SIS managers, especially Claude Dansey, believed that close collaboration in the field with the inexperienced Americans only risked compromising SIS's hard won assets. Moreover, Broadway was almost certainly loath to share with OSS the prestige and standing within the Alliance that it had achieved through its unique capabilities. It sought instead to exclude OSS from its field work as much as possible and was largely successful in doing so, despite the fact that it trained many aspiring OSS spymasters and shared some of the product of its labors. Even Sussex evolved from what was initially intended to be a Franco-British affair.

In many ways, OSS shared Britain's desire for independence and exclusivity in the realm of secret intelligence, even though it consistently sought to gain access to as much as SIS would divulge, principally through the OSS offices in London. Independence in SI work, in fact, was a cornerstone of Donovan's long-term plan to establish a wholly independent secret service, largely because OSS was more confined in the realm of special operations by virtue of its various working arrangements with SOE. These arrangements had come about in part because special operations were seen to be more directly applicable to conventional military operations, whereas intelligence collection was more intangible. Freedom in SI matters, moreover, gave OSS access to – and an enhanced standing with – the intelligence components of the various governments-in-exile that SIS had tried to exploit unilaterally.

Signs of Donovan's intent independently to pursue SI activities on an unrestricted basis date from the earliest days of COI – in unoccupied France and Vichy North Africa – and only increased over time, especially in the Far East. OSS and SIS surely suffered from the lack of field collaboration, which was all too evident in the many mistakes the former made that might have been avoided, and especially in the little the latter accomplished of consequence in the Far East through lack of resources, *inter alia*. Yet, both sides were willing to accept the shortcomings of a separate approach in the name of preserving flexibility to pursue their national and parochial agendas. This is not meant to imply that OSS and SIS never collaborated in non-French field activities; they did so frequently, but almost always in a very narrow and specific fashion, and these instances were by and large of a limited duration and on a case by case basis, rather than being the product of a broad collaborative program. It was only in the European 'Invasion Sphere' that the secret intelligence relationship was restricted or mutually dependent to any significant degree.

FINAL OBSERVATIONS

From 1940 to 1945, the British and American secret services had many goals in common, foremost among which was to win the war. Whilst the degree and composition of their collaboration during the conflict's various key phases varied sometimes greatly, they nonetheless managed to work together in a largely effective manner and for constructive ends when it mattered most, especially in France in 1943–4. Both sides, however, traversed what were steadily diverging paths almost from the outset of their contact in 1940 right through 1945. These paths may have begun as parallel ones, but they certainly did not finish as such.

While the two sides shared a common purpose, their often opposing organizational objectives invariably brought them into discord. The inevitability of this process was one of the most striking aspects of the evidence presented in this study. Donovan's organization, starting from scratch, sought to gain as much as it could from the British, but never lost sight of its ultimate goal, which was to create an organization that was capable of independent action on a global scale in all aspects of clandestine work. That capability was intended for use in safeguarding and pursuing US national interests both in war and peace, although OSS was disbanded at war's end and only reconstituted in 1947 – minus its special operations component – as the Central Intelligence Agency. Donovan's overarching goal posed a fundamental challenge to the key aspiration of the wartime British secret services, which was to harness the enormous resources of the United States to further Britain's national war aims – be these survival, the pursuit of a peripheral grand strategy, preservation of the Empire, or reconstitution of it. Where possible, SIS and SOE also naturally hoped to pursue more parochial interests in the process of using American resources for British policy ends.

The output of British energies directed toward achieving London's main objective in the first half of the war, however, made it increasingly difficult for SIS and SOE to maintain control over OSS in the second half in what was a distinctly *a priori* process. As US resources were steadily channeled into COI / OSS – stimulated somewhat by British actions – Donovan became increasingly capable and ambitious, and independence was a natural American objective. Thus, the anecdote of 'Frankenstein's monster' (OSS) returning to haunt its maker (Britain) is somewhat apropos, although in actual fact, the evolution of the relationship was much less sinister and calculated, and much more mutually beneficial as we have seen. The fact that clashing interests in places like India, Burma, North Africa, and Yugoslavia had little negative effect on practical clandestine cooperation in places like France, London, and Norway is indicative of the resilience of the overall relationship and the willingness of both sides to put their differences aside when necessary. Winston Churchill's observation of the 'changing of the guard' in the world from Britain to the United States at the end of the war, however, proved to be true not only in the military and political realms, but in the clandestine realm as well.

Notes

PREFACE

1. Bradley F. Smith, 'The OSS and Record Group 226: Some Perspectives and Prospects,' in George C. Chalou (ed.), *The Secrets War: The Office of Strategic Services in World War II*, (Washington, DC: National Archives and Records Administration, 1992).
2. Particularly useful sources on cryptanalytic cooperation include Bradley Smith's *The Ultra-Magic Deals*, Thomas Parrish's, *The American Codebreakers: The US Role in ULTRA*, F.W. Winterbotham's *The Ultra Secret*, David Kahn's *Codebreakers* and *Seizing the Enigma*, and Sir Harry Hinsley's five volume *British Intelligence in the Second World War*.

1 PLANTING THE SEEDS: 'WILD BILL' DONOVAN'S TWO EUROPEAN MISSIONS

1. Allen W. Dulles, *William J. Donovan and the National Security*, (Central Intelligence Agency: Studies in Intelligence, Summer 1959), adapted from an address delivered in tribute to William J. Donovan by Allen Dulles in 1959.
2. The British Secret Intelligence Service (SIS) dispatched Claude Dansey to Washington with Arthur Balfour's mission in 1917. Dansey assisted the nascent intelligence arm of the US Army to establish a viable capability to assist the British and French in the First World War; a capability that was largely abandoned by the US in the interwar years.
3. Telegram from Sir B. Newton of the British Mission in Baghdad to the Foreign Office (declassified from 'SECRET'), No. 134, E521/G, 14 February 1941, Foreign Office Papers (hereafter cited as 'FO') 371/27098, United Kingdom Public Record Office, London (hereafter cited as 'UKPRO').
4. The Coordinator of Information (COI) was established by Executive Order on 11 July 1941. 'Donovan was directed to "collect and assemble information and data bearing on national security from the various departments" . . . and "to analyze and collate such materials for the use of the President and such other officials as the President may designate."' Thomas F. Troy, *Donovan and the CIA: A History of the Establishment of the Central Intelligence Agency* (Frederick, Maryland: Althea Books, University Publications of America, 1981), p. 69 (first published in classified form by the Central Intelligence Agency's Centre for the Study of Intelligence in 1975). The COI was the forerunner of the Office of Strategic Services (OSS), which was established by Executive Order on 13 June 1942 and was itself the forerunner of the Central Intelligence Agency (CIA), established on 26 July 1947.
5. *War Report of the OSS* (declassified from 'TOP SECRET'), Prepared by History Project, Strategic Services Unit, Office of the Assistant Secretary of War, War Department, Washington, DC, (New York: Walker 1976), p. 5.
6. On 22 July 1940, the British War Cabinet formally approved a draft document signed three days earlier by Neville Chamberlain establishing SOE under the Ministry of

Economic Warfare and its head, Hugh Dalton. In a telling comment about SOE's mission, Dalton observed, 'Regular soldiers are not the men to stir up revolution, to create social chaos or to use all those ungentlemanly means of winning the war which come so easily to the Nazis.' Derrick Mercer (ed.), *Chronicle of the Second World War*, (Harlow, Essex: Longman, 1990), p. 107.

7. Radiogram from Lord Beaverbrook to Colonel William Donovan, photographically reproduced in Corey Ford, *Donovan of OSS*, (Boston: Little, Brown, 1970), p. 95.

8. Robert E. Sherwood, *The White House Papers of Harry Hopkins*, (New York: 1948), as quoted verbatim in Ford, op. cit., p.89.

9. C.H. Ellis, 'Mission Accomplished' (unpublished original manuscript), (Central Intelligence Agency: Historical Intelligence Collection, HIC.Y 151.E4), pp. 31–2.

10. John H. Godfrey, 'The Naval Memoirs of Admiral J.H. Godfrey, Vol. V, 1939–1942, Naval Intelligence Division, Part 1' (hereafter cited as 'Godfrey Memoirs'), Godfrey Papers (hereafter cited as 'GDFY'), Box 1, Folder 6, pp. 130–31, Churchill College Archive at Cambridge University (hereafter cited as 'CCA').

11. BSC was based in New York City and was initially established to 'bring under central control' the security responsibilities of the British Purchasing Commission, which procured war materiel for the UK, and for the overlapping jurisdiction of Britain's Ministries of Information, Economic Warfare, Supply and War Transport, and the intelligence branches of the armed forces. The Commission had a security division to liaise with various US and Canadian law enforcement agencies, immigration authorities, and military intelligence branches. Stephenson's BSC inherited the Commission's security functions, enlarged its contacts, and expanded its responsibility to include liaison with the US Federal Bureau of Investigation (FBI) and later with Donovan's organization. BSC became the British authority for all intelligence, special operations, and related liaison activities in the Western Hemisphere, including work undertaken by SIS, SOE, the Political Warfare Executive (PWE), and UK censorship components in Bermuda. Ellis, 'Mission Accomplished,' pp. 36–7 (including deleted passage), 40, 77–8, 96, 99–101, 103–5.

12. H. Montgomery Hyde, *The Quiet Canadian: The Secret Service Story of Sir William Stephenson* (London: Hamish Hamilton, 1962), p. 28. Hyde, incidentally, worked for BSC in New York and Bermuda during the war and was a close friend of Stephenson.

13. While on his honeymoon in 1919, Donovan visited Siberia with the US Ambassador to Japan to evaluate the state of the White Russian government. In 1920, he accompanied the American banker Grayson Murphy on a tour of war-ravaged Europe at the behest of various relief organizations. In 1932, he visited Germany on private business, and upon returning home argued for armed preparedness to counter European militarism. In 1935, he met Mussolini in Rome and toured Italian military camps in Libya and Abyssinia, later reporting to Roosevelt that Italy would win its war there. And in 1936, Donovan visited a Spain embroiled in civil war and returned home with a report on Germany's technical advances for the US Army Chief of Staff. See Ford, op. cit., pp. 59–83.

14. Ellis, op. cit., p. 48.

15. British Security Coordination Memorandum (declassified from 'PERSONAL AND CONFIDENTIAL') for Mr. James R. Murphy, Office of Strategic Services, Washington, DC, April 26, 1944 in the J. Russell Forgan Papers (hereafter cited as 'Forgan Papers'), Box 1, File 'Stephenson, William S.' Hoover Institution Archives on War, Revolution, and Peace (hereafter cited as 'HIA'), Stanford University.

16. Hyde, op. cit., p. 35.

17. *War Report*, p. 5.

18. Troy, op. cit., pp. 30–32.

19. Ford, op. cit., pp. 90–91.

20. Troy, op. cit., p. 36.
21. Thomas F. Troy, 'COI and British Intelligence (declassified from "SECRET"),' unpublished internal CIA paper, as quoted in Troy, op. cit., p. 36.
22. Troy, op. cit., p. 36.
23. Synopsized from Conyer Read, 'Pre-COI Period (declassified from "SECRET"),' internal CIA paper (Washington: OSS Records, Washington Historical Office), p. 23 as quoted in Troy, op. cit., p. 36.
24. Ellis, op. cit., p. 32.
25. Hyde, op. cit., p. 37.
26. Donovan carried letters from Knox and Clarence Dillon to Lord Beaverbrook, the Minister of Aircraft Production, from Dillon to Brendan Bracken, then Secretary to the Prime Minister, from a John D. Biggers to a British Colonel R.W. Weeks, from William Knudson of The Advisory Commission to the Council of National Defense to Mr. C.J. Bartlett, Managing Director of Vauxhall, from James Forrestal to Sir Hugh Seely at the Air Ministry, and from Hull to American Diplomatic and Consular officers abroad. 'List of Letters of Introduction,' The Donovan Collection (Donovan's personal papers, hereafter cited as 'Donovan Papers'), Box 81B, 'William J. Donovan – Personal, Volume 34,' US Army Military Historical Institute, Carlisle Barracks, Carlisle, Pennsylvania (hereafter cited as 'AMHI').
27. SOE resulted from the merger of the War Office's 'Military Intelligence Research' ('MIR') and the SIS sabotage unit, 'Section D' ('Destruction').
28. Mercer (ed.), op. cit., p. 107.
29. Nigel West, *MI6: British Secret Intelligence Operations, 1909–45*, (London: Weidenfeld & Nicolson, 1983), p. 204.
30. 'Program – July 1940 Trip (Col. D),' Donovan Papers, Box 81B, Vol. 34, (AMHI).
31. James Leutze (ed.), *The London Journal of General Raymond E. Lee, 1940–41* (Boston: Little, Brown, 1971), entry dated 2 August 1940, p. 27.
32. During 23–31 July 1940, Donovan received telephone calls from Labour Minister Ernest Bevin, Sir Charles Craven, Lord McGowan, the Duchess of Westminster, Lady Duff Cooper, Lady Astor, Lady Colefax, Lady Beatty, Lady Metcalf, and Lady Stanley. 'Telephone Messages,' Donovan Papers, Box 81B, Vol. 34 (AMHI). Evidently, his evenings were put to good use.
33. Beaverbrook, as Minister of Aircraft Production, asked Donovan for information on the secret American Sperry bombsight, which was ultimately made available to London, but only after British secret information that German agents had acquired the design in 1938 was provided to Washington. Hyde, op. cit., p. 40.
34. Ellis, op. cit., p. 50.
35. Ford, op. cit., pp. 91–2.
36. West, *MI6*, pp. 139 and 204.
37. Handwritten note on 'Bath Club' letterhead, 25 July 1940, with illegible signature, Donovan Papers, Box 81B, Vol. 34, (AMHI).
38. 'Program – July 1940 Trip (Col. D),' Donovan Papers, Box 81B, Vol. 34 (AMHI).
39. Note from Godfrey to Donovan, 28 July 1940, Donovan Papers, Box 81B, Vol. 34 (AMHI).
40. Godfrey Memoirs, GDFY, Box 1, Folder 6, p. 132, (CCA).
41. Bradley F. Smith, *The Ultra-Magic Deals and the Most Secret Special Relationship, 1940–46*, (Shrewsbury, England: Airlife Publishing, 1993), p. 38. See also *DNI Note of 2 August 1940 on Donovan's Visit*, Admiralty Papers (hereafter cited as 'ADM') 233/85, File 002376/40 (UKPRO) as cited in F.H. Hinsley, *British Intelligence in the Second World War: Its Influence on Strategy and Operations, Volume*

One (Official History), (London: Her Majesty's Stationery Office, 1979), pp. 312–13.

42. Hinsley, op. cit., p. 313.
43. Letter from Godfrey to Donovan, 20 July 1941, Donovan Papers, Box 81B, Vol. 34, (AMHI).
44. Godfrey Memoirs (GDFY) Box 1, Folder 6, pp. 132 & 129, (CCA).
45. Troy, op. cit., p. 33.
46. Paula G. Thornhill, 'Catalyst for Coalition: The Anglo-American Supply Relationship, 1939–1941,' (unpublished doctoral thesis, Oxford University, Trinity Term, 1991), p. 190.
47. *War Report*, p. 5.
48. Hyde, op. cit., p. 41.
49. Ellis, op. cit., p. 33.
50. Letter from E.R. Stettinius, Jr. to Donovan (undated, but included with other material dated August 1940), Donovan Papers, Box 81B, Vol. 34, (AMHI).
51. Letters from Miles to Donovan, 4 September, 5 and 26 October 1940, Donovan Papers, Box 81B, Vol. 34, (AMHI).
52. Letter from Donovan to FDR, 1 October 1940, and letter from Anderson to Donovan, 5 October 1940, Donovan Papers, Box 81B, Vol. 34, (AMHI).
53. Godfrey Memoirs (GDFY) Box 1, Folder 6, p. 131, (CCA).
54. Ellis, op. cit., pp. 33, 94–7.
55. Ibid., pp. 33–5.
56. B.F. Smith, op. cit., p. 14.
57. Spaatz was later promoted General and made Chief of Staff of the US Air Force.
58. Ellis, op. cit., p. 88.
59. Ellis, op. cit., p. 89.
60. Ibid., pp. 88, 99.
61. Thornhill, op. cit., p. 190.
62. Letters from Lord Halifax to Anthony Eden and to Archibald Sinclair, 5 December 1940, FO 371/24263/A4925/4925/45(1), p. 273, (UKPRO).
63. Letter from Donovan to Forrestal, 5 August 1940, Donovan Papers, Box 81B, Vol. 34, (AMHI).
64. Letter from Donovan to Sir Ronald Tree, 21 August 1940, and Tree's two replies, 28 August and 11 September 1940, Donovan Papers, Box 81B, Vol. 34, (AMHI).
65. Letter from Donovan to Brendan Bracken, 27 August 1940, Donovan Papers, Box 81B, Vol. 34, (AMHI).
66. Cable from Donovan to Bracken, 23 September 1940, Donovan Papers, Box 81B, Vol. 34, (AMHI).
67. Letter from Vansittart to Donovan, 28 October 1940, Donovan Papers, Box 81B, Vol. 34, (AMHI).
68. Letter from Donovan to Vansittart, 26 September 1940, Donovan Papers, Box 81B, Vol. 34, (AMHI).
69. Ellis, op. cit., p. 59.
70. After returning from Britain, Donovan tried to see Hoover to report on his meetings with a 'special intelligence unit which was working in South America and Mexico and was anxious to work with the FBI.' Précis of a memorandum from Hoover dated 6 August 1940, no caption, as cited in Dennis De Brandt, 'Structuring Intelligence for War,' *Studies in Intelligence*, (CIA: Historical Intelligence Collection, undated), p. 53. Note that earlier in 1940, Stephenson established a liaison relationship with the FBI in the spring of 1940 on matters concerning Nazi subversion in the Western Hemisphere. The British, through Stephenson, passed on specific information of operational interest to the FBI, which often intervened to arrest suspected

Nazi agents. The memo précis described above indicates that Donovan was not yet aware of this link when he returned from Britain, and is indicative of the unco-ordinated nature of intelligence activities on both sides of the Atlantic at this time.

71. Telegram from Churchill to Sir Miles Lampson, the British Ambassador in Cairo, for passage to Donovan, 12/604/604/G, 30 January 1941, FO 371/29792, (UKPRO).
72. Telegram from Lampson to Churchill on behalf of William Donovan, No. 268, R604/G, 8 February 1941, FO 371/29792, (UKPRO).
73. Hyde, op. cit., p. 43.
74. Ibid., p. 43.
75. Letter from Kirk to Donovan, 14 August 1940 (declassified from 'CONFIDEN-TIAL'), Donovan Papers, Box 81B, Vol. 34, (AMHI).
76. Telegram from the Marquis of Lothian of the British Mission in Washington, DC to the Foreign Office on the former's meeting with US Navy Secretary Frank Knox, No. 3281, 1 December 1940, FO 371/24263/272, (UKPRO).
77. Ellis, op. cit., pp. 62–63.
78. Telegram from Lothian to the Foreign Office, No. 2829, 27 November 1940, FO 371/24263/A4925/4925/45, p. 270, (UKPRO).
79. Telegram from Lothian to the Foreign Office, No. 2913, 4 December 1940, FO 371/24263/A4925/4925/45, p. 276, (UKPRO).
80. Letter from Halifax to Duff Cooper (declassified from 'SECRET'), (undated, but ad-ditional material in the file indicates that it was written on approximately 6 December 1940), FO 371/24263/A4925/ 4925/45(4), p. 281, (UKPRO).
81. Signal by Godfrey to Cunningham as quoted in Hyde, op. cit., p. 44.
82. Hyde, op. cit., p. 44.
83. Draft letter from COS to Commanders-in-Chief Mediterranean, Middle East, Gibraltar, and Malta, FO 371/24263, A51946/G, 26 December 1940 (declassified from 'SECRET'), p. 304, (UKPRO).
84. Letter from Sinclair to Halifax, 7 December 1940 (declassified from 'CONFIDEN-TIAL'), FO 371/24263, A5059/4925/45, (UKPRO).
85. Memorandum from J. Labouhere to 'J. B[alfour],' 7 December 1940, FO 371/24263, A4925/4925/45, p. 268, (UKPRO).
86. Handwritten note signed 'J. B[alfour].' at bottom of memorandum from J. Labouhere, 7 December 1940, FO 371/24263, A4925/4925/45, p. 268, (UKPRO).
87. Diary entry for 27 December 1940, Lt. Colonel Vivian Dykes, 'Personal Diary of Trip with Colonel William Donovan 26 December 1940 – 3 March 1941' (declassified from 'SECRET AND PERSONAL') (hereafter cited as 'Dykes Diary'), Donovan Pa-pers, Tab 2, Exhibit III, p. 2, (AMHI).
88. Telegram from the Foreign Office to Lampson in Cairo, 24 December 1940 (declassi-fied from 'SECRET'), FO 371/24263, A5194/G, p. 307, (UKPRO). This messages notes that expenses for Donovan's trip 'will be borne by His Majesty's Government, and Colonel Dykes has been told to draw on His Majesty's Embassy/Legations for funds which should be charged to the funds of the Assistant to the Oriental Secretary/Passport Control Officer.'
89. Dykes Diary, Entries for 1 March and 15, 21, and 24 January 1941, pp. 59, 20, 26, and 28.
90. Ellis, op. cit., p. 86.
91. Dykes Diary, pp. 1–4.
92. Ellis, op. cit., pp. 86–7.
93. Troy, op. cit., p. 39.
94. Ford, op. cit., p. 99.
95. West, *MI6*, p. 206.

96. David Mason, *Who's Who in World War II*, (London: Little, Brown, 1978), pp. 336–7.
97. Dykes Diary, Various entries from pp. 11–19 and 39–41, (AMHI).
98. Report by Donovan from meeting with Brigadier Pollack in Cairo, 21 February 1941, Donovan Papers, Box 94B, 'Balkan Trip 1941 of William J. Donovan,' (AMHI).
99. Dykes Diary, Entry for 14 January 1941, p. 19.
100. Ibid., Entry for 20 February 1941, p. 52.
101. Ibid., Entry for 19 February 1941, p. 51.
102. Telegram from the British Middle East Intelligence Center to the War Office drafted by Dykes, 13 February 1941 (declassified from 'MOST SECRET'), FO 371/27098, E514, (UKPRO).
103. Telegram from the British Ambassador in Baghdad, Sir B. Newton, to the Foreign Office, 14 February 1941 (declassified from 'SECRET'), FO 371/27098, E521G, (UKPRO).
104. Eden to the Prime Minister from Cairo, 22 February 1941 (declassified from 'SECRET'), FO 371/26194, A1728, p. 26, (UKPRO).
105. Ford, op. cit., p. 100.
106. Dykes Diary, Entries for 15–16 January 1941, pp. 20–21. Roosevelt signed the Lend-Lease Bill into law on 11 March 1941, paving the way for the provision of American war materiel – ostensibly in a leasing arrangement – to Britain and the other Allies. The first shipments went to the United Kingdom, Greece, and China. See Mercer (ed.), op. cit., p. 168.
107. Dykes Diary, Entry for 17 January 1941, p. 22.
108. Diary of Henry J. Morgenthau, (FDRL), pp. 23–4, as cited in Troy, op. cit., p. 40.
109. Ford, op. cit., p. 100.
110. See Hyde, op. cit., p. 46, Ellis, op. cit., p. 63, and Ford, op. cit., pp. 102–3.
111. Hinsley, op. cit., pp. 369–70.
112. Bickham Sweet-Escott's draft lecture notes titled, 'SOE in the Balkans,' Bickham Sweet-Escott Papers, Box 4, Folder 11A, Balliol College Archives, Oxford University (hereafter cited as 'BOA'), pp. 2–3.
113. 'Report to SO – On Certain SO2 Activities in Yugoslavia,' 24 June 1941, Bickham Sweet-Escott Paprs, Box 4, Folder A11, (BOA).
114. Ibid.
115. 'British Relations with OSS,' OSS Records, Job 62–242, Box 29, Folder 2 (typescript, I). See Thomas F. Troy, *Wild Bill and Intrepid*, (Yale University Press, 1996), p. 223.
116. See Eden to Prime Minister from Cairo, 22 February 1941, p. 26, FO 371/26194/A1728; Dykes to the War Office, 13 February 1941 (declassified from 'MOST SECRET'), FO 371/27098/E514; Newton to the Foreign Office from Baghdad, 14 February 1941 (declassified from 'SECRET'), FO 371/27098/E521/G and E538/G; Memorandum of Conversation of Dykes and Knabenshue with the Iraqi Minister of Foreign Affairs, 12 February 1941, FO 371/27098/E780G; and Palairet to the Foreign Office from Athens, 18 January 1941 (declassified from 'SECRET'), FO 371/29792/R1382/G and A/183/183/G, (UKPRO).
117. Minutes of a Foreign Office (American Department) meeting about Donovan, 25 February 1941, FO 371/26194/A1154, p. 24, and Troy, op. cit., p. 39.
118. Troy, op. cit., p. 40.
119. Hyde, op. cit., p. 42.
120. Letter from Donovan to Knox, 26 April 1941, excerpted as 'Appendix A' of Troy, op. cit., p. 417.
121. *War Report*, p. 7.
122. Godfrey Hodgson, *The Colonel: The Life and Wars of Henry Stimson*, 1867–1950, (Boston: Northeastern University Press, 1990), p. 203. See also Herbert O. Yardley, *The American Black Chamber*, (New York: Blue Ribbon Books, 1931), pp. 368–71.

2 AN UNEQUAL PARTNERSHIP: THE COORDINATOR OF INFORMATION AND BRITISH MENTORING

1.   William Stephenson as quoted by his biographer H.M. Hyde, *Quiet Canadian*, p. 155.
2.   COI had four principal components: Secret Intelligence (SI), Research and Analysis (R & A), Special Operations (SO), and the Foreign Information Service (FIS). To staff COI, Donovan recruited a remarkable group of individuals from America's elite. These included J.P. Morgan's sons Henry and Junius, Bill Vanderbilt, Andrew Mellon's son-in-law David Bruce, Atherton Richards, who was the president of the Hawaiian Pineapple Company, and Elmo Roper, who conducted the *Fortune Magazine* surveys. From literary circles came Pulitzer Prize-winning playwright Robert Sherwood and noted poet Archibald MacLeish. From academe came James Phinney Baxter of Williams, William Langer and Edward Mason of Harvard, Norman Holmes Pearson, Wilmarth Lewis, and Sherman Kent of Yale, G.T. Robinson of Columbia, Conyers Read of Pennsylvania, Maurice Halperin of Oklahoma, and Preston James of Michigan. From Hollywood came the great film directors John Ford and Merian Cooper, and the actor Douglas Fairbanks, Jr. Other prominent figures, such as G. Edward Buxton, the famous newspaperman, noted lawyers Russell Livermore, William Whitney, and Allen Dulles, and Roosevelt's son James, also joined COI. See Stewart Alsop and Thomas Braden, *Sub Rosa: The OSS and American Espionage* (New York: Cornwall Press, 1946), pp. 7, 18–19, and author's interview with SOE and SIS veteran Peter Lee, 12 September 1995, at the Special Forces Club in London.
3.   Ray S. Cline, *Secrets, Spies, and Scholars: Blueprint of the Essential CIA* (Washington, DC: Acropolis Books, 1976), p. 30.
4.   Mercer (ed.), *Chronicle*, p. 173.
5.   Hyde, op. cit., p. 152.
6.   Admiral John Godfrey, 'Godfrey Report', ADM 223/84, (UKPRO).
7.   Godfrey, 'Naval Memoirs,' Godfrey Papers, Box 1, Folder 6, pp. 132–133, (CCA).
8.   Ibid.
9.   Ibid., p. 137.
10. Ibid., p. 134.
11. Andrew Lycett, *Ian Fleming* (London: Weidenfeld & Nicolson, 1995), pp. 129–30.
12. The Assistant Chief of Staff for Intelligence of the US Army.
13. Memorandum from Miles to Marshall titled, 'Coordinator for the Three Intelligence Agencies of the Government,' 8 April 1941, Records of the Army Staff, Record Group 319, Washington National Records Center, Suitland, Maryland, as cited in Troy, *Donovan and CIA*, p. 42.
14. Otto Doering in taped interview with Anthony Cave Brown, William J. Donovan Papers (hereafter cited as 'Donovan Papers'), Box 1, Folder 1, transcript p. 66, (CCA).
15. See Troy, op. cit., pp. 49–52 and 55–9.
16. Historian Anthony Cave Brown may have overstated this point when he wrote the following on p. 58 of *'C': The Secret Life of Sir Stewart Menzies, Spymaster to Winston Churchill*, (New York: Macmillan, 1987): 'Such, indeed, was the alarm that Donovan was a British control that for a time FDR decided against Donovan's appointment as chief of the new secret service.'
17. J. Edward Lumbard, 'William J. Donovan,' pamphlet reprinted from Memorial Book, 1959, of The Association of the Bar of the City of New York, p. 7, Hyde Papers, Box 1, Folder 4 (CCA).
18. Doering interview, Donovan Papers, Box 1, Folder 1, 18 October 1977, p. 40 (CCA).
19. War Report, p. 7.
20. Ibid.

21. Untitled and undated document, RG 226, Entry 190, Box 239, Folder 544, (NARA).
22. Sherwood and Donovan both had considerable influence with Roosevelt, and the former struggled to retain his independent access to the President even after he became Donovan's subordinate. Largely as a result of Sherwood's maneuverings, he and his foreign propaganda element were transferred from COI to the new Office of War Information (OWI) in the summer of 1942. Sherwood's propagandists worked closely with Stephenson's BSC, which brought them into competition with the Research and Analysis Branch of COI/OSS.
23. Hyde, op. cit., p. 153.
24. Cave Brown, 'C', p. 359.
25. Letter from Dansey to Donovan, 15 July 1941, Donovan Papers, Microfilm Reel 32, (AMHI), as cited in Cave Brown, 'C', p. 360.
26. William Henoeffer, 'If Donovan Were Here Today,' Address delivered by the Curator of CIA's Historical Intelligence Collection at CIA Headquarters to French, British, and American World War II Jedburghs on occasion of the Second International Jedburgh Reunion organized by OSS Veterans in Washington, DC, 14 May 1988, p. 4 (author's personal collection).
27. Letter from Stephenson to H. M. Hyde, 18 September 1961, Hyde Papers, Box 1, Folder 5, (CCA).
28. Godfrey, 'Godfrey Report,' 7 July 1941, ADM 223/84, (UKPRO).
29. Ibid.
30. Lycett, op. cit., p. 130.
31. Troy, op. cit., p. 81.
32. Lycett, op. cit., p. 131.
33. Bradley H. Smith, *The Shadow Warriors: The OSS and the Origins of the CIA*, (London: André Deutsch, 1983), p. 90.
34. R. Smith, *OSS*, p. 19.
35. The fierce opposition from the US military, State Department, FBI, and various other official entities to the creation and activities of COI is a complex and fascinating example of bureaucratic warfare that is well documented in Troy, op. cit., pp. 43–71.
36. 'Appointments and Telephone Calls, August 9, 1941 – September 29, 1945,' Donovan Papers, (AMHI), as cited in Troy, op. cit., p. 83.
37. Ellis, op. cit., p. 123.
38. Ibid., pp. 120, 84–5.
39. David Bruce in interview with Thomas F. Troy, 30 December 1972, as cited in Troy, op. cit., p. 83.
40. Peter Grose, *Gentleman Spy: The Life of Allen Dulles*, (London: André Deutsch, 1994), pp. 145–6.
41. As a young diplomat in 1916, Dulles represented the US Government at the funeral of the Habsburg Emperor Franz Josef in Vienna.
42. Mr William Dwight Whitney interview with unidentified OSS officer, 6 June 1945, Record Group ('RG') 226, Entry 190, Box 220, Folder 247, p. 1, (NARA).
43. David Stafford, *Camp X: OSS, 'Intrepid,' and the Allies' North American Training Camp for Secret Agents, 1941–1945*, (New York: Dodd, Mead, 1987), p. 28.
44. Donovan to FDR, 'Excerpts from letter dated July 25, 1941, from Chairman of Joint Operations Group in England,' 6 August 1941, PSF 128, Folder 'COI 1941,' (FDRL).
45. Donovan to FDR, 'Letter from Polish Ambassador regarding Polish-Soviet relations (FYI),' 27 September 1941, PSF 128, Folder 'COI 1941,' (FDRL).
46. Donovan to FDR, 'Report on Germany – Spring and Autumn 1941,' PSF 128, Folder 'COI 1941' (FDRL).
47. Donovan to FDR, 'FYI re. coverage of Roosevelt letter to Stalin by United Press in Berlin,' 8 October 1941, PSF 128, Folder 'COI 1941,' (FDRL)

48. Donovan to FDR, 'FYI re. summary of Russian transport system,' 17 October 1941, PSF 128, Folder 'COI 1941,' (FDRL).
49. Donovan to FDR, 'Copy of a letter from British Naval officer to wife in England describing sinking of Bismarck,' 21 October 1941, PSF 128, Folder 'COI 1941,' (FDRL).
50. Donovan to FDR, 'Commandos,' 21 October 1941, PSF 128, Folder 'COI 1941,' (FDRL).
51. PSF 128, Folder 'COI 1941,' (FDRL).
52. Whitney interview with unidentified OSS officer, 6 June 1945, RG 226, Entry 190, Box 220, Folder 247, p. 1, (NARA).
53. Roosevelt to Churchill, 24 October 1941, OF 4485, Box 1, Folder 'Office of Strategic Services, 1940–October 1941,' (FDRL).
54. Troy, op. cit., p. 78.
55. Cave Brown, '*C*', p. 363.
56. Whitney interview with unidentified OSS officer, 6 June 1945, p. 1.
57. Author's interview with Fisher Howe, 13 August 1995, in Washington, DC.
58. Ibid.
59. Ibid.
60. Christopher Andrew, *Secret Service: The Making of the British Intelligence Community*, (London: William Heinemann, 1985), p. 467.
61. Whitney interview with unidentified OSS officer, 6 June 1945, p. 4
62. Whitney to Donovan, 2 December 1941, RG 226, Entry 190, Box 246, File 681, p. 1, (NARA).
63. Ibid., pp. 1–3, (NARA).
64. America's intelligence contribution to the Allied effort was pitifully small in 1940–41. Most of what was useful came from Robert Murphy's 12 vice-consuls in North Africa who were charged with collecting secret information on Vichy and Axis activities, although even this was considered by the British largely to be background material. Murphy had negotiated the Vichy-US trade accord in February 1941 and subsequently served as the US Consul in Algiers. His 'network' was eventually turned over to Donovan's organization and proved to be one of OSS's most important sources of information in its early days. See F. H. Hinsley, op. cit., p. 444, and Doolittle to the Secretary of State, 'Liaison with the British Intelligence Services (declassified from "STRICTLY CONFIDENTIAL"),' 30 January 1942, Goodfellow Papers, Box 2, Folder 'Algeria,' (HIA), pp. 1–4.
65. Whitney to Donovan, 2 December 1941, RG 226, Entry 190, Box 246, File 681, p. 3, (NARA).
66. Ibid.
67. Whitney interview with unidentified OSS officer, 6 June 1945, p. 3.
68. Ibid., p. 1.
69. Ismay was Churchill's personal Chief of Staff and deputy secretary to the War Cabinet.
70. Ismay to Churchill and Churchill's Reply, CAB 120/815, November 1941, (UKPRO).
71. Whitney interview with unidentified OSS officer, 6 June 1945, p. 2.
72. Cave Brown, '*C*', p. 364. ULTRA was what the British called intelligence derived from ENIGMA machine decryptions.
73. Troy, op. cit., pp. 117–18.
74. Whitney to Bruce (declassified from 'SECRET'), 28 February 1942, RG 226, Entry 190, Box 246, Folder 678, pp. 4–5, (NARA).
75. Whitney interview with unidentified OSS officer, 6 June 1945, p. 2.
76. Ibid.
77. Winner, a former newspaperman and friend of David Bruce, was one of Whitney's assistants.
78. Cave Brown, '*C*', p. 365.

79. Whitney to Bruce, 28 February 1942, RG 226, Entry 190, Box 246, Folder 678, p. 2, (NARA).
80. Ibid.
81. Anthony Read and David Fisher's *Colonel Z: The Life and Times of a Master of Spies*, (London: Hodder & Stoughton, 1984). p. 311.
82. Bruce to Whitney (declassified from 'SECRET AND PERSONAL'), 18 March 1942, RG 226, Entry 190, Box 246, Folder 678, p. 4, (NARA).
83. Whitney to Bruce, 28 February 1942, RG 226, Entry 190, Box 246, Folder 678, p. 3, (NARA).
84. Bruce to Whitney, 18 March 1942, RG 226, Entry 190, Box 246, Folder 678, pp. 1–4, (NARA).
85. Ibid., pp. 3–4.
86. 'Chronological Index,' Volume 2 (SI), RG 226, Entry 190, Box 251, Folder 739, p. 1, (NARA).
87. Untitled and undated document, RG 226, Entry 190, Box 239, Folder 544, pp. 30–31, (NARA).
88. Ibid.
89. Bickham Sweet–Escott, *Baker Street Irregular: Five Years in the Special Operations Executive*, (London: Methuen, 1965), p. 127.
90. Ibid.
91. *War Report*, p. 70. 'L' activities were associated with special operations and 'K' activities with espionage-related work. They were later separated under Goodfellow and Bruce, respectively.
92. Ibid.
93. Major General Rygor Slowikowski, *In the Secret Service: The Lighting of the Torch*, (London: Windrush Press, 1988), pp. 171–2.
94. Eric Dennis, untitled article from Paris in *The Chronicle Herald*, 28 May 1964, R. Harris Smith Papers, Box 1, Folder 'North Africa,' (HIA). The curator of the Central Intelligence Agency's Historical Intelligence Collection confirmed in a conversation with the author on 28 November 1995 that while little unclassified evidence exists to verify Solborg's story about his SIS work in 1939–40, it is believable and very consistent with related events of the period, Solborg's personality, and British targeting and tradecraft. Moreover, Ellis' involvement in arranging for Solborg's COI appointment augurs in favor of its authenticity.
95. Troy, op. cit., p. 106.
96. Stafford, op. cit., p. 60.
97. Donovan to Adjutant General 'Stephenson, William Samuel – Recommendation for Award of Distinguished Service Medal,' 19 June 1944, Forgan Papers, Box 1, Folder (unmarked envelope), (HIA).
98. R. Smith, *OSS*, pp. 91–2.
99. Stafford, op. cit., p. 63.
100. Ellis, op. cit., pp. 119–20.
101. Donovan to Goodfellow, 23 March 1942, Goodfellow Papers, Box 4, Folder 'OSS Memoranda 1941–March 1942,' (HIA) as cited in B. H. Smith, op. cit., p. 439. According to Smith, Solborg was suspected by the Germans in North Africa of being an American agent because of his work there in 1941.
102. Slowikowksi, op. cit., p. 172.
103. Solborg to Goodfellow sent from the Aviz Hotel in Lisbon, 21 March 1942, M. Preston Goodfellow Papers (hereafter cited as 'Goodfellow Papers'), Box 2, Folder 'Solborg, Bob – 1941–1954,' (HIA).
104. Solborg to Goodfellow sent from the US Consulate in Casablanca, 10 June 1942, Goodfellow Papers, Box 2, Folder 'Solborg, Bob – 1941–1954,' (HIA).

105.   Ernest Volkman and Blaine Baggett, *Secret Intelligence*, (New York: Doubleday, 1989), p. 31.
106.   Cline, op. cit., pp. 45–6.
107.   Ibid.
108.   R. Smith, *OSS*, p. 39.
109.   Troy, op. cit., pp. 106–7.
110.   Ibid.
111.   Cave Brown, '*C*', pp. 269, 357.
112.   Read and Fisher, op. cit., p. 311.
113.   Ibid., p. 312.
114.   Untitled and undated document, Donovan Papers, Box 87C, Volume 4, p. 1, (AMHI).
115.   Ellis, op. cit., pp. 141–2.
116.   Norwood F. Allman, 'December, Part I, History – Far East, SI,' Norwood F. Allman Papers, Box 6, Folder 'History – Far East, SI,' (HIA).
117.   Memorandum to QO, No. W-159, 'Chinese Scheme,' 7 January 1942, Goodfellow Papers, Box 4, Folder 'OSS Memoranda, 1941–March, 1942,' p. 1.
118.   Ibid., p. 2.
119.   Donovan to FDR, 24 January 1942, PSF 128, Folder 'Coordinator of Information 1942,' (FDRL).
120.   M.B. DePass Jr. to Donovan with copy to Solborg, 'Scheme OLIVA,' 27 January 1942, Goodfellow Papers, Box 4, Folder 'OSS Memoranda, 1941–March, 1942,' pp. 1–5.
121.   Maochun Yu, 'OSS in China – New Information About and Old Role,' *International Journal of Intelligence and Counterintelligence*, Spring 1994, Vol. 7, Number 1, p. 78. For second part of citation, see also John P. Davies to Ambassador Gauss, 'Anglo-American Cooperation in East Asia,' 15 November 1943, RG 226, Entry 110, Box 52, Folder 16, (NARA).
122.   Article by Eric Dennis on Solborg's exploits in the *Chronicle Herald* newspaper, 28 May 1964, R. Harris Smith Papers, Box 1, File 'North Africa,' (HIA).
123.   Biographical notes on Whitney Shepardson, Smith Papers, Box 1, File 'North Africa,' (HIA).
124.   R. Smith, *OSS*, p. 33.
125.   Nelson D. Lankford (ed.), *OSS Against the Reich: The World War II Diaries of Colonel David K.E. Bruce*, (Kent State, Ohio: Kent State University Press, 1991), p. 2.
126.   Howe interview, 13 August 1995.
127.   R. Smith, *OSS*, p. 33.
128.   Author's interview with Henry Hyde, 24 July 1995, in New York City. As a senior OSS officer based in London and North Africa in 1943, Hyde worked closely with his British counterparts.
129.   Untitled and undated document, RG 226, Entry 190, Box 246, Folder 678, (NARA).
130.   Robin Winks, *Cloak and Gown: Scholars in America's Secret* War, (London: Collins Harvill, 1987), p. 192.
131.   The most likely cause of any anti-American feelings harbored by Dansey was his fear that Donovan's aggressive and well-financed 'amateurs' would interfere with what he considered to be carefully planned, professional SIS operations in Europe and elsewhere. Dansey had been in the intelligence 'game' for a good portion of his life and had notoriously little patience for those possessing what he deemed to be insufficient experience. A good account of these views can be found in Read and Fisher, op. cit.
132.   Ibid., p. 308.
133.   Hyde interview, 24 July 1995.
134.   Cave Brown, '*C*', p. 324.
135.   Stafford, op. cit., pp. 53–5.

136. Author's interview with Sir Douglas Dodds-Parker, 26 May 1995, in Heyford, Oxfordshire. As the head of SOE's 'MASSINGHAM' base in Algiers and joint chief of the Anglo-American SO organization in North Africa from January 1943, and as head of SOE's activities in Italy in 1943, Dodds-Parker was an important figure in SOE-OSS relations during the war.
137. Ellis, op. cit., p. 160.

3 TRIAL BY FIRE: LONDON AND THE PROVING GROUNDS OF NORTH AFRICA AND BURMA

1. *War Report*, p. 104.
2. 'Directive – Functions of the Office of Strategic Services (declassified from "SECRET"),' 9 March 1943, RG 226, Entry 190, Box 228, Folder 388, (NARA).
3. Roosevelt's Executive Order establishing the OSS titled 'Office of Strategic Services,' 13 June 1942, RG 226, Entry 190, Box 229, Folder 406, (NARA).
4. 'Directive – Functions of the Office of Strategic Services (declassified from "SECRET"),' 9 March 1943, RG 226, Entry 190, Box 228, Folder 388, (NARA).
5. Nelson D. Lankford (ed.), *OSS Against the Reich: The World War II Diaries of Colonel David K.E. Bruce*, (Kent State, Ohio: Kent State University Press, 1991), p. 15.
6. Draft letter from Sir Charles Hambro to Donovan, 3 June 1942, RG 226, M1642, Roll 111, (NARA), p. 1.
7. Lankford (ed.), op. cit., pp. 17–8, 20–4, & 212, entries for 21–22 May, 25–31 May, and 1–5 June 1942.
8. Ibid., pp. 23–5, entries for 12–22 June 1942. Philby was already spying at this time for Moscow.
9. Draft letter from Hambro to Donovan, 3 June 1942, RG 226, M1642, Roll 111, (NARA), p. 2.
10. Hambro to Donovan (declassified from 'SECRET AND PERSONAL'), CH/2355, 23 June 1942, RG 226, M1642, Roll 111, (NARA).
11. 'Division of Territories and Other Collaboration between the British SOE and the United States OSS,' Memorandum for the Joint Chiefs of Staff, undated, RG 226, M1642, Roll 111, (NARA).
12. 'Agreements Between OSS and British SOE (declassified from "SECRET"),' Enclosure, undated, RG 226, Microfilm (hereafter cited as 'M') 1642, Roll 111, (NARA), pp. 1–2.
13. 'Division of Territories and Other Collaboration between the British SOE and the United States OSS,' Memorandum for the Joint Chiefs of Staff, undated, RG 226, M1642, Roll 111, (NARA).
14. Ibid. OSS Switzerland's French operations later complicated relations with SOE in London.
15. 'Record of Discussion regarding collaboration between British and American SOE,' 23 June 1942, No. 4, Goodfellow Papers, Box 4, Folder 'OSS Memoranda June–July 1942,' (HIA), p. 2.
16. 'Agreements Between OSS and British SOE (declassified from "SECRET"),' Enclosure, undated, RG 226, M1642, Roll 111, (NARA), p 2.
17. 'SOE Activity in North Africa (declassified from "MOST SECRET"),' June 1942, HS 3/56, (UKPRO).
18. 'Excerpt from JPWC Minutes, Agreement Between Office of Strategic Services and British Secret (*sic*) Operations Executive,' undated, RG 226, M1642, Roll 111, (NARA).

19. 'Joint Psychological Warfare Committee: Agreements Between OSS and British SOE (declassified from "SECRET"),' JPWC 27/3d Draft, 27 August 1942, RG 226, M1642, Roll 111, (NARA).

20. 'Relations with the British and Other Allies,' undated, Director's Office, RG 226, Entry 190, Box 220, Folder 248, (NARA), p. 1.

21. One of the major obstacles to achieving independence from the British concerned OSS London's reliance on SIS and SOE communications through mid-1942. In the autumn of 1942, the US State Department finally agreed to allow OSS coded messages to be transmitted privately from the US Embassy in London and to allow OSS to use the diplomatic pouch without OSS material being reviewed by State Department personnel. Once OSS London moved to its new offices at 72 Grosvenor Street in early 1943, it was able to establish a truly independent communications capability. See 'Introductory Survey of Establishment, Activities and Plans of SI London,' 15 January 1945, RG 226, Box 233, Folder 469, (NARA), p. 11.

22. 'Relations with the British and Other Allies,' undated, Diretor's Office, RG 226, Entry 190, Box 220, Folder 248, (NARA), p. 1.

23. A first group of three American SO officers were enrolled in Britain's 'Camp X' school in Canada between April and June 1942, and their positive experience prompted OSS to request that 64 officers be sent to 'various specialized training schools in Great Britain, and [that] American SO Officers be detailed . . . to the various operational stations and offices in England. Donovan believed that this 'not only [served] as a means of training . . . but [ensured] unity of doctrine and effort.' SOE agreed to take 48 OSS trainees. See 'Record of Discussion regarding collaboration between British and American SOE,' 23 June 1942, No. 6, RG 226, M1642, Roll 111, (NARA).

24. 'Procurement Period,' undated, RG 226, M1623, Roll 3, (NARA), p. 11.

25. Eisenhower was appointed to this position on 25 June 1942.

26. William Phillips to FDR, 13 August 1942, PSF 38 'Diplomatic Correspondence Great Britain: Office of Strategic Services,' (FDRL).

27. 'Introductory Survey of Establishment, Activities and Plans of SI London,' 15 January 1945, RG 226, Box 233, Folder 469, (NARA), p. 11.

28. 'The Functions and Requirements of SAB London (declassified from "SECRET"),' 12 August 1942, RG 226, Entry 190, Box 319, Folder 422, (NARA), p. 12.

29. William Phillips to Donovan, 12 August 1942, RG 226, Entry 190, Box 229, Folder 412, (NARA).

30. Ellery Huntington, 'SO Organization, Operations and Objectives, Based on London Trip, 9–27 September 1942,' RG 226, M1642, Roll 111, (NARA), p. 11.

31. 'French operations,' Captain [Donald] Downes to Goodfellow, Goodfellow Papers, Box 4, Folder 'OSS Memoranda 1941–March 1942,' (HIA), pp. 1–2.

32. 'American participation in SO in France and Western Europe,' internal COI memorandum for Goodfellow probably from a member of his staff, 10 June 1942, Goodfellow Papers, Box 4, Folder 'OSS Memoranda June–July 1942,' (HIA), pp. 1–2.

33. 'SOE and SO London (Operational Arrangements) (declassified from "SECRET"),' undated but almost certainly part of the follow on talks to the June 1942 accords, RG 226, M1642, Roll 111, (NARA).

34. Ellery Huntington, 'SO Organization, Operations and Objectives, Based on London Trip, 9–27 September 1942,' RG 226, M1642, Roll 111, (NARA), p. 7.

35. 'SOE and SO London (Operational Arrangements) (declassified from "SECRET"),' undated but almost certainly part of the follow on talks to the June 1942 accords, RG 226, M1642, Roll 111, (NARA).

36. William Phillips to Shepardson (declassified from 'SECRET'), 25 July 1942, RG 226, Entry 190, Box 246, Folder 683, (NARA).

37. Huntington, 'SO Organization, Operations and Objectives, Based on London Trip, 9–27 September 1942,' RG 226, M1642, Roll 111, (NARA), p. 7

38. Goodfellow had become Donovan's special assistant for organizing guerrilla groups.

39. Huntington, 'SO Organization, Operations and Objectives, Based on London Trip, 9–27 September 1942,' RG 226, M1642, Roll 111, (NARA), pp. 8–9.

40. Ibid., p. 24.

41. Ibid., pp. 13–14.

42. Ibid., p. 25.

43. Ibid., p. 22.

44. 'Introductory Survey of Establishment, Activities and Plans of SI London,' 15 January 1945, RG 226, Box 233, Folder 469, (NARA), p. 10.

45. Shepardson Memorandum, 'Office of Strategic Services – London,' 24 June 1942, RG 226, Entry 190, Box 233, Folder 469, (NARA), pp. 1 & 6.

46. Ibid., pp. 8–9.

47. Ibid., pp. 10–11.

48. William Maddox interview with unidentified OSS officer, 13 October 1944, RG 226, Entry 190, Box 251, Folder 739, (NARA).

49. De Gaulle's top lieutenants all took pseudonyms (from a Paris metro map) to conceal their identities from the Germans and thus protect their family members in France from reprisals.

50. 'Relations with the French,' undated, RG 226, Entry 190, Box 251, Folder 739, (NARA).

51. Shepardson interview with unidentified OSS officer, 2 November 1944, RG 226, Entry 190, Box 251, Folder 739, (NARA).

52. Ibid.

53. Ibid.

54. 'The Functions and Requirements of SAB London,' 12 August 1942, RG 226, Entry 190, Box 319, Folder 422, (NARA), p. 3.

55. SI London Branch Report SMR No. 4, 1 April 1943, 'Introductory Survey of Establishment, Activities and Plans of SI London,' 15 January 1945, RG 226, Box 233, Folder 469, (NARA), pp. 20–21.

56. Ibid., pp. 20–21.

57. William Phillips to FDR, 13 August 1942, PSF 38 'Diplomatic Correspondence Great Britain: Office of Strategic Services,' (FDRL).

58. 'Relations with Allied Governments in Exile,' undated, RG 226, Entry 190, Box 251, Folder 739, (NARA), p. 1.

59. Shepardson interview with unidentified OSS officer, 2 November 1944.

60. Ibid.

61. 'Relations with the French (declassified from "SECRET"),' undated, RG 226, Entry 190, Box 251, Folder 739, (NARA).

62. 'Relations with the French (declassified from "SECRET"),' undated, RG 226, Entry 190, Box 251, Folder 739, (NARA). See also 'Record of Meeting with OSS Representatives on North Africa (declassified from "MOST SECRET"),' 12 August 1942, HS 3/56, (UKPRO).

63. 'Introductory Survey of Establishment, Activities and Plans of SI London' 15 January 1945, RG 226, Box 233, Folder 469, (NARA), pp. 18–20. See also Shepardson interview with unnamed OSS officer, 2 November 1944.

64. 'Notes on Talk with General McClure (Roseborough) (declassified from "SECRET"),' 7 September 1942, and 'Supplementary Notes on talk with Philip, Billotte, Passy, and Bingen (Roseborough) (declassified from "SECRET"),' 10 September 1942, RG 226, Entry 190, Box 251, Folder 739, (NARA).

65. 'Relations with the French (declassified from "SECRET"),' undated, RG 226, Entry 190, Box 251, Folder 739, (NARA).

66. The American desire to exclude de Gaulle's organization from TORCH had its roots in December 1941, when Gaullist forces seized the French islands of St Pierre and Miquelon off Newfoundland, which were then under Vichy's authority. While de Gaulle's action was somewhat useful to the Allies – a powerful radio transmitter on St Pierre capable of broadcasting intelligence on Allied shipping and weather conditions to German naval units operating in the North Atlantic was seized – it was acutely embarrassing for the US Government, which had just concluded an agreement with Vichy Admiral Robert 'involving maintenance of the *status quo* in French possessions in the Western Hemisphere.' US Secretary of State Cordell Hull wrote to Roosevelt on 31 December 1941 that he believed '95 percent of the French people are not Gaullists and would not follow him,' which, according to Hull, 'leads straight to our plans about North Africa and our omission of de Gaulle's co-operation in that connection.' See Robert Sherwood (ed.), *The White House Papers of Harry L. Hopkins, Volume I, September 1939– January 1942,* (London: Eyre & Spottiswoode, 1949), pp. 456–62, including reproduction of Hull to FDR, 'Memorandum for the President,' 31 December 1941.

67. Maddox, 'Relations of OSS to Free French BCRA and British Broadway (declassified from "SECRET"),' 26 August 1942, RG 226, Entry 190, Box 251, Folder 739, (NARA).

68. 'Memorandum for Discussion with Colonel Huntington, Comments on OSS (declassified from "MOST SECRET"),' 23 October 1942, HS 3/61, (UKPRO).

69. War Report, p. 71.

70. Ibid., p. ix.

71. 'Record of Discussion Regarding Collaboration between British and United States SOE,' 17 June 1942, RG 226, M1642, Roll 111, (NARA), Appendix I.

72. Under a long-standing Anglo-US agreement, American diplomatic and intelligence organizations 'looked after contacts with Vichy France while Great Britain handled relations with Spain.' See F.H. Hinsley, *British Intelligence in the Second World War: Its Influence on Strategy and Operations, Volume II*, (London: HMSO, 1981), p. 470.

73. *The Overseas Targets: War Report of the OSS, Volume II* (declassified from 'TOP SECRET'), Prepared by History Project, Strategic Services Unit, Office of the Assistant Secretary of War, War Department, Washington, DC, (New York: Walker, 1976), p. 11.

74. SOE to Eddy (declassified from 'MOST SECRET'), LONMAY No. 4, 10 September 1942, HS 3/63, (UKPRO).

75. Named for its principal architects Robert Murphy (then US chargé d'affaires in Vichy) and Marshal Maxime Weygand (then Vichy Governor of North Africa), the accord also permitted the US to establish twelve consular positions to monitor imports of US goods. Known as 'Murphy's twelve apostles,' these 'consular officers' were used in conjunction with OSS representatives in Tunisia, Algeria, and Morocco to collect intelligence on Vichy and Axis activities; together they were taken over by Donovan's organization in January 1942 and formed the framework for OSS's SI and SO networks used in support of TORCH.

76. 'Record of Discussion Regarding Collaboration between British and United States SOE,' 17 June 1942, RG 226, M1642, Roll 111, (NARA), Appendix I.

77. 'Summary of Agreement between British SOE and American SO,' undated, Copy 23, RG 226, M1642, Roll 111, (NARA), pp. 11–12. See also 'Cipher Telegram No. 14,' 1 September 1942, HS 3/63, (UKPRO).

78. 'Record of a Meeting with OSS Representatives on North Africa (declassified from "MOST SECRET"),' 12 August 1942, HS 3/56, (UKPRO).

79. Nigel West, *Secret War: The Story of SOE, Britain's Wartime Sabotage Organization,* (London: Westintel, 1992), p. 134.

80. B.H. Smith, *Shadow Warriors*, p. 146.
81. *War Report, Volume II*, p. 11.
82. Eddy made no organizational distinction between SI and SO in North Africa, which meant that all of his charges were expected to perform all sorts of subversive activities, from spying and sabotage to propaganda and secret diplomacy.
83. ENIGMA decryptions and other SIGINT processed by SIS and disseminated to the TORCH military planners played a major role in the 8 November invasion and military campaign that followed. The effectiveness of Allied deception plans, for example, which sought, *inter alia*, to convince Berlin that Dakar, Italy, or the Aegean were more likely invasion points than the real landing areas in Algeria and Tunisia, was assessed in this manner. SIS also reported various other useful items, such as intelligence indicating that probable resistance to the Allies was weakest near Algiers, and that the Germans planned to occupy Vichy France in the event of an Allied invasion of North Africa. Moreover, the military commanders used throughout the North African campaign critical tactical intelligence on Axis movements provided by SIS, again, principally derived through SIGINT. See Hinsley, op. cit., pp. 468–74 & 481–505.
84. *War Report, Volume II*, p. 13.
85. 'Report of a Meeting with OSS Representatives on North Africa (declassified from "MOST SECRET"),' August 1942, HS 3/63, (UKPRO).
86. 'Minutes of SOE Working Committee held on 31st August 1942 to Consider Progress of LONMAY (declassified from "MOST SECRET"),' HS 3/63, (UKPRO).
87. 'SO Operation Instructions to Lieutenant Colonel W.A. Eddy (declassified from "SECRET"),' AFHQ, 14 October 1942, Rounds Papers, Box 1, Folder 'Landings in North Africa,' (HIA), pp. 1–2. SOE did have some human assets at its disposal in North Africa, particularly in Spanish Morocco, although it was forced to halt operations in the weeks leading up to TORCH because it had been compromised through a security lapse. The 'remnants' of this network were to be used as possible to assist the landings at Casablanca, while SOE agents in Casablanca who were not compromised were put under Eddy's control. See SOE to Eddy (declassified from 'MOST SECRET'), LONMAY No. 4, 10 September 1942, 'Minutes of SOE Working Committee Meeting Held on 13th August 1942 to Discuss Operation LONMAY (declassified from "MOST SECRET"), and Minutes of SOE Working Committee Meeting Held on 20th August 1942 to Discuss Operation LONMAY (declassified from "MOST SECRET"),' HS 3/63, (UKPRO).
88. 'Note on the discussions with General Mason-MacFarlane,' ADL/GL/118, 24 August 1942, HS 3/63, (UKPRO).
89. 'Preliminary Report on OSS/SOE Activities,' 8 December 1942, HS 3/56, (UKPRO), p. 6.
90. Cline, *Secrets, Spies and Scholars,* p. 70.
91. Mast was the deputy commander-in-chief of the French forces in Vichy North Africa and was a supporter of Giraud, whom he represented at this meeting. See Cipher Telegram from General Mark Clark to General Eisenhower, LONMAY No. 79–90, 24 October 1942, HS 3/63, (UKPRO).
92. Clark to Eisenhower, LONMAY No. 85, 24 October 1942, HS 3/63, (UKPRO).
93. Clark to Eisenhower, LONMAY No. 79–90, 24 October 1942, HS 3/63, (UKPRO).
94. 'SO Operation Instructions to Lieutenant Colonel W.A. Eddy (declassified from "SECRET"),' AFHQ, 14 October 1942, Rounds Papers, Box 1, Folder 'Landings in North Africa,' (HIA), pp. 1–2.
95. SOE to Eddy (declassified from 'MOST SECRET'), LONMAY No. 4, 10 September 1942, HS 3/63, (UKPRO).
96. Edward Hymoff, *OSS in World War II*, (New York: Richardson and Steirman, 1986), p. 75.

97. *War Report, Volume II*, p. 18.
98. OSS London to Donovan, 23 November 1942, RG 226, Entry 190, Box 229, Folder 412, (NARA), pp. 1–3.
99. Ibid.
100. David A. Walker, 'OSS and Operation Torch,' *Journal of Contemporary History*, Volume 22, Number 4, October 1987, p. 669.
101. OSS London to Donovan, 23 November 1942, RG 226, Entry 190, Box 229, Folder 412, (NARA), pp. 1–3.
102. Ibid.
103. 'MO to DCD (O) (declassified from "SECRET AND PERSONAL"),' MO/B10/508, 22 October 1942, HS 3/63, (UKPRO).
104. 'Preliminary Report on OSS/SOE Activities,' 8 December 1942, HS 3/56, (UKPRO), p. 7.
105. SOE to Phillips (declassified from 'MOST SECRET'), CH/3468, 9 November 1942, HS 3/63, (UKPRO).
106. 'Preliminary Report on OSS/SOE Activities,' 8 December 1942, HS 3/56, (UKPRO), p. 5.
107. 'CD to SO,' CD/3934, 12 December 1942, HS 3/56, (UKPRO).
108. 'Report by MG/A of Intervention with Brigadier Vogel, Deputy Head of G-3 Section, at Norfolk House on 8th September 1943 (declassified from "MOST SECRET"),' HS 3/63, (UKPRO).
109. 'Preliminary Report on OSS/SOE Activities,' 8 December 1942, and 'CD to SO,' CD/3934, 12 December 1942, HS 3/56, (UKPRO), pp. 1–3.
110. Ibid., p. 4.
111. Carleton Coon, *A North Africa Story: The Anthropologist as OSS Agent 1941–1943*, (Memoir), (Ipswich, Massachusetts: Gambit, 1980), pp. 131–3.
112. West, op. cit., p. 132.
113. Cline, op. cit., p. 70.
114. Hinsley, op. cit., p. 470. See also 'AD/W to C/CDO,' No. 2958, 9 November 1942, HS 3/63, (UKPRO). General Clark had promised General Mast in October that the Americans would evacuate Giraud from France via submarine, but did not subsequently have one available and used a British submarine instead. See 'Eisenhower to Murphy (declassified from "SECRET"),' HQS ETOUSA, and 'Clark to Murphy (declassified from "MOST SECRET"),' HS 3/63, (UKPRO).
115. CAB 121/497, folio 229A, (UKPRO) as cited in Hinsley, op. cit., p. 479.
116. Hinsley, op. cit., p. 484.
117. Shepardson interview with unidentified OSS officer, 2 November 1944.
118. 'Relations with the French (declassified from "SECRET"),' undated, RG 226, Entry 190, Box 251, Folder 739, (NARA).
119. SOE to BSC (New York), No. 2909, 2 November 1942, HS 3/63, (UKPRO).
120. 'Relations with the French (declassified from "SECRET"),' undated, RG 226, Entry 190, Box 251, Folder 739, (NARA).
121. SOE to BSC (New York), No. 2909, 2 November 1942, HS 3/63, (UKPRO).
122. Author's interview with Sir Douglas Dodds-Parker, 26 May 1995, in Heyford, Oxfordshire. Speculation by historians that SOE was secretly involved in Darlan's assassination have been vigorously denied by surviving veterans of both SOE and SIS. While the British certainly had the motive to kill Darlan, only circumstantial evidence points to their involvement. See also author's interview with Sir Patrick Reilly, All Souls College, May 1995.
123. 'Relations with the French (declassified from "SECRET"),' undated, RG 226, Entry 190, Box 251, Folder 739, (NARA).
124. Ibid.

125. 'Plan for Activities Based in Algiers,' HS 3/56, (UKPRO), p. 1.
126. 'Memorandum Indicating the Latest Position on MASSINGHAM,' 22 November 1942, HS 3/56, (UKPRO), p. 2.
127. 'AD to CD, North Africa Mission,' 23 October 1942, HS 3/56, (UKPRO).
128. 'CD to GM,' Telegram 0006 LONMAY to New York, 4 November 1942, HS 3/61, (UKPRO).
129. 'MO/A to Huntington (declassified from "MOST SECRET"),' 11 September 1942, HS 3/63, (UKPRO).
130. 'CD to G,' Telegram 2847 to New York, 6 November 1942, HS 3/61, (UKPRO).
131. 'AD to CD, North African Mission,' 23 October 1942, HS 3/56, (UKPRO), pp. 1–2.
132. 'G to CD,' Telegram 296/301 from New York, 10 November 1942, HS 3/61, (UKPRO).
133. The belief that SOE had claimed 'exclusive rights' came from a poorly worded telegram sent by SOE to BSC on 6 November in which this was implied. Baker Street later claimed that this was a misunderstanding and that it only desired *joint* activities into Europe to avoid working at cross purposes. 'The real cause of complaint,' wrote SOE on 19 November, 'is that we did not keep [Donovan] informed as to our day-to-day talks with General Eisenhower resulting in the final agreement with him.' See 'OSS/SOE "MASSINGHAM" Controversy,' 19 November 1942, and SOE to BSC No. 2847, 6 November 1942, HS 3/61, (UKPRO).
134. Eddy to Leland Rounds, 29 November 1942, Leland L. Rounds Papers, Box 1, Folder 'miscellaneous – correspondence,' (HIA).
135. The BRANDON mission performed tactical intelligence collection, sabotage behind enemy lines, and helped to defend the northern flank of the Allied line against 500 Italian troops in Tunisia. A few OSS operatives were subordinated to BRANDON and performed reconnaissance patrolling operations, but their role was minor. BRANDON was hampered throughout its work by a lack of training and aircraft; it was dissolved in May 1943. See 'M/CD to CD,' MCD/1120, 6 May 1943, HS 3/61, (UKPRO) and *War Report, Volume II*, p. 19.
136. Author's telephone interview with Sir Douglas Dodds-Parker, 27 February 1996, in London.
137. 'AMR to DCDO,' November 1942, HS 3/56, (UKPRO).
138. 'Memorandum Indicating the Latest Position on MASSINGHAM,' 22 November 1942, HS 3/56, (UKPRO), p. 4.
139. Ibid., p. 1.
140. Ibid.
141. 'AM to DCD (O),' 22 November 1942, HS 3/56, (UKPRO).
142. 'D/CD to CD – Supplemental Agreement No. 1,' 23 November 1942, HS 3/56, (UKPRO).
143. 'AM to DCD (O),' 22 November 1942, HS 3/56, (UKPRO).
144. 'U to AD/U regarding lunch with Heppner,' U/US/2729, 23 November 1942, HS 3/56, (UKPRO).
145. 'AD/U to CD (declassified from "MOST SECRET"),' 23 November 1942 and 'U to AD/U regarding lunch with Heppner,' U/US/2729, 23 November 1942, HS 3/56, (UKPRO).
146. From CD,' Local No. 533, 1 December 1942, HS 3/56, (UKPRO).
147. 'OSS and SOE in North Africa (declassified from "MOST SECRET"),' Copy No. 58, 9 January 1943, RG 226, M1642, Roll 111, (NARA).
148. Huntington, 'Operational Organization OSS/SOE,' 3 February 1943, RG 226, Entry 190, Box 90, Folder 25, (NARA).
149. 'J.W. Munn to OSS Representative, North Africa,' 14 February 1943, HS 3/57, (UKPRO).
150. Troy (ed.), *Secret OSS Diary of James Grafton Rogers*, p. 25, entry for 4 December 1942.

151. Ibid., p. 30, entry for 20 December 1942.
152. Robert B. Asprey, *War in the Shadows: History of Guerrilla Warfare from Ancient Persia to the Present*, (London: Little, Brown, 1994), p. 315.
153. Named for the Norwegian Second World War collaborationist Vidkun Quisling, this expression is now a commonly accepted term meaning traitor, especially one who agrees to govern on behalf of a conquering nation.
154. 'Relations with the French (declassified from "SECRET"),' undated, RG 226, Entry 190, Box 251, Folder 739, (NARA).
155. Following the Casablanca Conference of 17–27 January 1943 in which both Giraud and de Gaulle attended for talks with Roosevelt and Churchill, most of the leadership of OSS – including Eddy in Algiers – favored Giraud, although OSS Washington's SI chief Arthur Roseborough preferred de Gaulle. Eddy had established ties to the formerly pro-Vichy intelligence service in North Africa, the *Service de Renseignement*, or SR, and Roseborough was soon replaced by Henry Hyde, who was a friend of Giraud's *chef de cabinet* and secured permission from Giraud to recruit 35 Frenchmen for SI work. See Arthur Funk, 'The OSS in Algiers,' in George C. Chalou (ed.), *The Secrets War: The Office of Strategic Services in World War II*, (Washington, DC: National Archives and Records Administration, 1992), p. 168.
156. Munn had to be replaced because of the continuing confusion surrounding the question of whether MASSINGHAM was complicit in Darlan's assassination. See Peter Wilkinson and Joan Bright Astley, *Gubbins and SOE*, (London: Leo Cooper, 1993), p. 118.
157. Dodds-Parker interview, 26 May 1995.
158. Ibid.
159. Robert Pflieger to R. Davis Halliwell, 'SO Set-up in Algiers,' 6 August 1943, RG 226, Entry 190, Box 90, Folder 25, (NARA), pp. 1–2.
160. 'Relations with the British and Other Allies,' undated, Director's Office, RG 226, Entry 190, Box 220, Folder 248, (NARA), pp. 3–4.
161. Ibid.
162. Ibid., pp. 4–5.
163. Ibid., pp. 3–4.
164. 'Précis of Meeting at Kingston House of 11th January 1943, to Discuss OSS Activities in Norway (declassified from "SECRET"),' RG 226, M1642, Roll 111, (NARA), p. 1.
165. Donovan to CD – Ref. /4226 (declassified from 'MOST SECRET AND PERSONAL'), 14 January 1943, RG 226, M1642, Roll 111, (NARA), pp. 1–2.
166. 'Précis of Meeting at Kingston House of 11th January 1943, to Discuss OSS Activities in Norway (declassified from "SECRET"),' RG 226, M1642, Roll 111, (NARA), p. 1.
167. 'Relations with the British and Other Allies,' undated, Director's Office, RG 226, Entry 190, Box 220, Folder 248, (NARA), pp. 3–4.
168. R. Davis Halliwell to Donovan, 'Outline for SO Operations for Calendar Year 1943 (declassified from "SECRET"),' 30 December 1942, RG 226, M1642, Roll 111, (NARA), pp. 1–2.
169. Ibid.
170. Huntington to Major V. Lada-Mocarski, 'Arrangements Between SOE and OSS – Current Status (declassified from "SECRET"),' 23 March 1943, RG 226, M1642, Roll 111, (NARA).
171. 'Excerpts from Report of E.C.H., Jr. [Huntington], to W.J.D. [Donovan] covering European trip ending March 21, 1943 (declassified from "SECRET"),' RG 226, M1642, Roll 111, (NARA).
172. Ibid.

173. Robert Pflieger to R. Davis Halliwell, 'SO Set-up in Algiers,' 6 August 1943, RG 226, Entry 190, Box 90, Folder 25, (NARA), pp. 1–2.

174. *War Report, Volume II*, p. 357.

175. Thomas N. Moon and Carl F. Eifler, *The Deadliest Colonel*, (New York: Vantage Press, 1975), pp. 49–51.

176. Ibid., p. 40.

177. 'Preliminary Activities,' undated, RG 226, Entry 190, Box 41, Folder 70, (NARA), pp. 1, 5.

178. Ibid., p. 1.

179. 'Introduction,' undated, RG 226, Entry 190, Box 41, Folder 70, (NARA).

180. In 1942, OSS also dispatched two officers – one of whom was Ilia Tolstoy, grandson of the famous Russian writer of the same surname – overland from India to Tibet to explore the possibility of resupplying China via the Tibetan mountains. They met the Dalai Lama, who requested that the US supply him with a radio transmitter to communicate with his people, and finally arrived in Chunking in August 1943, reporting that it would take two years to construct a viable Tibetan supply route. See Carolle J. Carter, 'Mission to Yenan: The OSS and the Dixie Mission,' in Chalou (ed.), op. cit., pp. 302–3.

181. 'Burma (declassified from "SECRET"),' undated, RG 226, Entry 190, Box 205, Folder 46, (NARA), pp. 1–2. See also author's interview with Colonel Carl Eifler, 9 August 1995, in Salinas, California.

182. Moon and Eifler, op.cit, p. 62.

183. Eifler Memorandum, 'Major Eifler's Mission in Relation to SOE India,' undated, RG 226, Entry 190, Box 29, Folder 49, (NARA), p. 14.

184. 'Burma (declassified from "SECRET"),' undated, RG 226, Entry 190, Box 205, Folder 46, (NARA), pp. 2–7.

185. 'Preliminary Activities,' undated, RG 226, Entry 190, Box 41, Folder 70, (NARA), p. 6.

186. When SOE India's Colin MacKenzie discovered that Dorman-Smith had provided the rupees to Eifler *gratis*, he claimed that this was done improperly and that OSS should refund him, which Eifler subsequently did. See Eifler Memorandum, 'Major Eifler's Mission in Relation to SOE India,' undated, RG 226, Entry 190, Box 29, Folder 49, (NARA), p. 18.

187. There were instances of cooperation with SOE, such as on 9 December 1942 when Eifler's unit crossed into Burma dressed as British soldiers in an effort that had been coordinated with SOE to disguise their purpose and nationality from the Burmese. In this particular instance, however, the British commander of the Kachin Levies, Colonel Gamble, purposely exposed Eifler's men as Americans in the first of many unhappy incidents involving Gamble and Detachment 101 that probably dissuaded Eifler from pursuing any closer coordination than was absolutely necessary. In February 1943, Eifler complained to the US Rear Echelon Headquarters in Delhi that Gamble had attempted unsuccessfully to take operational control of his detachment. See Eifler to General Ferris, New Delhi, 11 February 1943, RG 226, Entry 190, Box 68, Folder 499, (NARA), and Eifler interview, 9 August 1995.

188. 'Meeting Held on Tuesday, 27th July, 1943, in London, to Discuss OSS/SOE Plans in the Far Eastern Theatre (declassified from "SECRET"),' RG 226, M1642, Roll 111, (NARA).

189. 'SOE-OSS Cooperation in the Far Eastern Theatre (declassified from "SECRET"),' undated, RG 226, M1642, Roll 111, (NARA).

190. 'Lieutenant-Colonel F.D. Merrill to Chief of Staff, "Coordination of Eifler Group with British,"' New Delhi, 17 September 1942, RG 226, Entry 190, Box 68, Folder 499, (NARA).

191. 'Merrill to General Ferris, "Conference with D.M.O. and D.M.I. on Eifler Group,"' New Delhi, 16 March 1943, RG 226, Entry 190, Box 68, Folder 499, (NARA), p. 1.

192. Eifler to Colin MacKenzie, 22 October 1942, RG 226, Entry 190, Box 68, Folder 499, (NARA), p. 2.
193. 'MacKenzie to P. Mason (declassified from "MOST SECRET"),' No. 2194, 18 December 1942, WO 106/6092, (UKPRO).
194. 'MacKenzie to P. Mason (declassified from "MOST SECRET"),' Appendix A, WO 106/6092, (UKPRO)
195. 'MacKenzie to P. Mason (declassified from "MOST SECRET"),' No. 2194, 18 December 1942, WO 106/6092, (UKPRO).
196. 'Private from VCIGS to F.M. Wavell (declassified from "MOST SECRET"),' Draft, 4 February 1943, WO 106/6092, (UKPRO).
197. 'AD4 to CD,' AD4/855, 19 May 1943, HS 1/202, (UKPRO).
198. 'Meeting to Decide Guidance for Viceroy,' UK Foreign Office Telegram No. 478–S, February 1943, Personal Papers of [confidential source who wishes to remain anonymous].
199. Ibid.
200. 'Viceroy to Secretary of State for India,' No. 178–S 'Personal,' 17 February 1943, Personal Papers of [confidential source who wishes to remain anonymous].
201. 'Meeting to Decide Guidance for Viceroy,' UK Foreign Office Telegram No. 478–S, February 1943, Personal Papers of [confidential source who wishes to remain anonymous].
202. Ibid.
203. Troy (ed.), *Secret OSS Diary of James Grafton Rogers*, p. 30, entry for 6 January 1943.
204. William Phillips to FDR, 17 December 1942, PSF 38 'Diplomatic Correspondence Great Britain: Office of Strategic Services,' (FDRL).
205. 'CD to S.O.,' CD/5195, 20 May 1943, HS 1/202, (UKPRO).
206. 'AD4 to CD,' AD4/855, 19 May 1943, HS 1/202, (UKPRO).
207. 'AD4 to CD,' AD4/783, 4 May 1943, HS 1/202, (UKPRO), p. 1.
208. 'DMO to VCIGS,' MO12/BM336, 3 February 1943, WO 106/6092, (UKPRO).
209. 'AD4 to CD,' AD4/783, 4 May 1943, HS 1/202, (UKPRO), p. 2.
210. 'DMO to VCIGS,' MO12/BM336, 3 February 1943, WO 106/6092, (UKPRO).
211. 'US Intelligence and Cognate Activities in India, Minute by the Commander-in-Chief India Command,' COS (T) 20, 17 May 1943, Personal Papers of [confidential source who wishes to remain anonymous].
212. 'Annex III, CCS 196/1,' 14 May 1943, Personal Papers of [confidential source who wishes to remain anonymous].
213. 'Annex IV, CCS 196/1,' 14 May 1943, Personal Papers of [confidential source who wishes to remain anonymous].
214. 'C-in-C India to War Office (declassified from "MOST SECRET"),' 029474, 29 January 1942, HS 1/202, (UKPRO).
215. India Office to Wavell (declassified from 'MOST SECRET'), 14 May 1943, HS 1/202, (UKPRO).
216. Ibid.
217. Ibid. Note also that the number of OSS personnel in India and China fluctuated significantly over time. The build-up in China, however, was considerably larger than in India, and focused mainly on special operations, althogh a smaller number of secret intelligence officers were also active. Moreover, OSS staffed its China and India missions with personnel dedicated to research and analysis, counterintelligence, and propaganda. See *War Report, Volume II,* pp. 393–419.
218. 'Combined US-British Intelligence Activity in India (declassified from "MOST SECRET"),' Annex B, 27 May 1943, HS 1/202, (UKPRO).
219. 'US Intelligence and Cognate Activities in India, Minute by the Commander-in-Chief India Command,' COS (T) 20, Personal Papers of [confidential source who wishes to remain anonymous].

220. Ibid.
221. India Office to Wavell (declassified from "MOST SECRET"), 14 May 1943, HS 1/202, (UKPRO).
222. 'Note by Major-General W. J. Cawthorn on Discussions in Washington on Anglo-US Intelligence Layout in India-China-Burma Commands (declassified from "MOST SECRET"),' 5 June 1943, HS 1/202, (UKPRO).
223. 'CD to Patrick Reilly, Broadway (declassified from "MOST SECRET"),' JGB/5386, 12 June 1943, HS 1/202, (UKPRO).
224. Internal SOE Memorandum on Difficulties between SOE and OSS in India, 18 June 1943, HS 1/202, (UKPRO), p. 1.
225. BSC to Baker Street, No. 0267, 11 June 1943, HS 1/202, (UKPRO).
226. Internal SOE Memorandum on Difficulties between SOE and OSS in India, 18 June 1943, HS 1/202, (UKPRO), p. 1.
227. The OSS position in China at this time was greatly complicated by the US Navy's independent efforts to conduct joint SI and SO missions with this organization under the direction of M.E. Miles. 'The partnership between Miles and Tai Li . . . director of China's internal security and counter-intelligence service . . . crystallized [in April 1943] into a joint Sino-American clandestine agency.' The Navy succeeded in getting Donovan to agree to designate Miles as chief of OSS China later in 1943, but OSS in reality had little control over Miles' activities. See *War Report, Volume II*, pp. 360–2.
228. The SIS presence in China was small, but did have a relationship with Chiang's intelligence service. Interestingly, in what was almost certainly a Chinese effort to play one ally off against the other, SIS had been 'expressly excluded from allowing or inviting any American participation in this.' See Internal SOE Memorandum on Difficulties between SOE and OSS in India, 18 June 1943, HS 1/202, (UKPRO), pp. 3–4.
229. Ibid., p. 3–4.
230. 'Policy, VI. French Indo-China,' 26 July 1943, HS 1/202, (UKPRO), p. 15.

4 COMING OF AGE: LONDON, NORWAY, AND THE JEDBURGH-SUSSEX NEGOTIATIONS

1. 'Memorandum for Discussion with Colonel Huntington, Comments on OSS (declassified from "MOST SECRET"),' 23 October 1942, HS 3/61, (UKPRO).
2. 'Director's Office, Part III, 1944 (declassified from "SECRET"),' undated, RG 226, Entry 190, Box 211, Folder 142, (NARA), p. 1.
3. Space constraints preclude a detailed examination of political warfare and analytical (R & A) cooperation in London, but these activities were important. Throughout 1943, OSS's R & A and Morale Operations branches worked closely with their British counterparts, especially the Political Warfare Executive (PWE). In March, SOE invited OSS to participate in its propaganda plan for the invasion of France. In May, OSS urged that all political warfare components be coordinated, and in June, PWE and OSS London experienced difficulties as the former felt threatened by OSS's superior resources. In September, the creation of the Combined Allied Staff prompted OSS to press for equality with PWE and the US Office of War Information in propaganda preparations for D-Day; by the end of the year, the Combined Staff appointed OSS to its Political Warfare Board. R & A, meanwhile, established the widest network of OSS liaison ties, exchanging information with nearly every key British Government body. Britain expected an informational *quid pro quo* – particularly

regarding the Far East – but was willing to wait, which explained R & A's effectiveness in 1943. See William Phillips to FDR, 13 August 1942, PSF 38 'Diplomatic Correspondence Great Britain: OSS,' (FDRL); Hackett Memorandum, 'Notes on the Need for the Organization of Politico-Military Duties,' 30 March 1943; Howe to Oeschner, 'Psychological Warfare Activities in London,' 15 May 1943; Rae Smith to Bruce, 18 June 1943; Donovan to the Theater Commander, 20 September 1943; and Bruce to Scribner, 17 December 1943, RG 226, Entry 190, Box 220, Folder 248, (NARA); 'Procurement Period,' undated, RG 226, M1623, Roll 3, (NARA), pp. 18–22, 83–84; Ian Fleming to Shepardson, 17 September 1942, RG 226, Entry 190, Box 318, Folder 393, (NARA).

4. 'Relations with the British and Other Allies,' undated, Director's Office, RG 226, Entry 190, Box 220, Folder 248, (NARA), pp. 5–6. The term 'moon operation' refers to the insertion of an agent or team by parachute into enemy-controlled territory with the aid of moonlight. According to SOE historian M.R.D. Foot, 'normally pilots required a moon more than half full, in a sky more than half clear of cloud, before they would contemplate going on a night operation for SOE' because it was very difficult to spot a drop zone. See M.R.D. Foot, *SOE: The Special Operations Executive, 1940–46*, (London: BBC, 1984), p. 104.

5. 'Relations with the British and Other Allies,' undated, Director's Office, RG 226, Entry 190, Box 220, Folder 248, (NARA), pp. 5–6.

6. Lloyd to Bruce, 16 February 1943, Director's Office, RG 226, Entry 190, Box 220, Folder 248, (NARA), p. 52.

7. Relations with the British and Other Allies,' undated, Director's Office, RG 226, Entry 190, Box 220, Folder 248, (NARA), pp. 5–6.

8. 'M to CD' and BSC (New York) to SOE, Nr. 25207, March 1943, HS 2/219, (UKPRO).

9. '(Draft) Memorandum on Collaboration between American Office of Strategic Services (OSS), the Norwegian Government, and the Special Operations Executive (SOE) in regard to Activities in Norway and Norwegian Waters (declassified from "MOST SECRET"),' 22 January 1943, HS 2/219, (UKPRO). See also 'CD to Huntington (declassified from "MOST SECRET AND PERSONAL"),' 14 January 1943, HS 2/219, (UKPRO).

10. 'OSS Operations in Norway – Chiefs of Staff Papers,' COS 43.117 (0), 12 March 1943, HS 2/219, (UKPRO).

11. Ibid.

12. Ibid.

13. 'D/Plans to CD,' Plans/501/120, 23 March 1943, HS 2/29, (UKPRO).

14. Handwritten note, 'CD to D/Plans regarding OSS (Norway) plan and COS decision to turn it down,' 23 March 1943, HS 2/219, (UKPRO).

15. 'D/Plans to Ismay, OSS Operations in Norway,' 24 March 1943, HS 2/219, (UKPRO).

16. Handwritten note, 'CD to D/Plans regarding OSS (Norway) plan and COS decision to turn it down,' 23 March 1943, HS 2/219, (UKPRO).

17. 'CD to Bruce,' CD/4766, 26 March 1943, HS 2/219, (UKPRO).

18. Ibid.

19. 'Relations with the British and Other Allies,' undated, Director's Office, RG 226, Entry 190, Box 220, Folder 248, (NARA), pp. 7–8.

20. Ibid., pp. 7–8.

21. Ibid.,

22. Ibid., pp. 8–9.

23. 'Excerpts from Report of E.C.H., Jr. [Huntington], to W.J.D. [Donovan] covering European trip ending March 21, 1943 (declassified from "SECRET"),' RG 226, M1642, Roll 111, (NARA).

24. Ibid.

25. Andrews died in late May 1943.
26. 'Establishment of OSS London as a Military Detachment,' undated, Director's Office, RG 226, Entry 190, Box 220, Folder 248, (NARA), pp. 73–4.
27. 'Relations with the British and Other Allies,' undated, Director's Office, RG 226, Entry 190, Box 220, Folder 248, (NARA), p. 11.
28. The Spartan exercise provided the first test of the Jedburgh concept. It began on 3 March 1943 and included British and Canadian regular forces. A mock invading force advanced from Salisbury Plain to Hungerford and established a bridgehead from which a break-out was effected. 'In haste, a dozen mock Jedburgh teams were put together and infiltrated into the battle zone . . . They were assigned specific targets for sabotage and required, after the first attack, to report results and to seek further orders by means of radio communications . . . Counter-intelligence groups were pitted against them.' The Jedburgh teams' performance was deemed a great success. See Arthur Brown, 'The Jedburghs: A Short History,' (unpublished paper drafted by British Jedburgh veteran held in the library of the Special Forces Club in London), p. 3.
29. 'Relations with the British and Other Allies,' undated, Director's Office, RG 226, Entry 190, Box 220, Folder 248, (NARA), pp. 11–12.
30. Ibid., p. 10.
31. Ibid., pp. 12–13.
32. Letter from Hambro to Bruce, 27 April 1943, Director's Office, RG 226, Entry 190, Box 220, Folder 248, (NARA), p. 13.
33. Bruce to Commanding General, ETOUSA, 'Aircraft for Special Operations in N.W. Europe,' 5 May 1943, Director's Office,' RG 226, Entry 190, Box 220, Folder 248, (NARA), pp. 85–7.
34. 'Establishment of OSS London as a Military Detachment,' Director's Office, RG 226, Entry 190, Box 220, Folder 248, (NARA), p. 88.
35. Report by Hambro to Donovan on the status of SOE and SO's contributions to the resistance movements in France, 24 June 1943, Director's Office, RG 226, Entry 190, Box 220, Folder 248, pp. 18–19.
36. 'Relations with the British and Other Allies,' undated, Director's Office, RG 226, Entry 190, Box 220, Folder 248, (NARA), pp. 17, 20.
37. 'Establishment of OSS London as a Military Detachment,' undated, Director's Office, RG 226, Entry 190, Box 220, Folder 248, (NARA), pp. 89, 91.
38. 'Relations with the British and Other Allies,' undated, Director's Office, RG 226, Entry 190, Box 220, Folder 248, (NARA), pp. 19–20.
39. Huntington to Mr. Scribner, 'SO Operations – Western Europe – Relations with North Africa (declassified from "SECRET"),' 28 August 1943, RG 226, M1642, Roll 111, (NARA).
40. Ibid.
41. David Eisenhower, *Eisenhower at War, 1943–1945*, (New York: Random House, 1986), p. 840.
42. 'Relations with the British and Other Allies,' undated, Director's Office, RG 226, Entry 190, Box 220, Folder 248, (NARA), p. 21.
43. Letter from Bruce to Buxton, 18 September 1943, Director's Office, RG 226, Entry 190, Box 220, Folder 248, (NARA), p. 21.
44. 'Introductory Survey of Establishment, Activities and Plans of SI London,' 15 January 1945, RG 226, Box 233, Folder 469, (NARA), p. 14.
45. 'Relations with the British and Other Allies,' undated, Director's Office, RG 226, Entry 190, Box 220, Folder 248, (NARA), p. 45.
46. 'SI London Branch Report SMR No. 4, 1 April 1943,' 15 January 1945, RG 226, Box 233, Folder 469, (NARA), p. 16.

47. 'Introductory Survey of Establishment, Activities and Plans of SI London,' 15 January 1945, RG 226, Box 233, Folder 469, (NARA), p. 17.
48. Letter from Maddox to Bruce, 1 April 1943, Director's Office, RG 226, Entry 190, Box 220, Folder 248, (NARA), p. 23.
49. 'Relations with the British and Other Allies,' undated, Director's Office, RG 226, Entry 190, Box 220, Folder 248, (NARA), p. 23.
50. 'Introductory Survey of Establishment, Activities and Plans of SI London,' 15 January 1945, RG 226, Box 233, Folder 469, (NARA), p. 15.
51. Ibid.
52. Letter from Maddox to Bruce, 1 April 1943, Director's Office, RG 226, Entry 190, Box 220, Folder 248, (NARA), p. 23.
53. 'Introductory Survey of Establishment, Activities and Plans of SI London,' 15 January 1945, RG 226, Box 233, Folder 469, (NARA), p. 17.
54. Ibid., p. 12.
55. 'Relations with the British and Other Allies,' undated, Director's Office, RG 226, Entry 190, Box 220, Folder 248, (NARA), p. 25.
56. Shepardson to Bruce, Cable No. 18098, 19 April 1943, 15 January 1945, RG 226, Box 233, Folder 469, (NARA), pp. 23–4.
57. Shepardson to Bruce, Cable No. 03105, 4 April 1943, 'Introductory Survey of Establishment, Activities and Plans of SI London,' 15 January 1945, RG 226, Box 233, Folder 469, (NARA), pp. 22–3.
58. Bruce to Shepardson, Cable No. 06175 and 06181, 5 and 6 April 1943, 'Introductory Survey of Establishment, Activities and Plans of SI London,' 15 January 1945, RG 226, Box 233, Folder 469, (NARA), p. 23.
59. 'Introductory Survey of Establishment, Activities and Plans of SI London,' 15 January 1945, RG 226, Box 233, Folder 469, (NARA), pp. 26–7.
60. Ibid.
61. The Sussex program is discussed in detail in Chapter 6.
62. 'Relations with the British and Other Allies,' undated, Director's Office, RG 226, Entry 190, Box 220, Folder 248, (NARA), p. 26.
63. Ibid., pp. 26–7.
64. Bruce to Shepardson, 18 June 1943, RG 226, Entry 190, Box 220, Folder 248, (NARA).
65. 'Relations with the British and Other Allies,' undated, Director's Office, RG 226, Entry 190, Box 220, Folder 248, (NARA), p. 28.
66. Bruce to Shepardson, 18 June 1943, RG 226, Entry 190, Box 220, Folder 248, (NARA).
67. 'Introductory Survey of Establishment, Activities and Plans of SI London,' 15 January 1945, RG 226, Box 233, Folder 469, (NARA), p. 29.
68. Bruce to Devers, 16 August 1943, RG 226, Entry 190, Box 220, Folder 248, (NARA).
69. Donovan to Colonel Nelson, US Pentagon, 7 August 1943, RG 226, M1642, Roll 111, (NARA).
70. Bruce to Donovan, 18 September 1943, Director's Office, RG 226, Entry 190, Box 220, Folder 248, (NARA), p. 56.
71. 'Relations with the British and Other Allies,' undated, Director's Office, RG 226, Entry 190, Box 220, Folder 248, (NARA), pp. 55–7.
72. Donovan to the JCS, 18 October 1943, RG 226, Entry 190, Box 220, Folder 248, (NARA), pp. 59–61.
73. Ibid.
74. Ibid., pp. 61–2.
75. 'Introductory Survey of Establishment, Activities and Plans of SI London,' 15 January 1945, RG 226, Box 233, Folder 469, (NARA), p. 12.
76. 'Relations with the British and Other Allies,' undated, Director's Office, RG 226, Entry 190, Box 220, Folder 248, (NARA), pp. 62–3.

5 THE YUGOSLAV MORASS: A CASE STUDY IN ANGLO-OSS DIVERGENCE

1. Written by George Moreton and quoted in Artemis Cooper, *Cairo in the War, 1939–1945,* (London: Penguin, 1989), p. 259.
2. Sweet-Escott, *Baker Street Irregular,* p. 145.
3. SOE Belgrade's George Taylor encouraged the nationalist Yugoslav military authorities during the German invasion to leave Mihailovic behind to rally resistance forces. See author's interview with Sir Douglas Dodds-Parker, Special Forces Club, 1 October 1996.
4. See WO 208/2014, Enclosure 1a, 'Summary of Events in Yugoslavia,' CAB 121/676, SIC file F/Yugoslavia/3F. F.H. Hinsley, *British Intelligence in the Second World War: Its Influence on Strategy and Operations, Volume III, Part 1* (Official History), (London: HMSO, 1984), p. 137.
5. Echoing Sir Harry Hinsley, a vast literature has grown up on this subject in recent years and it should be clearly understood that the following pages make no effort to survey it comprehensively. Instead, this section will address the Yugoslav-related specifics of the period 1942–44 that are critical to an examination of the Anglo-US dynamic in subversive warfare.
6. SOE's Bill Deakin, who later served with Tito, has claimed that two representatives of the Yugoslav government-in-exile traveling with Hudson had secret orders to direct him only to Chetnik bands loyal to King Peter and led by Mihailovic. See F.W.D. Deakin, *The Embattled Mountain,* (Oxford: Oxford University Press, 1971), p. 130.
7. From CAB 101/126 historical paper on Yugoslavia, pp. 1–5, as quoted in Hinsley, op. cit., p. 137.
8. The Yugoslav resistance eventually forced the Germans to commit some fifteen divisions and approximately 100 000 collaborationist Yugoslav troops to the occupation effort. Up to nineteen Italian divisions and six Bulgarian ones were added to these forces in 1942–3. See *OSS War Report*, Volume II, p. 127, and Hinsley, op. cit., p. 142.
9. 'The OSS in Yugoslavia,' R. Smith Papers, Box 2, (HIA).
10. OSS War Report, Volume II, p. 127.
11. Donovan to General George Marshall, 13 February 1942, Goodfellow Papers, Box 3, Folder 'Office of Strategic Services Correspondence, January 1942–May 1942,' (HIA).
12. 'Proposed Letter to Coordinator of Information (declassified from "SECRET"),' Brigadier General W.B. Smith, 26 March 1942, Goodfellow Papers, Box 2, Folder 'Balkan Countries,' (HIA).
13. 'The OSS in Yugoslavia,' R. Smith Papers, Box 2, (HIA).
14. 'Proposed Plan to Assist Yugoslavs (declassified fom "SECRET"),' 29 March 1942, Goodfellow Papers, Box 2, Folder 'Balkan Countries,' (HIA), p. 1.
15. 'Proposed Letter to Coordinator of Information (declassified from "SECRET"),' Brigadier General W.B. Smith, 26 March 1942, Goodfellow Papers, Box 2, Folder 'Balkan Countries,' (HIA).
16. 'Plan for Psychological Warfare in Jugoslavia and Transylvania (declassified from "SECRET"),' W.B. Smith, The Combined Chiefs of Staff, 30 March 1942, Goodfellow Papers, Box 2, Folder 'Balkan Countries,' (HIA).
17. 'Psychological Warfare (Jugoslavs and Transylvania), Note by the Secretaries (declassified from "SECRET"),' 29 March 1942, W.B. Smith, Joint Secretariat, Goodfellow Papers, Box 2, Folder 'Balkan Countries,' (HIA).
18. Nedic had been the commander of the Yugoslav Southern Army when Germany invaded.

19. Author's interview with Mihailo Protic, a veteran of Mihailovic's Chetnik movement, in Belgrade, 6 July 1996.

20. 'The OSS in Yugoslavia,' R. Smith Papers, Box 2, (HIA). When assessing Mihailovic's actions, however, it is important to note that the Chetniks were almost exclusively peasants who lived in the forests on the outskirts of their villages, and were bound by tradition to protect non-combatant interests. They were relatively immobile as they and their families continued to work the land, and were thus very vulnerable to reprisals. In contrast, the Partisans were mobile because most were displaced urban dwellers; 'they avoided reprisals by leaving areas at once after attacking.' Moreover, the Axis skillfully used propaganda that greatly exaggerated the number of ethnic Serbs killed in Croatia and Bosnia to demoralize the Chetniks by leading them to believe that they had 'lost the biological war *vis-à-vis* the Croats' and had to conserve their human resources until a general uprising could be coordinated with the decisive Allied assault on the Continent. Thus, Mihailovic's caution is more understandable, and Allied propaganda probably created unrealistic expectations. See 'Lt. Colonel Hudson's report on the Serbs,' 17 March 1944, WO 202/162, pp. 2–5, and the Seitz report, 'Basic estimate of American officers with British Missions attached to General Mihailovic requested by Gruenther,' 25 October 1943, FO 371/37618, (UKPRO). See also letter from Dusan Topalovic, who served with the Mihailovic forces, to author of September 1996.

21. Hudson report, op. cit., p. 5.

22. SOE's Bickham Sweet-Escott has identified 'the absence of reliable intelligence' in Yugoslavia as one of the major problems plaguing SOE during the war. See 'SOE in the Balkans,' draft lecture notes, Bickham Sweet-Escott papers, Box 4, Folder 11A, (BOA), pp. 8–9.

23. Letter from Basil Davidson to Bickham Sweet-Escott, 14 February 1966, Sweet-Escott Papers, Box 8, Folder B6, (BOA).

24. CX/MSS 495/T3, 564/T2, 575/T23, 903/T14, 911/T13, 1031/T14 and 16, 1033/T5, 1036/T8; WO 208/2014, Enclosure 19a; CAB 101/126, as quoted in Hinsley, op. cit., pp. 138–9.

25. Bickham Sweet-Escott, 'Some Factors in British Decision-making over Jugoslavia, 1941–44,' unpublished paper, Sweet-Escott Papers, Box 4, Folder A11, (BOA), p. 9.

26. Letter from Sweet-Escott to Basil Davidson, February 1966, Box 8, Folder B6, (BOA).

27. Author's interview with Dusan Marinkovic, a Cetnik veteran of the Belrade underground, in Belgrade, 6 July 1996. Marinkovic's research has revealed that Mihailovic ordered a senior subordinate, General Ostoic, to confiscate Hudson's radio set.

28. Very few British supplies ever reached the Cetniks. According to an OSS source, 'from commencement of operations [following Hudson's initial contact with the Chetniks] until May [1943], Mihailovic received [only] a few [aircraft] sorties a month' and precious few supplies. 'Personal observation of Cetnik troops [revealed] that they [wore] grossly inadequate clothing . . . In attack they [used] all kinds of old weapons . . . without sights or base plates.' The lack of supply was attributed principally to the lack of transport aircraft and of a long-term British supply program, but almost certainly also reflected Britain's growing uncertainty about the desirability of continuing to back Mihailovic – at least exclusively – even in 1942. See report of OSS Colonel Albert Seitz, 'Basic estimate of American officers with British Missions attached to General Mihailovic requested by Gruenther,' 25 October 1943, FO 371/37618, (UKPRO).

29. Marinkovic interview, 6 July 1996.

30. CAB 101/126, p. 12, and synopsis of Hudson's autumn 1942 reports as quoted in Hinsley, op. cit., p. 140. Note also that SOE 'officially condoned accommodations with the Italians by Montenegrin Cetniks . . . designed to facilitate the eventual take-

over of arms and positions.' See Michael Lees, *The Rape of Serbia*, (London: Harcourt Brace, 1990), p. 347.

31. 'Aid to Greeks and Jugoslavs,' Memorandum for Goodfellow probably from a member of his staff, 10 June 1942, Goodfellow Papers, Box 4, Folder 'Office of Strategic Services Memoranda June-July 1942,' (HIA).

32. Ibid.

33. These Yugoslavs were to have been recruited by Donovan's organization from suitable ethnic communities in North America.

34. 'Division of Territories and Other Collaboration between the British SOE and the United States OSS,' Memorandum for the Joint Chiefs of Staff, RG 226, M1642, Roll 111, (NARA).

35. 'Record of Discussion regarding collaboration between British and American SOE,' 22 June 1942, No. 3, RG 226, M1642, Roll 111, (NARA).

36. Huntington, 'SO Organization, Operations and Objectives, Based on London Trip, 9–27 September 1942,' RG 226, M1642, Roll 111, (NARA), p. 24.

37. 'AD's report, II. Cairo Mission,' 9 November 1942, HS 3/61, (UKPRO). Part of the reason for Britain's insistence on micromanaging Allied policy in Yugoslavia concerns its increasing doubts about the Chetniks. In July 1942, broadcasts by 'Radio Free Yugoslavia' alleged that the Chetniks were collaborating with the enemy and attributed various Chetnik military operations to the Partisans. The charges were generally accepted as fact by British and US propagandists, who began to use them for their reports on Yugoslavia. In reality, Radio Free Yugoslavia was a joint Partisan-Soviet clandestine transmitter located in the Soviet Caucasus, and as such was part of Tito's anti-Chetnik propaganda effort. Nonetheless, the Allies lacked the capability to accurately assess the truthfulness of the charges, but once they had been used in Allied broadcasts, they began to gain legitimacy. Deakin has argued in *The Embattled Mountain*, however, that there were many incidents in which Partisan operations were erroneously attributed to the Chetniks.

38. 'Memorandum for Discussion with Colonel Huntington, Cairo Mission (declassified from "MOST SECRET"),' 23 October 1942, HS 3/61, (UKPRO).

39. 'AD's report, II. Cairo Mission,' 9 November 1942, HS 3/61, (UKPRO).

40. 'Memorandum for Discussion with Colonel Huntington, Comments on OSS (declassified from "MOST SECRET"),' 23 October 1942, HS 3/61, (UKPRO)

41. 'AD's report, II. Cairo Mission,' 9 November 1942, HS 3/61, (UKPRO).

42. Internal OSS memorandum (untitled and declassified from 'SECRET'), 20 October 1942, RG 226, Entry 190, Box 205, Folder 47, (NARA).

43. Ibid.

44. Ibid.

45. Ibid.

46. WO 208/2104, Minute 31 of 15 September 1942; CX/MSS/1350/T12; CX/MSS/1559 para 37, as quoted in Hinsley, op. cit., p. 141.

47. Claims that pro-communist SOE officers and other 'leftist' British officials intrigued to distort the intelligence picture in Yugoslavia to favor Tito and unfairly discredit Mihailovic have increased in recent years. Michael Lees, who liaised with the Cetniks for SOE and married a cipher clerk who worked in SOE's Cairo and Bari missions, is one of the more thoughtful and outspoken claimants. He and others, such as David Martin, have charged that SOE Cairo's 'dominant' – if junior – personality, James Klugmann, was a likely ringleader. Klugmann – whose initial candidacy for membership in SOE had been rejected in London – was the historian of the British Communist Party. He attended public school with Soviet spy Donald MacLean, Cambridge University in the 1930s with Kim Philby and other noted communists, and is alleged to have recruited Anthony Blunt for the Soviets before Blunt in turn recruited Guy Burgess, who in turn

recruited Donald MacLean. Espionage historians Andrew Sinclair and Andrew Boyle believe Klugmann dominated the Cambridge Socialist Club, which was directed by the British Communist Party, as well as the infamous Trinity Hall communist cell. Klugmann is widely believed to have recruited many important agents for the Soviets in the 1930s, including John Cairncross, who interestingly later handled Yugoslav-related intercepts at GCHQ. Many British intellectuals sympathized with communism as fascism loomed, and Lees and others are convinced that SOE, SIS, the Foreign Office, PWE, and the BBC were almost certainly infiltrated by left-wing sympathizers who favored Tito on ideological grounds and were in a position to influence related events. Lees has described Hugh Seton-Watson, a Balkans expert seconded to SOE Cairo as an advisor on Yugoslav matters, as a 'hard-left socialist . . . if not forthrightly pro-communist' whilst at university. He has identified SOE Cairo's Frank Thompson as 'a dedicated, romantic, card-carrying communist,' who with Klugmann and Seton-Watson organized a failed mission to contact communist rebels in Bulgaria. Basil Davidson, a key British Liaison Officer with Tito, was, says Lees, 'unashamedly – indeed, proudly – of a strongly left-wing persuasion;' an observation that is shared by Sir Douglas Dodds-Parker. Ormand Uren, a junior Balkan desk officer at Baker Street, evidently leaked SOE secrets to the British Communist Party, was court-martialed on 21 October 1943 and jailed for seven years. Many have attempted to explain away this theme as consistent with the practice of SOE, and also OSS, of ignoring the ideological persuasion of staff and agents – so long as they were anti-fascist – and argue that it was not unusual given Moscow's status as an ally. Basil Davidson has completely rejected the 'communist conspiracy' theory and argues that Klugmann was the only communist on SOE Cairo's staff. Nonetheless, the implications of Lees' arguments – which are based not just upon recollections but upon informed personal interpretation of often purposely misleading documentary evidence – are considerable. While the evidence is mostly circumstantial, its profusion alone makes it worthy of note. See Lees, op. cit.; author's interview with Dodds-Parker on 1 October at the Special Forces Club; Andrew Sinclair, *The Red and the Blue: Cambridge, Treason, and Intelligence,* (London: Little, Brown, 1986); Andrew Boyle, *The Climate of Treason: Five Who Spied for Russia,* (London: 1979); Basil Davidson, *Special Operations Europe: Scenes from the Anti-Nazi War,* (London: Grafton Books, 1987); Letter from Basil Davidson to Bickham Sweet-Escott, 14 February 1966, Sweet-Escott Papers, Box 8, Folder B6, (BOA); David Martin, 'Churchill's Yugoslav Blunder: Precursor to the Yugoslav Tragedy,' *International Journal of Intelligence and Counterintelligence,* Winter 1991–92, Vol. 5, No. 4.

48. Lees, op. cit., p. 44.
49. 'The OSS in Yugoslavia,' R. Smith Papers, Box 2, (HIA).
50. 'Coordination of SOE and the American SO Mission in the Balkans and Middle East,' 9 January 1943, RG 226, M1642, Roll 111, (NARA), pp. 1–3.
51. 'AD's report, II. Cairo Mission,' 9 November 1942, HS 3/61, (UKPRO).
52. Bailey had worked for the Trepca Mines enterprise in Yugoslavia in the 1930s. In 1939, he helped SIS's 'Section D' with its operations in Yugoslavia. He was subsequently recruited by SOE. See 'Obituary, Colonel S.W. Bailey, Resistance in the Balkans,' *The Times,* 9 July 1974.
53. Deakin, op. cit., p. 177. See also letters from Dusan Marinkovic to author, 27 July and 1 October 1996.
54. 'The OSS in Yugoslavia,' R. Smith Papers, Box 2, (HIA).
55. Deakin, op. cit., p. 186.
56. Lees, op. cit., p. 349. See also Topalovic letter to author, September 1996.
57. Seitz report, op. cit.
58. Protic interview, 6 July 1996.

59. The depth of Mihailovic's disdain for Hudson is clearly evident in a letter the former wrote to Bailey in which he charged Hudson with 'secretly interfering in our internal affairs, talking our commanders into disobedience.' See Mihailovic to Bailey, 11 July 1943, Sig. Arch. VII, Cha, Box 20, Document No. 14/3, Archive of the Military Historical Institute in Belgrade (hereafter cited as 'AMHIB').

60. Protic interview, 6 July 1996.

61. Mihailovic's headquarters was divided into three different groups, one with Mihailovic, another with Major Ostojic, and a third with Major Lalatovic. See Marinkovic letter to author, 27 July 1996.

62. Major Ostojic to Captain Jelovac, Telegram No. 14, QEY 8/2, 14 April 1942, (AMHIB).

63. Protic interview, 6 July 1996.

64. See Marinkovic letter to author, 27 July 1996.

65. Bickham Sweet-Escott, Letter to the Editor, *The Times Literary Supplement*, 19 May 1972.

66. CX/MSS/2782/T21, CX/MSS/495 para 27, 1384 para 24, CX/MSS/1564 para 18, 2256/T10, 2574 para 6, 2597/T8 as quoted in Hinsley, op. cit., pp. 146–7.

67. 'Outgoing Telegrams of the Mihailovic Headquarters,' Document No. 72, 3 April 1942, Archive VII, CHA (Cetnik documents), (AMHIB).

68. These agents were part of a larger group of 30 ethnic Croats miners recruited in Canada by SOE's Bailey and SIS's William Stuart in 1942 with the help of Tim Buck, the leader of the Canadian Communist Party. Lees alleges in *The Rape of Serbia* (p. 35) that all of the recruits were Communist Party members and were placed in Klugmann's care at SOE Cairo until they could be deployed to Yugoslavia.

69. 'The OSS in Yugoslavia,' R. Smith Papers, Box 2, (HIA), and Lees, op. cit., p. 350.

70. The head of SOE in the Middle East.

71. Huntington to Glenconner, 15 February 1943, RG 226, M1642, Roll 111, (NARA).

72. Ibid.

73. McBaine to James Miller (declassified from 'SECRET'), 28 April 1943, RG 226, Entry 190, Box 205, Folder 47, (NARA), p. 2.

74. Ibid.

75. McBaine to Amoss (declassified from 'SECRET'), 31 May 1943, RG 226, Entry 190, Box 205, Folder 47, (NARA), p. 1. Interestingly, SOE London and Cairo often disagreed about policy toward OSS, as did elements within SOE London with each other. Hambro had even backed Huntington against Glenconner in March when the latter attempted to place severe restrictions on OSS Cairo personnel. See 'Excerpts from Report of E.C.H. to W.J.D. covering European trip ending March 21, 1943 (declassified from "SECRET"),' RG 226, M1642, Roll 111, (NARA).

76. COS (W)638, 10 June 1943, HS 3/199, (UKPRO).

77. Troy (ed.), *Secret OSS Journal of James Grafton Rogers*, p. 39, entry for 20 July 1943.

78. Ibid., p. 142, entry for 8 September 1943.

79. Deakin, op. cit., pp. 109–11.

80. OSS War Report, Volume II, p. 127.

81. Deakin, op. cit., pp. 109–11.

82. 'Messages from American Liaison Officer with General Mihailovic, No. 32, August 31st,' 13 September 1943, RG 226, Entry 190, Box 205, Folder 47, (NARA).

83. Ibid., No. 28, 13 September 1943.

84. Ibid., No. 19, 2 September 1943.

85. Ibid., No. 31, 13 September 1943.

86. Ibid., No. 22, 2 September 1943.

87. Ibid., No. 57, 60, 13 September 1943.

88. Ibid., Nos 61–64, 13 September 1943.

89. Ibid., No. 67, 13 September.
90. Seitz report, op. cit.
91. The town was Prijepolje and its seizure was erroneously attributed by the BBC to the Partisans.
92. Hudson report, op. cit., p. 3.
93. Kirk Ford, Jr., *OSS and the Yugoslav Resistance, 1943–1945,* (Texas: Texas A&M University Press, 1992), p. 18.
94. Lees, op. cit., pp. 101–3.
95. Letter from Dusan Marinkovic to author, 1 October 1996.
96. D/Plans to AD/E (declassified from "MOST SECRET"),' Plans/181/1334, 28 September 1943, HS 3/199, (UKPRO).
97. Deakin claims to have persuaded the Bergamo Division's commander to comply with Partisan demands. See Deakin, op. cit., pp. 232–6.
98. Miscellaneous notes, R. Smith Papers, Box 2, Folder 'Yugoslavia,' (HIA).
99. MacLean, *Eastern Approaches,* (London: Jonathan Cape, 1949), pp. 297–8.
100. 'Copy of Telegram AMW/JU/5589,' 13 December 1943, FO 371/37618, (UKPRO).
101. Miscellaneous notes, R.H. Smith Papers, Box 2, Folder 'Yugoslavia,' (HIA).
102. Mihailovic's claims of action should have been at least partially confirmed by the reports of *British* officers attached to the Chetniks. In late September, for example, 'a large bridge near Visegrad, probably the largest blown by resistance movements in the Balkans, was demolished by [British] Major Archie Jack, covered by Mihailovic forces and watched by . . . Armstrong. The BBC announced this as a *Partisan* success.' Similarly, on 30 September, Michael Lees and a Chetnik group destroyed a key section of the Belgrade–Salonika railway, 'which blocked traffic for seven to ten days, [but] was, within forty-eight hours of [Lees] reporting it to Cairo, attributed by the BBC to the Partisans.' In retrospect, Lees was confounded by the misrepresentation of these Chetnik operations and has argued that they are further proof of a pro-Tito conspiracy among key British decision-makers. See Lees, op. cit., p. 75.
103. 'The OSS in Yugoslavia,' R. Smith Papers, Box 2, (HIA).
104. Miscellaneous notes, R. Smith Papers, Box 2, Folder 'Yugoslavia,' (HIA).
105. Mihailovic saw both Armstrong and Bailey as 'dilettantes who were unable to understand that the war . . . was primarily between communists and monarchists, and the resistance to German occupation came second.' See letter from Dusan Marinkovic to author, 1 October 1996.
106. Hudson report, op. cit., p. 9.
107. Seitz report, op. cit.
108. 'The OSS in Yugoslavia,' R. Smith Papers, Box 2, (HIA).
109. Seitz report, op. cit.
110. In late September, SOE suggested that a 'clear but ad hoc boundary should be set, by which Serbia is recognized as Mihailovic's territory, and Slovenia, Croatia-Slavonia, Dalmatia, Bosnia-Herzegovina and Macedonia south of Skopje are recognized as Partisan territory.' See 'Balkan Politico-Military Situation (declassified from "MOST SECRET"),' 28 September 1943, HS 3/199, (UKPRO).
111. Seitz report, op. cit.
112. 'In Message Operational Log, Jugoslavia,' 17 November 1943, FO 371/37618, (UKPRO).
113. SOE's Sweet-Escott has noted that 'for a few months' in the summer of 1943, '[SOE Cairo] hadn't got nearly enough operators to handle the [message] traffic, or nearly enough [code clerks] to decode the messages. No wonder important signals were delayed, or even lost altogether.' See 'SOE in the Balkans,' draft lecture notes, Sweet-Escott papers, Box 4, Folder 11A, (BOA), p. 11.
114. Keble to West, 14 November 1943, FO 371/37618, (UKPRO).

115. 'Notes of a Meeting held at MO4 [SOE Cairo] at 1500 Hrs. on 17 November 1943 (declassified from "MOST SECRET"),' 17 November 1943, HS 3/199, (UKPRO).
116. Ibid.
117. AD to D/Plans, 26 November 1943, HS 3/57, (UKPRO).
118. 'Notes of a Meeting held at MO4 [SOE Cairo] at 1500 Hrs. on 17 November 1943 (declassified from "MOST SECRET"),' 17 November 1943, HS 3/199, (UKPRO).
119. 'The OSS in Yugoslavia,' R. Smith Papers, Box 2, (HIA).
120. With the exception of his presence during the Partisan escape from German encirclement at Mount Durmitor and the disarming of the Bergamo Division, Deakin spent his time at Tito's headquarters where he almost certainly was inundated with Partisan propaganda.
121. Lees, op. cit., pp. 212–15.
122. Martin, 'Churchill's Yugoslav Blunder,' *International Journal of Intelligence and Counterintelligence*, Winter 1991–92, Volume 5, No. 4, pp. 422–3.
123. Ibid., p. 421.
124. MacLean sent Farish to a remote village after the latter made his initial favorable report on the Partisans. Interestingly, Farish's radio set proved faulty and he was unable to report on events in Partisan territory or at Tito's headquarters during an important period. Historian Kirk Ford believes that this was a diplomatic means of removing Farish from the center of events. See K. Ford, op. cit.
125. 'The OSS in Yugoslavia,' R. Smith Papers, Box 2, (HIA).
126. Ibid.
127. OSS Cairo's Turner McBaine had actually set up the OSS base in Bari that Huot later used for his resupply operation.
128. Deakin, op. cit., pp. 245–56.
129. 'OSS, SO, Shipping Operation – Italy to Yugoslavia, 1943,' Tofte, Personal Collection of Ward Warren, Curator, HIC, CIA.
130. Ibid.
131. Ibid.
132. Dodds-Parker interview, 1 October 1996.
133. Due to personal animosities between MacLean and SOE Cairo's Keble, the former had been placed under the direct authority of General Henry Maitland Wilson, which for all intents and purposes relegated SOE Cairo to the role of a supporting element. Both MacLean and Wilson had a low opinion of SOE Cairo and vice-versa; this estrangement might explain why the former were not properly informed.
134. 'GHQ Middle East Forces Directive No. 187, To Brigadier Stawell, Force 133,' 26 November 1943, HS 3/199, (UKPRO).
135. 'OSS, SO, Shipping Operation – Italy to Yugoslavia, 1943,' Tofte, Personal Collection of Ward Warren, Curator, HIC, CIA.
136. 'Loan to SOE,' Internal OSS letter, 24 November 1943, RG 226, M1642, Roll 111, (NARA).
137. 'OSS, SO, Shipping Operation – Italy to Yugoslavia, 1943,' Tofte, Personal Collection of Ward Warren, Curator, HIC, CIA.
138. Sterling Hayden, *Wanderer*, (New York: Alfred Knopf, 1963), pp. 313–14.
139. 'Summary, OSS, SO, Shipping Operation – Italy to Yugoslavia, 1943,' Hans V. Tofte, Personal Collection of Ward Warren, Curator, Historical Intelligence Collection (HIC), Central Intelligence Agency (CIA).
140. Harold Macmillan, *The Blast of War: 1939–45*, (London: Macmillan, 1967), p. 526.
141. Robert Sherwood (ed.), *The White House Papers of Harry L. Hopkins, Volume II, January 1942–July 1945,* (London: Eyre & Spottiswoode, 1949), p. 770.
142. Ibid., p. 775.

143. 'Anthony Webb to M. Rose, Foreign Office,' ECL/JU/5517, 4 December 1943, FO 371/37618, (UKPRO). The evidence to which Webb was referring appears to have come from a report about a delegate from Nedic who approached one of Mihailovic's field commanders with an offer from the Germans to 'clothe, equip, and pay Mihailovic forces for anti-Partisan activities.' This was probably sent to the Foreign Office via SOE Cairo, then was repeated by the British Ambassador to King Peter's government. As it fails to mention the Chetnik response, nor does it directly implicate Mihailovic, it is scarcely damning. See Stevenson to Foreign Office (declassified from 'SECRET'), No. 155, 6 December 1943, FO 371/37618, (UKPRO).
144. 'From His Majesty's Ambassador to the Yugoslav Government Cairo to Foreign Office (declassified from "SECRET"),' No. 152, FO 371/37618, (UKPRO).
145. 'Minutes,' 14 December 1943, FO 371/37618, (UKPRO).
146. Stevenson to Eden (declassified from 'SECRET'), No. 51, 29 November 1943, FO 371/37618, (UKPRO).
147. Stevenson to Foreign Office (declassified from 'SECRET'), No. 155, 6 December 1943, FO 371/37618, (UKPRO).
148. Stevenson to Foreign Office (declassified from 'SECRET'), No. 160, 8 December 1943, FO 371/37618, (UKPRO).
149. 'Minutes,' Foreign Office cover note, 12 December 1943, FO 371/37618, (UKPRO).
150. Stevenson to Foreign Office (declassified from 'SECRET'), No. 171, 11 December 1943, FO 371/37618, (UKPRO).
151. 'Minutes,' 14 December 1943, FO 371/37618, (UKPRO).
152. Stevenson to Foreign Office (declassified from 'SECRET'), No. 175, 12 December 1943, FO 371/37618, (UKPRO).
153. Stevenson to Foreign Office (Immediate), 15 December 1943, FO 371/37618, (UKPRO).
154. 'Report by Captain R.P. Wade, 2nd Northants Yeo., on his stay in Jugoslavia (declassified from "TOP SECRET"),' March–December 1943, WO 202/162, (UKPRO), p. 2.
155. Hudson report, op. cit., p. 8.
156. 'Report by Captain R. P. Wade, 2nd Northants Yeo., on his stay in Jugoslavia (declassified from "TOP SECRET"),' March–December 1943, WO 202/162, (UKPRO), pp. 2–3.
157. Lt. Colonel S.B. Cope, 'Neronian Mission (declassified from "TOP SECRET"),' 25 May 1944, WO 202/162, (UKPRO).
158. Hudson report, op. cit., p. 9.
159. Captain Purvis to SOE Cairo, 'Roughshod Report (declassified from "SECRET"),' 1 January 1944, WO 202/162, (UKPRO).
160. 'Appendix to General Report FUGUE Mission,' May 1944, WO 202/162, (UKPRO). Note that FUGUE was a code name for Captain Michael Lees.
161. 'War Diary of Major J. Sehmer from 19 April 1943 to 13 December 1943 (declassified from "TOP SECRET"),' WO 202/162, (UKPRO), p. 3.
162. Letter from Sir Douglas Dodds-Parker to author, 17 September 1996.
163. MacLean, op. cit., p. 403.
164. Sir Peter Wilkinson and Joan Bright Astley, *Gubbins and SOE*, (London: Leo Cooper, 1993), p. 163.
165. Eden to Churchill, Grand No. 74, 22 December 1943, FO 371/37618, (UKPRO).
166. Wilkinson and Astley, op. cit., p. 163.
167. Hudson report, op. cit., p. 13.
168. 'COS to Wilson,' 28 January 1944, HS 3/173, (UKPRO).
169. 'Foreign Office to Mideast Defence Committee regarding OSS-SOE in the Mideast,' February 1944, HS 3/173, (UKPRO).

170. 'Mideast Defence Committee to Air Ministry,' CCL/386, 1 February 1944, HS 3/173, (UKPRO).

171. 'The OSS in Yugoslavia,' R. Smith Papers, Box 2, (HIA).

172. Roosevelt to Donovan, 22 March 1944, RG 218, Geographical Files 1942–45, Box 736, (NARA).

173. Donovan to Eisenhower, 31 March 1944, RG 226, Entry 116, Box 6, Folder 45, (NARA).

174. Churchill to Roosevelt, 1 April 1944, and Roosevelt to Churchill, 8 April 1944, in Walter Kimball (ed.), *Churchill and Roosevelt: The Complete Correspondence, Volume III,* (Princeton, NJ: 1984), pp. 80–82.

175. 'The OSS in Yugoslavia,' R. Smith Papers, Box 2, (HIA).

176. 'Colonel Bailey's Report on the Situation in Yugoslavia (declassified from "MOST SECRET"),' 14 March 1944, DHI 70/JU/6375, WO 202/162, (UKPRO), p. 4.

177. 'Report on Vera Pesic by Major Raw,' 27 May 1944, WO 202/162, (UKPRO).

178. Bailey report on Jevdjevic, September 1943, WO 202/162, and B1/X/72/174, 23 September 1943, WO 202/162, (UKPRO).

179. Stevenson to FO, No. 155, 6 December 1943, FO 371/37618, (UKPRO).

180. 'Colonel Bailey's Report on the Situation in Yugoslavia (declassified from "MOST SECRET"),' 14 March 1944, DHI 70/JU/6375, WO 202/162, (UKPRO), p. 5.

181. In late December 1943, the first two SI teams to carry their own radios were deployed to Slovenia and proceeded to collect valuable intelligence on Axis military facilities and movements. The Slovenian operation – with the help of the Partisans – was greatly expanded through 1944, and in June one OSS officer and two Partisans crossed into Austria, collecting intelligence on rail movements for 44 days before disappearing. See *OSS War Report, Volume II,* p. 128.

182. 'The OSS in Yugoslavia,' R. Smith Papers, Box 2, (HIA).

183. 'Mideast Defence Committee to Air Ministry,' CCL/386, 1 February 1944, HS 3/173, (UKPRO).

184. SOE to Bruce (declassified from 'TOP SECRET'), CMC VG16868, 22 June 1944, HS 3/199, (UKPRO).

185. 2677 Regiment, September 1944, RG 226, Entry 99, Box 20, Folder 106, (NARA).

186. 'Independent American Military Mission,' July 1944, RG 226, Entry 154, Box 23, Folder 321, (NARA).

187. Donovan to J.E. Toulmin, 19 July 1944, RG 226, Entry 143, Box 7, Folder 68 'Caserta,' (NARA).

188. Ford, op. cit., p. 101.

189. Ibid., p. 113. Note also that McDowell was a notorious anti-communist and was thus predisposed to favor Mihailovic. See B. Smith, *The Shadow Warriors,* p. 282.

190. Toulmin to Green, 21 July 1944, RG 226, Entry 136, Box 33, Folder 360, (NARA).

191. Donovan to Colonel Edward Glavin, 19 September 1944, RG 226, Entry 136, Box 21, Folder 219, (NARA).

192. Green to McDowell, 15 August 1944, RG 226, Entry 99, Box 35, Folder 176, (NARA).

193. Protic interview, 6 July 1996. See also Marinkovic letter to author of 1 October 1996.

194. Dusan Biber, 'Failure of a Mission: Robert McDowell in Yugoslavia, 1944,' in Chalou (ed.), *The Secrets War,* pp. 197, 204–7. Note also that the Partisans assisted in evacuating Allied airmen from Yugoslavia during the war.

195. Donovan to Toulmin, 13 September 1944, RG 226, Entry 136, Box 30, Folder 310, (NARA).

196. Commando units which operated in American military uniforms and conducted all sorts of SO work.

197. *OSS War Report, Volume II*, pp. 129–30.
198. The partial evacuation of Cairo was ordered when it was feared that Rommel's advancing *Afrika Korps* would capture the city.
199. 'SOE in the Balkans,' draft lecture notes, Bickham Sweet-Escott, Sweet-Escott Papers, Box 4, Folder A11, (BOA), p. 10.

6   THE LIBERATION OF FRANCE: A CASE STUDY IN ANGLO-OSS
    CONVERGENCE

1.   'Part Played by Britain and America in Helping French Resistance (3rd draft),' 14 November 1944, RG 226, Entry 190, Box 285, Folder 1265, (NARA), p. 1.
2.   Letter from Paul van der Stricht to R.H. Smith, 14 April 1971, Paul van der Stricht Papers, Box 1, (HIA).
3.   Bickham Sweet-Escott, *Baker Street Irregular*, (London: Methuen, 1965), p. 39.
4.   Douglas Porch, *The French Secret Services: From the Dreyfus Affair to the Gulf War*, (London: Macmillan, 1996), pp. 178–9.
5.   'Brief History of [French] Resistance,' undated, RG 226, Entry 190, Box 741, Folder 2, (NARA).
6.   Porch, op. cit., p. 184.
7.   Sweet-Escott, op. cit., p. 108.
8.   Letter from André Dewavrin, former chief of de Gaulle's BCRA intelligence apparatus, to Bickham Sweet-Escott, 20 May 1966, Bickham Sweet-Escott Papers, Box 8, Folder B6, Balliol College Archives, Oxford University (hereafter cited as 'BOA'), pp. 3–4.
9.   Van der Stricht, 'Resistance Support for Overlord,' unpublished and undated paper, Van der Stricht Papers, Box 1, (HIA), p. 14.
10.   'British Participation (Brief History),' undated, RG 226, Entry 190, Box 741, Folder 2, (NARA).
11.   'Part Played by Britain and America in Helping French Resistance (3rd draft),' 14 November 1944, RG 226, Entry 190, Box 285, Folder 1265, (NARA), p. 2.
12.   'Supplies and Personnel,' undated, RG 226, Entry 190, Box 741, Folder 2, (NARA).
13.   'RF-Section Methods,' undated, RG 226, Entry 190, Box 741, Document Series 12, (NARA).
14.   Arthur Brown, 'The Jedburghs: A Short History,' unpublished and undated paper drafted by British Jedburgh veteran held in the library of the Special Forces Club in London, p. 7.
15.   'Part Played by Britain and America in Helping French Resistance (3rd draft),' 14 November 1944, RG 226, Entry 190, Box 285, Folder 1265, (NARA), p. 4.
16.   'DF-Section,' 1 January 1944, RG 226, Entry 190, Box 741, Document Series 11, (NARA), pp. 1–4.
17.   Intelligence section of the French General Staff.
18.   'Brief History of [French] Resistance,' undated, RG 226, Entry 190, Box 741, Folder 2, (NARA).
19.   Ibid.
20.   Jean Moulin, 'Report on the Activities, Plans and Requirements of Groups formed in France with a view to the eventual liberation of the country,' October 1941, found in Appendix E of M.R.D. Foot's *SOE in France: An Account of the Work of the British Special Operations Executive in France, 1940–1944*, (London: HMSO, 1966), pp. 488–9, 180. Moulin was appointed by de Gaulle as his personal representative

charged with establishing a unified resistance command; he made significant progress before being betrayed. He was tortured to death by the Germans.

21. The *Maquis* operated mostly in southern France, but later established themselves throughout the country. Members lived as outlaws in the wild to escape Vichy mobilization orders or German labor deportation efforts. They resisted throughvarious acts of aggression, including sabotage, ambush, etc.

22. The *Sedentaires* were resisters who stayed at home and continued to work in their normal civilian occupations, but were armed and prepared to rise up during the invasion. See 'RF-Section Components,' undated, RG 226, Entry 190, Box 741, Document Series 12, (NARA).

23. 'Brief History of [French] Resistance,' undated, RG 226, Entry 190, Box 741, Folder 2, (NARA).

24. De Gaulle claims to have first instructed Frenay and d'Astier to help organize a National Council of Resistance inside France around Jean Moulin in the autumn of 1942, but the Council was not formally established until May 1943. See Charles de Gaulle, *The War Memoirs of Charles de Gaulle: Unity, 1942–1944*, (New York: Simon & Schuster, 1959), p. 42.

25. 'RF-Section Chronological Summary,' undated, RG 226, Entry 190, Box 741, Document Series 12, (NARA).

26. 'RF-Section Parachute Supply Organizations,' undated, RG 226, Entry 190, Box 741, Document Series 12, (NARA).

27. 'Part Played by Britain and America in Helping French Resistance (3rd draft),' 14 November 1944, RG 226, Entry 190, Box 285, Folder 1265, (NARA), p. 5.

28. 'RF-Section Agreements,' undated, RG 226, Entry 190, Box 741, Document Series 12, (NARA).

29. Ibid.

30. 'RF-Section Chronological Summary,' undated, RG 226, Entry 190, Box 741, Document Series 12, (NARA).

31. 'RF-Section Agreements,' undated, RG 226, Entry 190, Box 741, Document Series 12, (NARA).

32. Bernard D. Rifkind, 'The OSS and Franco-American Relations: 1942–1945,' unpublished doctoral thesis, (Washington, DC: George Washington University, 1983), p. 122.

33. One of the most notorious incidents involving the Gaullists concerned Britain's disastrous intervention at Dakar in September 1940. The British blamed the Gaullists for compromising their plans through poor security practices, which resulted in the dispatch by Vichy of a naval squadron from Toulon to Dakar. These French sailors were anti-British because of the Royal Navy's earlier attack on the French fleet at Mers-el-Kebir, and they succeeded in stiffening the will of the Dakar garrison to resist British and Gaullist overtures to come over to their side. As a result of this incident and other security lapses, 'de Gaulle was kept in ignorance about every major operation involving France for the rest of the war.' See Porch, op. cit., pp. 181–2.

34. 'British Representative, Free French National Committee, to Foreign Office (declassified from "MOST SECRET"),' No. 92, 17 June 1942, WO 106/5416A, (UKPRO).

35. 'Foreign Office to Washington (declassified from "MOST SECRET"),' No. 3813, 16 June 1942, WO 106/5416A, (UKPRO).

36. 'French Equatorial Africa (British Embassy) to Foreign Office (declassified from "CONFIDENTIAL"),' No. 345, 29 August 1941, WO 106/5416A, (UKPRO).

37. 'Arrival of General de Gaulle (declassified from "SECRET"),' Offices of the War Cabinet, 30 August 1941, WO 106/5416, (UKPRO).

38. 'C-in-C Middle East to War Office (declassified from "SECRET"),' No. 40987, 2 September 1941, WO 106/5416A, (UKPRO).

39. De Gaulle, op. cit., p. 4.
40. 'RF-Section Agreements,' undated, RG 226, Entry 190, Box 741, Document Series 12, (NARA).
41. 'RF-Section Chronological Summary,' undated, RG 226, Entry 190, Box 741, Document Series 12, (NARA).
42. Ibid.
43. 'RF-Section Pre-D-Day Operations,' undated, RG 226, Entry 190, Box 741, Document Series 12, (NARA).
44. Arthur L. Funk, 'American Contacts with the Resistance in France,' February 1970, R. Smith Papers, Box 1, (HIA), p. 6.
45. 'Notes on Talk with General McClure (Roseborough) (declassified from "SECRET"),' 7 September 1942, and 'Supplementary Notes on talk with Philip, Billotte, Passy, and Bingen (Roseborough) (declassified from "SECRET"),' 10 September 1942, RG 226, Entry 190, Box 251, Folder 739.
46. 'Relations with the French (declassified from "SECRET"),' undated, RG 226, Entry 190, Box 251, Folder 739.
47. 'Part Played by Britain and America in Helping French Resistance (3rd draft),' 14 November 1944, RG 226, Entry 190, Box 285, Folder 1265, (NARA), p. 6.
48. From November 1942, all of France was occupied by the Germans in response to the Allied invasion of North Africa. For the purposes of this paper, however, the 'occupied zone' refers to that area occupied by the Germans since the fall of France in 1940, excluding the northern (coastal) occupied zone and the area administered by the Vichy authorities.
49. 'Chronological Summary RF-Section,' undated, RG 226, Entry 190, Box 741, Document Series 12, (NARA).
50. 'RF-Section Components,' undated, RG 226, Entry 190, Box 741, Document Series 12, (NARA).
51. 'RF-Section Chronological Summary,' undated, RG 226, Entry 190, Box 741, Document Series 12, (NARA).
52. 'RF-Section Components,' undated, RG 226, Entry 190, Box 741, Document Series 12, (NARA).
53. 'RF-Section Methods,' undated, RG 226, Entry 190, Box 741, Document Series 12, (NARA).
54. Letter from Van der Stricht to R.H. Smith, 14 April 1971, Van der Stricht Papers, Box 1, (HIA). Van der Stricht refers here to the 'F-Section' of SOE, led from late-1941 by Maurice Buckmaster, which dealt with non-Gaullist French resisters and eventually established nearly 100 agent networks inside France. See Foot, op. cit., pp. 20, 178–9.
55. Letter from Van der Stricht to A.L. Funk, 8 July 1968, Van der Stricht Papers, Box 1, (HIA). See also 'Job Description,' 5 June 1944, Van der Stricht Papers, Box 1, (HIA).
56. Letter from Van der Stricht to William J. Casey, 23 December 1977, Van der Stricht Papers, Box 1, (HIA).
57. 'American Participation (Brief Summary),' undated, RG 226, Entry 190, Box 741, Folder 2, (NARA).
58. Van der Stricht, 'Resistance Support for Overlord,' unpublished and undated paper, Van der Stricht Papers, Box 1, (HIA), p. 14.
59. 'RF-Section Agreements,' undated, RG 226, Entry 190, Box 741, Document Series 12, (NARA).
60. Funk, 'American Contacts with the Resistance in France,' February 1970, R. Smith Papers, Box 1, (HIA), p. 10.
61. 'RF-Section Summary of Sabotage in 1943,' undated, RG 226, Entry 190, Box 741, Document Series 12, (NARA).
62. 'Sabotage,' undated, RG 226, Entry 190, Box 741, Folder 2, (NARA).

63. Letter from Van der Stricht to R.H. Smith, 14 April 1971, Van der Stricht Papers, Box 1, (HIA).

64. 'American Participation (Brief Summary),' undated, RG 226, Entry 190, Box 741, Folder 2, (NARA). Virginia Hall was actually the first American agent operating in France, having traveled to Lyon in 1941, but she was employed by SOE. See Foot, op. cit., pp. 259–60. Note also that Floege successfully ran an agent circuit called 'SACRISTAN' that carried out numerous acts of sabotage and gathered valuable intelligence until it was broken up by the Germans in late December 1943. See *War Report, Volume II*, p. 178.

65. Ibid., p. 179.

66. Letter from Van der Stricht to A.L. Funk, 21 June 1967, Van der Stricht Papers, Box 1, (HIA).

67. Van der Stricht, 'Resistance Support for Overlord,' unpublished and undated paper, Van der Stricht Papers, Box 1, (HIA), p. 6a.

68. Ibid, p. 13.

69. Letter from Hambro to Bruce, 19 May 1943, RG 226, Entry 190, Box 220, Folder 248, (NARA).

70. Ibid.

71. 'Relations with the British and Other Allies,' undated, Director's Office, RG 226, Entry 190, Box 220, Folder 248, (NARA), p. 16.

72. These successes included operating an effective clandestine courier service between France and Switzerland, and financing *Maquis* and other resistance groups operating in Savoy and along the Franco-Swiss frontier. See *War Report, Volume II*, pp. 179–80.

73. Van der Stricht, 'Resistance Support for Overlord,' unpublished and undated paper, Van der Stricht Papers, Box 1, (HIA), p. 13.

74. Ibid, p. 12a.

75. German military intelligence.

76. For a comprehensive and authoritative account of the operational difficulties experienced by SOE in France during 1943–4, see Foot, op. cit., pp. 289–349.

77. Van der Stricht, 'Resistance Support for Overlord,' unpublished and undated paper, Van der Stricht Papers, Box 1, (HIA), p. 6b–9. See also Lauran Paine, *The Abwehr: German Military Intelligence in World War II*, (London: Robert Hale, 1984), pp. 15–16.

78. 'Part Played by Britain and America in Helping French Resistance (3rd draft),' 14 November 1944, RG 226, Entry 190, Box 285, Folder 1265, (NARA), pp. 7–8.

79. 'Report on OG's, Company B, 2671st Special Recon Battalion Separate (Provisional) (declassified from "SECRET"),' 20 September 1944, RG 226, Entry 190, Box 741, Folder 7, (NARA), p. 9.

80. 'Maquis,' undated War Office document, WO/106/4321, (UKPRO).

81. It was estimated in January 1944 that only 10 per cent of all the Maquis fighters were armed, and in some areas, only 5 per cent. See 'Appreciation of the Strength and Organization of the French Maquis as at 26 [January] 1944 (declassified from "MOST SECRET"),' DRP/151, WO 106/4321, (UKPRO).

82. 'Part Played by Britain and America in Helping French Resistance (3rd draft),' 14 November 1944, RG 226, Entry 190, Box 285, Folder 1265, (NARA), p. 11.

83. 'Appreciation of the Strength and Organization of the French Maquis as at 26 [January] 1944 (declassified from "MOST SECRET"),' DRP/151, WO 106/4321, (UKPRO).

84. Van der Stricht, 'Resistance Support for Overlord,' unpublished and undated paper, Van der Stricht Papers, Box 1, (HIA), p. 14.

85. 'Part Played by Britain and America in Helping French Resistance (3rd draft),' 14 November 1944, RG 226, Entry 190, Box 285, Folder 1265, (NARA), p. 11.

86. 'RF-Section Special Maquis Missions,' undated, RG 226, Entry 190, Box 741, Document Series 12, (NARA).

87. 'Appreciation of the Strength and Organization of the French Maquis as at 26 [January] 1944 (declassified from "MOST SECRET"),' DRP/151, WO 106/4321, (UKPRO).

88. 'RF-Section Special Maquis Missions,' undated, RG 226, Entry 190, Box 741, Document Series 12, (NARA).

89. 'RF-Section Special Maquis Missions,' undated, RG 226, Entry 190, Box 741, Document Series 12, (NARA).

90. 'Chronological Summary RF-Section,' undated, RG 226, Entry 190, Box 741, Document Series 12, (NARA).

91. 'Appreciation of the Strength and Organization of the French Maquis as at 26 [January] 1944 (declassified from "MOST SECRET"),' DRP/151, WO 106/4321, (UKPRO).

92. 'RF-Section Special Maquis Missions,' undated, RG 226, Entry 190, Box 741, Document Series 12, (NARA).

93. Ibid.

94. Ibid.

95. The RF-Section of SOE alone claimed that in 1943, its French networks seriously disabled factories for rubber regeneration, tire production, ether, cellophane, railway wagons, cement, gun powder, steel, aluminum, ballbearings, small arms, needle-bearings, motors, pistons, and automotive axles. Railway traffic was interrupted through the destruction or damage of viaducts, numerous locomotives and rolling stock, railway repair shops, and train derailments – '150 trains on average were immobilized daily, half of which were for more than 6 hours.' Transformers and power stations were damaged, as well as dams, numerous canal locks and forage depots. See 'RF-Section Summary of Sabotage in 1943,' 'Sabotage of Railways,' 'Sabotage of Transformers, Power Stations, Pylons, Electric Installations in 1943,' 'Destruction of Dams, Canals, and Locks in 1943,' all undated, RG 226, Entry 190, Box 741, Document Series 12, (NARA).

96. *War Report, Volume II*, pp. 194–5.

97. At Tehran, it was decided that ANVIL should consist of a two-division assault into southern France and a ten-division follow-up to be launched simultaneously with OVERLORD. This was later scaled back and the date postponed to mid-summer 1944. See Sherwood (ed.), *The White House Papers of Harry L. Hopkins, Vol. II*, p. 778.

98. Funk, 'American Contacts with the Resistance in France,' February 1970, R. Smith Papers, Box 1, (HIA), p. 13.

99. 'JCM to War Cabinet Office (declassified from "MOST SECRET"),' JSM 1526, 19 February 1944, WO 106/4321, (UKPRO).

100. Arthur L. Funk, *Hidden Ally: The French Resistance, Special Operations, and the Landings in Southern France, 1944*, (New York: Greenwood Press, 1992), p. 9. See also A.L. Funk, 'Churchill, Eisenhower, and the French Resistance,' *Military Affairs*, February 1981, pp. 31–3.

101. Dewavrin later claimed the independent work of SOE's F-Section prompted him to ask Yeo-Thomas to accompany him to France in 1943 to help to organize and unify the resistance groups. See Letter from André Dewavrin to Bickham Sweet-Escott, 20 May 1966, Bickham Sweet-Escott Papers, Box 8, Folder B6, (BOA), pp. 3–4.

102. Van der Stricht, 'Resistance Support for Overlord,' unpublished and undated paper, Van der Stricht Papers, Box 1, (HIA), pp. 15–16.

103. 'British COS to General Wilson (declassified from "MOST SECRET"),' COSMED 27, 10 February 1944, WO 106/4321, (UKPRO).

104. 'JSM to War Cabinet Office (declassified from "MOST SECRET"),' JSM 1509, 12 February 1944, and 'U.S. Aircraft for SOE Purposes (declassified from

"MOST SECRET")," COS Committee Meeting Extract, COS (44), WO 106/4321, (UKPRO).

105. In January 1944, the British Chiefs tried in vain through their representatives in Washington to get the U.S. War Department to allocate more aircraft for special operations. See 'Air Ministry to Britman Washington,' OZ 451, 25 January 1944, WO 106/4321, (UKPRO).
106. Van der Stricht, 'Resistance Support for Overlord,' unpublished and undated paper, Van der Stricht Papers, Box 1, (HIA), pp. 15–16.
107. 'Part Played by Britain and America in Helping French Resistance (3rd draft),' 14 November 1944, RG 226, Entry 190, Box 285, Folder 1265, (NARA), p. 6.
108. 'Chronological Summary RF-Section,' undated, RG 226, Entry 190, Box 741, Document Series 12, (NARA).
109. 'American Participation (Brief Summary),' undated, RG 226, Entry 190, Box 741, Folder 2, (NARA).
110. Letter from Van der Stricht to William J. Casey, 23 December 1977, Van der Stricht Papers, Box 1, (HIA). See also 'SFHQ and OSS (SO) and SOE Missions to countries in Supreme Commander, AEF's sphere (declassified from "TOP SECRET"),' SHAEF/17515/ops(C), November 1944, RG 226, Entry 190, Box 285, Folder 1264, (NARA).
111. 'Part Played by Britain and America in Helping French Resistance (3rd draft),' 14 November 1944, RG 226, Entry 190, Box 285, Folder 1265, (NARA), pp. 7–8.
112. The performance of the Gaullist forces, in particular, was enhanced considerably during this period. See 'Tenth Monthly Progress Report to SHAEF from SFHQ London (declassified from "TOP SECRET"),' MUS/715/1437, June 1944, WO 106/4322A, and 'Casualties Inflicted on the Germans by French Resistance (declassified from "TOP SECRET"),' PHO H/1100, 24 April 1944, WO 106/4320, (UKPRO).
113. 'Role of Resistance Groups in the South of France (declassified from "TOP SECRET"),' SHAEF/17240/13/OPS, 21 May 1944, and 'Operational Directive to SOE/SO (SFHQ) (declassified from "TOP SECRET"),' 23 May 1944, WO 106/4321, (UKPRO). The new chain of command was thus: 1. SHAEF; 1A. SFHQ-London; 2. AFHQ-Algiers; 2A. SPOC-Algiers; 3. SOE and OSS in Algiers; 4. Resistance Groups in France. See 'Resistance in South France Operational Control and Communications (declassified from "TOP SECRET"),' Appendix A to SHAEF/17240/13/OPS, 21 May 1944, WO 106/4321, (UKPRO).
114. 'RF-Section, Preliminary Explanation,' undated, RG 226, Entry 190, Box 741, Document Series 12, (NARA).
115. Van der Stricht, 'Resistance Support for Overlord,' unpublished and undated paper, Van der Stricht Papers, Box 1, (HIA), pp. 5–6.
116. Funk, 'American Contacts with the Resistance in France,' February 1970, R. Smith Papers, Box 1, (HIA), p. 120.
117. 'SO/SOE Activities in France – Relations with the French Authorities ('declassified from "SECRET"),' Paul van der Stricht, 14 December 1943, Van der Stricht Papers, Box 1, (HIA).
118. 'Aide-Mémoire on SOE Collaboration with the French (declassified from "SECRET"),' 25 November 1943, Van der Stricht Papers, Box 1, (HIA).
119. 'SO/SOE Activities in France – Relations with the French Authorities ('declassified from "SECRET"),' Paul van der Stricht, 14 December 1943, Van der Stricht Papers, Box 1, (HIA).
120. Ibid.
121. Ibid.
122. Ibid.

123. Van der Stricht, 'Resistance Support for Overlord,' unpublished and undated paper, Van der Stricht Papers, Box 1, (HIA), pp. 32–3.

124. For details, see Foot, op. cit., pp. 289–349.

125. 'SO/SOE Activities in France – Relations with the French Authorities ('declassified from "SECRET"),' Paul van der Stricht, 14 December 1943, Van der Stricht Papers, Box 1, (HIA).

126. *War Report, Volume II*, p. 177.

127. 'RF-Section, D-Day Operations,' undated, RG 226, Entry 190, Box 741, Document Series 12, (NARA).

128. Van der Stricht, 'Resistance Support for Overlord,' unpublished and undated paper, Van der Stricht Papers, Box 1, (HIA), pp. 29–31.

129. *War Report, Volume II*, p. 178.

130. 'Sabotage,' undated, RG 226, Entry 190, Box 741, Folder 2, (NARA).

131. *War Report, Volume II*, p. 192.

132. 'Military Action,' undated, RG 226, Entry 190, Box 741, Folder 2, (NARA).

133. Author's interview with Sir Douglas Dodds-Parker, Special Forces Club, 1 October 1996.

134. 'JSM Washington to WCO London (declassified from "MOST SECRET"),' JSM 1396, January 1944, WO 106/4321, (UKPRO).

135. Dewavrin – 'Colonel Passy' – had by this time relocated his headquarters to Algiers, where he remained as overall chief of the BCRA. Dewavrin spent a great deal of time in France during 1943, helping to organize the various resistance groups, particularly after Jean Moulin's capture.

136. Letter from Van der Stricht to R.H. Smith, 17 September 1971, Van der Stricht Papers, Box 1, (HIA).

137. Brown, Op. cit., pp. 12–13. Note that the Communist *Francs Tireurs et Partisans* remained independent of FFI as did some of the *Maquis*.

138. In the week ending 12 March 1944, for example, nearly 1300 containers and 239 packages were dropped to the resistance in France – a significant increase over earlier supply efforts. See 'Chronological Summary RF-Section,' undated, RG 226, Entry 190, Box 741, Document Series 12, (NARA).

139. Van der Stricht, 'Resistance Support for Overlord,' unpublished and undated paper, Van der Stricht Papers, Box 1, (HIA), pp. 23–4.

140. 'JSM to WCO (declassified from "MOST SECRET"),' JSM 1639, 14 April 1944, WO 106/4321, (UKPRO).

141. 'Theatre Report (declassified from "SECRET"),' 1 May 1944, RG 226, Entry 190, Box 241, Folder 590, (NARA).

142. 'AGWAR to ETOUSA (Eisenhower) (declassified from 'TOP SECRET"),' WAR-20343, 8 April 1944, 'Activities of OSS in European Theatre (declassified from 'MOST SECRET"),' JSM 1623, 7 April 1944, and 'Air Ministry to Britman Washington (declassified from 'MOST SECRET"),' COS(W) 1246, 30 May 1944, in WO 106/4321, (UKPRO). Note also that this close coordination included the complete sharing of information about operations. See Donovan to Marshall (declassified from 'TOP SECRET'), 12 July 1944, and Scribner to Buxton, 'Situation Reports (declassified from 'TOP SECRET"),' 29 June 1944, RG 226, M1642, Roll 111, (NARA).

143. 'Theatre Report (declassified from "SECRET"),' 1 May 1944, RG 226, Entry 190, Box 241, Folder 590, (NARA).

144. 'AGWAR (Marshall) to SHAEF (Eisenhower) (declassified from "MOST SECRET & PERSONAL"),' SH.130, W30283, 30 April 1944, WO 106/4321, (UKPRO).

145. 'AGWAR (Joint COS) to ETOUSA (Eisenhower) (declassified from "MOST SECRET"),' SH.111, W24345, 17 April 1944, WO 106/4321, (UKPRO).

146. 'SHAEF (Eisenhower) to AGWAR (Marshall) (declassified from "MOST SE-CRET"),' S-51396, SH156, 6 May 1944, WO 106/4320, (UKPRO).

147. 'SHAEF (Eisenhower) to AGWAR (Marshall) (declassified from "MOST SE-CRET"),' 17 May 1944, WO 106/4321, (UKPRO).

148. 'Aircraft Available to SFHQ (declassified from "TOP SECRET"),' Appendix A to MUS/705/6/1053, 4 June 1944, RG 226, M1642, Roll 111, (NARA).

149. 'SHAEF (Eisenhower) to AGWAR (Marshall) (declassified from "TOP SECRET"),' S-51396, 6 May 1944, WO 106/4321, (UKPRO). Note also that OSS acquired most of its equipment for packing and delivery from British sources, and much of this was delivered to the resistance by SOE 'irrespective of whether OSS operations [were] conducted jointly with SOE or separately.'

150. *War Report, Volume II*, p. 191.

151. 'Theatre Report (declassified from "SECRET"),' 1 May 1944, RG 226, Entry 190, Box 241, Folder 590, (NARA).

152. *War Report, Volume II*, p. 191.

153. Koenig's appointment as Commander-in-Chief, FFI, and the official establishment by SHAEF of EMFFI occurred on 2 June 1944, although EMFFI was not made operational until D-Day.

154. 'OSS (SO) Comments on SHAEF Draft Paper on SFHQ Missions to Countries in SHAEF's Sphere (declassified from "SECRET"),' 17 October 1944, RG 226, Entry 190, Box 285, Folder 1264, (NARA).

155. Koenig's appointment resulted in the assignment of Gaullist officers, senior of whom was Colonel A. Ziegler, to SFHQ with joint responsibility for operations in France. See 'Administration,' April–June 1944, RG 226, Entry 190, Box 740, Document Series 3, (NARA).

156. 'Situation Report,' July–September 1944, RG 226, Entry 190, Box 740, Document Series 4, (NARA).

157. William P. Davis to Joseph M. Scribner (declassified from 'SECRET'), 14 June 1944, RG 226, Entry 190, Box 90, Folder 25, (NARA).

158. Brown, Op. cit., pp. 12–13. See also 'Situation Report,' July–September 1944, RG 226, Entry 190, Box 740, Document Series 4, (NARA).

159. Letter from Van der Stricht to William J. Casey, 23 December 1977, Van der Stricht Papers, Box 1, (HIA).

160. 'Command and Control of Resistance,' 26 May 1944, Van der Stricht Papers, Box 1, (HIA).

161. Funk, 'American Contacts with the Resistance in France,' February 1970, R. Smith Papers, Box 1, (HIA), p. 18.

162. Letter from Dewavrin to Sweet-Escott, 20 May 1966, Bickham Sweet-Escott Papers, Box 8, Folder B6, (BOA), p. 6. See also 'Administration,' April–June 1944, RG 226, Entry 190, Box 740, Document Series 3, (NARA).

163. Letter from Van der Stricht to R.H. Smith, 14 April 1971, Van der Stricht Papers, Box 1, (HIA).

164. Van der Stricht said that Millet, whom he described as de Gaulle's *eminence grise*, 'distrusted the British.' See letter from Van der Stricht to William J. Casey, 23 December 1977, Van der Stricht Papers, Box 1, (HIA).

165. Letter from Van der Stricht to William J. Casey, 23 December 1977, Van der Stricht Papers, Box 1, (HIA).

166. Letter from Van der Stricht to R.H. Smith, 14 April 1971, Van der Stricht Papers, Box 1, (HIA).

167. 'Jedburghs,' undated, RG 226, Entry 190, Box 740, Document Series 5, (NARA), p. iii.

168. Brown, op. cit., p. 5. Brown also notes that the Jedburgh Section was initially jointly led by SOE Major A. Coombe-Tennant (British) and OSS Major H.B. Cox, and

from D-Day onwards was staffed by four British, three American, and two French officers.

169. Potential recruits were tested for intelligence, physical conditioning, problem solving, teamwork, psychiatric suitability, etc. See author's interview with William Colby, OSS Jedburgh veteran and former director of CIA, 19 July 1995, Washington, D.C.

170. Brown, op. cit., pp. 6–9.

171. Ibid.

172. Radio operators were trained first at the SOE Special Training School (STS) 54 before joining the officers at Milton Hall. See Major Wyman W. Irwin, 'A Special Force: Origin and Development of the Jedburgh Project in Support of Operation Overlord,' unpublished MA thesis, U.S. Command and General Staff College, Fort Leavenworth, Kansas, 1991, p. 118. There were many other special operations and secret intelligence schools in England and Scotland for infiltration, explosives, counterespionage, etc. These were all run by the British, sometimes with instructor staffs that included members of OSS. See author's interview with William Morgan, an OSS veteran who served both as a psychiatric evaluator for the Jedburgh program and as a Jedburgh officer, 16 July 1995, Great Falls, Maryland.

173. Colby interview, 19 July 1995.

174. Major Wyman W. Irwin, 'A Special Force: Origin and Development of the Jedburgh Project in Support of Operation Overlord,' unpublished MA thesis, US Command and General Staff College, Fort Leavenworth, Kansas, 1991, pp. 118, 129.

175. Brown, op. cit., p. 5. OSS's William Morgan makes similar observations. See Morgan interview, 16 July 1995.

176. Colby interview, 19 July 1995.

177. Morgan interview, 16 July 1995.

178. Ibid.

179. Ibid.

180. Colby interview, 19 July 1995.

181. 'Supplies and Personnel,' undated, RG 226, Entry 190, Box 741, Folder 2, (NARA).

182. 'Jedburgh Teams (declassified from "TOP SECRET"),' MA/VOIGS, 2 July 1944, WO 106/4322A, (UKPRO).

183. Irwin, op. cit., p. 134.

184. Colby interview, 19 July 1995.

185. 'Supplies and Personnel,' undated, RG 226, Entry 190, Box 741, Folder 2, (NARA). Other OSS sources put these numbers at 103 French, 90 British, and 83 Americans, respectively, for all of France, Belgium, and Holland during the same period. See *War Report, Volume II*, p. 199.

186. Brown, op. cit., p. 13 and Annex A.

187. 'Jedburghs,' undated, RG 226, Entry 190, Box 740, Document Series 5, (NARA), p. i.

188. Ibid., p. ii.

189. Brown, op. cit., p. 4.

190. 'Jedburghs,' undated, RG 226, Entry 190, Box 740, Document Series 5, (NARA), p. ii.

191. Ibid., p. iv.

192. Ibid., p. ii.

193. 'Dispatch of Jedburgh Teams and Operational Groups to France from United Kingdom and North Africa (declassified from "TOP SECRET"),' 23 August 1944, RG 226, M1642, Roll 111, (NARA). See also 'Appendix E to MUS/715/1437 (declassified from "TOP SECRET"),' 10 July 1944, WO 106/4322A, (UKPRO).

194. 'Sabotage,' undated, RG 226, Entry 190, Box 741, Folder 2, (NARA).

195. Brown, op. cit., p. 14. See also Major Michael R. King, 'Jedburgh Operations: Support to the French Resistance in Central France From June Through September 1944,' un-

published MA thesis, US Command and General Staff College, Fort Leavenworth, Kansas, 1991, p. 6.

196. 'Introductory Summary Account of SUSSEX Operation (declassified from "SE-CRET"),' undated, RG 226, Entry 190, Box 234, Folder 471, (NARA).

197. Ibid.

198. 'Sussex Plan Drafted (declassified from "SECRET"),' undated, RG 226, Entry 190, Box 234, Folder 471, (NARA).

199. German countermeasures were indeed increased as D-Day approached. See 'State of the Resistance as of 30 June 1944,' April–June 1944, RG 226, Entry 190, Box 740, Document Series 3, (NARA).

200. 'Minutes of meeting of Tuesday, 7 September 1943, on "Sussex Training Scheme,"' and 'Minutes of Meetings of Tuesday, 5 October; of Thursday, 14 October; of Saturday, 30 October; of 11 December; and of 31 December, 1943 (all declassified from "SECRET"),' RG 226, Entry 190, Box 234, Folder 471, (NARA).

201. This plan was submitted by OSS to the US Theater Commander on 5 July 1943; approval was received on 5 October. See 'Sussex Plan Drafted (declassified from "SE-CRET"),' undated, RG 226, Entry 190, Box 234, Folder 471, (NARA).

202. 'Initial Difficulties (declassified from "SECRET"),' undated, RG 226, Entry 190, Box 234, Folder 471, (NARA).

203. 'Sussex Plan Drafted (declassified from "SECRET"),' undated, RG 226, Entry 190, Box 234, Folder 471, (NARA).

204. 'Sussex (declassified from "SECRET"),' undated, RG 226, Entry 190, Box 234, Folder 471, (NARA), p. 1.

205. 'Sussex Plan Drafted (declassified from "SECRET"),' undated, RG 226, Entry 190, Box 234, Folder 471, (NARA).

206. 'SMR #6 (declassified from "SECRET"),' 1 May 1943, RG 226, Entry 190, Box 234, Folder 471, (NARA), p. 2B.

207. 'Minutes of Sussex Committee Meeting,' 7 September 1943, RG 226, Entry 190, Box 234, Folder 471, (NARA).

208. 'Recruiting of Agents (declassified from "SECRET"),' undated, and 'Cable from Washington to London No. 0994 (declassified from "SECRET"),' 16 October 1943, RG 226, Entry 190, Box 234, Folder 471, (NARA).

209. 'SMR No. 13 (declassified from "SECRET"),' 15 August 1943, RG 226, Entry 190, Box 234, Folder 471, (NARA).

210. 'Recruiting of Agents (declassified from "SECRET"),' undated, RG 226, Entry 190, Box 234, Folder 471, (NARA).

211. Ibid., and 'SMR No. 18 (declassified from "SECRET"),' 1 November 1943, RG 226, Entry 190, Box 234, Folder 471, (NARA).

212. O'Brien to Shepardson, File SA-12243, 30 October 1943, RG 226, Entry 190, Box 234, Folder 471, (NARA).

213. 'SMR No. 20 and 21 (declassified from "SECRET"),' 1 and 15 December 1943, RG 226, Entry 190, Box 234, Folder 471, (NARA).

214. 'SMR No. 22 (declassified from "SECRET"),' 1 January 1944, RG 226, Entry 190, Box 234, Folder 471, (NARA).

215. 'Recruiting of Agents (declassified from "SECRET"),' undated, RG 226, Entry 190, Box 234, Folder 471, (NARA).

216. Ibid., and 'Preparations for Carrying out Plan (declassified from "SECRET"),' undated, RG 226, Entry 190, Box 234, Folder 471, (NARA).

217. 'Recruiting of Agents (declassified from "SECRET"),' undated, RG 226, Entry 190, Box 234, Folder 471, (NARA).

218. Ibid.

219. Ibid.

220. 'Minutes of meeting held in Room 501, Broadway, on Tuesday, 4 January 1944 (declassified from "SECRET"),' RG 226, Entry 190, Box 234, Folder 471, (NARA).

221. Letter from Major General J.F.M. Whitely to Lt. Colonel W– of SIS (declassified from 'SECRET'), 28 February 1944, File SX-76, RG 226, Entry 190, Box 234, Folder 471, (NARA).

222. 'Cover Stories (declassified from "SECRET"),' undated, RG 226, Entry 190, Box 234, Folder 471, (NARA).

223. 'Meeting at TS-7 (declassified from "SECRET"),' 7 December 1943, RG 226, Entry 190, Box 243, Folder 614, (NARA).

224. 'Documents (False Papers) (declassified from "SECRET"),' undated, RG 226, Entry 190, Box 234, Folder 471, (NARA).

225. 'Meeting at TS-7 (declassified from "SECRET"),' 7 December 1943, RG 226, Entry 190, Box 243, Folder 614, (NARA).

226. Ibid.

227. 'Selection of Points and Division of Teams (declassified from "SECRET"),' undated, RG 226, Entry 190, Box 234, Folder 471, (NARA).

228. Note that other separate OSS and SOE packing stations were in operation during this time in Holme, England and in Algiers.

229. 'Dispatch,' undated, RG 226, Entry 190, Box 234, Folder 471, (NARA), p. 4.

230. Ibid., p. 3.

231. 'Selection of Points and Division of Teams (declassified from "SECRET"),' undated, RG 226, Entry 190, Box 234, Folder 471, (NARA).

232. 'Field Detachments (declassified from "SECRET"),' undated, RG 226, Entry 190, Box 234, Folder 471, (NARA).

233. 'Arrangements for Reception (declassified from "SECRET"),' undated, RG 226, Entry 190, Box 234, Folder 471, (NARA).

234. 'Pathfinder Mission (declassified from "SECRET"),' June 1944, RG 226, Entry 190, Box 236, Folder 516, (NARA).

235. 'Dispatch,' undated, RG 226, Entry 190, Box 234, Folder 471, (NARA), pp. 5–7.

236. 'SMR No. 29 (declassified from "SECRET"),' 15 April 1944, RG 226, Entry 190, Box 234, Folder 471, (NARA).

237. 'Operations (declassified from "SECRET"),' undated, RG 226, Entry 190, Box 234, Folder 471, (NARA).

238. 'First Messages (declassified from "SECRET"),' undated, RG 226, Entry 190, Box 234, Folder 471, (NARA).

239. 'Supplies and Personnel,' undated, RG 226, Entry 190, Box 741, Folder 2, (NARA).

240. 'Sussex (declassified from "SECRET"),' undated, RG 226, Entry 190, Box 234, Folder 471, (NARA), p. 1.

241. 'Situation on D-Day (declassified from "SECRET"),' undated, RG 226, Entry 190, Box 234, Folder 471, (NARA).

242. 'End of Operation (declassified from "SECRET"),' undated, RG 226, Entry 190, Box 234, Folder 471, (NARA).

243. 'SI Branch Monthly Report, No. 33 (declassified from "SECRET"),' 15 June 1944, RG 226, Entry 190, Box 234, Folder 471, (NARA), p. 3.

244. 'J.T. Betts, Brigadier General, GSC, D/A, C of S, G-2, to Colonel John Haskell, Chief, SI Branch, [OSS/ETOUSA] (declassified from "SECRET"),' 27 July 1944, RG 226, Entry 190, Box 234, Folder 471, (NARA).

245. 'Further Commendation from SHAEF (declassified from "SECRET"),' undated, and 'SMR No. 35 (declassified from "SECRET"),' 15 July 1944, RG 226, Entry 190, Box 234, Folder 471, (NARA).

246. Letter from Colonel E.J. Foord for K.W.D. Strong to CO/OSS/ETO (declassified from 'SECRET'), 19 August 1944, RG 226, Entry 190, Box 234, Folder 471, (NARA).

247. 'Sussex (declassified from "SECRET"),' undated, RG 226, Entry 190, Box 234, Folder 471, (NARA).

248. 'Supplies and Personnel,' undated, RG 226, Entry 190, Box 741, Folder 2, (NARA).

249. 'Jedburghs,' undated, RG 226, Entry 190, Box 740, Document Series 5, (NARA), p. v.

250. 'Report on OG's, Company B, 2671st Special Recon Battalion Separate (Provisional) (declassified from "SECRET"),' 20 September 1944, RG 226, Entry 190, Box 741, Folder 7, (NARA), p. 3. OSS determined in June 1944 that the 4 French sections were 'highly trained' and 'thoroughly satisfactory,' but the Italian sections were rated as less effective and placed in reserve. See Davis to Scribner (declassified from 'SECRET'), 14 June 1944, RG 226, Entry 190, Box 90, Folder 25, (NARA). Note also that two Norwegian, four Greek, four Yugoslav, and three additional Italian OG sections were held in reserve by OSS. See 'Appendix E to MUS/715/1437 (declassified from "TOP SECRET"),' 10 July 1944, WO 106/4322A, (UKPRO).

251. 'Supplies and Personnel,' undated, RG 226, Entry 190, Box 741, Folder 2, (NARA).

252. 'Report on OG's, Company B, 2671st Special Recon Battalion Separate (Provisional) (declassified from "SECRET"),' 20 September 1944, RG 226, Entry 190, Box 741, Folder 7, (NARA), p. 2.

253. 'Jedburghs,' undated, RG 226, Entry 190, Box 740, Document Series 5, (NARA), p. vi.

254. 'Supplies and Personnel,' undated, RG 226, Entry 190, Box 741, Folder 2, (NARA).

255. 'Report on OG's, Company B, 2671st Special Recon Battalion Separate (Provisional) (declassified from "SECRET"),' 20 September 1944, RG 226, Entry 190, Box 741, Folder 7, (NARA), p. 13.

256. Some OGs were placed under the tactical authority of SPOC in June 1944 for use in support of the ANVIL/DRAGOON operation. Ibid., p. 4.

257. 'SAS Operations in Connection with OVERLORD (declassified from "TOP SECRET"),' MO3/BM/2063, 5 July 1944, WO 106/4322A, (UKPRO), pp. 2–3.

258. 'Report on OG's, Company B, 2671st Special Recon Battalion Separate (Provisional) (declassified from "SECRET"),' 20 September 1944, RG 226, Entry 190, Box 741, Folder 7, (NARA), pp. 6–7.

259. 'Supplies and Personnel,' undated, RG 226, Entry 190, Box 741, Folder 2, (NARA).

260. 'Report on OG's, Company B, 2671st Special Recon Battalion Separate (Provisional) (declassified from "SECRET"),' 20 September 1944, RG 226, Entry 190, Box 741, Folder 7, (NARA), p. 10.

7 KEY FINDINGS

1. Author's telephone interview with Sir Douglas Dodds-Parker in London, 18 September 1996.

2. 'SFHQ and OSS (SO) and SOE Missions to countries in Supreme Commander, AEF's sphere (declassified from "TOP SECRET"),' SHAEF/17515/ops (C), November 1944, and 'OSS (SO) Comments on SHAEF Draft Paper on SFHQ Missions to Countries in SHAEF's Sphere (declassified from "SECRET"),' 17 October 1944, RG 226, Entry 190, Box 285, Folder 1264, (NARA).

3. Douglas Dodds-Parker dates the start of virtually autonomous OSS and SOE operations there back to the Allied invasion of Sicily. Moreover, he has observed that

throughout 1944, 'a summons from [Allied military or political authorities in Italy] would find me as short of information on OSS activities as they were.' Dodds-Parker, *Setting Europe Ablaze*, pp. 179–80. See also Max Corvo, 'The OSS and the Italian Campaign,' in George Chalou (ed.), *The Secrets War*, pp. 183–93.

4. See E. Bruce Reynolds, 'The Opening Wedge: The OSS in Thailand,' in Chalou (ed.), op. cit., pp. 328–44, and Richard Aldrich, 'Imperial Rivalry: British and American Intelligence in Asia, 1942–46,' *Intelligence and National Security*, Volume 3, No. 1, January 1988, (London: Frank Cass, 1988).

5. E. Bruce Reynolds has observed that the British sought to 'check-rein the OSS [in Thailand] because of suspicions that it was promoting an anticolonial political agenda . . . OSS, [meanwhile], sought to carve a niche for [itself] by taking full advantage of Thailand's independent status [so that it] might serve as the opening wedge for postwar American economic and political influence in Southeast Asia.' See Reynolds, op. cit., pp. 328–9.

6. Aldrich, op. cit., pp. 22–3.

7. Ibid., p. 8.

8. Churchill's minute to Eden quoted in a minute by J.R. Colville, Private Secretary to Churchill, 18 April 1945, CAB 120/827, (UKPRO), as cited by Aldrich, op. cit., p. 5.

9. Author's interview with Geoffrey Jones, President of the Veterans of the OSS, in New York, July 1995.

War Chronology of Key Events

1939	**September**	Germans invade Poland; Britain and France declare war on Germany. FDR ask Congress to repeal the US Neutrality Act. Poland capitulates in less than a month of fighting.
	November	British SIS chief Hugh Sinclair dies and is replaced by Stewart Menzies. US Neutrality Act replaced by 'cash and carry' law for arms sales to UK. Red Army invades Finland, quickly bogs down.
	December	*Stephenson / SIS plan to sabotage Swedish ore shipments to Germany.*
1940	**February**	Hitler orders unrestricted submarine warfare. *Stephenson plot foiled when Swedish King intervenes with British King. Stephenson offers Finnish Field Marshal Mannerheim sabotage support.*
	March	Finland sues for peace; accepts tough Soviet terms.
	April	*Stephenson sent to US to start SIS-FBI liaison; returns to London.* Germans invade Denmark and Norway; Denmark surrenders in 24 hours. British and French troops land in Norway, German counterattacks force retreat.
	May	Allies evacuate Norway; Germans invade Low Countries, France. As Allies fall back in France, Churchill becomes new British Prime Minister. FDR warns Congress of German Fifth Column threat in America. Churchill appeals to FDR for US aid. *Stephenson returns to US to lead British Security Coordination (BSC).* British Expeditionary Force flees France in Dunkirk sealift.
	June	French General Charles de Gaulle appointed French defense undersecretary. Japanese forces advance into the heart of China. Italy invades France; de Gaulle begins to organize resistance from London. France surrenders on the 22nd after just six weeks of fighting.
	July	Collaborationist French government set up at Vichy under Pétain and Laval. British destroy French Navy at Oran; Vichy severs relations with Britain. *FDR sends Donovan on first special mission to London.* 'Battle of Britain' begins as Luftwaffe attacks Royal Air Force bases in UK. *British create Special Operations Executive (SOE) to 'set Europe ablaze'.*
	August	RAF barely winning Battle of Britain in desperate fight with the Luftwaffe.

Donovan returns to US, urges support for UK, transfer of old destroyers.

US tells UK that it has broken Japanese diplomatic codes; offers cooperation.

September US transfers 50 old destroyers to UK for free lease on British Caribbean bases.

Hitler postpones invasion of Britain, shifts air tactics to bombing of UK cities.

US conscription bill passes in Congress by one vote; Japan joins the Axis.

October Hitler abandons UK invasion plans, intensifies U-boat offensive in the Atlantic.

US secretly agrees to give Britain arms; FDR announces US will not enter war.

Italy invades Greece against German wishes, quickly bogs down.

November Greek army counterattacks, driving back Italian invaders.

FDR wins third presidential term in a landslide; Chamberlain dies in Britain.

British air attack devastates Italian fleet at Taranto.

Romania and Hungary join Axis; Germans plan invasion of Russia.

December Defeatist US Ambassador to UK, Joseph Kennedy, resigns and returns home.

US-UK conclude limited cryptanalytic cooperation accord.

FDR sends Donovan on mission to Britain, Mediterranean, and Balkans.

British defeat Italians at Sidi Barrani in major Western Desert victory.

Greeks chase Italians into Albania; Germans begin Balkan buildup of forces.

Donovan visits UK, Gibraltar, Malta, and the Western Desert.

FDR outlines 'Lend-Lease' concept; says US to be the 'arsenal of democracy'.

1941 January *Donovan visits Greece, Albania, Bulgaria, and Yugoslavia.*

FDR sends Harry Hopkins to London; Lend-Lease negotiations begin.

Allies capture Tobruk; Churchill to send troops to support Greece.

Secret US-UK staff talks (ABC1) cover possible future joint war strategy.

February *Donovan visits Turkey, Cyprus, Palestine, Egypt, Iraq, and Syria.*

Donovan-supporter John Winant named US Ambassador to UK.

Bulgaria joins Axis; German troops enter Bulgaria.

British capture Benghazi and 250 000 Italians; Rommel sent to Tripoli.

March Yugoslavia's regent, Prince Paul, agrees to join Axis.

US passes Lease Act; US-Vichy trade accord signed.

Donovan visits Spain, Portugal, and UK; returns to Washington.

British deploy Allied Expeditionary Force to Greece.

British Navy, alerted by ULTRA, smashes Italian fleet at Cape Matapan.

Yugoslav nationalists overthrow Prince Paul, repudiate pact with Axis.

April UK warns USSR of impending German invasion; Stalin ignores warning.

Rommel launches counteroffensive against British in North Africa.

Nazis invades Yugoslavia, Greece; Hitler postpones attack on USSR.

Allies evacuate 50 000 troops from Greece in 'Second Dunkirk' disaster.

May Draza Mihailovic begins to organize Cetnik resistance in Serbia.
British deploy first agents to France.
Hitler declares 'Thousand Year Reich'; Rudolf Hess flies to Scotland.
German paratroopers seize Crete from British.
German battleship *Bismarck* sinks HMS *Hood*, then is itself sunk.

June Free French and British forces invade Vichy-controlled Syria.
John Godfrey, UK naval intelligence chief, sent on mission to US.
FDR agrees to establish COI and to appoint Donovan as COI chief.
Germans invade USSR on the 22nd in massive attack.
French Communist Party begins to organize anti-German resistance.

July Stalin adopts scorched-earth policy in face of German onslaught.
Tito organizes pro-Communist Partisan resistance in Yugoslavia.
COI established on the 11th by FDR with Donovan as chief.
British-Soviet alliance formed against Germany.
Japan occupies French Indochina with Vichy's consent.

August Germans drive deep into USSR, crushing Red Army formations.
US and UK sign Atlantic Charter of democratic principles.
Stephenson assigns Dick Ellis to liaise with COI in Washington.
COI begins sending intelligence reports, mostly from BSC, to FDR.

September *Donovan recruits Bill Whitney and Bob Solborg into COI.*
First Mihailovic-Tito meeting; *SOE sends Bill Hudson to Yugoslavia.*
US Navy begins escorting British convoys in the western Atlantic.
Whitney, Solborg, and Sherwood dispatched to London for survey.
Germans surround Leningrad, capture Kiev.

October US-UK agreement to send planes and tanks to USSR.
Donovan promotes North Africa as suitable proving ground for COI.
Germans mount assault on Moscow; Siberian troops reinforce Moscow.
Whitney, Sherwood return from London; debriefed about SO and SI.
General Hideki Tojo becomes Prime Minister of Japan.
David Bruce and Wallace Phillips recruited into COI.
Whitney opens first COI overseas station in London.

November US isolationists throw eggs at British ambassador visiting Detroit.
Wallace Phillips named COI's SI chief.
Japan secretly plans Pearl Harbor attack.
COI's Howe instructed to secretly pass $100 000 to SOE in London.
British back Mihailovic; Cetniks and Partisans attack each other.
Severe cold and snow hit Russia; Germans reach outskirts of Moscow.

December Japanese surprise attack sinks US fleet at Pearl Harbor on the 7th.
Red Army counterattacks at Moscow; drive Germans back on wide front.
COI London staff augmented.
Japan invades Philippines, Burma, Malaya, captures Hong Kong.
Churchill goes to Washington for talks with FDR (ARCADIA staff talks).

1942 January   Japan captures Kuala Lumpur; invades Dutch East Indies.
US General Stilwell named to command US forces in China.
Wallace Phillips replaced by Bruce; Solborg returns to Washington.
Jean Moulin organizes pro-Gaullist resistance inside France.
Ismay curtails COI London's access during Whitney's absence.

February   Japan captures Singapore.
Solborg departs for Lisbon and North Africa.

March   Japan captures Java, Rangoon, advances in the Philippines.
Russia appeals for 'Second Front' against Germans in Europe.
Carl Eifler recruited into COI.

April   U-boats continue to sink huge amounts of Allied merchant shipping.
Japan captures Bataan, closes 'Burma Road'; Doolittle raid on Tokyo.
Eifler, key subordinates, trained by British at Camp X in Canada.
French General Giraud escapes from German captivity.

May   Strategic victory for US Navy in Battle of Coral Sea.
Russian victory at Kharkov reversed; five Russian armies trapped.
Bruce arrives in London, lays groundwork for Donovan visit.
Stilwell and his troops evacuate Burma and retreat to India.
Rommel launches North Africa offensive, intends to capture Cairo.
OSS Detachment 101, led by Eifler, dispatched to Far East.
Czech resistance wounds Reinhard Heydrich, who dies on 4 June.

June   *Shepardson arrives London as new SI Chief (1 June).*
US Navy defeats Japanese in decisive Battle of Midway (4–6 June).
Solborg returns to Washington, replaced by Goodfellow.
Nazis destroy Soviet 'Red Orchestra' spy network in Germany.
OSS created on 13 June to replace COI; FIS part of COI joins OWI.
Donovan and Goodfellow arrive in London for OSS-SOE-SIS talks.
Churchill goes to Washington for talks with FDR.
King Peter of Yugoslavia meets FDR, Donovan in Washington.
Rommel captures Tobruk, drives on towards El Alamein.
Formal OSS-SOE accords to 'divide the world' for SO work.
Eisenhower appointed commander of US forces in Europe.
Gustav Guenther made interim Chief of SO London.
Germans launch Caucasus/Stalingrad offensive.

July   *Detachment 101 arrives in India; Eifler meets with Stilwell in China.*
British burn classified papers in Cairo; Rommel halted at El Alamein.
William Phillips made overall chief of OSS London.
Hitler makes Stalingrad a major objective of southern offensive.
SOE accelerates efforts to build French resistance networks.
William Maddox made Shepardson's deputy at SI London.
Tito launches major Partisan offensive against fascist Croatian Ustashi.
OSS London establishes link to Gaullist BCRA.

August   General Montgomery takes over British Eighth Army at El Alamein.
Ellery Huntington replaces Goodfellow as OSS's SO chief.
Germans approach Stalingrad, crush Canadian raid on Dieppe.
OSS's Bill Eddy made chief of joint OSS-SOE element in North Africa.
Churchill meets with Stalin in Moscow.

	OSS London establishes links to other governments-in-exile.
September	*Detachment 101 trains natives in India and Burma for SO work.*
	German Sixth Army fights its way into Stalingrad.
	Huntington extensively surveys SOE's facilities and methods.
	OSS-SIS-French tripartite intelligence arrangement agreed upon.
October	Allied forces for 'TORCH' invasion of North Africa assemble.
	Gaullist security lapses threaten Anglo-OSS-BCRA tripartite work.
	US Navy surprises Japanese at Guadalcanal.
	Tripartite intelligence activity suspended.
	Germans forced to halt Caucasus offensive.
November	Germans beaten at El Alamein; Hitler refuses to evacuate North Africa.
	TORCH invasion begins on the 8th; US co-opts Vichy Admiral Darlan.
	Germans occupy Vichy France; French scuttle fleet at Toulon.
	SOE, Greek resistance destroy key viaduct on main Athens rail line.
	German Sixth Army surrounded and trapped by Soviets in Stalingrad.
December	*Shepardson made SI Washington chief.*
	Darlan assassinated; Giraud named new high commissioner in North Africa.
	Britain's Bailey sets up mission to Mihailovic.
	Allied troops advance in Burma.
	OSS's Canfield arrives in London for joint French operations.

1943	**January**	*Donovan visits Algiers; Huntington, Hambro revise joint accord.*
		Japan evacuates Guadalcanal; Allies capture Tripoli.
		OSS's Van der Stricht arrives in London to run French desk for SO.
		FDR, Churchill, and Stalin meet at Casablanca; de Gaulle–Giraud talks.
		USSR offensives at Stalingrad, Leningrad; Axis offensive against Tito.
		SOE agrees to OSS participation in Norwegian operations.
		German Sixth Army surrenders at Stalingrad on the 31st.
	February	*British complain about Eifler's independent work in Burma, India.*
		Red Army recaptures Kursk, Kharkov.
		First 'Sea Horse' mission sent by British to survey French resistance.
		Mihailovic criticizes British for not providing sufficient supplies.
	March	*Maddox made SI London Chief.*
		Germans retake Kharkov; Stalin demands immediate second front.
		SOE-OSS Norway operation blocked; compromise gives OSS role.
		Two attempts by German coup plotters to assassinate Hitler fail.
		Allies break Axis line in Tunisia; Hitler–Mussolini meeting on North Africa.
	April	*Maddox offers 'Lloyd Plan' to Bruce, Donovan.*
		Warsaw ghetto uprising by Jews is ruthlessly crushed by Germans.
		US JCS issues 155/7/D, which restricts OSS operations.
		US fighter planes kill Japan's Admiral Yamamoto in secret ambush.
	May	*SIS, SOE agree to include OSS in Sussex, Jedburgh plans.*
		FDR and Churchill hold 'TRIDENT' talks in Washington on North Africa.
		Bruce formally requests airlift from US ETO commander.

Allies capture 250 000 Axis troops in final major battle in North Africa.
SIS agrees to renew tripartite activities with OSS, BCRA.
Allied offensive in Burma collapses, British retreat to initial positions.
SOE sends first mission to Tito; FDR wants OSS to be represented.
British and US sign new accord to share 'ULTRA' intelligence.

June   *Donovan visits London, rejects Lloyd Plan.*
French resistance committee gives Giraud command of French Army.
First OSS officer parachutes into France.
Tito barely evades capture by Axis.
SI London provides more reports to SIS than receives for first time.
French resistance leader Moulin captured, tortured, killed by Germans.
SIS decides that dual agent network in France now desirable.

July   Huge German offensive at Kursk smashed by Russian counter attack.
Allies invade Sicily; Mussolini overthrown, arrested; Badoglio leads Italy.

August   *OSS's Benson joins Tito, Mansfield joins Mihailovic.*
US and UK agree to share atomic secrets.

September *Second Sea Horse mission dispatched to France.*
Allies invade Italian mainland; Italians sign secret armistice, surrenders.
Tito seizes Italian arms; SOE's Bailey stops Cetnik weapon seizure.
German SS commandos rescue Mussolini; new puppet state in North Italy.
Maclean, Armstrong take over Allied missions to Tito, Mihailovic.
OSS's Farish joins Maclean, Seitz joins Armstrong.
Russians recapture Smolensk.
Donovan authorizes Adriatic resupply of Tito; Huot work begins.
OSS/SOE subordinated to COSSAC for French operations.
Hambro replaced by Gubbins as chief of SOE.

October   Allies capture Naples; Badoglio government declares war on Germany.
OSS London renews request for airlift from US ETO.
US JCS overturns 155/7/D; 155/11/D gives OSS wider powers.
Lord Wavell becomes viceroy in India.
'Cantinier-Xavier' mission deployed to the Maquis.
Allied Italian campaign bogs down; Italian partisans operate in North Italy.

November   *SOE Cairo undermines key report by OSS's Seitz on Cetniks.*
Russians recapture Kiev.
OSS 'loans' SOE $2.5 million for Yugoslav operations.
Maclean gives 'Blockbuster' report on Tito to Eden, Churchill.
De Gaulle ousts Giraud as co-chair of French Resistance Committee.
SOE exfiltrates 12 French agents, including François Mitterrand
Sussex school becomes operational.
FDR, Churchill, Chiang Kai-shek meet in Cairo ('Sextant' conference).
Donovan meets with SOE in Cairo; FDR-Donovan meeting in Cairo.

December   FDR, Churchill, Stalin meet in Tehran, effectively abandon Mihailovic.
British devise 'test' for Mihailovic as pretext to break off relations.
Eisenhower becomes Supreme Allied Commander in Europe.
Churchill writes to Tito, promises full aid and end of support for Cetniks.
Red Army launches major winter offensive; Germans retreating.

1944 January   *Churchill wants French supply doubled; gives SOE more planes.*
Allies launch offensive in Italy; Russian troops drive into Poland.
OSS/SOE in London combined for OVERLORD support operations.
UK General Wilson named Supreme Allied Commander Mediterranean.
SOE's Mockler-Ferryman, OSS's Haskell to jointly lead SFHQ.
Allies advance in Burma, Italy, land at Anzio; Russians relieve Leningrad.
Tripartite Sussex and Maquis committees set up in London.
Tripartite Sussex recruitment commission set up in Algiers.
SOE / OSS / BCRA 'UNION' mission deployed to Maquis.

February   Germans counterattack in Italy; Red Army drives into Estonia.
Sussex committee asks SHAEF to designate intelligence targets.
Finland asks for peace with USSR after heavy Soviet air raids.
First Pathfinders deployed to France.

March   Germans abandon offensive against Allies at Anzio; occupy Hungary.
SHAEF assumes full control of SFHQ.
Allies advance in Burma, divert to stop Japanese advance in India.
Red Army drives through Ukraine; Germans attack Maquis in Southern France.

April   *First Sussex teams deployed to France.*
Red Army enters Rumania, recaptures Crimea, advances in Poland.
Giraud formally ousted by de Gaulle as head of French Army.
Allies halt Japanese advance in India, renew offensive in Burma.
De Gaulle publicly gives all credit to British for resistance resupply.
Finland rejects Soviet peace demands; Russians retake Yalta.
Donovan supporter US Navy Secretary Knox dies of heart attack.
Allied troops assemble in southern Britain for D-Day invasion of France.

May   *Eisenhower gives OSS more aircraft for French operations.*
Tito sends delegation to London, seizes Axis weapons cache in Zagreb.
AFHQ creates SPOC in Algiers; SHAEF creates EMFFI in London.
Allies capture Cassino, drive on Rome.
SHAEF takes over all Allied operations in southern France.
SFHQ receives its formal mandate from SHAEF.
Jedburgh teams begin deploying to France.
OSS's Musulin forced by British to leave Mihailovic.

June   Allies capture Rome on the 4th, invade Northern France on the 6th.
Jedburghs, OGs continue deployments; Allies capture Cherbourg.
Red Army launches offensive in Byelorussia.

| | US Navy defeats Japanese in Battle of Philippine Sea. |
| **July** | *OSS creates air rescue unit for downed Allied pilots with Cetniks.* |

US Navy defeats Japanese in Battle of Philippine Sea.

July   *OSS creates air rescue unit for downed Allied pilots with Cetniks.*

Red Army captures Vilna, Minsk, nears Warsaw; British stall at Caen.

Hitler survives assassination attempt, crushes anti-Nazi conspiracy.

Tojo ousted as Japanese premier; US marines invade Guam.

Bretton Woods conference establishes IMF, global development bank.

August   *OSS's Musulin recontacts Cetniks; OSS's McDowell joins Cetniks.*

US breaks out from Normandy beachhead, Patton drives into Brittany.

Jedburghs, OSS OGs, and British SAS deployed to Southern France.

Allies invade Southern France, liberate Marseilles, Paris.

Romania declares war on Germany; Red Army enters Bucharest.

September Allies liberate Brussels; US troops enter Germany.

Red Army enters Yugoslavia, captures Tallinn; Russo-Finnish armistice.

FDR, Churchill meet in Quebec to discuss Pacific strategy.

Allied 'Market Garden' operation in Holland fails to achieve its objectives.

Dumbarton Oaks conference discusses UN, post-war security regime.

October   British troops recapture Crete, liberate Athens.

Churchill, Stalin meet in Moscow, secretly agree on division of Balkans.

MacArthur returns to the Philippines; FDR recalls Stilwell from China.

Red Army captures Riga, enters East Prussia, occupies Bulgaria.

Tito liberates Belgrade, signs accord of cooperation with King Peter.

US Navy defeats Japanese in Battle of Leyte Gulf.

November *McDowell mission to Mihailovic withdrawn at Churchill's request.*

FDR reelected for fourth time as US President.

British launch offensive in Burma; Allies enter Rhineland, stall in Italy.

December Stalin, de Gaulle meet in Moscow; Hungary declares war on Germany.

Germans launch surprise 'Battle of the Bulge' offensive in the Ardennes.

OSS backs Ho Chi Minh's 'People's Army' in Indochina.

Patton leads Allied counteroffensive in the Ardennes.

Churchill, Eden fly to Athens to try to avert Greek civil war.

SS General approaches OSS's Dulles to discuss German surrender.

1945 January   Germans lose Battle of the Bulge; Allies reopen Burma Road.

Red Army captures Warsaw, liberates Auschwitz concentration camp.

February FDR, Churchill, Stalin meet in Yalta, decide future of post-war Europe.

Red Army offensive in Germany stalls; Russians capture Budapest.

March   Eisenhower slows western offensive to allow Russians to capture Berlin.

April   FDR dies on 12 April; Truman becomes US President.

Allies launch major new offensive in Italy; Vienna captured by Red Army.

US and Russian troops meet at Elbe; Germans in Italy surrender to Allies.

		Mussolini killed; Hitler commits suicide; Red Army captures Berlin.
	May	Germany surrenders; Prague liberated; Churchill resigns.
	June	US captures Okinawa; UN charter signed in San Francisco.
	July	Truman, Churchill, Stalin meet at Potsdam; Germany dismembered.
		Churchill loses general election; Attlee new Prime Minister.
	August	US drops atomic bombs on Hiroshima, Nagasaki; Japan surrenders.
	September	*OSS disbanded.*
1946	**January**	*SOE disbanded.*

Bibliography

PRIMARY SOURCES

I. ARCHIVAL MATERIAL

United States of America

Central Intelligence Agency, Historical Intelligence Collection, Langley, Virginia

- Hans Tofte Reports
- William Henoeffer's CIA Address
- OSS Documents (miscellaneous)
- Studies in Intelligence Series (unclassified articles)

Hoover Institute Archive, Stanford University

- Norwood F. Allman Papers
- Oliver J. Cadwell Papers
- Russell Forgan Papers
- Gero von Schulze Gaevernitz Papers
- Preston Goodfellow Papers
- David Wooster King Papers
- Kostas Kouvaras Papers
- Franklin A. Lindsay Papers
- Joseph E. Persico Papers
- Leland L. Rounds Papers
- Richard Harris Smith Papers
- Paul van der Stricht Papers

Franklin D. Roosevelt Memorial Library and Archive, Hyde Park, New York

- Harry Hopkins Papers
- Henry J. Morgenthau, Jr. Papers
- Franklin D. Roosevelt Papers
    - Coordinator of Information, 1942 (PSF 128)
    - Diplomatic Correspondence Great Britain (PSF 38)
    - Office of Strategic Services (PSF 148, PSF/OSS, OF 4485)

- ***U.S. Army Military Historical Institute Archives, Carlisle, Pennsylvania***

- William J. Donovan Papers
- Vivian Dykes Diary

U.S. National Archives and Records Administration, College Park, Maryland

- Microfilm Series 1642 (W. J. Donovan's OSS Records)
- Record Group 94 (ANVIL / DRAGOON)
- Record Group 218 (Geographical Files)
- Record Group 226 (OSS Documents – Principal Holdings)
- Record Group 407 (Army, 1940–42)

Other

• Personal papers of an OSS veteran who wishes to remain anonymous

United Kingdom

Balliol College Archive, Oxford University

• Bickham Sweet-Escott Papers

Churchill College Archive, Cambridge University

• William J. Donovan Papers
• H. Montgomery Hyde Papers
• John Godfrey Papers/War Diaries

Imperial War Museum, Department of Sound Recordings, London

• Recorded Interviews with Sir Douglas Dodds-Parker
• Recorded Interviews with Sir Peter Wilkinson

Public Record Office, Kew, London

• Admiralty
    Naval Intelligence Papers, 1939–47 (ADM 223)
• Cabinet Office
    War Cabinet Minutes (CAB 65)
    Ministry of Defence Secretariat Files, 1938–47 (CAB 120)
    British Joint Staff Mission, Washington (CAB 122)
• Foreign Office
    General Correspondence, Political (FO 371)
• Prime Minister's Office
    Correspondence and Papers (PREM 1)
    Confidential Papers (PREM 4)
• Special Operations Executive
    Far East; Office of Strategic Services; Misc. (HS 1)
    Scandinavia; Office of Strategic Services; Misc. (HS 2)
    North Africa; Middle East; Balkans; Office of Strategic Services; Misc.
    (HS 3)
• War Office
    Directorate of Military Operations and Intelligence, 1837–1961 (WO 106)
    World War II Military Headquarters Papers, Military Missions, 1938–52
    (WO 202)
    Directorate of Military Intelligence, 1917–1956 (WO 208)

Special Forces Club Library, London

• Miscellaneous unpublished papers (see section IV below)

Federal Republic of Yugoslavia

Military Historical Institute Archive, Belgrade

• Cetnik Documents

II. INTERVIEWS

Office of Strategic Services (US)

- William Colby
- Carl Eifler
- Fisher Howe
- Henry Hyde
- Geoffrey Jones
- William Morgan
- Bronson Tweedy

Special Operations Executive / Secret Intelligence Service (UK)

- Vera Adkins
- Sir Douglas Dodds-Parker
- Peter Lee
- Gwen Lees
- Stephen Mann
- Sir Patrick Reilly

Yugoslav Resistance

- Dusan Marinkovic
- Mihailo Protic
- Dusan Topalovic
- Zvonomir Vuckovic

Other

- M.R.D. Foot

III. MAGAZINES AND NEWSPAPERS

- The Chronicle Herald
- The Economist
- McLean's Magazine
- The New York Times
- The Times
- The Times Literary Supplement

IV. DIARIES, MEMOIRS, UNPUBLISHED PAPERS, PRIMARY SOURCE ARTICLES

Alsop, Stewart, and Braden, Thomas. *Sub Rosa: The OSS and American Espionage*, (New York: Reynal & Hitchcock, 1946)

Astley, Joan Bright. *The Inner Circle: A View of War at the Top*, (London: Hutchinson, 1971)

Beevor, J. G. *SOE: Recollections and Reflections, 1940–45*, (London: Bodley Head, 1981)

Boulle, Pierre. *The Source of the River Kwai*, (London: Secker & Warburg, 1966)

Brook, Sir Robin. 'The London Operation: the British View,' in George C. Chalou (ed.), *The Secrets War: the Office of Strategic Services in World War II*, (Washington, DC: National Archives and Records Administration, 1992)

Brown, Arthur. 'The Jedburghs: a Short History,' (unpublished memoir, Special Forces Club Library, undated)

Buckmaster, Maurice. *Specially Employed*, (London: Batchworth, 1952)

The Campaign in Burma, Prepared for South-East Asia Command by the Central Office of Information, (London: HMSO, 1946)

Casey, William. *The Secret War Against Hitler*, (Washington, DC: Regnery Gateway, 1988)

Churchill, Winston S. *The Second World War*, 6 vols., (Boston: Houghton Mifflin Company, 1979)

Cline, Ray S. *Secrets, Spies, and Scholars: Blueprint of the Essential CIA*, (Washington, DC: Acropolis, 1976)

Coon, Carleton S. *A North African Story*, (Ipswich, Massachusetts: Gambit, 1980)

Crosby, Colonel M.G.M. 'Irregular Soldier,' (unpublished memoir, Special Forces Club Library, undated)

Danchev, Alex (ed.). *Establishing the Anglo-American Alliance: the Second World War Diaries of Brigadier Vivian Dykes*, (London: Brassey's, 1990)

Davidson, Basil. *Special Operations Europe: Scenes from the Anti-Nazi War*, (London: Victor Gollancz, 1981)

Deakin, F.W.D. *The Embattled Mountain*, (Oxford: Oxford University Press, 1971)

De Gaulle, Charles. *The War Memoirs of Charles de Gaulle, Unity 1942–44*, (New York: Simon & Schuster, 1959)

Dodds-Parker, Sir Douglas. *Setting Europe Ablaze*, (Surrey: Springwood Books, 1984)

Dulles, Allen W. 'William J. Donovan and the National Security,' *Studies in Intelligence*, (CIA: Historical Intelligence Collection, Summer 1959)

Eisenhower, Dwight D. *Crusade in Europe*, (London: Heineman, 1948)

Ellis, C.H. 'Mission Accomplished,' (unpublished memoir, CIA's Historical Intelligence Collection, 14 September 1972)

Hamilton-Hill, Donald. *SOE Assignment*, (London: William Kimber, 1973)

Hayden, Sterling. *Wanderer*, (New York: Alfred Knopf, 1963)

Hyde, H. Montgomery. *The Quiet Canadian: the Secret Service Story of Sir William Stephenson*, (London: Hamish Hamilton, Ltd., 1962)

Hymoff, Edward. *The OSS in World War II*, (New York: Richardson & Sterman, 1986)

Kimball, Walter (ed.). *Churchill and Roosevelt: The Complete Correspondence,* Vol. III, (Princeton, NJ: 1984)

Lankford, Nelson D. (ed.). *OSS Against the Reich: The World War II Diaries of Colonel David K.E. Bruce*, (Kent State University Press, 1991)

Lees, Michael. *The Rape of Serbia: the British Role in Tito's Grab for Power, 1943–44*, (New York: Harcourt, & Brace, 1990)

Lees, Michael. *Special Operations Executed*, (London: William Kimber, 1986)

Leutze, James (ed.). *The London Journal of General Raymond E. Lee, 1940–41*, (Boston: Little, Brown, 1971)

MacLean, Fitzroy. *Eastern Approaches*, (London: Jonathan Cape, 1949)

Macmillan, Harold. *The Blast of War, 1939–45*, (London: Macmillan, 1967)

Millar, George. *Maquis*, (London: Cedric Chivers, 1945)

Moon, Thomas, and Eifler, Carl. *The Deadliest Colonel*, (New York: Vantage Press, 1975)

Obolensky, Serge. *One Man in His Time*, (London: Hutchinson, 1960)

Philby, Kim. *My Silent War*, (London: Granada Publishing, 1969)

Sherwood, Robert E. (ed.), *The White House Papers of Harry L. Hopkins* 2 vols., (London: Eyre & Spottiswoode, 1949)

Slowikowski, Rygor. *In the Secret Service: The Lighting of the Torch*, (London: Windrush Press, 1988)

Sweet-Escott, Bickham. *Baker Street Irregular*, (London: Methuen, 1965)

Tito, Josip Broz. *Selected Military Works*, (Belgrade: Vojnoizdavacki Zavod, 1966)

Top Secret War Report of the OSS, 2 vols. Prepared by History Project, Strategic Services Unit, Office of the Assistant Secretary of War, War Department, Washington, DC, with introduction by Kermit Roosevelt, (New York: Walker, 1976). Declassified on 17 July 1975

Troy, Thomas F. (ed.). *Wartime Washington: the Secret OSS Journal of James Grafton Rogers, 1942–1943*, (Frederick, Maryland: University Publications of America, 1987)

Wilkinson, Sir Peter, and Astley, Joan Bright. *Gubbins and SOE*, (London: Leo Cooper, 1993)

Yardley, Herbert O. *The American Black Chamber*, (New York: Blue Ribbon Books, 1931)

SECONDARY SOURCES

BOOKS

Andrew, Christopher. *Secret Service: The Making of the British Intelligence Community*, (London: William Heinemann, 1985)

Asprey, Robert B. *War in the Shadows: the Guerrilla in History*,Vol. 1, (New York: Doubleday, 1975)

Beloff, Nora. *Tito's Flawed Legacy: Yugoslavia and the West, 1939 to 1984*, (London: Victor Gollancz, 1985)

Boyle, Andrew. *The Climate of Treason: Five Who Spied for Russia*, (London: 1979)

Cave Brown, Anthony. *'C': The Secret Life of Sir Stewart Menzies, Spymaster to Winston Churchill*, (New York: Macmillan, 1987)

Cookridge, E.H. *Set Europe Ablaze: the Story of Special Operations in Western Europe, 1940–45*, (London: Pan Books, 1966)

Cooper, Artemis. *Cairo in the War, 1939–1945*, (London: Penguin, 1989)

Cruickshank, Charles. *SOE in the Far East*, (Oxford University Press, 1986)

Cruickshank, Charles. *SOE in Scandinavia*, (Oxford University Press, 1983)

Eisenhower, David. *Eisenhower at War, 1943–45*, (New York: Random House, 1986)

Feis, Herbert. *Churchill, Roosevelt, Stalin: the War they Waged and the Peace they Sought*, (Princeton University Press, 1967)

Foot, M.R.D. *European Resistance to Nazism 1940–45*, (London: Eyre Methuen, 1976)

Foot, M.R.D. *SOE in France: an Account of the Work of the British Special Operations Executive in France, 1940–44*, (London: HMSO, 1966)

Foot, M.R.D. *SOE: The Special Operations Executive, 1940–46*, (London: BBC, 1984)

Ford, Corey. *Donovan of OSS*, (Boston: Little, Brown, 1970)

Ford, Kirk. *OSS and the Yugoslav Resistance, 1943–45*, (Texas A&M University Press, 1992)

Funk, Arthur. *Hidden Ally: the French Resistance, Special Operations, and the Landings in Southern France, 1944*, (New York: Greenwood Press, 1992)

Funk, Arthur. *The Politics of TORCH: the Allied Landings and the Algiers Putsch, 1942*, (University Press of Kansas, 1974)

Garlinski, Jozef. *Poland, SOE and the Allies*, (London: Allen & Unwin, 1969)

Garlinski, Jozef. *The Swiss Corridor*, (London: Dent, 1981)

Gilbert, Martin. *Second World War*, (London: Phoenix Giant, 1996)

Grose, Peter. *Gentleman Spy: The Life of Allen Dulles*, (London: André Deutsch, 1995)

Heimark, Bruce. *The OSS Norwegian Special Operations Group in World War II*, (London: Praeger, 1994)

Hinsley, F.H. et al. *British Intelligence in the Second World War*, 5 vols. Official History, (London: HMSO, 1979–90)

Hinsley, F.H., and Stripp, Alan, (eds). *Code Breakers: the Inside Story of Bletchley Park*, (Oxford University Press, 1993)

Hodgson, Godfrey. *The Colonel: the Life and Wars of Henry Stimson*, 1867–1950, (Boston: Northeastern University Press, 1990)

Howarth, Patrick. *Intelligence Chief Extraordinary: the Life of the Ninth Duke of Portland*, (London: Bodley Head, 1986)

Lysett, Andrew. *Ian Fleming*, (London: Weidenfeld & Nicolson, 1995)

Marshall, Bruce. *The White Rabbit: the Story of Wing Commander F.F.E. Yeo-Thomas*, (London: Evans Brothers, 1952)

Mason, David. *Who's Who in World War II*, (London: Little, Brown, 1978)

Mercer, Derrik (ed.), *Chronicle of the Second World War*, (London: Longman, 1990)

Paine, Lauran. *The Abwehr: German Military Intelligence in World War II*, (London: Robert Hale, 1984)

Parrish, Thomas. *The American Codebreakers: the U.S. Role in ULTRA*, (London: Scarborough House, 1991)

Persico, Joseph E. *Casey: From the OSS to the CIA*, (New York: Viking, 1990)

Porch, Douglas. *The French Secret Services: From the Dreyfus Affair to the Gulf War*, (London: Macmillan, 1996)

Read, Anthony, and Fisher, David. *Colonel Z: the Life and Times of a Master of Spies*, (London: Hodder & Stoughton, 1984)

Ruby, Marcel. *F Section SOE: the Story of the Buckmaster Network*, (London: Leo Cooper, 1988)

Shoenbrun, David. *Soldiers of the Night: the Story of the French Resistance*, (New York: E.P. Dutton, 1980)

Sinclair, Andrew. *The Red and the Blue: Cambridge, Treason, and Intelligence*, (Boston: Little, Brown, 1986)

Smith, Bradley F. *The Shadow Warriors: the OSS and the Origins of the CIA*, (London: André Deutsch, 1983)

Smith, Bradley F. *The Ultra-Magic Deals and the Most Secret Special Relationship, 1940–46*, (Shrewsbury, England: Airlife Publishing, 1993)

Smith, R. Harris. *OSS: The Secret History of America's First Central Intelligence Agency*, (University of California Press, 1972)

Stafford, David. *British and European Resistance, 1940–45: A Survey of the Special Operations Executive with Documents*, (London: Macmillan, 1980)

Stafford, David. *Camp X: OSS, 'Intrepid', and the Allies' North American Training Camp for Secret Agents, 1941–1945*, (New York: Dodd, Mead, 1986)

Troy, Thomas F. *Donovan and the CIA: a History of the Establishment of the Central Intelligence Agency*, (Frederick, Maryland: University Publications of America, 1981)

Troy, Thomas F. *Wild Bill and Intrepid: Donovan, Stephenson, and the Origin of CIA*, (Yale University Press, 1996)

Volkman, Ernest and Baggett, Blaine. *Secret Intelligence*, (New York: Doubleday, 1989)

West, Nigel. *MI6: British Secret Intelligence Service Operations, 1909–45*, (London: Westintel, 1983)

West, Nigel (ed.). *The Faber Book of Espionage*, (London: Faber & Faber, 1993)

West, Nigel. *Secret War: the Story of SOE, Britain's Wartime Sabotage Organization*, (London: Westintel, 1992)

Wheeler, Mark C. *Britain and the War for Yugoslavia, 1940–43*, (Boulder, Colorado, 1980)

Wilhelm, Maria de Blasio. *The Other Italy: the Italian Resistance in World War II*, (New York: Norton, 1988)

Winks, Robin. *Cloak and Gown: Scholars in America's Secret War*, (London: Collins Harvill, 1987)

Young, Peter (ed.), *The World Almanac Book of World War II*, (New York, Bison, 1981)

ARTICLES

Aldrich, Richard. 'Imperial Rivalry: British and American Intelligence in Asia, 1942–46,' *Intelligence and National Security*, (Vol. 3, No. 1, January 1988)

Anderson, Scott. 'With Friends Like These . . . The OSS and the British in Yugoslavia,' *Intelligence and National Security*, (Vol. 8, No. 2, April 1992)

Andrew, Christopher. 'Churchill and Intelligence,' *Intelligence and National Security*, (Vol. 3, No. 3, July 1988)

Biber, Dusan. 'Failure of a Mission: Robert McDowell in Yugoslavia, 1944,' in George C. Chalou (ed.), *The Secrets War: the Office of Strategic Services in World War II*, (Washington, DC: National Archives and Records Administration, 1992)

Calvi, Fabrizio. 'The OSS in France,' in George C. Chalou (ed.), *The Secrets War: the Office of Strategic Services in World War II*, (Washington, DC: National Archives and Records Administration, 1992)

Carter, Carolle J. 'Mission to Yenan: the OSS and the Dixie Mission,' in Chalou (ed.), *The Secrets War: the Office of Strategic Services in World War II*, (Washington, DC: National Archives and Records Administration, 1992)

Corvo, Alex. 'The OSS and the Italian Campaign,' in George C. Chalou (ed.), *The Secrets War: the Office of Strategic Services in World War II*, (Washington, DC: National Archives and Records Administration, 1992)

Courier, Leonard C. 'OSS Mission to the Burgundian Maquis,' *Studies in Intelligence*, (CIA: Historical Intelligence Collection, undated)

De Brandt, Dennis. 'Structuring Intelligence for War,' *Studies in Intelligence*, (CIA: Historical Intelligence Collection, undated)

Foot, M.R.D. 'OSS and SOE: an Equal Partnership?,' in George C. Chalou (ed.), *The Secrets War: the Office of Strategic Services in World War II*, (Washington, DC: National Archives and Records Administration, 1992)

Foot, M.R.D. 'Was SOE Any Good?', (pp. 239–54), in Walter Laqueur (ed.), *The Second World War: Essays in Military and Political History,* (London: Institute of Contemporary History, 1982)

Funk, Arthur. 'Churchill, Eisenhower, and the French Resistance,' *Military Affairs*, (February 1981)

Funk, Arthur. 'The OSS in Algiers,' in George C. Chalou (ed.), *The Secrets War: the Office of Strategic Services in World War II*, (Washington, DC: National Archives and Records Administration, 1992)

Georgia, Scudder. 'Agent Radio Operations in World War II,' *Studies in Intelligence*, (CIA: Historical Intelligence Collection, Winter 1959)

MacPherson, B. Nelson. 'Inspired Improvisation: William Casey and the Penetration of Germany,' *Intelligence and National Security*, (Vol. 9, No. 4, October 1995)

Martin, David. 'Churchill's Yugoslav Blunder: Precursor to the Yugoslav Tragedy,' *International Journal of Intelligence and Counterintelligence*, (Vol. 5, No. 4, Winter 1992–93)

McDonald, Lawrence H. 'The OSS and its Records,' in George C. Chalou (ed.), *The Secrets War: the Office of Strategic Services in World War II*, (Washington, DC: National Archives and Records Administration, 1992)

Pfeiffer, Jack. 'OSS Propaganda in Europe and the Far East,' *Studies in Intelligence*, (CIA: Historical Intelligence Collection, undated)

Reynolds, E. Bruce. 'Opening the Wedge: the OSS in Thailand,' in George C. Chalou (ed.), *The Secrets War: the Office of Strategic Services in World War II*, (Washington, DC: National Archives and Records Administration, 1992)

Smith, Bradley F. 'Admiral Godfrey's Mission to America, June/July 1941', *Intelligence and National Security*, Vol. 1, No. 3, September 1986, pp. 445–50. (Godfrey's original report produced in its entirety)

Stafford, David. 'SOE and British Involvement in the Belgrade Coup d'Etat of March 1941,' *Slavic Review*, (Vol. 36, No. 3, September 1977)

Walker, David A. 'OSS and Operation Torch,' *Journal of Contemporary History*, (Vol. 22, No. 4, October 1987)

Wheeler, Mark. 'The SOE Phenomenon,' in Walter Laqueur (ed.), *The Second World War: Essays in Military and Political History*, (London: Institute of Contemporary History, 1982)

Winks, Robin W. 'Getting the Right Stuff: FDR, Donovan, and the Quest for Professional Intelligence,' in George C. Chalou (ed.), *The Secrets War: the Office of Strategic Services in World War II*, (Washington, DC: National Archives and Records Administration, 1992)

Yu, Maochun. 'OSS in China – New Information About an Old Role,' *International Journal of Intelligence and Counterintelligence*, (Vol. 7, No. 1, Spring 1994)

THESES, DISSERTATIONS, AND MISCELLANEOUS

Irwin, Wyman W. 'A Special Force: Origin and Development of the Jedburgh Project in Support of Operation OVERLORD', (unpublished MA thesis, US Command and General Staff College, Combat Studies Institute, Fort Leavenworth, Kansas, 1991)

Jones, Matthew C. 'The Politics of Command: Britain, the United States and the War in the Mediterranean, 1942–44' (unpublished DPhil. thesis, Oxford University, St Antony's College, 1992)

King, Michael R. 'Jedburgh Operations: Support to the French Resistance in Central France from June through September 1944,' (unpublished MA thesis, US Command and General Staff College, Combat Studies Institute, Fort. Leavenworth, Kansas, 1991)

Lewis, S.J. 'Jedburgh Team Operations in Support of the 12th Army Group, August 1944,' (unpublished paper, US Command and General Staff College, Combat Studies Institute, Fort Leavenworth, Kansas, 1991)

Rifkind, Bernard D. 'The OSS and Franco-American Relations: 1942–1945,' (unpublished PhD thesis, George Washington University, 1983)

Thornhill, Paula. 'Catalyst For Coalition: the Anglo-American Supply Relationship, 1939–41,' (unpublished DPhil thesis, Merton College, Oxford, 1991)

Weiss, Steve. 'Anglo-American Negotiations, 1938–44: Strategy and the Road to ANVIL,' (unpublished PhD thesis, King's College, London, 1995)

Wise, Edward Tayloe. 'Vietnam in Turmoil: the Japanese Coup, the OSS, and the August Revolution,' (MA thesis, University of Richmond, May 1991)

Index

Abwehr, 156
Abyssinia, 81
ACRU, 142
Adkins, Vera, xx
Admiralty, 95
Adriatic, xiv, 124, 129–30, 133–4,
    139, 141, 190, 193
Aerodrome, 84
Afghanistan, 81
AFHQ, xiii–xiv, 69–71, 75, 141, 168
Africa, 75, 107
Afrika Korps, 10
Agent(s), 31, 33–4, 39, 41, 44, 57, 64,
    66, 68, 71–2, 75, 85, 87, 94, 98, 100,
    103–6, 108, 114, 123, 147–9, 153–7,
    170, 175, 177–9, 183, 188–9, 194–5
  chain(s), 56, 68
  contacts, 68
  networks, 22, 100, 102, 105
  personnel, 105
  radios, 67
  system, 105
Agents provocateurs, 159
Ain Taya, 75
Air
  bases, 83
  Chief Marshal, 14
  Commodore(s), 5
  Corps, 8
  cover, 190
  Crew Rescue Unit, 142
  delivery, 155
  dispatch unit, 179
  dropped, 165
  field(s), 69, 94, 97, 169, 177–8
  Force(s), xv, 17, 67, 114, 141,
    152, 156–7, 159, 162
  Intelligence, 61
  Marshals, 156
  Ministry, 9, 160, 178
  operations, 14, 153
  raid(s), 14, 44
  routes, 178
  Secretary of State for, 5
  sorties, 161, 166
  transport, xii, 79, 168, 190
  support, xiv
Airborne, 13, 101, 171
Aircraft, 8, 59, 60, 64, 69, 71, 96, 99,
    107,114, 117, 119, 152, 155,

156–7, 158, 160–2, 166–7,
    173, 178–9, 184, 190
Airlift, 98, 139, 166
Airmen, 141–3, 181
Airport, 13
Albania(ns), 16, 112
Albemarle (bombers), 160
Aldrich, Richard, xviii, 195
Aleutians, 81
Alexander, Crown Prince, xx–xxi
Alexander, General, 70
ALFRED, 155
Algeria, 75
Algiers, xiii–xv, xx, 46–7, 68–9, 72–9,
    81, 96, 107, 110, 133–4, 150,
    153, 162, 175–7, 181, 190–1
Alliance, 8, 23, 31, 93, 111, 149,
    151, 191, 194, 196
Allied, 32, 45, 49, 54, 65,
    67, 73, 98, 105, 111
  activities, 25
  advance, 160
  agencies, 104
  agent networks, 64, 105
  air attacks, 143
  Air Force(s), 142, 156, 178
  airmen, 142, 181
  armies, 40, 106, 147, 173
  arrangements, 109
  assistance, 111, 139–40
  base, xiv, 135
  camp, 15, 73, 109, 112, 116
  cause, 24, 73, 124
  clandestine activities, 183
  Command, 74, 90, 162, 169, 173–5
  Commander, 50, 133
  coup d'état, 17
  covert supply program, 116
  dealings, 133
  deception plan, 68
  decision-making, 119
  deliberations, 130
  differences, 88
  effort(s), 112, 119, 136
  espionage, 42, 48
  favor, 113, 142
  force(s), 51, 69–70, 75, 160, 192
  Forces Headquarters, xiii, 69,
    75, 122, 135, 141, 168
  governments, 123, 152

groups, 123
headquarters, 158
help, 132
High Command, 158–9
insurgent efforts, 113
intelligence gathering, 42; services, 36
intentions, 74
interlocutors, 15
invasion, 42, 45, 49, 51, 59, 69,
    74, 94, 100–1, 105, 150,
    153, 174, 183, 192
landing(s), 68–9, 72, 74, 165, 192;
    at Salerno, xiv
leadership, 146
materiel assistance, 132; support, 110,
    122
Mediterranean Command, 162
military action, 184; arrangements, 146;
    authorities, 98, 133; campaign, 144;
    command, 180, 192; forces,
    158–9; planners, 156; policy, 195;
    position, 195; power, 195
Military Command, 78
mines, 164
missions, 126, 191
move(ment), 77, 142
officer(s), 64, 158
opinions, xv
organization, 88–9
parachute supply operations, 150
personnel, 115, 131, 140
plan(s)(ners)(ning), 76, 133, 157, 162–3
policy, 115, 129, 131
political battleground, 195
position, 89
preparations, 122
prisoners of war, xiv
program, 112
propaganda, 113
push, 136
relationship, 127
resources, 84, 189
secret services, 38
services, 106, 174
shipping, xiii
ship(s), 69, 72
special forces, 159; operations, 82,
    117, 192
strategic diversions, 135
subversive policy, 115
support, xx, 135, 138
Task Force, 70
timetable, 136
troops, 146, 165, 174
undertaking, 134

unity, 142
victory, 1, 24, 147
war effort, 109
Allies, xiii–xiv, 2–3, 16–17, 49, 65, 72–3,
    78, 83, 91, 96, 112–13, 120–1, 126–7,
    133, 139, 143, 158, 163, 165, 182
Allman, Norwood, xix, 43
Ally, 130, 151
Alsop, Stewart, xvii
Ambassador, 37, 71, 136–7
Ambush, 84
American Rolling Mill Company, 39
Ammunition, 9, 60, 99, 111, 116,
    133, 135, 138, 154, 159, 164
Andrew, Christopher, xviii
Andrews, Frank, 97
Angers, 155
Anglophile, 2, 13, 33, 46
Ankara, 16
Anti-aircraft, 14–15, 178
Anti-American(ism), 47
Anti-Axis, xv, 95, 102
Anti-Fascists, xii
Anti-Japanese, xv
Anti-Nazi, 2, 68, 147
Anti-Partisan, 119
ANVIL/DRAGOON, xx, 143, 160,
    168, 173–4, 178, 181, 189, 191
Appeasement, xii
Arab(ic)(s), 67–8, 71, 86
Armament, 8, 153
Armco, 39
Armed forces, 32, 70
Armed services, 10, 14, 19, 43
Armed uprisings, 164
Armée Secrète, 149
Armistice, 66, 127, 147–9
Arms, 67, 99, 111, 116, 120–1, 127–8, 131,
    133–5, 150, 154, 156–7, 165–6, 168, 173
Armstrong, Charles, 126–9,
    131–2, 136, 139–40
Army, 25, 39, 47, 67, 73, 75, 83, 88,
    111, 128, 134, 149, 171, 174,
    176, 178, 180, 182
Army Air Force, 162
Army group(s), 107, 178–9, 181
Army in exile, 114
Army Intelligence, 8, 14, 40
Army signals, 70 ; schools, 171
AS, 149
Asia(s), 24, 45, 87, 195
Astley, Joan Bright, xvii
Astor, Vincent, 42
Athens, 13, 16, 18
Atherton, Terrence, 116

Atlantic, 51
Atomic bomb, xv
Attaché(s), 5–6, 11, 17, 19, 38, 43, 67
Attorney General, 27
Australia(n), 15, 51, 81
Austria, 140, 160
Axis, xii, 1, 15, 17–18, 24, 31, 44–5, 49,
    68, 74, 112–14, 120, 122–3, 125–6,
    128, 130, 132, 142, 165
Azores, 51

Back-channel, 46
Baghdad, 18
Bailey, William ('Bill'), 121–2, 125–7, 140–1
Baker Street, 38, 50–3, 57–9, 63, 70, 74–6,
    79, 82, 84–5, 88–9, 91, 95, 98, 113, 117,
    119–20, 122, 139, 148, 150, 152–6, 158,
    160–1, 163–4, 169–70, 178, 182–3, 187
Balkan(s), xiv, 1–2, 10, 13–18, 24, 51–3, 58–9,
    81–2, 109–11, 114, 116–23, 127–9, 134,
    136, 141, 144–7, 165, 182, 193–4
Baltic Europe, 81
Bari, xiii, xv, xx, 133–5, 139, 141–2, 190
Battle, 73, 87, 113, 143
Battle of Britain, 1, 5
Battle order, 179
Battleship, 32
BBC, 115, 120, 127, 130, 132, 136, 149, 179
BCRA, 62, 64–5, 148, 150, 153,
    162, 164, 169, 176
Beach(es), 69, 71
Beaumont-Nesbitt, Paddy, 5
Beaverbrook, Lord, 2, 5, 12–13
Bedell Smith, Walter, 114
Belgi(um)(an), 51, 61, 63, 80, 104, 149, 171–2
Belgrade, xiv, xix–xx, 13, 16–17, 113, 122
Beloff, Nora, 114
Benelux, 57
Benson, Melvin ('Benny'), 124–5, 127, 134
Benson, Rex, 47
Bergamo Division, 127
Berlin, 10, 16–17
Bermuda, 13
Berne, 155–156
Bismarck, 32
Black Chamber, 20
Black operations, 167
Black propaganda, 32, 38, 40
Bletchley Park, xx
Blitzkrieg, 147
Blockbuster, 131–2, 135, 138
Boat(s), 59, 71, 83, 135
Bolshevik Revolution, 39
Bomb(ers)(ing), 60, 99, 114, 157–8

Bomber base, 44
Bomber Group, 179
Bomber operations, 156
Boris, King (of Bulgaria), 16–17
Bosnia, 112, 120, 123
Brabonica, 138
Bracken, Brendan, 9, 78
Braden, Thomas, xvii
BRANDON, 75
BRAL, 150
Bridge(s), 69, 84, 138, 173, 181
Bridgehead, 101
Brindisi, xiv
Brissex, 177–9, 183
British American Group, 46
British Purchasing Commission, 46
British Security Coordination, xix, 3, 22
Brittany, 174
Broadway, 6, 50, 53, 61–4, 66–7, 71–2,
    78, 87, 91–2, 101–5, 148, 156,
    174–7, 183, 187–8, 195–6
Brook, Robin, 82, 161, 165
Brooke, Alan, 150
Brown, Arthur, 171, 174
Bruce, David, xiii, 28, 31, 36–7, 41–2,
    46, 50, 54, 94–100, 102–5, 107,
    109, 155–6, 161, 169
BSC, xix, 3–5, 8, 10–11, 13–14, 17, 19, 22–3,
    30–4, 36–40, 43, 50, 89, 185–8
Buckmaster, Maurice, 165, 168–9
Bulgar(ia)(ian)(s), 16, 112, 138, 143
Bureau Central de Renseignements et
    d'Action, 62
Bureau de Renseignements et d'Action
    Londres, 150
Bureau d'Operations Aëriennes, 150
Bureaucratic, 19, 188
    breakthrough, 27
    difficulty, 94
    enemies, 26, 30
    entities, 48
    infighting, xviii
    interests, 187
    minefield, 28, 30
    obstacles, 22
    rivals, 28
    soil, 45
    struggle, 42
    survival, 28
    truce, 64
    warfare, 26
Bureaucra(cy)(ts)(tically), xiii, 48, 68, 186–7
Burma, xv, xx, 44, 48–9, 51, 81, 83–6, 88–93,
    109–11, 144, 182, 194–5, 197

Burma Road, 49, 83, 124
Burmese, 84
Buxton, Edward, 31

C, 5, 28
CD, 100
Cadre(s), 40, 47, 96, 147–8, 194
Cadwell, Oliver J., xix
Caen, 170
Cairo, xiv, xx, 14–16, 18, 34, 59–60,
    67, 82, 99, 110, 113–18, 120–1,
    123–7, 129–34, 136–45, 191
Calcutta, 84
Calvi, Fabrizio, xviii
Cambridge, 46
Camp 'X', 40, 47, 83
Campaign(s), 67, 69–70, 97, 110–11,
    113, 122, 144, 157, 160,
    174, 179, 193
Canada, 22, 31, 40, 47, 83, 123
Canadian, xv, 3, 128
Canaries, 51
Canfield, Franklin, 154–5,
    158, 182, 190
Cantinier-Xavier, 158–9
Cape Verdes, 51
Caribbean, 14
Casablanca, 40, 68, 70, 72, 176
Casablanca Conference, 122
Case Officer, 20
Caserta, 142
Catholic, 11, 149
Cavendish-Bentinck, Victor, 50
Cavendish-Bentinck, William, 38
Cawthorn, W.J., 86, 88
CBI, 86, 88
Censorship, 13, 18, 86–7, 129
Central Intelligence Agency, xiii,
    xviii, 23, 30–1, 197
Chetnik(s), xiv, xx, 111–16, 119–23, 125,
    127–33, 136–45, 163, 165, 193
Ceux de la Libération, 149
Ceux de la Résistance, 149
CFLN, 150, 162
Chamber of Commerce, 41
Chartres, 149, 180
Chiang Kai-shek, 43–4, 83, 89
Chicago Daily News, 7
China, xii, 23, 43–4, 49, 51, 53, 81,
    83–4, 86, 88–90, 182, 194–5
China-Burma-India Theater, 86, 88
Chinese, 83
    authorities, 89
    government, 44, 89

nationalist(s), 49
    Scheme, 43–4
Chunking, 83, 89
Churchill, Winston Spencer, xiv–xv, 2, 5,
    9–10, 12–16, 28, 32, 34–5, 38, 46, 49, 73,
    86, 92, 122, 127, 131–2, 135–40, 142,
    144, 147, 151, 160–1, 184, 195, 197
Churchill College, xviii
CIA, xviii, xix–xxi, 1, 4, 7, 23, 28
Cinquième Bureau, 168
Cipher(s)(ing), 123, 125
    machines, 34
Civil
    uprisings, 68
    war, 113
Clamorgan Affair, 64
Clandestine(ly), xi, xiv–xv, xvii, xxi, 2, 6,
    14, 25, 39–41, 46, 67–8, 72, 83, 101,
    111, 143, 148–9, 158, 160, 183–4,
    186, 188, 191–3, 197
Clark, Mark, 68–9
Clarke, Brien, 68, 70, 192
Cline, Ray S., 23
Club de Pins, 77
CNR, 150
Coastal artillery, 69
Coastal defenses, 6
Code(s), 65, 125, 164, 177, 179, 183
Code name(d), 64, 72, 98, 101, 150,
    153, 155, 159, 178
Cohabitation, OSS-SOE, 57
COI, xii–xiii, 2, 7, 22–50, 54, 83,
    185–8, 196–7
Colby, William ('Bill'), xx, 172
Cold War, xix, xxii
Collaborat(ed)(ors)(ion)(ist)(ive), 4, 7–8,
    10, 13–15, 17–18, 20, 22–5, 29, 43, 45,
    51–2, 57–8, 64–6, 68, 72–3, 77, 81,
    89–91, 93, 95–6, 98, 110, 113, 115–16,
    120(, 122–3, 125, 129–30, 137, 141,
    144–7, 157, 159, 161, 171, 177, 180,
    182–3, 185–6, 189, 191–2, 196
Colonial(ism), 45, 49, 83,
    89–90, 151, 182, 195
Colony, 13, 67
Combined Operations Staff Supreme Allied
    Commander, 100, 157, 161–2, 170
Comité d'Action, 158
Comité Français de la Libération Nationale,
    150, 162, 176
Command, 69, 72, 74, 78, 80, 85, 87–8, 90, 93,
    98–100, 103, 106, 109, 114, 124, 133–5,
    140, 144, 158–9, 162, 167–9, 171, 173,
    178, 180, 184, 189–90, 192–195

Commandant, 47
Commando(s), 14, 30, 32, 39, 44, 66,
    69, 128, 137, 143, 180
Committee(s), 104
    of National Liberation, 73
    on Equipment for Patriot Forces, 95
Commonwealth, xi–xii, xvi, 189
Communicati(ons)(ng), 37, 40, 50, 54, 56,
    58–9, 63, 65, 69–70, 77, 79, 84, 87, 102,
    106–9, 112, 114, 123–5, 129–31, 143,
    148, 158–9, 163–4, 168, 171–3, 177,
    180–1, 187–9, 191–2, 195
Communis(m)(t)(ts), xii–xv, 68, 111–12,
    122, 128, 132, 141, 149
Congress, 4, 7
Conseil National de la Résistance, 150
Consulate(s), 41, 67
Convoy(s), 10, 84
Coon, Carlton, 71–2
Cooper, Duff, 11
Coordinator, 29, 40, 42
    of Information, 2, 19, 22, 24, 48, 53
    of Intelligence, xii, 7, 28
Corsica(n), xiii, xv, 157
Corvo, Max, xviii
COSSAC, 100, 107, 157, 161, 170
Couchet, General, 168
Counter-espionage, 3, 30, 48, 108, 186
Counter-intelligence, xx, 50,
    107–8, 168, 189
Counter-propaganda, 6
Counter-subversi(on)(ve), 107, 157, 159, 165
Coup d'état, Yugoslavia, 17–18
Cover, 102, 105, 177
Covert, 1, 7, 14, 20, 47, 71, 109,
    116, 182, 186, 195
Cowell, Gervase, xxi
Cowgill, Felix, 50
Croat(ian)(ia), 111–12, 119, 123
Crockett, General, 97–8, 106
Cross-Channel, 91–2, 94, 97,
    100, 109, 136, 153
Cryptograph(y)(ic), 20, 84
Cunningham, Admiral Andrew, 11, 15
Cyprus, 14
Czech(oslovakia), 51–2, 61, 63

d'Astier de la Vigerie, Emmanuel, 149, 160
D-Day, 146, 152, 155, 158–60, 164, 166,
    168, 171, 173, 179–80, 182, 184
D-Organization, 13
D-Section, xii, 13, 147
Dakar, 66, 72, 151
Dalmatia(n), 134–5, 142–3

Dalton, Hugh, 9
Dansey, Claude, 28, 36, 42, 47, 50,
    54, 61, 92, 156, 183, 186, 195
Darlan, Jean, 66, 72–3, 76–8,
    92, 101, 146, 152
Davidson, Basil, 115, 123
Deakin, William ('Bill'), xvii,
    114, 123–7, 132–3
Decoded, 178
Deciphering, 130
Decryptions, 122
de Gaulle, Charles, 40, 56, 62, 64–6,
    73, 78, 146–54, 160–3, 165–6,
    169–70, 176, 182, 184, 189
Debrett's, 46
Defection(s), 69
Defense(s), 69
    Advisory Commission, 8
    Committee, 161
    Savings Program, 26
Delhi, 83–6, 88–9
Demarche, 62
Democracies, xii
Democracy, xv
Demolition(s), 56, 84, 138,
    159, 164, 171, 181
Denmark, 98
Destroyers, 4, 8–9, 11, 14
Detachment '101', xx, 44, 83–5, 90, 194
Deuxième Bureau, 149, 168
Devers, Jacob, 97–9, 106–7
Dewavrin, André, 62, 73, 78,
    148, 153, 162, 169
DF-Section, 149, 155
Dictator(ial), 16, 71, 129
Dill, Field-Marshal John, 14–15
Diploma(t)(tic)(cy), 1, 6, 11, 15, 18, 20, 23,
    30–1, 34, 41, 49, 62, 67, 86, 121, 186
Disarmament, xii
Djebel Hallouf, 75
Djuric, General, 138, 141
Dock(s), 69
Dodds-Parker, Sir Douglas, xi, xvii, xix–xxi,
    47, 78–9, 81, 134, 190–1
Doering, Otto, 26
Donovan, William ('Bill' or 'Wild Bill'),
    xii–xiii, xv–xvi, xviii, xix, 1–61, 64–7, 70,
    74–9, 81–4, 86, 88–90, 94, 97–8, 102–4,
    106–11, 113–14, 116–21, 123–4, 128,
    130–6, 139–40, 142–5, 150, 153–4, 161,
    163, 166, 171, 176, 182–97
Dorman-Smith, Sir Reginald, 84
Double agent, 156
Drina, 138

Drop zone(s), 71, 142
Dulles, Alan, 1, 31, 37, 156
Dunderdale, Wilfred, 47
Dunkirk, 8–9
Dutch, 61, 63, 104, 172
Dutch East Indies, 44, 195
Dykes, Vivian, 12–13

East Africa, 51
East Asia(n), xv, 43–4, 83
Eastern Front, 39
Eastern Russia, 44
Eccles, David, 25
Eddy, (Colonel William 'Bill'), xiii,
    67–8, 70, 72, 75–7, 79, 153, 192
Eden, Anthony, 9, 15–16, 132, 136, 139,
    195
Egypt, 11, 15, 81, 99, 124
Eifler, Carl, xx, 44, 83–90, 110, 194
Eisenhower, Dwight David, xiii, 55, 57–8,
    67–70, 72–6, 78–9, 81, 100, 108–9,
    140, 146, 154, 161, 166, 168, 180, 190
Ellis, Dick, 4–5, 7–8, 17, 30–1,
    33, 38–40, 47, 50, 186–7
Ellis, Toby, 67, 71–2
EMFFI, xv, 167–70
Empire(s), xi, xvi, 45, 91, 145, 151, 197
Engineering Corps, 128
English Channel, xviii, 147
Engraving, 94
ENIGMA, 122
Equip(ment)(ping)(ped), 51–2, 56,
    60, 67–8, 70, 75, 94–7, 99,
    101–2, 117–20, 135, 148, 154–5, 160,
    164, 166, 171, 173, 177, 193–4
Eritrea, 81
Escape routes, 149
Espionage, xx, 2, 26, 30, 39,
    42, 89, 102, 106–8
Etat-Major Forces Françaises de l'Interieur,
    167–8
Ethiopia, xi–xii
ETO, 51
Europe, 4–5, 13, 20, 22, 24–5, 32, 39, 42, 44,
    49, 51, 54–6, 58–9, 74–5, 77, 81, 83, 87,
    91–3, 97–8, 100, 102, 104, 106, 111–12,
    128, 136, 146, 152, 155, 170, 190, 192
European(s), 1, 7–8, 31, 113, 154
    Command, 99
    continent, 111
    fighting movements, 56
    flank, 59
    Invasion Sphere, 196
    nationals, 56

Theater, 101, 106; Commander, 97,
    100, 106, 147
Theater of Operations, 51, 154
    war, 53, 65, 110–11
Execut(ed)(ion)(ing), 155, 161, 180
Executive Committee, 118
Executive Order, 27
Exfiltrat(e)(ed)(ion), 130, 141, 149, 154–5
Exile groups, 61, 64–5
Expatriate(s), 43
Explos(ive)(ives)(ion), 60, 72,
    121, 124, 148, 173

F-Section, 154, 158, 163–5, 168, 189
Factory(ies), 152, 159, 164
Fake(d) papers, 56
FALAISE, 72
Far East(ern), xx, 13, 42–3, 49,
    52–3, 58, 81, 83, 86–7, 89–90,
    109, 188, 191, 194–6
Farish, Lyn ('Slim'), 126, 128, 132–4, 141–2
Farouk, King, 15
Fascists, xii, 112
FBI, 10, 14, 19, 23, 25–6, 28, 30, 186–7
FDR, xix
Fedala, 69
Federal Bureau of Investigation, 10, 23
FFI, 165
Field Detachments, 178, 184
Field Headquarters '501', 122
Fifth Column, 3–4, 7
Finland, 51, 59
First World War, 4–5, 39, 42,
    46–7, 67, 111–12, 142
Fleet, 60, 133–5
Fleming, Ian, 27, 29–30, 50, 186–7
Floege, E.F., 155
Flying boat(s), 14, 80
Foot, Michael, xviii, xx
Force '133', 134–5
Forces Françaises de l'Intèrieur, 165
    Unies de la Jeunesse, 149
Ford, Corey, 4, 6, 17
Ford, Kirk, 114
Foreign
    agencies, 37
    governments, 123
    groups, 123
    information activities, 48
    intelligence, 31; sources, 61
    language, 96
    Minister, 15
    nationality groups, 48
    occupiers, 112

Foreign – *continued*
  Office, 11–12, 35, 61, 85, 110, 115–16,
        120–1, 127, 131, 136–40, 142, 145, 151
  policy, 140
  Secretary, 9, 11, 132
Forgan, J. Russell, xix
Formosa, 43–4
Forrestal, James, 9
Fortress (bomber), 166
Franc, 56
France, xi, xiii, xv, xviii, xx, 2, 8, 33, 42,
        46, 51–3, 56–8, 65–6, 73–4, 76–7, 80,
        82, 91–2, 94, 96–101, 105–9, 111,
        136, 143, 146–58, 160–5, 167–9,
        171–5, 177–84, 189, 192, 194, 196–7
Franc Tireurs et Partisans, 149
Franco, Francisco, 71
Free French (France), 61, 64, 148, 152, 155
Frenay, Henri, 149
French(man), xx, 6, 34, 38, 40, 45, 49,
        61–73, 76–8, 83, 86, 89, 91, 103–6, 110,
        129, 146–7, 149–58, 161, 163–73, 175–7,
        179–80, 182–3, 188–9, 192, 194–5
Front National, 149
FTP, 149
Fuel, 68, 84
FUJ, 149
Funk, Arthur, xviii, 169
Fuses, 60

'G-2', 8, 38, 41, 97, 106, 154, 178–80
Gambier-Perry, Richard, 50
Gaullist(s), 64–6, 72–3, 77–8, 91–2, 101,
        103, 108, 146–54, 158, 160, 162–5,
        167–70, 175–7, 182–4, 187
Genocide, 112
George, King (of Greece), 16
George VI, King, 5
German(s), xiv, 3–4, 10, 16, 18, 32, 39–40,
        49, 64, 66, 69, 71, 77, 80, 91, 102, 105,
        111–12, 114–15, 120–3, 127, 132,
        135–7, 139, 141–3, 146–7, 152, 156–7,
        159, 164–5, 170, 173–4, 180, 189
Germany, xii, 10, 15, 23–4, 51–3, 57, 72, 81,
        107, 123, 136, 140, 149, 160, 180, 194
Gestapo, 157
Gibraltar, 14, 34, 51, 56, 67–8,
        70, 72, 75, 79, 191–2
Giraud, Henri, 40, 65–6, 72–3, 78, 146,
        149–52, 162–3, 176, 182, 189
Giraudist(s), 40, 153
Glenconner, Lord, 82, 123, 134
Godfrey, (John), xix, 3, 6–8, 11,
        13, 18, 24–30, 41, 50, 186

Goodfellow, M. Preston, xix, 38–40,
        50, 55–6, 58, 67, 83, 90, 116–18
Government(s)-in-exile ('exiled
        governments'), 32, 34, 36, 49,
        54, 61, 63–4, 77–8, 90–1, 104,
        111–12, 119, 121, 123, 136,
        147, 150, 187, 189, 193, 196
Governor General (Burma), 84
Grabonica, 138
Grand Alliance, 23
Grand Mufti of Jerusalem, 15
Grand plan, 102
Grand strategy, 20, 91–2, 111, 197
Great Britain, 2
Greece, xv, 16, 18, 23, 96, 112, 128
Greek(s), 16, 46, 63, 110, 112
  Army, 16
  contacts, 59
  sources, 61
Grell, William, 165
Grendon Hall, 178
GRENOUILLE, 164
GRIS, 164
Gubbins, Colin, xv, xx, 5, 50, 58–9, 78–9,
        81–2, 94, 97, 100, 131, 134, 140, 169
Guenther, J. Gustav, 54, 57–8
Guerrilla(s), 43, 44, 112, 174
  action, 66, 160
  activities, 39, 66, 173, 180
  bands, 158
  campaign, 111
  groups, 44
  nuclei, 57, 80
  tactics, 171
  threat, 160
  units, 39
  warfare, 43, 48, 80, 152, 157, 164, 180–1
Guest, Ray, 46
Gurdelica, 138

Halifax (bomber), 148, 166
Halifax, Lord, 9, 11–12
Hambro, Charles, 50, 51, 55–6, 58–9, 67, 74–5,
        77, 79, 81–2, 84–5, 89, 92, 94–6, 98–100,
        117–19, 150, 155–6, 186, 189, 192–3
Harriman, Averell, 47, 50
Harris, Arthur ('Bomber'), 156, 158
Haskell, Joseph, 161–162, 169, 179, 184
Hayden, Sterling, 135
Headquarter(s)(ed), 14, 30, 37, 41, 46, 50,
        56–7, 60, 63, 74–5, 77, 81, 83–4, 93,
        122–3, 125, 129, 131–2, 135, 139–42,
        146, 152, 155, 158, 161, 164–9, 171,
        173, 177–8, 181–2, 184, 191, 194

Henhoefer, William, 28
Heppner, Richard ('Dick'), 37, 54, 76–7
Hewitt, Colonel, xv
Hinsley, Harry, xviii, 17, 114
Hitler, (Adolf), 2, 6, 10, 16–17
Hoare, Sir Samuel, 71–72
Ho Chi Minh, xv, 195
Hokkaido, 44
Holdsworth, Gerry, xiv
Holland, 51, 80, 149, 156, 171
Home Security, 18
Hong Kong, 89
Hoover, J. Edgar, 10, 14
Hopkins, Harry, 8, 18
Howe, Fisher, xx, 33–4, 37, 46
Hudson, William ('Bill'), 111, 114–16,
    120–2, 129–30, 135, 138
Hull, Cordell, 4–5, 11
Human contribution, 99
Human facilities, 101
Human Intelligence, 68, 109, 186, 188
Human resources, 99, 101
HUMINT, 68
Hungar(y)(ians), xii, 81, 112
Huntington, Ellery, 54–5, 58–60, 79–82, 90–2,
    94, 96–7, 99–100, 118, 121, 123
Huot, Louis, xiv, 133–4, 143, 145, 190
Hyde, H. Montgomery, xvii, xix, 4–5, 11, 17
Hyde, Henry, xx, 46

Iberia, 40, 46, 53, 57, 67, 80, 91, 107
Iceland, 80–1
Imperial(ism)(ist), 44–5, 71,
    86, 90, 150–1, 182, 195
Independence, xiii, 49, 53, 56, 67, 76, 80,
    82, 86, 89–91, 96, 103, 107–10, 119,
    124–5, 131, 134, 143, 151, 153, 161,
    163, 182–3, 185, 190, 192–7
India(ns), xv, xx, 51–2, 81, 83–90,
    110, 124, 144, 182, 194–5, 197
India Office, 87–8
Indochina, xv, 44, 51, 81, 89–90, 195
Indochinese, 89
Infiltrat(ing)(ion)(ed), 31, 52, 77,
    114, 123, 131, 140, 153
Inform(er)(ants)(s), 67–8
Insertion, 134
Instructor(s), 58, 106, 158, 171–2,
    177, 181
Insurgent(s), 111–13
Intelligence, xi–xiii, xv, xvii–xix, 2–3, 8,
    10, 13–15, 18–20, 22–6, 28–32, 36–9,
    41, 43, 45–6, 54, 61–4, 66, 69–70, 78,
    85–8, 91, 101–2, 104–5, 107–9, 113–15,
    123, 129, 131, 139–40, 142, 144,
    147, 152–4, 165, 167–8, 174–6,
    178–81, 183, 186–7, 189–90
activities, xvii, 17, 19, 25, 41–2,
    101, 103, 107, 131
agenc(y)(ies), 19, 102, 108, 153
agenda, 30
alliance, 20
agents, 108
apparatus, 148
arm, 153
authority, 131
branch, 43
capabilities, 24
capability, 24
centralization, 25
chief, 42, 148
clearinghouse, 9
collection, xxi, 15–16, 18–19, 22,
    28, 40–1, 45, 103, 109, 140,
    148, 174, 178, 188, 196
collector(s), 1, 20, 173–4, 186
community, 1, 5, 19, 25
components, 49, 54, 196
consumer, 174
contingent, 143
contribution, 42
cooperation, 1, 6, 20
coordination, 3, 7
credentials, 19
departments, 29
digests, 103
entity, 3, 19–20, 22, 24, 45
establishment, 19
exchanges, 20
experience, 41
experiment, 49
folklore, 10
function(s), 41, 48, 102
functionaries, 6
gathering, 41–2, 101, 148
groups, 101
historian, xvii
history, xvii
house, 20
infiltration operations, 39
information, 105
investment, 33
liaison, 78, 100
links, 90
material, 73, 108, 185
matters, 23, 62, 64, 67
messages, 179
mission, 140

Intelligence – *continued*
  network(s), 53, 105, 156
  officer(s), 29, 42, 113, 131, 141, 143
  operations, 75, 104, 146, 174, 179, 195
  organization(s), xvii, 6, 8, 19, 27,
        29, 31, 47, 88, 90, 103
  penetration, 66
  picture, 88, 110, 116
  problem, 19, 27
  protocols, 49–50
  purposes, 152
  relations(hip), 34, 47, 64, 153
  reports, 68, 101, 179
  representation, 67
  requirements, 21
  research, xvii, 22
  role, 6
  security, 25
  service(s), 4, 18, 22, 25, 29, 36, 41, 61–2,
        70, 73, 87, 91, 104, 108, 175
  sharing, 194
  shortfall, 116
  situation, 115–16
  sources, 61
  Staff, 29
  standpoint, 66
  story, 47
  summary, 35
  surveys, 36
  system, 23
  targets, 175
  teams, 101, 180
  training, 171; facilities, 22
  work(ers), 19, 83, 100, 131
  writing, xviii
Inter-Allied
  Maquis Missions, 155, 182–3
  Missions, 157–9, 165, 168, 173, 189
  organization, 88–9
Intercept(s)(ed), 64
Interceptor planes, 6
Invade(d), 122, 160, 165
Invad(ing)
  armies, 154–5
  forces, 68, 80, 98, 124
Invasion, 64–8, 70, 72–4, 80, 91–4, 97,
        99, 101–2, 104–6, 109, 122, 136,
        143, 146, 149–150, 153, 156–9, 162,
        164, 168, 174, 182–4, 193, 196
  force(s), 65, 69–70, 100, 153
  plan(s), 105, 157, 164
  Sphere, 51–2, 57, 80, 90–1, 103, 190, 196
  units, 96
  zones, 69

Iraq(i), 15, 81
Iraqi Regent, 15
Iran, 81
Ireland, xii, 95
Irish, 11, 47
Ismay, Hastings, 35–6, 50, 95, 187
Isolationist(s), 26, 28
Italian(s), xiii, 14, 69, 77, 112, 115–16, 120–2,
        127–9, 131, 133, 135, 144, 160, 180, 193
  armistice, xiii–xiv
  navy, 10
Italy, xiii–xiv, 37, 51–3, 57–9, 76–7, 80–1,
        92, 107, 122–3, 127, 133–5, 139, 142,
        156, 160, 190, 192–4

Jackson, Robert, 27
Japan(ese), 39, 42–5, 49, 83–4,
        88, 124, 136, 195
JAUNE, 164
Java, 124
JCS, 48, 88, 102
JCS directive, 103; 155/7/D, 102–103,
        108; 155/11/D, 108–109
Jedburgh(s), xv, xx, 93–4, 97–9, 103, 105,
        159, 165, 168, 170–6, 180–4, 189–90
Jerusalem, 15, 144
Jevdjevic, General, 141
Joint
  activities, 96, 99, 113, 171, 183, 190
  affair, 193
  Allied undertaking, 134
  Anglo-US mission(s), 126, 128
  assessment, 171
  British-American headquarters, 146
  clandestine operations, 184
  command apparatus, 182
  effort(s), 109, 113
  endeavors, 188
  enterprise, 186
  entity, 154
  field operations, 100, 180
  headquarters, 161
  Intelligence Committee, 29, 35, 38, 50
  intelligence center, 88; effort, 102;
        gathering, 94, 101; operation, 101
  Jedburgh Section, 168
  military headquarters, 184
  missions, 143
  operation(s), 63, 91–2, 94,
        99, 101, 143, 155, 168
  operational agreements, 94
  parachute and equipment packing
        station, 177
  participation, 103

planning, 106, 184
Psychological Warfare Committee, 53
recruiting team, 171
regional command structure, 192
responsibility, 162
school, 106
secret activities, 146
SIS/OSS, 176
SIS-OSS-French teams, 105
SOE/OSS, 157, 171, 175, 178
special operations, 97; teams, 94
Staff(s), 88, 114, 154
stake, 109
status, 91
structure, 172, 192–3
subversive activities, 150
supervision, 104
Sussex Selection Board, 176–7
training, 90, 194
venture, 96
Jones, Geoffrey, xix–xxi
Jordan, 81
Jungle, 84, 195
Junglecraft, 84
Justice Department, 32

Keble, C.M., 82, 130, 144
Keswick, David, 158
Karachi, 83
Kennedy, Joseph P., 3, 5, 10, 25
Kharkov, 49
King, David Wooster, xix, 176
Knight, Ridgeway, 69
Knox, Frank, 3–7, 11, 14, 18–20, 27, 41
Koenig, Pierre, xv, 167–70
Korea, 43–44, 81
Kouvaras, Kostas, xix
Kun, Bela, xii

Langley, xxi
Larson, Mr., 43
Latin America, 14, 31, 41
Law, Prime Minister Bonar Law
Law, Dick, xv
Lebanon, 81
Lee, Peter, xx
Lee, Raymond, 5
Lees, Gwen, xx
Lees, Michael, xvii, 114, 132
Lehr Panzer Division, 179
Lemnitzer, Lyman, 69
Lend-Lease, xiii, 8, 16, 19, 23,
    26, 29, 47, 50, 188
Lescovac, 138

Liais(e)(on), 32–3, 35, 37–8, 47, 50–1, 53–5,
    57–8, 61–3, 77–8, 80, 83–6, 89–90,
    100–1, 104, 110, 127–8, 134, 137–40,
    142, 150, 155, 158–9, 161, 171,
    173, 178, 181, 183–4, 186
Liberat(e)(ion)(ed), 44–5, 73, 80, 96–7,
    108, 111, 132, 138, 146, 151, 153,
    157, 166, 169, 174, 180, 182, 189, 192
Libération Nationale, 149
Liberator (bombers), 160, 166
Liberté, 149
Libya, 10, 16
Lim valley, 127
Limpet mine, 72
Lindsey, Franklin A., xix
Lisbon, 5, 13, 40
Lloyd, Stacey, 101–104
London, xv, xix–xxi, 3–4, 6–9, 10–14, 18,
    20, 22–5, 27–9, 31–41, 43, 45–58, 60–5,
    70, 72, 76–84, 86–90, 92–110, 115–19,
    123–7, 130–1, 138, 144, 146–7, 149–51,
    153–8, 160–3, 165–9, 173–9, 181–2,
    187–92, 196–7
Longmore, Air Chief Marshal, 14–15
Lothian, Lord, 5, 11
Low Countries, 2, 58, 96, 98–100, 107–8, 194
Luftwaffe, 10, 178
Lycett, Andrew, 29
Lyons, 159
Lyttleton, Oliver, 50

MAAF, 142
MacArthur, Douglas, 50
MacDonald, Larry, xix, xxi
Macedonians, 112, 132
MacKenzie, Colin, 85, 88–9
Macklin, Gilbert, 0
MacLean, Fitzroy, 126–8, 131–2,
    134–6, 138–9, 141
McBaine, Turner, 131
McDowell, Robert, 142–143
Maddox, William ('Bill'), 54, 61,
    63–4, 78, 90, 101–5, 109
Madeira, 51
Madrid, 13, 40, 71, 175
Malaya, 51, 81, 195
Malta, 14, 68
Manchukuo, 43, 81
Manchuria(n), 43–44
Manfredonia, 135
Mann, Stephen, xx
Mansfield, Walter, 125–9, 131–2, 134, 139
Manuel, P.E.J., 165
Maquis, 149, 155, 157–61, 165, 180–3

Marine, 44, 125
  volunteers, 44
Marinkovic, Dusan ('Duka'), xx, xxii, 122
Markovitch, General, 141
Marrakech, 160
Marshall, George, 26, 41, 113, 166
Mason-MacFarlane, General, 68
MASSINGHAM, 47, 74–9, 82, 90, 96, 191
Mast, Charles, 69
Mayfair, 46
Mediterranean, xiii, xv, xx, 1–2, 10–13, 18,
    21, 23, 25–6, 68, 74, 96, 112, 124,
    128, 133–4, 140–2, 144, 160, 162
  Allied Air Force, 142
Medjedja, 138
Menzies, Robert, 15
Menzies, Stewart, xx, 5–6, 14, 18, 28,
    33, 36, 42, 47, 50, 61–2, 64, 78,
    92, 103, 105, 109, 186
Mers-el-Kebir, 66
Message, Terry, xxi
Metaxas, Ioannis, 16
MEW, 14, 25, 32
MID, 39
Middle East, 1, 10, 14–15, 51–2, 59, 81–2,
    86–7, 90–1, 99, 114, 117–18, 124,
    131, 133, 144, 152, 182, 194
Midget submarine, 39
MIDHURST, 94–5
Mihailovic, Draza, xiv–xv, xxi, 95, 110–16,
    119–30, 132–3, 135–42, 144–5, 193
Miles, Sherman, 8, 26, 41
Milice, 159
Military, 3, 19, 48, 51, 55, 58, 79–80, 87,
    90, 103, 109, 111, 114, 145–6, 149,
    162, 180, 184, 191, 194, 197
  accomplishments, 138
  action, 95, 115, 148
  activities, 97
  advisors, 160
  aircraft, 69
  approach, 126
  arm, 149
  attache(s), 38–9, 43, 66
  authorities, 49, 51, 60, 75, 87, 97, 100,
      107, 140, 161, 178, 184, 189, 194
  background, 172, 175
  cadre, 96
  campaign, 144, 193
  catastrophe, 186
  channels, 70
  chief(s), 46, 159
  climate, 49
  collection assets, 105

  Command, 78, 180, 184, 192
  communications, 122
  considerations, 192
  convoy route, 43
  destruction, 98
  direction, 170
  directives, 162
  effectiveness, 115
  effort, 51
  elements, 106
  equipment, 185
  establishment(s), 41, 48, 93, 110, 157
  exercise, 98
  expedien(t)(ce), 65, 78
  experience, 175
  facilities, 18
  forces, 73, 98, 158–9, 183
  formations, 158
  headquarters, 184
  information, 103
  installations, 14, 40, 68
  Intelligence, 5, 25–6, 33, 41, 61,
      86, 142; chief, 42, 154;
      Division, 39; Service, 108
  intelligence, 88, 106, 113
  liaison authority, 150
  leader(ship), 73, 78, 112
  Masters, 48
  objectives, 96
  officers, 68
  operations, 23, 35, 48, 56, 65–6, 73, 99,
      122, 152, 165–6, 173–4, 179, 196
  organization, 102
  participation, 56
  plan(ners), 68, 156–7
  policy, 195
  political warfare program, 103
  position, 195
  power, 127, 195
  presence, 55
  pressure, 126
  program, 102
  realities, 128
  recognition, 65
  requirement(s), 105, 174, 176, 183
  role, 148
  services, 23, 70, 82, 170, 186–7
  setback, 65
  situation, 24, 158, 173
  staff(s), 88, 150
  standing, 162
  standpoint, 65
  strategy, 48
  sources, 38

success(es), 42, 44
support, 69, 139, 189
training, 175
uniforms, 180
unit(s), 69, 189
value, 121
Militia, 159
Miller, Francis, 177
Millet, Jean, 170
Milton Hall, 171–2
Minister(s), 46
  of Economic Warfare, 50, 160
  of Information, 5
  of State, xv
  of War, 111
Ministry, 179
  of Economic Warfare, 7–8,
    14, 25, 32, 35, 61
  of Information, 7–9, 32
  of Supply, 7
MIR, xii
Mirkovic, General, 114
Missionaries, 86–87
Mockler-Ferryman, E.E.,
    154, 160–2, 169, 184
MOI, 9, 32
Molfetta, 135
MOMIE, 164
Monarchist, 112, 128
Mongol(ia), 43
Monopoli, 135, 141
Montenegr(ins)(o), 112, 126–7, 139
Moon
  cycles, 179
  operation, 94
  period, 160
Moorhouse, Chris, xxi
Morale, 32, 65–6, 71, 99, 122,
    152–3, 159, 165, 167, 181
Morand, Frank, 113–114
Morgan, William, xx, 172
Morgenthau, Henry, 16, 26
Morocco, 40, 67–68, 75
Morton, Desmond, 5, 28, 35–36, 187
Morton, Perry, xxi
Moscow, 111
Most Secret, 35
Moulin, Jean, 149–150
Mountbatten, Lord Louis, 50, 90
Mouvements Unis de Résistance, 149
Munn, James, 50, 77–78
MUR, 149
Murphy, Robert, 67–69,
    72, 76, 188

Muslims, 112
Musulin, George, 123, 140–2

Naples, xiii, xv
National(ist)(ity), 73, 141, 148, 171–2, 195–6
  defeat, 186
  group(s), 82, 111
  imperatives, 185
  interests, 49, 60, 110, 197
  Liberation movement, 127, 133
  military authorities, 178, 189
  military elements, 106
  papers, 147
  policy, 51
  revolt, 111
  security, 27, 38
  war aims, 197
Nationalist(s), 44, 49, 83
Naval, 11, 19, 141
  attache, 67
  base, 80
  escorts, 10
  forces, 66
  Intelligence, 5, 8, 41, 61, 88, 108
  Operations, 7–8
  offices, 6
  signals school, 14
  Staff, 5
  strategists, 31
Navy, 25, 67, 99
  Department(s), 10, 36
  Intelligence, 40
  representative, 11
  Secretary, 3, 6, 27
  ships, 99
Nazi(s), xiii–xiv, 1, 3–4, 7–8, 10, 24, 112, 114
Nazira, 84
Near East, 12, 59, 87, 113
Nedic, Milan, 115, 123, 136–7
Nelson, Frank, 5, 18
New York, 22, 24–7, 30–1,
    37, 39, 46–7, 51, 188
Newfoundland, 34
NOIR, 164
Non-Invasion Sphere, 51–2
Normandy, xv, 146, 150, 168,
    170, 174, 179, 183–4, 189
North Africa(n), xx, 22, 24, 38–42, 45, 48–51,
    53, 59, 64–81, 86–7, 89–93, 96–7, 100,
    104, 144, 148, 152–3, 156, 166, 168,
    171, 175–7, 188, 190, 192, 194, 196–7
North America(n), 4, 13, 47, 105
  American Military Purchasing
    Commission, 39

North America(n) – *continued*
  Atlantic, xiii, 24
  Vietnam, xv
North Sea operations, 99
Norway, 2, 51, 57, 59, 80, 92–6,
  98, 109, 192–3, 197
Norwegian(s), 63, 80–1, 104, 193
  activities, 94–95
  coast, 95
  Collaboration Committee, 81
  government, 57
  Groups, 59
  network, 81
  operations, 94
  service, 61
  special operations, 109
  work, 95

Occup(y)(ation)(ied), xii–xiv, 65, 77,
  81, 88, 93, 95, 99, 102, 105, 107,
  110, 111–12, 114, 146–8, 152–3,
  155, 157, 159, 161, 171, 175, 195
OCM, 149
O'Connor, Richard, 14
Office
  of Civilian Affairs, 23
  of Inter-American Affairs, 23
  of Naval Intelligence, 41, 108
  of Strategic Services, xii, xxii, 2, 23, 48
  of the Coordinator of Information, 48
  of War Information, 86, 145
OG, 143, 180–1
O'Neill, Robert J., xxi
Operation(s), 13, 40, 58, 69, 94, 96
Operational, 51, 84, 99, 106,
  143, 153, 166, 179
  activities, 39
  agreements, 94
  approval, 94
  areas, 37, 52, 133
  arrangements, 97
  base, 80
  control, 98, 100
  coordination, 40
  direction, 67, 170
  disengagement, 90
  domain, 91
  endeavors, 191
  ends, 185
  environment, 40
  facilities, 80
  failures, 156, 164
  Groups, xv, 57, 80, 96, 143, 180–1
  headquarters, 74

  leads, 37
  level, 162
  matters, 57, 144, 156
  objectives, 117
  partnership, 52
  plan(ning)(ner), 89, 103, 161
  preeminence, 117–18
  presence, 190
  protocols, 50
  purposes, 34, 51
  requirements, 166, 190
  restrictions, 34
  revisions, 79
  role, 104
  Staffs, 98
  status, 82
Operative(s), 13, 44, 57, 68, 70–1, 96,
  98, 102, 107, 111, 148, 171
ORA, 149
Oral History Unit, 31
Oran, 69
Organisation Civile et Militaire, 149
Organisation de Résistance de l'Armée de
  l'Armistice, 149
OSS, xii–xv, xvii–xviii, xix–xxi, 2, 4, 23,
  31, 33, 36–8, 42, 44–68, 70–5, 77–89,
  91–104, 106–10, 113, 117–21, 123–6,
  128–31, 133–6, 139–42, 144–6, 148,
  150–1, 153–8, 160–85, 188–97
  activities, 42, 147
  agent(s), 94, 102
  assessment, 161
  base, 134
  collection, 87
  contingent, 143
  document, 18
  maritime operations, 46
  network(s), 66, 101
  operative, 1
  operational records, xviii
  policy, 145
  records, xviii
  teams, 105
  unit, 90
  war report, 2, 4, 19, 66, 114
OSS/SOE, 69–70, 75, 81, 89,
  107, 123, 190, 192
Ossex, 177–9, 183
Ottawa, 43
OVERLORD, xx, 143, 150, 153, 162,
  168–9, 173–4, 178, 180–1, 189
Overt, 3, 19, 62, 74
OWI, 86–7
Oxford, 32, 46–7

Pacific, 42–4, 51
Palestine, 14–15, 81
Papagos, Alexander, 16
Parachut(es)(ed)(ing), 84, 99, 106,
    114, 123–6, 128, 142, 148, 150,
    155, 158, 175, 177–8, 180–1
Paramilitary, xv, 143, 149, 154–155,
    158, 163, 168, 170
Paratroops, 96
Paris, 39, 157
Parliamentary Secretaries, 5
Partisan(s), xiv, xx, 110–13, 115–16, 119–24,
    126–35, 137, 139, 141–5, 160, 190, 193
Passy, Colonel, 62, 165, 168
Passport Control Officer(s), 13
Pathfinders, xv, 178–9, 189
Patriot(s)(ic), 59, 95–6, 118,
    155, 157, 163, 166
Patton, George, 174
Paul, Prince (of Yugoslavia), 17–18
PCO, 13
Pearl Harbor, xiii, 29–32, 34–5, 39, 43, 124
Pearson, Norman Holmes, 46
Pelabon, Commandant, 176
Penetrat(ion)(ions)(ed), 43, 88, 108, 157, 159
    activities, 15
Persia, 87, 128
Persico, Joseph, xix
Pescadores, 43
Peter, King (of Yugoslavia), 111–12,
    114, 116, 119, 137, 143
Peterborough, 171
Philby, Kim, 50
Philippines, 44, 50
Phillips, Wallace, 40–2, 46, 53, 188
Phillips, William, 37, 54–5,
    57, 63, 70, 77, 86, 90
Plane(s), 59, 107, 156–7, 161
Pleydell-Bouverie, Barty, 30, 187
Plymouth, 14
Poland, xiv–xv, 2, 51–2, 194
Poles, xiv, 63
Policy Committee, 77, 97
Polish, xiv, 32, 34, 61
    Secret Army, 96
Political(ly), 29, 49, 62, 65, 68, 72–3,
    76, 78–80, 82–3, 87, 96, 106, 111,
    113–14, 116, 119–20, 126–8, 140–3,
    146, 148–50, 159, 161, 163–4, 166,
    186, 189, 191–2, 194–5, 197
    intelligence, 113
    Warfare, 3, 103; Executive, 14, 22,
        32, 50, 54, 61, 120, 145, 167
Politicians, 128

Port(s), 68–9, 135
Port Lyautey, 69
Portugal, 13, 18, 40, 51, 59, 107, 149
Post-Cold War, xix, xxii
Post-war, 136, 148, 151, 195
Premier Bureau, 168
Prime Minister, xv, 5, 12,
    15–16, 139–40, 160–1
Printing, 94
Prisoner(s), 73
    of war, 56, 175
Propaganda, 2, 6, 19, 22, 24, 26–7,
    30, 32, 34–5, 38, 40, 42–3, 45, 54,
    66, 68, 70, 86–8, 94, 103, 111, 113,
    119–20, 132, 145, 167, 186
Protic, Mihailo ('Bata'), xx, xxii, 122
Psychological, 71
    attacks, 27
    warfare, 34, 102
    Warfare Board, 70
PWE, 14, 22, 32, 88, 120

Quatriéme Bureau, 168
Quisling(s), 78, 112, 115, 136

Radar, 6
Radio, xii, 7, 14, 18, 56, 59–60, 66–8, 70,
    72, 84, 88, 94, 101, 105–7, 111, 116,
    118–19, 124–6, 131, 141–2,
    148–9, 154–6, 158, 160, 171–3,
    175, 177, 181, 183, 188
Rail(way)(ways), 69–70, 84, 122,
    136, 164, 173, 177, 181
Ravna Gora Division, xx
Rebellion, 112
Reception
    committee, 171, 178–9
    parties, 71
Reconnaissance, 143
    intelligence groups, 101–2
Recruit(ed)(s)(ing)(ment), 23, 32, 34, 40, 44,
    46–7, 52, 56–7, 63, 68–9, 80–1, 84, 94,
    101–2, 104–6, 113, 117, 128, 135, 148,
    153–4, 159, 162, 170–2, 175–8, 183, 193
Red Army, 49
Red Cross, 50
Refugee(s), 31, 61, 108, 175
Reilly, Patrick, xx
Reprisals, 84, 115, 121, 125, 165
Republican(s), 11, 47
Resistance, xii, 38–40, 56, 63, 65–6, 69,
    73, 77–8, 95–7, 99, 105, 111–15, 120,
    122, 125–6, 135, 144, 146–50, 152–8,
    160–70, 173–4, 180–4, 189, 191

Resupply(ing), 122, 133, 135, 144, 171, 181, 190, 193
Revolt, 119
Revolution, xii
RF-Section, 151, 154, 158, 160, 163–4, 168, 189
Richmond, Wally, 84
Rhodes Scholar, 46
Rif, 68
Road(s), 69–70, 83–4
Roadblock, 84, 164
Rodgers, Sue, xxi
Rogers, James Grafton, 77, 86, 124
Romania(ns), 16, 112, 143
Rome, 160
Rommel, Erwin, 49
Roosevelt, Franklin (Delano), xiv, xviii, xix, 2, 4, 7–10, 12, 16, 18–19, 23–8, 30, 32, 35, 40–2, 44–5, 48–9, 55, 65–6, 72, 86, 90–1, 116, 122–3, 133, 135–6, 138, 140, 142, 146, 151, 160, 182, 186–7, 195
Roosevelt, Teddy, xii
Roper-Caldbeck, Terence, 47
Roseborough, William Arthur, 46, 65, 153–4
ROUGE, 164
Rounds, Leland, xix
Royal(ist), 12, 95
  Army, 111
  Canadian Mounted Police, 128
  Engineers, 128
  Navy, 4, 67
  Yugoslav Army, 111
Royal Air Force, 7, 34, 67
Russia(n), xii, 39, 44, 111–12, 114, 124

Sabotage, xiv, 3, 24, 26, 38–40, 43–4, 48, 57, 68–70, 72, 80, 89–90, 97, 105, 121, 137–8, 142, 148, 150, 152, 155, 159–60, 164, 169, 173–4, 180, 186
Saboteur(s), 1, 23, 44, 72, 91, 183
Safi, 69
Salerno, xiv, 144
Sanjak, 126
Sardinia, 77
SAS, xv, 180–1
Saudi Arabia, 81
Scandinavia, 46, 51–2, 59, 81, 95, 107–8, 194
Scheme 'OLIVA', 44
Schmitt, Amy, xix, xxi
School(s), 39–40, 52, 58, 60, 99, 106, 113, 148, 171, 175–7, 181
Scientific, 9, 27
SEA HORSE, 153
Sea Lord, 5

SEAC, 90
Seaman, Mark, xix, xxi
Second front, 49
Second World War, xi, xv, xvii, xxi, 185
Secret(s), xvii, 2, 5–6, 8, 10, 12–13, 15, 23, 32, 94, 152, 155, 187
  agencies, 46
  agent(s), 39
  airfield, 97
  Army, 96
  base, 99
  diplomat, 15
  fact, 28
  group, 17
  information, 9–10, 12, 24, 39, 61
  intelligence, xi–xii, 3, 27, 30, 32, 34–5, 40, 43, 47, 54, 58, 61, 66, 71–2, 75, 86, 93, 100–1, 103–6, 108–9, 140, 142, 174, 179, 182, 188, 194–6
  Intelligence Service(s), xii, xviii, xxii, 2, 62, 108
  lines of communication, 131
  material, 34
  negotiations, 68
  operations, 69
  service(s), xi–xii, xvii, xx, xxii, 2, 18–20, 22, 24, 29, 31, 36–8, 45–6, 49, 87, 90, 92–3, 106, 110–11, 143, 147–9, 161, 182, 185–9, 194–7
  staff talks, 23
  warfare, 31, 83
  weapons, 179
Secretary
  of State, 20; for the Colonies, 50
  of State for Air, 12
  of War, 7, 20
Section d'Attérrissages et Parachutages, 150
Security, 6, 15, 28, 57, 64–6, 68, 71, 77, 84, 87–8, 99, 102, 105, 108, 151, 156, 159, 164, 166, 176
Sédentaires, 149
Seitz, Albert, 126, 128–32, 134, 139, 142
Selbourne, Lord, 50, 160
Self-determination, 86, 145
Serbia(n), xix, 112, 115, 123, 126, 132, 136, 138, 140, 142–4
  nationalist group, 111
  Peasant Party, 17
Serb(s), 113, 115, 119, 128–9
SFHQ, 161, 166–9, 172–3, 181
SHAEF, 161, 165–6, 168–9, 179–80, 184
Shanghai, 89
Shepardson, Whitney, 37–8, 46, 54, 57, 61–5, 90, 101, 103–4, 186

Sherwood, Robert, 27, 32, 35, 43, 45
Shetland Islands, 99
Ship(ping)(s), 68–9, 72, 84, 99, 133, 135
SI, xi, 35, 43, 58–64, 67, 79, 86, 88–9,
    101, 104, 107–8, 113, 131, 196
Siam, 51
Sicil(y)(ian)(ians), 77, 122, 135, 193
Sidi Barrani, 10, 14
Sidi Ferruch, 77
SIGINT, 68, 115, 120
Signal(s), xiii, 11, 14, 71, 141, 171
    intelligence, xx, 68
    parties, 70
Silent killing, 171
Simovic, Dusan, xiv, 17–18
Singapore, 34, 45
SIS, xii–xiii, xx–xxi, 2–3, 5–6, 13–14, 18,
    20, 22–4, 28–9, 31–2, 35–6, 39, 41–2,
    46–7, 49–50, 54, 60–63, 65, 67–8, 70–2,
    77–8, 83–5, 87–95, 99–109, 143,
    146–8, 151, 153, 156, 167, 174–80,
    182–5, 188–9, 191–2, 194–7
Sinclair, Archibald, 9, 12
Sixiéme Bureau, 168
Skopje, 122
Sloven(es)(ia), 112, 123
Smith, Bradley, xvii–xviii
Smith, R. Harris, xviii, xix
SO, xi, 17, 35, 55–60, 63, 69, 77, 79–82,
    89–90, 98, 100, 117–18, 131, 133–4
'SO2', 17
Socialist(s), xii, 149
SOE, xi–xiv, xviii, xx–xxi, 2, 5, 9, 13–14,
    17–18, 20, 22–4, 31–3, 35, 37–40,
    43, 45, 47, 49–61, 66–85, 87–88, 100,
    105, 107, 109–11, 113, 115–21,
    123–7, 129–40, 142, 144–73,
    180–5, 187, 189–93, 195, 197
    SOE/OSS, xiii–xiv, 89, 131, 155,
        160, 165–6, 170, 191
Sofia, 13, 16
Solberg, Robert, 38–40, 46, 188
Soscice, Victor, 155
Southeast
    Asia, 50, 83, 90
    Asian Command, 90
Southwest Pacific, 51
Soviet, xv, 32, 49, 132, 136, 138, 143
    Front, 112
    Union, xiv, 149
Spaatz, Carl, 8, 156, 158, 161
Spain, xii, 18, 51, 56, 59, 64, 71–2, 107, 149
Spanish, 67–68
SPARTAN, 98

Spearhead(s), 96
Special
    access, 35
    Activities – K and L Funds, 38
    Air Service, 180
    coups, 180
    equipment, 189, 194
    Forces, xx, 159, 168, 180; Headquarters,
        161–2, 166–7, 168, 171,
        181–2, 184, 190
    Forces Club, xix, xxi
    Inter-Allied Missions, 158, 189
    Jedburgh Signals Section, 171
    Maquis Missions, 158
    mission(s), 10, 169, 186
    observer, 14
    Observers Group, 8–9, 85
    operations, xi, xiv–xv, xvii, xviii, 2–3,
        13–15, 17, 20, 22, 27, 30, 32, 34–40,
        43–5, 47, 49–51, 53–4, 60, 66–7, 69,
        71–2, 74–7, 79, 81–3, 86, 91, 93–4, 97,
        100, 106–7, 109, 113, 117–18, 123–4,
        140–1, 143, 146, 153–5, 161–2, 165–8,
        173–4, 178–9, 186, 188–90, 192–4,
        196–7; training facilities, 22, 47;
    Operations Branch, 154, 188; Center, xv;
        Committee, 136; Executive, xi,
        xxii, 2
    Projects Operations Center,
        168, 171, 181, 190
    relationship, xi, 1, 143
    Service(s), 5, 14, 29, 48, 98, 163
    support, 49
    training, 59; school, 172
    units, 178
    warfare, 143
Sperry bomb-sight, 11
Sphere(s), 53, 80, 84, 86, 93, 117,
    119, 126, 129, 156, 193, 195
    of control, 84
    of influence, 67, 110, 124
    of interest, 146
    of strategic responsibility, 165
Spies, 42, 183
Split, 127
SPOC, 168, 181
Spy(ing), 1, 24, 41, 164
    agency, 106
    network(s), 41, 100, 102
Spymaster(s), 23, 31, 106, 196
Stafford, David, xviii
Stalin, (Josef), xiv, 49, 135–6, 140
Stanley, Oliver, 50
State Department, 6, 23, 25, 30, 35, 68, 187

Station, 32–3, 37, 50, 54–5, 59
Station 'IX', 148
Stawell, W.A.M., 134
Stephenson, William ('Bill' or 'Little Bill'),
   xviii, 3–6, 8, 10–14, 17, 19–20,
   22–5, 27–31, 33–4, 37, 39–40,
   45, 47, 50, 56, 75, 186–7
Stirling (bomber), 160
Stettinius, Jr., Edward, 8
Stevenson, Ralph, 136–7
Stilwell, Joseph, ('Vinegar Joe'),
   83–6, 88–90, 194–5
Stimson, Henry, 3–4, 11, 18, 20, 27, 41
Strateg(ic)(y)(ally), 4, 12, 23, 27, 32,
   43, 48, 51, 55, 61, 65, 78, 81, 92,
   95, 105–6, 111–12, 118, 120,
   127, 135, 145, 147, 153,
   158, 160, 162, 164–5, 170,
   173, 185, 192
Stockholm, 34
Street, Vivian, 126
Strings, 68
Strong, General, 64–5, 103, 180
Stuart, Duncan, xxi
Sub-chasers, 99
Submarine, xiii, 69, 71, 80, 111
Subver(t)(sion)(sive), 2–3, 5, 10, 19–20,
   26–7, 39–40, 66, 68–9, 110–13,
   116–17, 120, 124, 146–8, 152, 157
Suez Canal, 15
Sumatra, 51
Suppl(y)(ies)(ing)(ier), 51–3, 56–60, 65,
   67, 71, 77, 80, 83, 95–7, 104, 108,
   112, 114–16, 118–23, 125–6,
   129–30, 133–5, 139, 141, 148, 150,
   153–4, 157, 160, 166–8, 173, 175,
   177, 180, 185, 190–1
Surrender, 127, 142
Sussex, xv, 93–4, 100–1, 105–6, 108,
   165, 171, 173–80, 182–4,
   189–90, 194, 196
Supplementary activities, 27
Supreme
   Allied Commander, 50, 107–9,
      133, 140, 166, 190
   Command, 52, 174
   Commander in Europe, 146
   Headquarters, 171, 177, 179, 184; Allied
      Expeditionary Force, 161–2,
      165, 168, 171
Sweden, 51–2, 59, 107
Sweet-Escott, Bickham, xvii, xix,
   xxi, 17, 110, 115, 122, 144
Swinton, Lord, 6

Switzerland, 31, 51–3, 58, 72,
   107, 149, 155–6, 184, 192
Syria, 15, 81

Tactical, 92, 105–6, 168, 170,
   175, 178, 181, 185, 192
Tangier, 40, 64, 66–8, 71–2, 75, 192
Taranto, 10
Target(s)(ed)(ing), 32, 42, 49, 51, 66, 70,
   84, 101, 107, 109, 166, 175, 184
Tassels, 68
Taylor, George, 119
Taylor, John, xix, xxi
Technical, 9, 51, 54, 70, 101, 173, 180
Tehran, 129–33, 135–8, 160
Telex, 30
Thailand, xv, 44, 81, 195
Theater(s), 55, 57, 63, 67, 75, 77, 79–80,
   84, 86, 88, 94, 101, 104, 106–7,
   114, 124, 141, 154, 160, 182
Theater Commander(s), 48, 57, 97, 100,
   104, 106, 108, 123–4, 147, 158, 175
Thompson, Robert, 133
Tito, (Josip Broz), xiv, 111–13, 115–16,
   119, 121–4, 126–28, 131–9,
   141–5, 160, 190, 193
Titoist, 126
Tofte, Hans, xix, 133–4
Tokyo, 42, 45
Top Secret, 6
Topalovic, Dusko, xx, xxii
TORCH, xx, 45, 65–77, 80, 91, 101, 103,
   109, 146, 149, 152–4, 182–3, 191–2
TORTUE, 164
Tours, 155
Train(s)(ed)(ing)(ees), 14, 22, 29, 31–3,
   39–40, 44–5, 47, 50–4, 57–60, 63, 65,
   75–8, 80–1, 83–4, 86, 90, 94, 96, 102–6,
   108, 111, 113, 117–18, 124, 134, 138,
   141, 148, 150, 152–4, 157–8, 164–6, 168,
   170–3, 175–7, 180–1, 188–91, 193, 196
Transatlantic, 3, 20, 23, 64, 185, 187
Transport(ation), 40, 54, 58–60, 63, 65, 67, 77,
   79, 99, 102, 109, 117–19, 131, 134–5,
   141–2, 149, 159, 168, 189–91, 193–4
Treaty, 89
Treasury Secretary, 16, 26
Tree, Ronald, 9
Tripartite, 158, 162, 193
   activit(y)(ies), 64–5, 91, 103, 105
   agreements, 104
   arrangement, 163, 192
   basis, 167, 173, 177
   commission, 177

committees, 177
cooperation, 64–5, 165, 174
  discussions, 104
  initiative, 64
  intelligence arrangement, 64
  Jedburgh program, 182
  Maquis missions, 159
  mechanism, 64
  operations, 189
  Pact, 18
  participants, 178
  partner(s), 163–4
  planning, 189
  relations, 101
  representation, 173
  scheme, 65
  staff, 170
  structure, 158
  unit, 168
  work, 64, 103
Troisième Bureau, 168
Troy, (Thomas), xviii, 4, 7, 26
Tsar(ist), 39
Tunis, 68
Tunisia, xiv, 69, 75
Turkey, 18, 81
Turk(s), 16, 112

U-boats, 10
ULTRA, 35
UN, 151
Unarmed combat, 84
Undercover, 13, 41, 68, 104
Underground, 48, 56, 63, 102, 108, 122
Underwood, Mr., 43–4
UNION, 159–160
Union Jack, 45
United Nations, 88, 93
Unoccupied, 147, 149, 155, 196
Ustashi, 112–13, 132
USSR, 24, 51
Uzica, 138

van der Stricht, Paul, xix, 146, 154–8, 161–5,
  168–70, 182, 190
Venezia Division, 127
Vansittart, Robert, 9
Versailles, 46
VERT, 164
Vice Consul(s), 41, 68–9, 188
Viceroy, 87
Vichy, 22, 34, 40–1, 56, 65–9, 72–5, 77–8,
  146–9, 151, 175, 182, 188, 192, 196
Viet Minh, 195

Vietnamese, 195
VIOLET, 164
Vis, 135
Visegrad, 138
von Schultze Gaevernitz, xix
VJ-Day, xv
Vuckovic, Zvonomir, xx, xxii

War, 23–26, 28–30, 32, 38–9, 41, 44–7, 49–50,
  56, 65, 73, 76–7, 79, 83, 91, 93, 96, 110,
  115, 122, 128, 136, 139, 142–3, 146, 148,
  151, 155, 169, 175, 183, 185–7, 192–7
  aims, 23
  Cabinet, 5, 33, 50, 137
  Department(s), 26, 30, 36, 41, 47, 85, 106
  effort, 23, 32, 82, 109, 120,
    145, 152, 185, 187
  fighting, 90
  machine, 91
  materiel, 10, 15–16, 20, 116–17,
    135, 150, 164
  Office, 9, 85, 95
  Office Intelligence Section, xii
  preparations, 10
  Secretary, 25, 27
  years, 28
Warren, Ward, xix, xxi
Washington, xiii, xviii, 1–2, 6–10, 13, 15–20,
  22, 24–6, 28, 30, 33, 36–7, 40, 42–3, 45,
  47–8, 50–1, 53–4, 58, 61, 64–6, 74,
  76–7, 81, 85–9, 102–4, 107, 116, 123–4,
  126, 129–30, 136, 139, 147, 151, 164,
  166, 175, 177, 187
Wavell, Archibald, 14–16, 84–9
Weapon(s), 9, 28, 56, 65, 69, 84,
  135, 148, 155, 159, 170–1
Weil, Richard, 141
Welles, Sumner, 5
West, Paul, 130
West Africa, 51
West Point, 162
Western
  Alliance, 151
  Allies, 91
  Directorate, 161
  Europe, 51, 56, 82, 91, 98–9, 102, 158, 167
  Europe(an) Section, 154, 158
  Desert, 14–15, 49
  Front, 67
  Hemisphere, 3, 10, 14, 43, 108
  Mediterranean, 96
Weygand, Maxime, 67
Wheeler, Mark, xviii, 114
White House, 4, 9, 25–6, 30, 41–2

White propaganda, 34
Whitehall, 33, 41, 85
Whitney, William ('Bill'), 32–8, 46, 53–4, 186
Wilkinson, Gerald, 50
Wilkinson, Peter, xvii, xx
Wilson, Henry Maitland, 14, 140, 142
Winant, John, 25–6, 50
Winks, Robin, xviii
Winner, Percy, 36
Wireless, xii, 56, 68–70, 105
Wiseman, William, 25–6
Woodruff, Freddie, xxii
World War I, 25, 39

World War II, 114
Wuchinich, George, 123

Yankees, 77
Yeo-Thomas, F.F.E., 160
Yorkshire, 46
Yu, Maochun, 45
Yugoslav(s)(ia), xiv–xv, xx–xxii, 16–17, 59, 61, 63, 82, 95–6, 109–14, 116–18, 120–5, 127, 129–35, 137–41, 143–6, 148, 156, 160–1, 163, 165, 191–3, 197

'Z', Colonel, 28
Ziegler, A., 168, 170